TOWARD LEXINGTON

*The Role of the British Army in the
Coming of the American Revolution*

Toward Lexington

The Role of the British Army in the Coming of the American Revolution

BY JOHN SHY

PRINCETON, NEW JERSEY

PRINCETON UNIVERSITY PRESS

1965

F O R

Sally

Preface

MILITARY history is not simply a bloody chronicle of attacks and retreats, victories and defeats; it is also the story of unresolved ambiguities and contradictions. Armies are meant to defend a state against an external threat, but historically they have been almost as important as instruments of internal control. Among politicians, those in power have frequently been embarrassed by the enormous expense of even a modest military force, while those in opposition have as often feared (or pretended to fear) the danger of an army managed by their rivals. To farmers and burghers, an army was usually a nasty and wasteful institution which became especially troublesome when any of it was nearby, but which sometimes became especially convenient if law or property were in danger or invasion threatened, and especially profitable if it bought what farmers and burghers sold. Thinking men long have recognized the need to make the army a healthy organ rather than a cancer in the body politic. Simultaneously they have recognized the weaknesses of militiamen when faced by professional soldiers. Of even greater importance, these same men have usually recoiled at the thought of performing extended military service themselves, and thus have tended to accept a standing army as the least of the evils presented to them.

Anglo-American history in the century or so before the American Revolution can be read as a testimonial to the truth of these statements. Inability to solve the problem of colonial defense eventually raised fundamental issues of political organization. In turn, failure to resolve these issues by force brought about the disruption of the first British empire. The problems connected with the standing army were central in both failures, and illustrate how closely the second failure was tied to the first. Inadequate defense kept the colonies free from any serious attempt by the imperial administration to govern forcibly, and this led to an explosive reaction when coercion was first tried in a timid and inexperienced way. Moreover, defense had been inadequate largely because the key to utilizing colonial manpower was never found; in the American Revolution, this meant that the potentially enormous military strength of Loyalism remained inert, almost untapped as a means to put down rebellion.

Viewed from today all of this has turned out happily; the thirteen colonies became the United States, Great Britain was deflected toward a subtler but sounder concept of empire, and both nations maintained, even strengthened, a healthy military tradition. But this last point, the Anglo-American military tradition, has another aspect. While praetorianism has never been a serious threat in either state, neither has the problem of military security been adequately solved. Until this century, both nations could rely on their geographical isolation, and on their economic and sea power; they could afford to accept military unpreparedness as falling within their tradition. This time has passed, however, and it has become apparent that, as in France, the existence of a strong military force within a free society continues to raise the same unanswered questions.

What follows is an exploration of some of these questions as they arose in the colonies before the American Revolution. This book is not meant to be a complete account of the British regular army in North America, nor is it a full history of American attitudes and behavior toward the army. Although both subjects are discussed wherever they are relevant to the main theme, they are of considerable importance in themselves and deserve further treatment elsewhere. The main theme, however, is posed by the question: What was the army doing in America? If one is willing to be colloquial as well as literal, the question is ambiguous. It asks what the army was *meant* to do, as well as what it *actually* did. Answers to both questions have been essayed, with close attention given to the way in which the answers continually interacted. The result, it is hoped, not only provides a study in the military history of early America, but also elucidates one aspect of the breakdown of the first British empire.

John Shy

Princeton, New Jersey
January 1965

Contents

CONTENTS

TOWARD LEXINGTON

*The Role of the British Army in the
Coming of the American Revolution*

I · Soldiers in North America Before 1760

Two names known to every American schoolboy—John Smith and Miles Standish—illustrate a neglected truth about the English settlement of North America: colonization was a military operation. Captains Smith and Standish were soldiers, and their military expertise was not the least reason for their presence among the first settlers. At a time when the more advanced European states were increasingly dependent on long-service, mercenary armies, Smith and Standish and some other professional soldiers not so well known were helping Virginians and Pilgrims to revive a decaying medieval institution—the militia.

It was all the Virginians and Pilgrims, not just a few, that these soldiers organized and trained. Unlike England, where militia duty was highly selective, liability to service was nearly universal in the colonies, and militia organization was a mirror of early American political and social structure. The boundaries of towns and counties defined the membership of companies and regiments; militia officers, whether elected or appointed, were invariably leading citizens therein. Nearly every man owned his weapon and equipment as nearly every man owned land. The wealthy organized themselves as cavalry, and the very poor labored to pay for a weapon from the armory in the same way that the workhouse demanded some compensation for charity. The governor, a military title in its most common English usage, was the commander, and one or more of his councillors were his military lieutenants. In time of war, committees of the town selectmen, the county court, and the provincial legislature took care of logistics and even advised the governor on strategy.[1]

[1] The best brief account of the colonial militia system is in Louis Morton, "The Origins of American Military Policy," *Military Affairs*, XXII (1958), 75-82. A provocative essay is found in Daniel Boorstin, *The Americans; the Colonial Experience* (N.Y., 1958),

The simplicity and comprehensiveness of the militia were attractive qualities to a few hundred people trying to stay alive in an inhospitable wilderness, but the colonists would surely have forsaken the militia and all its virtues if Smith and Standish had been but soldiers of the King with some troops and with orders to protect His Majesty's plantations against Indians, Dutchmen, Frenchmen, and Spaniards. Instead, the first British soldiers in America were private adventurers rather than servants of the Crown because the King assumed no responsibility for colonial defense, just as he offered little else except company charters and proprietorial grants. Under these circumstances, British colonies defended themselves, and the militia, whatever its intrinsic qualities or historic connection with the Anglo-Saxon *fyrd*, was a necessity for survival.

With time, American necessity became British policy; the precedent of colonial self-defense repeatedly guided imperial decisions. Only a few years after Britain and France had begun what has been called the "Second Hundred Years War," John Locke made the point explicit in a report written for the Board of Trade: "There is force enough in those Colonies to repel all attempts made by the French and Indians, nor can it be imagined that so great a number of English should think it much to employ their own hands and purses in the defence of their estates, lives and families, . . ." Locke recommended, not that British soldiers be shipped to America, but that a royal governor be commissioned to raise, unite, and employ the militia of charter and proprietary as well as Crown colonies.[2]

Clearly a policy of colonial self-defense rested on the mercantilist assumption that colonies were not to drain but to contribute to the military strength of the mother country. It can then be argued that the British government capitulated 58 years after Locke's report by adopting a broader view of empire. In 1754, it decided that continued reliance

---

341-372. The fullest treatment of militia in the seventeenth century is presented in Darrett B. Rutman, "A Militant New World, 1607-1640" (Unpublished thesis, U. of Virginia, 1959).

[2] *CSPC, 1696-1697*, #286. See Abbreviations, page 427.

4

on colonial self-defense would mean the loss of the Ohio Valley, and it proceeded to reverse a century-and-a-half of precedent by pouring men and money into North America during the Seven Years War. Whether the fault lay in America or in England, the militia system apparently had failed, and the consequences of that failure were to lead to a constitutional dispute that triggered the American Revolution.[3] Such an argument is not wrong; it is, however, too simple.

The truth is more complex because practice was more complicated than theory. The militia system was not a single system at all; though the law read much the same everywhere, there were important differences among the colonies in what the law meant. Moreover, militia law and its meaning changed through time, as new military demands arose and as colonial societies themselves changed. Finally, the "failure" of the militia was relative; it must be seen in its contemporary context, when most military undertakings "failed," when many ended disastrously, and none could be called efficient by the standards of modern warfare.

Similarly, the British policy of colonial self-defense was something less than the unchanging rock that John Locke would lead one to believe. A few months after Locke had written his report, the Board of Trade recommended that three companies of troops be stationed in Newfoundland, and two years before a company had gone to garrison Jamaica.[4] The policy that colonists must defend themselves might better be understood as a myth useful to both colonists and officials; it stiffened the will of the one, and was a convenient excuse to the other.

---

[3] This is basically the view of Professor Lawrence H. Gipson, expressed at various points in his massive scholarly work, *The British Empire before the American Revolution* (N.Y., 1936—), which has now reached ten volumes. For an excellent account of American defense problems before 1756, written from the imperial point of view, see Stanley M. Pargellis, *Lord Loudoun in North America* (New Haven, 1933), Chapter I.

[4] On Jamaica: *CSPC, 1693-1696*, #1478. On Newfoundland: *CSPC, 1696-1697*, #583; and *APCC*, II, #670.

In fact, the most important, as well as most complex, aspect of colonial defense may not have had much to do with defense at all. It is a truism to say that society shapes and is shaped by the way it makes war; nevertheless, this particular truism was full of meaning for early America. The closer one looks at how these colonies were defended, the more the clear distinction between "regulars" and "militia" blurs, the more the connection between military experience and political behavior stands out. The British army stationed in America after the Seven Years War played a major role in the outbreak of the Revolution, and that is what this book is about, but the nature of that role can be comprehended only in the perspective of 150 years of colonial warfare.

The Changing Face of Colonial Militia

There is no way to distinguish between soldiers and planters in earliest Virginia, Plymouth, or Massachusetts Bay. When John Smith took "soldiers" on an exploring expedition, he took part of the colony equipped and instructed, on this particular occasion, to fight.[5] Of course every man's duty easily became no one's responsibility, especially since nothing is more wasteful than soldiering in peacetime, and waste was intolerable in communities where men died of starvation. But by the end of the first generation, when food had become more ample and some Indian tribes plainly hostile, military organization was beginning to diverge from the militia ideal.

For example, every Sunday was military training day in Virginia in 1632; ten years later, training was required every month; in 1674, mandatory training dropped to three times annually. The Indian threat to the existence of the colony had indeed diminished, but not as much as the decline in training would indicate. The threat was simply

[5] The basic study of early Virginia militia is found in Philip A. Bruce, *Institutional History of Virginia in the Seventeenth Century* (N.Y., 1910), II, 4-120. Except where noted, the following account is based on it. For John Smith and his "soldiers," see Rutman, "Militant New World," 121-122.

being met in new, more convenient, and more economical ways. As early as the 1620's, the incidence of active military service was beginning to be more discriminate. Individual volunteers, not militia companies, were raised for an expedition against the Indians. In case of attack or alarm, county commanders did not simply call out the militia; rather, they were empowered to levy, or draft, the kind and number of men they needed. In 1639, Negroes were specifically exempted from service, and a generation later the same was done for all but a few white servants. Small, paid, more or less permanent guards soon became necessities at forts like Point Comfort.[6]

Military organization in the early decades was largely determined by relations with the Indians. Between the two great massacres of 1622 and 1644, Virginia was implacably hostile toward all Indians as a matter of deliberate policy. The military demands of such a policy were great, for experience had taught that continual harassment was essential to keep the enemy from seizing the initiative.[7] Continual harassment in turn required sizeable forces serving for extended periods, too many men to pay as the fort garrisons were paid, and service too long to draft unpaid men from the militia as was done in the case of attack. At first a system of military districts was tried, each district to fill a quota of three expeditions annually. A later law required that every 15 "tithables" (that is, persons subject to poll tax) maintain one of their number under arms in the colony's service, the unlucky man to be drafted if the 15 could not agree among themselves.[8] Perhaps the impracticability of such schemes led to the gentler Indian policy of 1646, which required only small garrisons at a few forts in the backcountry.[9]

[6] Bruce, *Institutional History*, II, 5-6, says slaves were excused, but *The Statutes at Large: Being a Collection of All the Laws of Virginia . . .* , ed. William W. Hening (Richmond, 1810-23), I, 226, says "negroes."

[7] See Wesley Frank Craven, "Indian Policy in Early Virginia," 3 *WMQ*, I, 73.

[8] Hening, *Statutes at Large*, I, 140-141, 292-293.

[9] Craven, "Indian Policy," 3 *WMQ*, I, 75-76.

During about the same period, New England was also trying to adapt an amorphous militia organization to more specialized tasks. Because Virginia and New England faced their last great Indian uprising at the same time, in 1675-1676, it provides a convenient means of comparing the military condition of the two areas. The war gravely damaged both of them, and the social structure of each came near cracking under the strain. In fact, comparison of the two regions at war easily yields a catalogue of similarities in their response to the threat; but the number of differences are equally impressive, and perhaps of greater significance.[10]

In the beginning Governor William Berkeley of Virginia adopted a defensive strategy, which required the minimum number of paid soldiers, but even so the tax burden was one of the major causes of the subsequent insurrection led by Nathaniel Bacon. Under pressure from Bacon, the Virginia Assembly in 1676 called for twice as many soldiers as had been raised by Berkeley the previous year, but Bacon nevertheless attracted broad popular support because his offensive strategy promised a chance to hit back at the Indians, plunder for volunteers who followed him, and freedom from the militia draft for the rest of the colony if there were sufficient volunteers.[11] The appeal of the last point is suggested by the fact that widespread resistance to the impressment of men for military service had forced an explanatory Act of the Virginia Assembly on the subject in 1648.[12]

New Englanders did not like to be drafted either, but the important point is that they put up with it. Of course there was grumbling and evasion as war-weariness set in,

[10] See Wilcomb E. Washburn, *The Governor and the Rebel: A History of Bacon's Rebellion in Virginia* (Chapel Hill, 1957), and Douglas Leach, *Flintlock and Tomahawk: New England in King Philip's War* (N.Y., 1958). Leach, "The Military System of Plymouth Colony," *New England Quarterly*, XXIV (1951), 342-364, is the best account of a particular militia undergoing change.

[11] Hening, *Statutes at Large*, II, 326-336, 341-350; and Washburn, *Governor and the Rebel*, 35-63.

[12] Hening, *Statutes at Large*, I, 355.

but, facing a much larger attack than did Virginia, the New England colonies were better able to translate their available manpower into military force, and did not suffer political breakdown in the process. As one ponders the differences between Massachusetts and Virginia at war, the more clearly does the pattern of settlement seem crucial. New England towns were more scattered than Chesapeake farms, but each town had a capacity for military resistance that was lacking in an individual plantation. A town could bear the burden of a military draft and still hope to maintain itself against attack, while the loss of a man or two from a single, remote household often meant choosing between abandonment or destruction. Despite their shortages and complaints, New England towns could usually quarter and feed a company of soldiers beside their own, thus acting as advanced military bases. Even the meeting-house, large and centrally located, often served as a "garrison house," a strong point and refuge in case of attack. Although New England also promised its soldiers plunder in the form of scalp bounties, profits from the sale of Indian prisoners, and postwar land grants, these promises were contributory, and not essential as they were in Virginia, to the prosecution of the war. The cohesive and disciplined atmosphere of the town, a product of its religious and social origins, enabled Boston to wage war as Jamestown never could. Virginia was too poor and too atomized to defend itself; it could only retaliate.

The case of New York sharpens the comparison. The Dutch West India Company made the mistake of attracting settlers with the promise of defending them at Company expense. Successive revisions of the "Freedoms and Exemptions" of the colony put increasing stress on the need for self-defense, but the damage had already been done.[13] Organized solely as a commercial enterprise, New Netherland acquired an ethnic heterogeneity and an attitude toward war that subverted militia organization. As quickly as guns were issued to the inhabitants, they were passed on to the Indians for the furs they would bring.

[13] *NYCD*, II, 112, 123.

Even if they had been retained as intended, Governor Peter Stuyvesant would have been unhappy about the number of rebellious subjects with arms in their hands.[14] More sparsely populated than Virginia, New Netherland had much less of the sense of community that makes men fight for one another.

With the English conquest of 1664 came the stereotyped militia law.[15] Conditions, however, could not change as quickly as law. Only the New England towns on Long Island seem to have had an effective militia, but could a royal governor trust unruly Yankees?[16] As for the capital of the colony, a visitor who observed militia training in New York City in 1680 recorded that he had "never seen anything worse," while he was favorably impressed by a sham battle he saw staged by the militia of Boston.[17] Moreover, an accident of geography gave New York not the 200-mile frontier of Massachusetts or Virginia, but a single center of danger—the Anglo-Dutch city of Albany. The fur trade of Albany was the nexus of New York's vital and unusual relationship with the Iroquois Confederation, but it may be that both the Iroquois connection and the lucrative fur trade were valuable results of military weakness.[18] New Yorkers on the frontier had no choice but to get along with their neighbors; unlike Virginia, they were so vulnerable that, if struck, they could not even retaliate.

With the close of the seventeenth century, the problem of colonial defense took on a new dimension. Indians be-

[14] *Ibid.*, I, 427-428, 438.

[15] *Colonial Laws of New York from the Year 1664 to the Revolution* (Albany, 1894-96), I, 49-55.

[16] Ellis L. Raesly, *Portrait of New Netherland* (N.Y., 1945), 110. In 1667, Governor Richard Nicolls reported that he had transformed one-third of the country militia into cavalry, but it appears that only the towns on eastern Long Island were concerned. *NYCD*, III, 156, 167.

[17] *Journal of Jasper Danckaerts, 1670-1680*, eds. Bartlett B. James and J. Franklin Jameson (N.Y., 1913), 239, 271.

[18] Allen W. Trelease, "The Iroquois and the Western Fur Trade: A Problem in Interpretation," *MVHR*, XLIX (1962), 32-51, argues that the Iroquois connection cannot be understood in purely economic terms.

came an additional danger to the danger from France and Spain. For Virginia, however, the problem actually became simpler. The decimated tribes on her frontiers, now "tributary" to the colony, provided warriors who served with a few dozen paid, mounted rangers to scout the backcountry for signs of trouble. A desultory debate between the Governor and House of Burgesses over the value of frontier forts continued for years without important results. Virginia was becoming more thickly settled—the principal requirement for a workable militia system. But the colony was also becoming richer and less threatened, with the Appalachian barrier and the Carolinas to protect her, and so could afford to let a handful of hired soldiers man the defenses, dispensing with the military organization she at last had the capability of maintaining. Under these circumstances, when the Tuscarora threatened the colony momentarily in 1712, the Governor found diplomacy a more available instrument than force, and so made peace instead of war.[19]

The military situation in South Carolina was reminiscent of an earlier Virginia. Poverty and the sparseness of population were serious obstacles to the development of an effective militia. In 1720 the Assembly told the Board of Trade that South Carolina had 2,000 "bold, active, good woodsmen" who were "excellent marksmen," but that settlements scattered over 150 miles made it difficult and expensive to assemble them.[20] Eighteen years later Governor William Bull reiterated this judgment: Carolinians and Georgians were "as Brave as any People whatsoever," he wrote, but they were too thinly settled and too busy with agriculture to defend the southern colonies against French or Spanish regulars. He concluded that "Military Discipline is Inconsistent with a Domestick or Country Life."[21]

[19] On the vicissitudes of Virginia defense, see *CSPC, 1689-1692*, 308, 339ff., 379, and 394; *CSPC, 1699*, 202. On the Tuscarora crisis, see the *Official Letters of Alexander Spotswood*, ed. R. A. Brock, I, 131-133, 194, 197, 204-207.

[20] 29 January 1719/20, *CSPC, 1719-1720*, #531.

[21] To the Board of Trade, 25 May 1738, PRO 30/47 (Egremont MSS.), XIV, 55-56.

But the military difficulties of South Carolina were not merely a repetition of those of Virginia; there were other troubles shared only by New York.

In both New York and South Carolina, the engrossment of large blocks of land inhibited the more compact settlement that was militarily desirable. The need to compete with sister colonies for immigrants further complicated the defense problem. The New England and Chesapeake colonies had forged their militia when men either fought or died, but in turn-of-the-century New York and South Carolina, when danger became too great or government too harsh in its demands for military service, men could and did move to another colony—to Pennsylvania, for example, where there was no militia law.[22] Finally, both colonies were unusually concerned with the danger of insurrection.

Selected Negro slaves fought beside their white masters to defend South Carolina against the Yamassee Indians in 1715, but a slave uprising in 1739 led the Assembly to a terrified reexamination of the militia question. "It appears absolutely necessary to get a sufficient Number of white Persons into this Province," an investigating committee reported, and it then proposed legislation to force large landowners to import and maintain white soldiers in proportion to acreage held.[23] Increasingly the military laws of South Carolina concerned themselves with slave patrols.

New Yorkers likewise feared Negro insurrection, if for different reasons, since both slave and free Negroes were regarded as a most dangerous segment in the unruly capital. An uprising in 1741 appeared to justify these fears. Other varieties of disorder seemed even more likely in a colony that never achieved the homogeneity of Virginia or Massachusetts. Twenty years after Leisler's rebellion, the Governor discovered that the impressment clause of the militia act was being abused to settle old scores.[24] At

[22] See *CSPC, 1714-1715*, 301; *NYCD*, iii, 373, and iv, 185; *PROSC, 1685-1690*, 87.
[23] *CSPC, 1714-1715*, 351; *JCHA, 1739-41*, 25-26.
[24] Governor Hunter to the Board of Trade, 7 May 1711, *NYCD*, v, 202-203.

about the same time, he had to disarm the newly arrived Palatine German immigrants because of their threatening behavior. He soon had to rearm them, however, when the Assembly met its quota of troops for the expedition against Canada by raising 350 "Christian" volunteers, 150 Long Island Indians, and 100 Palatines. Such a response was a far cry from the concept of militia.[25]

New York and South Carolina occupied critical geographical positions in the European struggle for North America, but internal weaknesses led them away from militia defense, and toward reliance on semiprofessional soldiers like Peter Schuyler and John Barnwell, and on periodic pleas to Whitehall for assistance.[26] Only the New England and Chesapeake colonies had the social and historical basis for more than a paper militia in the eighteenth century, but comparison of the two areas forty years after the Indian wars of 1675 reveals an even wider divergence in practice than had existed in the earlier period.

At the end of Queen Anne's War, Governor Alexander Spotswood thought "the Virginians to be capable of being made as good a militia as any in the World, Yet I do take them to be at this time the worst in the King's Dominions." He had tried to order the militia out in 1713 without much success. A year later, in disgust, he had tried to scrap the whole system. Finding that "no Man of an Estate is under any Obligation to Muster, . . . even the Servants or Overseers of the Rich are likewise exempted," and that "the whole Burthen lyes upon the poorest sort of people," Spotswood sought to reduce the militia to one-third its paper strength, but to train it ten times annually and to pay it by a small tax on those exempted from service. His plan suggests the Reserve or National Guard of today, but it was defeated, he thought, by "Persons of Estates who would not come off so easily as they do now."[27] Instead,

[25] Hunter to St. John, 12 September 1711, *ibid.,* 253.

[26] On Schuyler, see *NYCD,* IV, 968; on Barnwell, see Verner W. Crane, *The Southern Frontier, 1670-1732* (Ann Arbor, 1929; 1956 edn.), *passim.*

[27] To the Board of Trade, 7 February 1716, *Spotswood Letters,* II, 194-212.

Virginia would rock along until the French had worked their way up the Ohio Valley, when the anguished letters of Governor Robert Dinwiddie and young Colonel Washington leave no doubts about the virtual nonexistence of the colony's militia.

It would be wrong to idealize the New England militia, but it would be equally mistaken not to recognize that there the institution had retained its vitality. While Spotswood was despairing of the Virginia militia, Governor Joseph Dudley could boast of having recruited several large expeditions against Nova Scotia and at the same time of having protected the colony against continual Indian attack. To guard the frontier, 16 towns from Hadley to Wells (in Maine) were designated as the outpost line. In each, Dudley reinforced the militia with 50-100 infantry and cavalry. Ten or twelve of the best houses were stockaded. The infantry conducted weekly patrols to the adjacent frontier towns, while the cavalry raided deep into Indian country, harassing the enemy, cutting his corn when still green, and seeking him out on snowshoes during the winter months. In case of serious emergency, every fourth or fifth man in the colony could be called out. Though a man might be excused for a £10 fine, the draft was still a reality. The whole system was not a perfect one, but, after the destruction of Deerfield in 1704, it was effective.[28]

To sum up: during the first half of the eighteenth century, New England defended itself. Virginia did not have to defend itself though it could have done so given time and incentive. New York, South Carolina, and Georgia could not defend themselves, and so relied on combinations of neutrality, Indian diplomacy, and help from home. Quaker-controlled Pennsylvania was neither able nor required to defend itself.

The European wars in North America were not, however, wars of defense. Since the beginning of the century, Americans had been writing proposals for the total elimina-

[28] To the Board of Trade, 8 April 1712, *CSPC, 1711-1712,* #375. See also *CSPC, 1702,* 709; *CSPC, 1706-1708,* 344, 678; and *CSPC, 1708-1709,* 240-241.

tion of French and Spanish power from the continent, and they had been trying, sometimes with assistance from England, sometimes without it, to carry out these proposals by offensive operations.

A few hundred troops were needed to wage war against Indians, but to attack Nova Scotia, Florida, Cape Breton, or Quebec required thousands of men ready to serve six months or longer. These expeditions were composed of volunteers. What made men volunteer, and what relation did the volunteer armies bear to the militia?[29]

It is not possible to answer these important questions with anything like precision, but the sources suggest a few conclusions. Most of the expeditions began as a mixture of crusade and migration, with the element of "adventure for its own sake" strong in both. The men who received commissions as officers may also have been officers in the militia, but volunteer rank was almost always higher, and invariably the officers were men who could communicate their own enthusiasm to other men. Military experience was seldom an important factor. The chance for the officer to raise his position in the community was a salt that added savor to adventure. The private soldier's reason for risking gunshot, gangrene, dysentery, smallpox, and scurvy might be as simple as admiration for the man who asked him to join, hatred of Catholicism, the chance to escape for a while from parental supervision or indentured servitude, or the prospect of getting rich.

When the King sent out blank commissions to his royal governors for officers who would recruit companies to serve in the West Indian expedition of 1741, Americans snapped them up. They relished the idea of an authentic military title as well as half-pay for life after the campaign. Other Americans enlisted in the ranks because they knew their

[29] See Howard H. Peckham, "Speculations on the Colonial Wars, 3 *WMQ*, XVII (1960), 463-472, for general thoughts on the subject. The word "militia" is conventionally used to describe both types of military organization, and thus obscures the important differences between them.

officers and had heard of the streets of gold in Havana.[30] These units were nominally regulars, but the pattern was similar for most of the other expeditions. Enlistment bounties, high pay, freedom from impressment for a number of years, and permission to keep issued clothing and muskets—all were used to attract recruits, but a more powerful lure seems to have been the chance to preempt a large piece of land in Nova Scotia or to plunder Saint Augustine.

However ferocious an army assembled in this manner might be, it lacked staying power. When Yankee soldiers learned in 1745 that they were not to be allowed to sack Louisbourg, they decided to go home rather than protect their conquest against recapture during the winter months.[31] Such an army made up in zeal what it lacked in skill and discipline. It was customary for a volunteer officer to request that a court-martial suspend sentence of a soldier convicted of disrespect or disobedience toward him; the men had joined his company with the understanding that justice would be gentle.[32]

One might imagine that, with every man legally obligated to military service, volunteers must have been militiamen. But the militia laws themselves indicate that there was always a drifting segment of the population not enrolled; many volunteers came from this group, usually the poorest inhabitants of a colony. Indentured servants were a second group not on the rolls who provided volunteers, and local Indians and free Negroes were a third. To be sure, when Massachusetts sent perhaps 6,000 men—3 per cent of her population and almost 20 per cent of her militia strength—in the land and sea service to Cape Breton in 1745-1746, most of them had to come from the militia proper. At other

[30] Governor Clarke to Newcastle, 8 July and 25 July 1740, *NYCD*, VI, 164, 167.

[31] Governor Shirley to William Pepperrell, 29 July 1745, *Correspondence of William Shirley*, ed. Charles H. Lincoln (N.Y., 1912), I, 260.

[32] For example, see the orderly book of Sgt. John Grant, kept at Fort Cumberland, Nova Scotia, entries for 8 August and 13 September 1761, HM 595.

times and places, there was less coincidence between the legal and the improvised military organizations. Militia companies everywhere had tended to become social clubs of the white male citizenry, and, especially outside of New England, they bore little relation to the wilder, less affluent men who went soldiering in the eighteenth century.[33]

One question remains: how and why did this system— militia for protection, volunteers for expeditions—fail at the beginning of the Seven Years War? The answer is that it did not truly fail, that it was hardly tested, and that only the standard by which failure was measured had changed. The war began in the upper Ohio Valley, where Virginia and Pennsylvania were most concerned. In the past, it had been enough for a colony to fight when it was injured, but neither colony had yet been directly attacked in 1754; only some Pennsylvania fur traders and a Virginia land company had suffered from the French move. The majority of the House of Burgesses could not see that an immediate, forceful reaction was necessary, and the Quakers preferred to rely on their conciliatory Indian policy for protection.[34]

Governor Robert Dinwiddie, however, held a broader view of empire, a view reinforced by his personal interest in the Ohio Company of land speculators and fur traders. Unfortunately, Dinwiddie was as militarily inexperienced as his colony. In his haste to recruit troops and to move them to the forks of the Ohio before the French had dug in, he made a mess of it. When the Assembly balked at voting the funds needed to mount an expedition, Dinwiddie ordered a draft from the nonexistent militia. This step

[33] For the drifting white population, see *Acts and Resolves, Public and Private, of the Province of Massachusetts Bay* (Boston, 1869-1922), IV, 193, and Hening, *Statutes at Large,* VII, 70. For servants, see Richard B. Morris, *Government and Labor in Early America* (N.Y., 1946), 279-290; and Abbot E. Smith, *Colonists in Bondage* (Chapel Hill, 1947), 279-282. For Negroes, see Benjamin Quarles, "The Colonial Militia and Negro Manpower," *MVHR,* XLV (1959), 643-652. Further discussion is in John W. Shy, "A New Look at Colonial Militia," 3 *WMQ,* XX (1963), 181-184.

[34] Gipson, *British Empire,* IV, 299-306, and VI, 20-45.

created so much antagonism among local magnates and mutinous behavior among the men that it was difficult to enlist volunteers even after money became available.[35] Pennsylvania, of course, did nothing in a military way.

The point is that a colonial governor in 1754 could not afford to try to move faster on matters of war and peace than his political support and the popular temper would allow. The historical shift in importance from militia to vounteers was tightly bound up with the shift of power from the colonial executive to the legislative and local parts of government. When Dinwiddie tried to turn the clock back, he succeeded only in crippling his colony's ability to fight. His proper course was to let the situation ripen, to take the time needed to convince Virginia that she was in danger and that her destiny lay over the mountains, and then to launch a crusade like the one Massachusetts had sent against Louisbourg in 1745. Instead, he thought in more modern and less realistic terms; he was obsessed with "speed, speed, speed," as Washington's biographer puts it.[36] As a result, Dinwiddie failed in an attempt to accomplish too much too quickly, and then called loudly for regulars from England as Virginia's only salvation.

Even Pennsylvania was not as militarily hopeless as she is often depicted. Quakers had voted money for war-making in the past.[37] In 1746 when Philadelphia was in danger from Spanish warships, Benjamin Franklin had published *Plain Truth*, a pamphlet that persuaded many eastern Pennsylvanians—including Quakers—to form a defensive "association," an extralegal militia.[38] Western Pennsylvanians, especially the Scotch-Irish, though without a militia law or financial assistance from the East, already knew how to defend themselves.

[35] Douglas S. Freeman, *George Washington* (N.Y., 1948-1954), I.

[36] *Ibid.*, I, 328.

[37] Isaac Sharpless, *A Quaker Experiment in Government* (Philadelphia, 1898), 194-211.

[38] See *The Papers of Benjamin Franklin*, eds. Leonard W. Labaree, *et al.* (New Haven, 1959-), III, 180-212.

But to let the Americans fight their own battles demanded of British ministers a certain callousness and considerable patience. The beginning would be bloody while the Americans were learning what had to be done. It would mean urging the colonies to unify their efforts, begging Virginia to help South Carolina and Georgia if necessary, New England to help New York. This had been done before, usually with less than satisfactory results. The capability and the willingness of the Americans to use force would determine imperial strategy, and not the other way around. There would also be some unpleasant repercussions if the Americans carried the burden of what promised to be the biggest colonial war yet.

All these requirements were intolerable. They ran against the grain of mid-eighteenth-century political economy. Dinwiddie's call fell on receptive ears, perhaps because experience seemed to disprove the premises of the defense policy of the preceding century. Regular troops had not in fact been kept out of the colonies, so a wiser mercantilism indicated that those regulars, if augmented and united, would provide a more rational, more responsive, and in the long run more economical instrument for the defense of North America.

Regulars and the Erosion of Policy

The Seven Years War was fought and won by these regulars, with the American provincials performing, in each successive campaign, more of an auxiliary function.[39] At the end of the war, a sizeable part of the regular army remained in America, a situation unprecedented in the first century and a half of its existence. But as one looks back over that century and a half, the cornerstone of imperial

[39] Casualty figures can best show the role to which the American provincials were relegated. At the bloody battle of Ticonderoga in 1758, there were 1,522 casualties among less than 6,000 regulars; 8 of 11 field officers and over half the captains among the regulars were killed or wounded. On the other hand, over 9,000 provincials at the battle suffered 334 casualties. Inclosure in Maj. Gen. James Abercromby to William Pitt, 12 July 1758, CO 5/50.

military policy, which should have kept regulars out of the colonies, appears to have been eroded here and there, softened for the final disintegration. In fact, there were British troops in North America very early in our history. Why and where were they sent, and what did they do?

The first experience of the American colonies with imperial military force was in 1651-1652 when Virginia and Barbados were brought to heel by an expedition from the Puritan Commonwealth.[40] But these soldiers soon departed, so that the first important injection of British troops into the colonial scene came with Cromwell's "Western Design" of 1655. Twenty-five hundred soldiers—"a disorderly mob made up of rejected men from the English regiments supplemented by vagabonds forcibly recruited from the London slums"[41]—set out with Admiral Sir William Penn and General Robert Venables; landed at Barbados where they were supplemented by almost 5,000 recruits from the Lesser Antilles who were, if anything, even worse; and, after a mismanaged campaign, those who had not died on the way eventually reached Jamaica. With military operations at an end, land was distributed, and settlement became as important as soldiering, but disease and Spanish counterattack took a terrible toll.[42] The situation had become critical by 1660. The Governor-General in Jamaica was embittered and discouraged, mutiny appeared imminent, and there was a dangerous antagonism between troops and civilians. "Souldiers," wrote their commander, "in time of peace, are look'd upon in the worst sense."[43] After the restoration of the monarchy in 1660, the Council

[40] Thomas J. Wertenbaker, *Virginia under the Stuarts 1607-1688* (Princeton, 1914), 99-100; Vincent T. Harlow, *A History of Barbados 1625-1685* (Oxford, 1926), 62-79.

[41] Arthur P. Newton, *The European Nations in the West Indies 1493-1688* (London, 1933), 216. See also Sir Charles Firth and Godfrey Davies, *The Regimental History of Cromwell's Army* (Oxford, 1940), II, 699-729.

[42] Charles M. Andrews, *The Colonial Period of American History* (New Haven, 1934-38), III, 23-26.

[43] Quoted in A. P. Thornton, *West-India Policy under the Restoration* (Oxford, 1956), 42.

for Foreign Plantations directed the new Governor to disband all but 400 infantry and 150 cavalry, and to retain even this small force on partial pay.[44] Because of the Cromwellian cast of this Jamaican army, it was deemed wiser to rely primarily on militia.[45]

Four hundred more regular soldiers came to America with Richard Nicolls, who accepted the surrender of New Amsterdam on behalf of the Duke of York in 1664.[46] These men were in the Duke's pay; the Duke in turn received some financial aid from the King for New York defenses.[47] Nicolls and his successor, Francis Lovelace, used detachments to garrison and control the frontier settlements of New York, but after the Dutch recapture of the province and its subsequent retrocession to the Duke as a result of the third Anglo-Dutch war (1673-1674), the garrison—then only 100 men—appears to have been divided between Albany and New York City.[48] The experiment in military control, 1664-1673, had had some interesting results: one was the brutal treatment of the Dutch inhabitants of Esopus by its garrison, and another was the later use of that same garrison to take up land in the "furthest dorp" in order to defend the main settlement. Once settled, these soldiers were dropped from the Duke's pay. The pattern may have been repeated in other towns of the province. This scheme of settling regular soldiers on small, con-

[44] The Council for Foreign Plantations recommended half-pay, 3 July 1661, but the cost of the garrison was eventually calculated "at a ffourth part pay," 4 April 1662. The total cost was £3,539. *APCC*, I, #522, #559. Because troops could never support themselves in the West Indies, even on full pay, it is obvious that the soldiers were primarily farmers and not a regular garrison.

[45] Thornton, *West-India Policy*, 50.

[46] Andrews, *Colonial Period*, III, 61.

[47] £1,000 in 1678. *APCC*, I, #1288.

[48] There were garrisons at Newcastle on the Delaware (20 men), Albany (20-100), Esopus (15-16), and Pemaquid (20). *NYCD*, XII, 461-462, 488, XIII, 309, 563; *CSPC, 1661-1668*, #1219; Andrews, *Colonial Period*, III, 115; Stanley M. Pargellis, "The Four Independent Companies of New York," *Essays in Colonial American History Presented to Charles McLean Andrews by his Students* (New Haven, 1931), 97.

tiguous parcels of land in order to provide a defensive barrier is one that recurs frequently in later memoranda on the colonies. It never seemed to work; the Governor of New York soon wrote that the soldiers at Esopus "are becoming more the nursery of Newgate, then persons who have taken on them a settled and resolved life."[49]

When the French entered the second Anglo-Dutch war in 1666, the English Privy Council commissioned Sir Tobias Bridge to command a regiment of 800 men in the most valuable of the British West Indies—Barbados. Earlier, Barbados had granted a 4½ per cent export duty to the Crown in exchange for a confirmation of land titles. It was from this fund that the regiment was to be paid.[50] The regiment was placed on half-pay after the war in 1667, and was finally reduced to two companies of 80 men each and moved to St. Christopher, an island that the English uneasily shared with the French.[51] The Barbadians had feared the regiment, but they had also tried to prevent its being sent to the Leeward Islands.[52]

As the Privy Council saw it, Bacon's rebellion in Virginia in 1676 required a large military force from England to restore order. The Guards regiments furnished 425 men, and the remainder of an expedition of 1,130 was quickly recruited. The rebellion was over when the troops arrived, and their presence was reckoned a disaster by the inhabitants of the strife-torn and economically depressed colony who had to house and feed them.[53] The first soldiers to land

[49] *NYCD*, XIII, 426, as well as 406-417, 419-422, and 428.

[50] Thornton, *West-India Policy*, 129. The troops were not recruited on the island, but were sent from England. *CSPC, 1661-1668*, #1446.

[51] Thornton, *West-India Policy*, 246. The 4½ per cent duty was also collected in the Leeward Islands (Nevis, Monserrat, Antigua, and St. Christopher), and this was added to the fund for payment of the regiment in 1668. *APCC*, I, #792.

[52] Thornton, *West-India Policy*, 244-245; *CSPC, 1661-1668*, #1446.

[53] Washburn, *Governor and the Rebel*, 95-100; *CSPC, 1675-1676*, #1053, #1059. It does appear that compensation was paid by the Crown to the Virginians for rations, *CSPC, 1675-1676*, #1060.

found themselves "quite destitute of quarters; no place fit to receive them, much less the number that are coming after, whereat the Governor, who believed a frigate or two would have been sufficient, and never desired soldiers, is much amused, and the whole people startled, and many ready to quit their plantations."[54] An order arrived from England to send back all but 100 soldiers and any others who "of their own free will desire to stay as planters or servants."[55] This order was soon changed, for, by 1677, it appears that the British government had begun to put its colonial house in order.

The threat of war with France together with the energy and system which the Earl of Danby brought to the ministry may have furnished the impulse for a reform of colonial administration in general, and of military forces in the plantations in particular. The two companies at St. Christopher, under-strength and with pay three years in arrears "so that they are naked and have onely subsisted by the charity of the planters, and the care of their colonell," were sent money and recruits.[56] Early in 1678, two more companies of 100 men each were sent to Jamaica along with the new governor of that island. It was evident that there was a close connection between the presence of these troops in Jamaica and the Crown's desire for a permanent revenue, and Jamaicans were never certain whether the regular troops were intended for defense or repression.[57]

[54] Sir John Berry and Col. Francis Moryson (two of the three commissioners) to Sir Joseph Williamson (Secretary of State) 2 February 1677, *CSPC, 1677-1680*, #32.

[55] 13 May 1677, *CSPC, 1677-1680*, #240.

[56] *APCC*, I, #1028, #1148. For a general description of the new interest in colonial affairs by the Privy Council after 1675, see Charles M. Andrews, *Colonial Self-Government, 1652-1689* (N.Y., 1904), 25-32. The exact nature of this new interest is unknown, but it is particularly evident in military matters. Andrew Browning, *Thomas Osborne, Earl of Danby* (Glasgow, 1951), sheds no light on the question, but, considering Danby's concern with financial problems, it may have been aimed at tightening colonial control in order to raise revenue. See Philip S. Haffenden, "The Crown and the Colonial Charters, 1675-1688," 3 *WMQ*, xv (1958), 297-300.

[57] Thornton, *West-India Policy*, 251. The 550 troops on partial

By the end of the year, two similar companies had been established in Virginia from the forces sent to quell Bacon's rebellion.[58] There was even some discussion of troops for Newfoundland.[59] Thus, in 1679, there were small but fixed garrisons in Jamaica, the Leeward Islands, Virginia, and New York at an annual cost to the Crown of about £15,400.[60]

But the new plan had hardly been drawn before it was dropped in the political turmoil and financial straits that resulted from the disclosure of the "Popish plot." Evidently a larger force was needed in the Leeward Islands, but when the Captain General in England, the Duke of Monmouth, submitted an estimate of £6,054 for the annual maintenance of 1,000 soldiers there, the government gave up the idea as impracticable. Soon the pay of the two companies left at St. Christopher was again several years in arrears. The Crown was unable to secure from Jamaica the permanent revenue which it sought for military purposes, and the two companies there were disbanded in 1680.[61] Finally, in the following year, the Lords of Trade considered disbanding the Virginia troops whose pay was also in arrears. The Governor of Virginia, Lord Culpeper, testified that the presence of these companies would have prevented Bacon's rebellion; that a future insurrection would cost five times as much to put down from England; that the unsettled state of North Carolina and Maryland, the Indian threat, and internal unrest due to economic de-

---

pay, the remnants of the "Western Design," appear to have been converted into a "minute man" element of the Jamaica militia by this time.

[58] *APCC*, I, #1235.

[59] George L. Beer, *The Old Colonial System 1660-1754*, Part I (N.Y., 1912), II, 218-220.

[60] This figure consists of the pay of the troops in the first three places and the allowance to the Duke of York for the defense of his colony in 1679, and of the average expenses of ordnance delivered to the various colonies between 1660 and 1677. Beer, *Old Colonial System*, I, 115n., 128n. It had cost about £12,700 to send the troops to Virginia in 1676. *CSPC, 1675-1676*, #1062, #1077.

[61] Thornton, *West-India Policy*, 249, 252.

pression all argued for retention of a regular force; and that a scattered population made militia more expensive and less effective.[62] But the Privy Council ordered disbandment unless Virginia would undertake the financial burden, and, after long debate in the Assembly, Virginia decided it was too poor to do this. So ended the only comprehensive plan before 1720 to use regulars as the backbone of colonial defense.[63]

It is surprising to find that the grandiose ideas behind the scheme for a "Dominion of New England" (1685-1689) apparently did not include a sizeable regular garrison for the colonies. The Duke of Albemarle, the new governor of Jamaica, did propose that the two companies previously stationed in that island be revived to prevent Negro rebellion,[64] and Sir Edmund Andros, Governor of the Dominion, did bring 100 soldiers with him in 1686,[65] to which were added the New York regulars. But Albemarle's proposal was never considered, and Andros's force was too small and too dispersed to play any important part in the upheavals of 1689 in Massachusetts and New York; his companies put up no resistance and simply melted away in the course of the provincial versions of the "Glorious Revolution."[66] What was happening in the meantime to the

[62] Beer, *Old Colonial System*, I, 117-118; *CSPC, 1681-1685*, #268.

[63] Order-in-council, 22 November 1681, and Sir Henry Chicheley to Sir Thomas Chicheley, 12 June 1682, *CSPC, 1681-1685*, #299, #550. The upshot can be used as evidence to argue either that the troops should have been disbanded or that they should have been retained, for the soldiers, disgruntled at the news of their pay ending on 1 April 1682, made common cause for a time with the rebellious tobacco plant cutters and refused to give up the main guard and the magazine. Observers said that the troops were "quite out of control," and that the danger to the Virginia government during the rebellion was great. After it was over, most of the discharged soldiers remained in Virginia. Chicheley letter above, and Virginia Secretary to Sir Leoline Jenkins, 8 May and 7 June 1682, *CSPC, 1681-1685*, #495, #546.

[64] [6 July] 1686, *CSPC, 1685-1688*, #759.

[65] Warrant of 30 August 1686, *CSPC, 1685-1688*, #832.

[66] Viola F. Barnes, *The Dominion of New England* (New Haven, 1923), 243-244; Pargellis, *Essays Presented to C. M. Andrews*, 98.

troops on St. Christopher typifies the fate of colonial garrisons before 1689: they had not been paid in four years, and 40 to 50 recruits were needed to replace men who had become "very ancient" and had "already turned planters."[67]

The Revolution of 1688 and the beginning of the long struggle with France wrought a change, not in policy, for there had been little worthy of the name; rather, it produced something resembling a policy. No longer did the Crown appear to toy with the idea of imperial government backed by force. It is true that the Attorney General opined, in 1694, that the Crown might appoint a single colonial Captain General over the forces of even private colonies, and Lord Bellomont's commission of 1697 as governor of New York and Massachusetts was the result of this opinion, but the aim in this case was to make full use of the colonial militia so that regular troops would not be required.[68] It is also true that regular troops were sent to the colonies in 1689 and after in numbers unprecedented since the "Western Design," but always either to the war-torn West Indies, which pleaded for military assistance, or to areas on the continent which were strategically critical but had insufficient population to form an effective militia. Continual warfare or the threat of war made defense the paramount consideration in distributing regular forces, and when they were sent to the colonies it was always with reluctance. Only in the suppression of Leisler's rebellion in New York in 1689-1690 were regulars sent for any other reason.

The two companies sent with Governor Henry Sloughter to put down the Leislerians became four companies of 100 each by 1701; their mission was to block the key invasion

[67] Gov. Johnson to the Lords of Trade, 10 August 1687, *CSPC, 1685-1688*, #1387. Albemarle, on a tour of the West Indies later in the same year, reported the St. Christopher companies "in very good order," *CSPC, 1685-1688*, #1567, but I suspect that this was of a piece with his advocacy of a garrison for Jamaica. The Lords of Trade considered these same companies hopeless five months later, for they planned their disbandment, and the dispatch of two fresh ones from England. *CSPC, 1685-1688*, #1742. This order was never executed because of the Revolution and the outbreak of war.

[68] Pargellis, *Loudoun*, 9.

routes along the Mohawk and Champlain valleys.[69] A regiment of 780 went to the Leeward Islands in 1689 to recapture St. Christopher, and, as always in the West Indies, disease did more damage than the enemy. Financing the regiment by the 4½ per cent duty proved unsatisfactory, but the inhabitants were so anxious to keep soldiers there that they gave men and officers free quarters.[70] Two years later, Barbados begged for a regiment of its own, and stressed the danger of a Negro insurrection. While it claimed to be too poor to provide free quarters, the Assembly voted a daily additional allowance of ninepence for the 500 men sent out in 1694.[71] At about the same time, Jamaica received an independent company, but the islanders soon asked for a regiment of 1,500, which they did not get.[72] In fact, with peace in the offing in 1697, the Jamaica merchants concurred in the disbandment of even this company, because the men would be less expensive and just as effective serving as militia. What Jamaicans, and perhaps colonists elsewhere, had in mind when they asked for regular troops in peacetime is revealed in a surprisingly frank memorandum from the Jamaica agent to the Board of Trade later in 1697. He asked that four companies of soldiers be sent to the island at Crown expense, to be given their full discharge as soon as they found employment. In effect, Jamaica sought government-financed white immigration.[73]

Finally, a new colonial garrison was added after the French capture of the Newfoundland harbors in 1696. The Board of Trade prepared a report which said that at least three companies were necessary for the defense of the island, and 510 men were sent with an expeditionary force

[69] Pargellis, *Essays Presented to C. M. Andrews*, 98-99.

[70] *CSPC, 1689-1692*, #113, #531, #634; Gov. Codrington to the Lords of Trade, 13 July 1691, *CSPC, 1689-1692*, #1643.

[71] *CSPC, 1693-1696*, #759, #884, #928, #997, #1371, #1401. A private soldier's daily pay was 8 pence.

[72] *CSPC, 1693-1696*, #1478; Petition to the Board of Trade, 16 December 1696, *CSPC, 1696-1697*, #598.

[73] *Ibid.*, #1154, #1406.

in 1697.[74] There was even a proposal to maintain a garrison in Acadia (Nova Scotia), but the Board of Trade called this idea "altogether unreasonable."[75] After the peace, a company of 43 soldiers manned Fort William at St. John's, Newfoundland.[76]

These garrisons were a source of continual trouble, both to the colonists and to the British government. There was a rumor that William III had sent discontented soldiers to the West Indies to be rid of them, and it was not long before the truth of the warning that "the military government [of Newfoundland] should be in the hands of a good and experienced officer, not too much given to self-interest, for he will meet with great temptations," was borne out by events.[77] In New York and Newfoundland, the troops were cruelly neglected by British administration, and in the West Indies by the colonial governments themselves. Jamaica by this time had become the most important of the British islands, and the lull between King William's and Queen Anne's Wars, and perhaps a sense of its own importance, led the Jamaican Assembly to act as if it would not renew its 21-year grant of revenue to the Crown. Under the combined threats from France of war, and from the Governor to rule Jamaica as Ireland was ruled, the Assembly capitulated at the eleventh hour.[78] But acts for quartering and granting additional pay to the troops were subjects of hot controversy until 1708, because the Assembly repeatedly tried to "tack" obnoxious provisions onto

[74] 13 January 1697, *ibid.*, #583. This report was never presented. *APCC*, II, #670.

[75] 14 May 1697, *CSPC, 1696-1697*, #1024.

[76] 30 March 1698, *CSPC, 1697-1698*, #333.

[77] William T. Morgan, "The British West Indies during King William's War (1689-97)," *Journal of Modern History*, II (1930), 391n; Col. John Gisborne (commander of troops in the expeditionary force) to the Board of Trade, 10 March 1698, *CSPC, 1697-1698*, #286. For the correctness of his estimate, see *APCC*, II, #865, #992, #1063, #1134.

[78] Ruth Bourne, *Queen Anne's Navy in the West Indies* (New Haven, 1939), 27, 33-35.

them.[79] Conditions were somewhat better for the regiment in the Leeward Islands, although the military was involved in an ugly incident there which will be discussed later, but Barbados was too poverty stricken to support the regiment that it vainly demanded as essential to its survival.[80] A new colonial garrison became necessary after Colonel Francis Nicholson and 400 royal marines, supplemented by a body of New England volunteers, captured Port Royal, Acadia, in 1710.[81] This, and the ease with which the French had overpowered the single company at St. John's in 1705, were sufficient reason to distribute henceforth a regiment between Newfoundland and Nova Scotia.

In the details of this account of troop movements, a trend begins to emerge by the end of Queen Anne's War. The doctrinaire assertion that colonies should defend themselves disappears, and the British government considers each case on its own merits. The Crown is willing at least to consider stationing regular garrisons overseas if any one or a combination of three conditions exists in a particular colony: (1) little capability for self-defense, (2) substantial strategic or financial value, and (3) colonial willingness to pay part of the costs of a regular garrison. Even though the Jamaica garrison was reduced in 1715 to two companies, Great Britain was maintaining a North American military establishment of almost 2,000 men at an annual cost of about £40,000 after the Treaty of Utrecht.[82]

By 1721, Lord Townshend, Secretary of State and

[79] *Ibid.*, 38-39. See also, among others, *CSPC, 1702-1703,* #1150; *1704-1705,* #107, #440, #547, #554, #557, #603, #754, #872, #1168, #1421, #1459, #1461; *1706-1708,* #1339, #1423.

[80] *CSPC, 1704-1705,* #554; Bourne, *Queen Anne's Navy,* 42, 46.

[81] G. M. Waller, *Samuel Vetch, Colonial Enterpriser* (Chapel Hill, 1960), 179-186.

[82] Estimates for 1714 and 1715, *Commons Journals,* XVIII, 47 and 636. This establishment included a company each at Bermuda and Providence (Bahamas). The estimates are for £34,743 and £35,766 respectively, but ordnance costs were estimated separately and lumped together in such a way that the North American items cannot be distinguished.

brother-in-law to Robert Walpole, had injected a new imagination and dynamism into the supervision of colonial affairs. With Spain hostile and France expanding and strengthening her occupation of the periphery of British settlement in America, he called for reports and recommendations on the continental colonies. In perhaps the most daring document it ever produced, the Board of Trade recommended that key points in the New York, Virginia, and the Carolina backcountry be fortified, and that eight infantry regiments be dispatched, four to Nova Scotia and four to South Carolina. The Board countered the obvious objection to this radical plan by a simple statement: "We are very sensible that this proposal will be attended with expense; but we hope it may be fully justify'd by the necessity thereof, for the preservation of the British colonies in America."[83] In fact, the recommendation to send troops had been made in the previous year, and regulars went to South Carolina in 1721.[84] But instead of the four regiments recommended by the Board of Trade, or even the single regiment hoped for by the Carolinians, Governor Francis Nicholson brought with him one ridiculous company, 100 "invalids"—pensioners discharged from active duty because of age or infirmity— and half of these were ill with scurvy. Like the regulars elsewhere, they were neglected by the colonists, although Nicholson said that the trouble was that they were too old and morose to look after themselves. If they did not burn down the fort and barracks at their outpost on the Altamaha River in early 1726 so that they could winter more comfortably at Port Royal, at least they did not endanger their lives in fighting the fire.[85] This was the only tangible result of the Board of Trade report.

[83] September 1721, *CSPC, 1720-1721*, #656, pp. 440-442.
[84] *Ibid.*, 425.
[85] Crane, *Southern Frontier*, 235, 245-246. The captain of this company, in excusing its behavior to the British Secretary at War, reported that the fort was about as militarily useful to South Carolina as if it had been in Japan, and that its location was so unhealthy that over 130 men had died there in the previous 6 years. *CSPC, 1726-1727*, 265-266.

Little more is heard of this South Carolina company: the Board of Trade was informed in 1729 that but for the presence of these few troops and some ships of the Royal Navy, the province "must have been lost by the ignorance, dishonesty, mutiny, and rebellion of the inhabitants. . . ." Sometime later, the governor requested another 100 regulars, there "being but few white men in the province and they require to be paid treble the charge of common soldiers sent from hence. . . ."[86] He did not get them.

In the West Indies, military service was miserable after 1715, but that represented a substantial improvement over the abominable conditions that had existed previously. Jamaica treated its two companies well enough to get six more in 1734 when the threat of rebellious and runaway slaves had become acute.[87] Antigua, which already had five companies of the Leeward Islands regiment stationed in it, made similar requests in 1737 and 1739. After some hard bargaining, during which the islanders were forced to agree to build barracks and a hospital, to provide heat and light for them, to grant extra pay to officers and men, and even to provide for discharged veterans, Antigua got its additional troops.[88] The pattern was clear: the West Indies could have soldiers whenever they were willing to pay for them, and the West Indies were increasingly pleased at the presence of regulars because of the mounting danger of slave insurrection.[89]

As for the continental colonies, a refreshing aberration occurred in the waning years of Walpole's ministry. Sir Robert told James Oglethorpe in early 1737 that he was

[86] Sir Alexander Cuming to Newcastle [December 1729], *CSPC, 1730*, #33li; #643.

[87] *APCC*, III, #68, #303.   [88] *Ibid.*, #400.

[89] Richard Pares, *War and Trade in the West Indies 1739-1763* (Oxford, 1936), 257-263. See also *APCC*, III, #599. This concern with domestic disorder is frequently mentioned in the reports from and on the West Indies. The case of St. Christopher in 1745 shows that it was the slaves and not the French the islanders feared: the Assembly tried to deprive the soldiers of their additional pay during an invasion scare, because the troops had occupied the island's citadel, and so had been unable to do nightly guard duty in the town.

at a loss how to defend North America. Oglethorpe, himself never at a loss for either words or ideas, replied "that if the defence were left to a militia it would cost dear, because they must be paid when in service for the neglect of their own affairs, and therefore it were more eligible and safe to have regular troops." When Walpole bridled at the cost of this, and rejected the alternative of simply levying two men from every infantry company and dragoon troop in the British army for colonial defense, Oglethorpe countered: "Then there must be a certain number new raised, and he believed that if a battalion of 500 men were allowed to each colony the colonies would themselves pay them, for the uneasiness they are now under proceeds from observing that the companies now there are not kept full, but have onely the name of a company, the officers putting the money of vacant soldiers into their pockets, so that the regular forces there are only nominal and of no service."

Although Walpole supposedly "relished the proposal," and subsequently appointed Oglethorpe to the office of Captain General for Georgia and South Carolina, it was the House of Commons which forced Walpole to add troops to the American garrison.[90] Oglethorpe had requested and soon obtained a Parliamentary grant of £20,000 for Georgia; he then threatened to resign his Captain Generalcy if Walpole did not let him raise a regiment for service on the southern frontier. Walpole consented reluctantly but then tried everything to prevent it: pleading the need for economy, he first planned to form the regiment by withdrawing troops from the West Indies, a scheme which the islanders vehemently opposed; then, pleading the need not to antagonize Spain, he urged Oglethorpe to drop the whole idea and to accept the

[90] *Diary of the First Earl of Egmont* (*HMC, Egmont MSS.*, London, 1923), II, 339-340. Pargellis, *Loudoun*, 5, is somewhat unfair to Oglethorpe by implying that he saw no alternative to British regulars paid by the Crown or to colonial militia. It is clear that Oglethorpe had in mind the very plan which Pargellis considers to be the only practicable and effective one—an "American" army.

colonelcy of a regiment in England. Oglethorpe refused the bribe, and "desired to know whether Georgia was to be given up, yea or nay? If so, it would be kind and just to let the Trustees know it at once, that we might write immediately over to the inhabitants to retire and save themselves in time." Wearily, "Sir Robert replied he did not see the necessity of that," and finally agreed to give him soldiers then in service.[91] Oglethorpe persuaded the Trustees to grant 3,000 acres for the support of his men, and then proceeded to lead them in an abortive attack on St. Augustine. They were more successful in defending the southern frontier.[92]

After Oglethorpe himself left the scene in 1743, an Order-in-Council established three infantry companies under the control of the Governor and Council of South Carolina, and, when Oglethorpe's regiment was disbanded in 1748-1749, some of the soldiers were absorbed by these companies.[93] As in New York after 1712, the companies were recruited in America, and as in the West Indies, an expressed fear of Negro revolt and a prior agreement by the Assembly to grant additional pay and to build barracks were factors in the decision to establish the garrison.[94]

King George's war also brought more troops to the North. Governor George Clarke sought a regiment of regulars for New York in vain.[95] But in 1745 a New

[91] *Egmont Diary*, II, 415, 418, 421, 429; Amos A. Ettinger, *James Edward Oglethorpe, Imperialist Idealist* (Oxford, 1936), 192-199.

[92] *Egmont Diary*, II, 438; Trevor R. Reese, "Britain's Military Support of Georgia in the War of 1739-1748," *Georgia Historical Quarterly*, XLIII (1949), 1-10.

[93] *APCC*, III, #592; Ettinger, *Oglethorpe*, 207-254. Officially, the South Carolina companies were disbanded, and three new companies raised for South Carolina from the remains of Oglethorpe's regiment. See *Colonial Records of the State of Georgia*, ed. A. D. Chandler (Atlanta, 1904-1916), VI, 353, 397, 450.

[94] PRO-SC, XXI, 397; Pargellis, *Essays Presented to C. M. Andrews*, 118; Gov. Glen to Newcastle, 28 May 1745 and 11 February 1746, PRO-SC, XXII, 104, 133; *JCHA, 1745-1946*, 76-79, 104, 109, 115-117, 161, 201.

[95] Clarke to Newcastle, 19 June 1743, *NYCD*, VI, 228.

England force performed the incredible feat of capturing Louisbourg. Governor William Shirley of Massachusetts and the commander of the force, Sir William Pepperell, were each ordered to raise a regiment of regulars from among the troops. Though the order was intended as a reward for their services, Shirley expressed doubt that he could recruit a regiment of Americans on the pay scale of the British army.[96] After the peace of Aix-la-Chapelle in 1748, these regiments, like Oglethorpe's, were disbanded, but one of the two regiments sent from Gibraltar in 1746 to reinforce the Louisbourg garrison was placed under the command of the new Governor of Nova Scotia, who had instructions to build a fortress and naval base on the site of Halifax.[97] The Governor reported shortly after his arrival that the other regiment, which had been stationed in Nova Scotia since 1711, was in a shocking condition: "The management in that Regiment has been so shameful that 'tis almost incredible—there never was such another in any service. . . . General Phillips deserved the highest punishment for what he did here . . . his receiving money for public works without disbursing one penny particularly for Canso where private men [soldiers] at their own charges were obliged to provide magazines for the stores, his never allowing the Regiment half their clothing, I am told not one of them ever had a knapsack or haversack."[98] In 1750 a third regiment, much smaller than the other two but with 130 women and children, came from Ireland to reinforce the Halifax settlement.[99] By 1754, before the dispatch of Braddock's expedition, the annual cost of over 4,000 soldiers in America and the West Indies was about

[96] Governor Shirley to Newcastle, 2 September 1745, *Shirley Correspondence*, I, 266ff.

[97] *Commons Journals*, xxv, 441, 898; John B. Brebner, *New England's Outpost* (N.Y., 1927), 166ff.

[98] Gov. Cornwallis to the Board of Trade, and to the Duke of Bedford, 11 September 1749, *Selections from the Public Documents of the Province of Nova Scotia*, ed. T. B. Akins (Halifax, 1869), 584, 586.

[99] Pargellis, *Loudoun*, 31.

£95,000. Of this, however, the 790 men stationed between Maine and Georgia cost only £13,500.[100]

In a way, the beginning of the final round in the colonial struggle between France and Great Britain was like that of King George's war: the Duke of Cumberland in 1754, like Oglethorpe in 1737, urged preparedness; the result was the dispatch of two under-strength regiments from Ireland under Major General Edward Braddock, and the reactivation of Shirley's and Pepperell's regiments. In fact, the government did not intend a policy reversal in 1754; it contemplated no large, long-term commitment of regular forces to North America. The cabinet saw its action as grounded on the precedent of previous wartime expeditions to help the colonies, only this time help would be timely, sufficient, and unhampered by divided control.[101]

Two disasters put the seal on a permanent change in both wartime strategy and peacetime policy. In 1755, the French and Indians nearly destroyed the two regiments from Ireland just south of modern Pittsburgh, and they killed Braddock himself, thus throwing Governor (and Colonel) William Shirley into the supreme command. A colonial governor without sufficient military experience was the wrong man for this job. While he was being replaced and the American army reinforced, the second disaster occurred: Oswego—strategic key to frontier New York and to control of the Iroquois Confederation—fell to Montcalm, and with it were captured Shirley's and Pepperell's regiments. These defeats made traditional military policy seem irrelevant, and they initiated a British reaction that saw at least 32 regiments containing over 30,000 regulars in North America at the peak of warfare, 1758-1759, most of them on the continent south of Nova Scotia.[102]

The colonies felt the political effects of this great mili-

---

[100] *Commons Journals*, XXVI, 847-848, 850, 930. This excludes the exceptional shipments of ordnance to Massachusetts, Maryland, Virginia, and for the Iroquois Confederacy.

[101] Pargellis, *Loudoun*, 31ff.

[102] Gipson, *British Empire*, VII, 177; Marshall Smelser, *The Campaign for the Sugar Islands, 1759* (Chapel Hill, 1955), 188-189.

tary force when the British government appointed a Commander in Chief, Lord Loudoun, for all except the West Indian troops, and gave him broad discretionary powers. Loudoun spent considerable time and effort in a partially successful attempt to force the continental colonies to support the war. He proved both inept and unlucky as a field commander, however, and when he was recalled, Maryland's governor could write: "You must know that His Lordship began to be regarded among us as a Vice Roy and to have great Influence in all the Colonies which I am apt to think his Successors will never have."[103] The governor was right; with Loudoun's departure, William Pitt took full charge of the war in North America and subsequent Commanders in Chief were little more than lieutenants for the execution of his military orders. Of even greater importance, Pitt's promise of monetary reimbursement eliminated the need to cajole and coerce most of the colonies into furnishing men and material. Thus the apparent threat of Cromwellian military rule to colonial liberties was, for the moment, averted.[104]

Fighting was substantially over on the continent in 1760, although the West Indian theater was the scene of major campaigns in the following two years. But as early as 1760 the British government had once again to ponder the perennial question: What regular forces shall be kept in North America in peacetime?

Regulars, Militia, and the Maintenance of Order: The Parke Affair

If anyone searched the record in order to let experience guide the formulation of a postwar military policy for North America, certain points should have stood out. The most striking characteristic of British regular forces in the colonies before the Seven Years War was the way they were neglected by the British government. Troops were

---

[103] Gov. Sharpe to William Sharpe, 27 August 1758, quoted in Pargellis, *Loudoun*, 278.

[104] This paragraph is a statement of the thesis elaborated by Pargellis, *Loudoun*.

dispatched to America and the West Indies, only to be forgotten in time of peace. Occasionally recruits were sent to fill vacancies. Occasionally money was sent to pay arrears, or clothing sent to cover nakedness. Occasionally the Board of Trade would exert pressure on an assembly that failed to meet a colony's commitment to support its regular garrison. But never were units in the colonies relieved, after several years service, by other units from England or Ireland, and never was there any sort of continuous administrative effort to look after these regular forces. Part of the reason for this was governmental immaturity; the bureaucratic machinery simply did not exist to handle such difficult problems. There was another and more important reason, however, and it was financial. It cost money to relieve regiments, to keep them up to strength, to equip and pay them. And these were expenditures which could be, and were, put off, if not forgotten. The system of creating and running an army by "farming" the regiments to proprietorial colonels, which was intended to obviate both the administrative and financial weaknesses of the state, proved inadequate for extended overseas service.

The result of this neglect was that regular forces in the colonies were largely ineffectual. The accounts of the South Carolina and St. Christopher companies and the Nova Scotia regiment, previously mentioned, were typical. During the Seven Years War, the Commander in Chief had more trouble than help from the weak and disorganized New York companies, and the commander of the expedition against Martinique in 1759 could expect little or no assistance from the Leeward Islands regiment which had been 60 years in the Caribbean.[105] In peacetime, the soldiers quite literally vegetated. It was a necessity if they were to survive. From sparetime employment, to reporting only

[105] Pargellis, *Essays Presented to C. M. Andrews*, 120-121; Smelser, *Campaign*, 18. At the beginning of the Seven Years War, the South Carolina companies were better than most; see Governor Dinwiddie to Henry Fox, 24 July 1754, *The Official Records of Governor Robert Dinwiddie*, ed. R. A. Brock (Richmond, 1883-84), I, 244-245.

for necessary guard duty, to full-time farming while the captain "padded" the muster-roll—these seem to have been the usual stages. At best, regular soldiers became little different from colonial militia.

A second point which becomes clear from a perusal of the record is that the companies and regiments in the colonies were almost always under the control of the governor concerned. It is true that the governor's council usually had a voice in the employment of these troops, but perhaps of greater importance to the typical governor was the income he received as colonel or captain. If there was more than one regiment (as in Nova Scotia) or company (as in New York), the commanders of the additional corps usually became or already were politically prominent in the colony. Seldom were the civil and military powers divided.

Both these features—administrative neglect and the absence of a distinct military power center—can be attributed to the smallness of the colonial garrisons. Except for Nova Scotia after 1750, the garrisons were no more than driblets scattered over America and the West Indies, nor were there 1,000 soldiers within an area of manageable size. The traditional "independent company" of the British army—the garrison unit that never moved from its fort, that seldom saw the "Governor" who nominally controlled it, and that was administered directly by the War Office—had made it possible to send small numbers of troops to America on a piecemeal basis without creating any new organizational forms or administrative procedures. For many years, these companies in America were treated as if they *were* British garrison units, looking after themselves, unsupervised by any general officer. Only in the Seven Years War did it become clear that the system was rotten because it was inapplicable—Albany was not Windsor Castle. Reform was evidently needed.

Reform would remedy neglect and improve efficiency, but it would also end control of regular forces by colonial governors. To anyone trying to look ahead in 1760, the political consequences of this change might have seemed negligible. The colonial governor had long since ceased to be an active "Captain General" of his province, so that others were already commanding both regulars and provincials in time of war. But what of the use of troops to maintain order within the colony?

The first British empire of course did not rely on force; rather, it depended on law and the consent of the governed. The paucity of troops in America and the West Indies before 1755 seems to prove the proposition, and even these few regulars had been sent to defend, not coerce, their provincial hosts. But a second look at the distribution of the forces raises a doubt. Regulars were in South Carolina and the West Indies largely because these colonies were willing to support them, and they were willing to support them because Carolinians and West Indians were becoming more frightened of slave insurrection every year. Regulars had first come to New York in order to conquer the province, and they had received a reinforcement in 1691 to put down a rebellion; they had remained, at least in part, because successive governors reported that the province was too unruly to defend itself. Regulars were in Nova Scotia primarily to pacify 10,000 sullen Acadians. The regulars in Newfoundland kept the French out of British harbors, but they also policed those harbors when they were filled with disorderly English fishermen.

It is not suggested that the British government had been following a devious military policy in the colonies; on the contrary, documents prove that defense was always the primary and often the only consideration in Whitehall. But through the years, the peacetime garrisons had tended to appear where they might be of use in peacetime; that is, in maintaining law and order. One might think that the near-pathological English fear of a standing army would brake any attempt to rule by force, but this same fear did not prevent the use of regular troops against the disturbers of the peace in Ireland and Scotland, or even in England against smugglers, strikers, grain rioters, and the London "mobility." In other words, military reform had political implications which, if not altogether clear, were at least worth pondering.

Militia could also maintain law and order. Puritans and Virginians had branded hostile Indians as "rebels," and one of the few times the New York militia quickly responded to the call and performed brilliantly was in the slave insurrection of 1741. Militia put down riots in both town and countryside. On the occasions when it did not quell disorder, the reason was usually simple: the militia was doing the rioting, or was in sympathy with the rioters. It seems reasonable to say that the militia was not a means of defense at all, but an instrument of either order or insurrection, depending on circumstances.

If the colonies failed to defend themselves, it was the volunteer system that had failed, because the militia had been useful for only the most primitive kind of defense; on the other hand, the militia had never failed to start or stop a civil war, as it chose. If the regular troops stationed in America were to be reformed and perhaps increased in number after the war, they were bound to affect the internal police of the empire. These considerations were not nearly as obvious as some others already mentioned—the need to abolish independent companies, for example—but they take on concrete meaning when seen in terms of one of the most lurid incidents in British colonial history.

Queen Anne had received the news of the victory of Blenheim from Colonel Daniel Parke, an aide-de-camp of Marlborough. This particular mark of the Duke's favor—for so it was—was reaffirmed in 1706 when Parke received a commission as Governor of the Leeward Islands. The job was no sinecure, because the British West Indians had suffered severely in their fight with the French. Parke's task was to organize for self-defense a population which was torn by internal dissension and nearly panic stricken by the fear of invasion, and whose attitude was tending dangerously toward an apathetic *sauve qui peut*.[106] Soon

---

[106] Bourne, *Queen Anne's Navy*, 210-223, and *passim*. Parke was also the father-in-law of William Byrd of Westover, Virginia. He was, in fact, unhappy that he had not been given the governorship

Parke, a vigorous but heavy-handed soldier, was in trouble in Antigua. He complained in 1708 that the island's Assembly refused to enact a quartering law without tying it to an unacceptable electoral law.[107] In the following year, the Assembly together with some freeholders and merchants formally accused the Governor of having "several times employed parties of armed soldiers not only in the business properly belonging to . . . civil officers, but likewise in the highest acts of violence and injustice, particularly in ejecting persons out of their freeholds and possessions, and in order to it [*sic*] breaking open doors and windows."[108] By then, charge and countercharge were flying, and the careful recording and preserving of both has made the historian's task very difficult.[109] The Governor's paramount concern was with the military situation, but his avarice and lechery did not endear him to his subjects; the majority of Antiguans were certain that they had fallen into the hands of a monster who would stop at nothing. Aside from these conclusions, the complexity of the situation and the conflicting statements made about it hinder any very certain judgments. Three times Parke just missed assassination. Finally, in early December of 1710, the dispute came to a head. When the lower house of the Assembly forced its way into the presence of the Governor and Council, Parke used his bodyguard of regulars to adjourn them at the point of bayonet. The assemblymen dispersed into the country where they raised several

---

of Virginia; Vere L. Oliver, *The History of the Island of Antigua* (London, 1894), I, lxxviii.

[107] *CSPC, 1708-1709*, #116, #245.

[108] *Ibid.*, #443.

[109] Two modern accounts of Parke and this affair are by Bourne, *Queen Anne's Navy*; and by Thomas Seccombe, *DNB*, XLIII, 225. The former is strongly anti-Parke, the latter as strongly pro. Parke's principal contemporary apologist was George French, who wrote a lengthy *History of Col. Parke's Administration* (London, 1717), and *An Answer to a Scurrilous Libel, Intitled a Letter to Mr. G. French* (London, 1719). These are fascinating and untrustworthy documents. I have not found the "Letter to Mr. G. French," which prompted his second pamphlet.

hundred militiamen. By the time they returned, the Governor, with some 70 regulars, had barricaded himself. He also had some artillery and did not hesitate to use it on his fellow Englishmen as they tried to storm the house. This goaded the Antiguans into fury. Of their two captains, Parke personally killed one as he broke into the house, but the other shot the Governor in the thigh. According to the account of one of Parke's few friends, a wild scene ensued, "The barbarous multitude, (for so I must call them) killing and wounding all they met giving no quarter to those in the house, and killed many of H.M. troops on the[ir] knees begging for quarter. . . ." They stripped and dragged Parke into the street, broke his back with a musket butt, and spat in his face as, dying, he called for water. That this account is not too exaggerated is borne out by the fact that 44 of the 70 regulars were killed or wounded, while there were only 12 casualties among the militiamen.[110]

The aftermath was, if possible, more bizarre. An investigating commission came to nothing. Parke's successor, ordered to pardon all but the principal leaders of the insurrection, was recalled within two years and imprisoned

[110] Thomas Morris (an Antigua councillor) to the Board of Trade, 27 February 1711, *CSPC, 1710-1711*, #683. Troop strength, casualty figures, and other accounts are in *ibid.*, #674, #676. Morris, in the letter cited above, wrote that the participants undoubtedly "will endeavour to alleviate their base actions by loading the Generall's [Parke's] memory with all the black crimes that is possible, but the onely thing they can charge him with, to give them any colour for what they have done, is his debauching many of their wives and daughters (which was indeed very dishonourable). . . ." He adds, however, that the rebels could not have known this until after his death unless some of them had rifled his papers beforehand! Parke's sexual activities alone would account for the brutality of the militia, and this passage in Morris's letter reads as if it may have been a left-handed defense of the governor which would in fact extenuate the conduct of the Antiguans. Oliver, *History of Antigua*, lxxxi, argues that Parke was not abused, but was humanely treated while dying of a wound in his thigh. This version is suspect as favoring the Antiguans; the weight of evidence is strongly against it.

for selling the Queen's mercy to affluent Antiguans. The murder of Parke occurred just as Marlborough, his patron, was losing out to the Tories in the British political struggle, and apparently there was the less zeal to bring the murderers to justice. But even the Whigs, after the Hanoverian accession, could not overcome the legal obstacles to the trial in England of several men who stood accused of "high treason outside His Majesty's dominions"; this was the same obsolescent law of Henry VIII which the government would consider reviving in the 1770's for the benefit of Sam Adams. No one was ever punished for the murder of Parke.[111]

Parke's murder is more than a colorful story. It exemplifies the problems which the British government faced if it contemplated coercive control of the colonies. In the first place, unlike English, Irish, and Scots, the Americans were armed and were more or less trained for war. Perhaps these militiamen were not very impressive when enlisted or drafted to fight the French or Indians, but they were at their best when fending off what they took to be an immediate threat to their liberty or property. An armed populace would be a serious problem for a military governor today, but how much more so in the eighteenth century when he could not technologically multiply the effective size of a comparatively small garrison with automatic weapons, tear gas, armored vehicles, radio, and telephone. When Bostonians had besieged Governor Andros and his handful of regulars on Fort Hill in 1689, the soldiers failed to open fire as the colonials advanced. Andros began to beat his men, presumably with the flat of his sword, until an exasperated Dutchman exclaimed:

[111] *CSPC, 1710-1711, #750; APCC,* ii, #1143; *DNB,* xliii, 225. In 1774, when Crown lawyers were searching for precedents, Thomas Hutchinson, former governor of Massachusetts, recalled the Parke affair and stated that two men were tried, one of whom died in Newgate, the other having been pardoned. The former must have been awaiting final action, for all other available evidence indicates that no one was punished. *The Diary and Letters of . . . Thomas Hutchinson,* ed. P. O. Hutchinson (Boston, 1884-1886), i, 207-208.

"What the Devil should I fight against a tousand men?"[112] It was a pertinent question.

Moreover, the anti-redcoat tradition could be and was more intensively nurtured in America than in England, for there the army was occasionally a welcome sight to the supporters of law and order, while here the militia performed many of the police duties that had to be done and fear of regular soldiers could be unequivocal. Finally, the governors had early lost the right to declare martial law without consulting their councils, so that the protection of soldiers from civil prosecution and the judicial conviction of rebels when an entire colony was bent on resistance were problems almost insoluble without rending the whole fabric of English law.[113] Thus the case of Daniel Parke suggests, if hazily and on a small scale, some of the difficulties that would later arise when the British government decided to maintain an army in America.

[112] Samuel Prince to John Prince, 27 April 1689, *Narratives of the Insurrections, 1675-1690,* ed. Charles M. Andrews (N.Y., 1915), 188.

[113] On martial law, see *Royal Instructions to British Colonial Governors, 1670-1776,* ed. Leonard W. Labaree (N.Y., 1935), I, 396-397.

II · The Decision of 1763

"PEACE is talk'd," Cecilius Calvert had written from London to Governor Horatio Sharpe of Maryland in 1760, but he added that "it seems not likely this year." Furthermore, Calvert continued, " 'tis hinted when, Act of Parliament will be moved for amendment of [colonial] Government and a Standing Force in America and that the Colonies must bear at least the greatest share of Charge for whose Protection the Force will be established, this will occasion a Tax."[1] Calvert then warned Governor Sharpe: "Being Preparative is best."

Calvert's letter does not mark the moment when the decision was made to keep a large regular army in North America. It is no more than one of many pieces of evidence that can be adduced to show that such ideas—an army for the colonies, a colonial revenue to support it, and reform of colonial government—were in the air during and even before the Seven Years War.[2] They were explicit in plans submitted to the British government by men interested in America; perhaps they were implicit in Pitt's method of waging war in the colonies, abandoning the traditional (and therefore constitutional?) but unworkable requisition system, and substituting a promise of Parliamentary reimbursement of colonial expenditures. Pitt's new policy was of considerable financial benefit to the colonies, but it was an innovation which weakened their claim, in equity if not in law, to be exempt from imperial taxation.[3] As will be seen, the decision to keep an army in America was not really *made*, it was simply assumed by the time the preliminaries of a peace settlement had been worked out in

[1] 19 January 1760, *Archives of Maryland*, eds. William H. Browne *et al.* (Baltimore, 1883—), XXXI, 527-528.

[2] See the citations in George L. Beer, *British Colonial Policy, 1754-1765* (N.Y., 1907), 261n., 266n., 271n.

[3] On this subject, see Lawrence H. Gipson, *The British Empire before the American Revolution, Vol. X: The Triumphant Empire: Thunder Clouds Gather in the West, 1763-1766* (N.Y., 1961), especially Chap. II, but also chaps. III-V.

late 1762. But the reasons *why* an army was to be kept there, and how those reasons changed and shifted in importance from 1763 to the outbreak of Revolutionary War, are not so easily discovered.

The Political Roots of Military Policy

To discuss policy without reference to politics is always dangerous, and never more so than when dealing with British policy before 1775. In those years the smoothly linked chain of rational decisions and supervised execution that the word "policy" suggests never appeared. There were, however, a few British officials who actually held some such vision of policy for the army in North America. To understand why reality fell so far short of their vision requires a general assessment of the political circumstances that shaped colonial military policy after the death of George II.

The pressures generated by the initial disasters of the Seven Years War had permitted William Pitt to force his way into power, and thus to threaten seriously the Walpole-Pelham system of carefully "managed" government. Under wartime conditions Pitt and Newcastle had maintained an uneasy coalition, with responsibility divided between themselves for strategy and politics, respectively. It is difficult to imagine that this alliance would not have exploded at the end of the war, with Pitt's function shrunk to a size commensurate with neither his talents nor his pretensions, and with Newcastle's continued management of the political machine giving him control of Parliament and administration. But before the war could be concluded, George III had ascended the throne—an immature king of no more than average intelligence, full of carefully nursed grievances against those who had served his grandfather, and almost wholly dependent on a well-intentioned but weak and politically inexperienced advisor; but, withall, a King anxious to restore the monarchy to what he regarded as its proper constitutional position. That political chaos was the result is not surprising, and historians have labored to reduce it to some sort of order. Their efforts cannot wholly succeed, because the chaos was real and not an illusion born of complexity. There were, however, certain persistent elements in the political situation, especially as it pertains to military policy, elements which, if kept in mind, are valuable aids to understanding. Three of these elements are visible in British politics during most of the eighteenth century; three others are particularly evident in the early years of the reign of George III. Several of them have been mentioned at one point or another in the preceding discussion. Other historians have noticed them, so there is no originality in pointing them out again, but it does seem worthwhile to reconsider them in the context of colonial military policy.

The first element is the traditional British fear of a standing army, a fear reinforced rather than attenuated by a number of legal safeguards. The burden of the British army upon the Englishmen who had to pay and house it was certainly less than the military burden borne by the people of the European continent. But in a Parliament that had once been quashed and later been threatened by an army under control of the executive, the British public had an instrument receptive to its grievances against the military.[4] When soldiers were used to maintain order in England, they were dispatched and employed only with the advice and consent of local magistrates. Woe to the king or minister who sought to use them otherwise. To do so was sure to incur odium, if not worse.

The second element was the demand for economy. This too was a traditional factor in the political equation, but the cost of the Seven Years War led contemporaries to see fiscal retrenchment as more necessary than ever before. The cost of the wars to come at the end of the century make these fears expressed after 1760 for the health of the British economy appear ill-founded to say the least, but the fears were no less real. And the pressure to economize did not

[4] See, for example, the protest of the House of Lords in 1718, and petitions from Lancaster in 1746 and Winchester in 1759, in David C. Douglas (ed.), *English Historical Documents, Vol. X: 1714-1718*, eds. D. B. Horne and Mary Ransome (N.Y., 1957), 622-628.

end with the postwar reduction of military and naval forces: in 1770 the Adjutant General would ask the military governor of Gibraltar to "Bear one thing in your mind, that Guineas from the Treasury are drops of Blood."[5] His advice might have been the motto of British peacetime commanders everywhere.

The Treasury and War Office had to carry their estimates and expenditures before a House of Commons that had built its power on an ability to control money; every Member who considered himself a "man of business" was interested in financial questions. The atrophy of political issues after 1715 intensified this situation, and the annual consideration of the estimates and voting of supply were normally the high points of each Parliamentary session. With the public debt at an unprecedented level and the usual postwar demand for tax reduction evident, the common weal and private political interest appeared to agree in arguing for rapid fiscal retrenchment.

The third element is one often attached to British colonial government in the Walpole-Pelham period under the title of "salutary neglect." To be sure, the beginning of the American Revolutionary period is usually associated with the end of this neglect. In another sense, however, British politicians continued to neglect the colonies, for almost all of them were both ignorant of and apathetic toward colonial matters. Reprehensible as it may seem to a modern historian, especially one with an American point of view, it is fairly understandable that a peerage for a prominent political colleague or opponent should be of far greater interest, and of greater immediate political importance, than the settlement of the New York-New Hampshire boundary controversy, for example. Even with a more elaborate administrative organization to handle the colonies, this situation would have persisted, for basically it was a failure of communication. One could expect at least three months to elapse between asking a question about the colonies and having it answered by someone on the spot. Few men in government had the time or the occasion to visit North

[5] Edward Harvey to Governor Boyd, 15 June 1770, WO 3/23, 64.

America—there were so many other matters of more immediate concern to command attention; nor was there need for dangerous sea-voyaging as long as the imperial machinery continued to operate.

Into this partial vacuum of information came the colonial "experts," men who invariably had some ax to grind or private interest to serve. The information and recommendations offered by these "experts" were usually and justifiably treated with caution, if not suspicion, by the few politicians who were interested in or responsible for American affairs, but the "experts" remained important because there was no available alternative to them. For a major politician to become a colonial expert himself was too difficult and unremunerative to justify the time and effort. Domestic and diplomatic problems always appeared more urgent, and so it happened that as late as 1774 the American question never received the attention, except sporadically, that its world-shaking consequences would seem to earn for it.

Of the other three keys to an understanding of the political background of colonial military policy, the three elements peculiar to the early reign of George III, the first is William Pitt himself. Pitt had acquired great political power in an unconventional way, that is by gaining the support of the country "independents" in the House of Commons, and of the commercial community, especially in the City. These two groups, together with a rising press, constituted the effective part of what passed for public opinion in eighteenth-century Britain. Pitt had resigned in late 1761 when he found that he could not carry the cabinet with him in approving an immediate declaration of war against a threatening Spain. From that time until he again resigned in 1768, after an abortive two-year period as chief minister, almost every other politician walked in fear of offending Pitt. The disturbing effect of this was compounded by Pitt's neurotic unwillingness to expound his own views on policy and by his repeated refusal to form a government unless given carte blanche. When he finally received it in 1766, he either would not or could not exercise the leadership that was so badly needed. Even after 1768, out of office, health broken, and popularity and power diminished by his acceptance of a peerage and a pension, he was an unpredictable force to be considered by anyone who planned to take a stand, especially on a question concerning the colonies or the military.

The fifth element was the Indian problem. The unprecedented employment of regular forces in North America after 1754 made imperial interference in Indian affairs essential. During the war, the problem was one of winning various tribes from their friendship with the French, and, if possible, of gaining their assistance or at least neutrality. The problem had a large part of its origin in the mismanagement of Indian affairs by American colonial governments, and its wartime solution required solemn promises by the British government on many counts. After the war, the problem was tied closely to the pressure for economy, and essentially was one of avoiding the heavy cost of a major Indian war; success in avoiding war with the Indians seemed to depend on keeping the wartime promises made to them.[6]

The last element is a description of the essence of British politics after 1760 in the following terms: Pitt and young George III—each in his way an unorthodox politician—had a splintering effect on the old system, creating violent personal animosities among leading politicians in the process. The "splinters," however, and their leaders could no longer present legitimate opposition to those in power by grouping themselves around the "reversionary interest"— the heir to the throne—as they had for the previous 45 and more years. Thus, the only available justification for opposition became specific issues or "measures." This situation tends to give a deceptively modern look to British politics in the age of the American Revolution; at the time, it deceived many Americans and some Englishmen into thinking that a liberal colonial policy was a political pos-

[6] The most thorough presentation and documentation of this point is in Jack M. Sosin, *Whitehall and the Wilderness: the Middle West in British Colonial Policy, 1760-1775* (Lincoln, Nebraska, 1961), especially 4ff.

sibility. But actually issues, including American issues, were seldom more than the excuse for previously determined factional divisions. Perhaps the American Revolution itself changed this situation, sobering some of those who had previously used the American question for the political "mileage" they found in it. Their letters and speeches from 1760 to 1775, however, are good evidence that most of them, and especially the "liberal" opposition, had acted, by modern standards, irresponsibly.

The questions may be asked, what, if not strong commitments on issues, kept politics so chaotic in the 1760's? And, attacking the problem on its other flank, why did the notorious, self-seeking flexibility of British politicians in this decade not operate quickly to heal the wounds inflicted in the first years of the new reign? The answer to both lies in the fact that by 1760 British politics had become a game, a game which offered tangible rewards to be sure, but one which demanded of all participants (except a few who willingly forfeited the approval of their peers) that the game be well played. "To make a figure" was the way Chesterfield described the raison d'etre of politics to his son, and the political correspondence of the times is shot through with a cant which, whether hypocritical or sincere, reveals a common body of assumptions about the game of politics: the appeal is always to personal honor, consistency, reputation, loyalty, trust, obligations, but rarely is it suggested that any of these might not be identical with national interest or public welfare. The desire "to make a figure" often nurtured rather than allayed the personal animosities so characteristic of 1763, and the felt need to justify such selfish attitudes created controversy where, as on the problem of the American colonies, there was basically little difference of opinion about what should be done.[7] Of course a certain amount of such behavior is

[7] "You will be of the House of Commons as soon as you are of age, and you must make a figure there if you would make a figure in your country," Chesterfield to Philip Stanhope, 5 December 1749, quoted in the first sentence of Sir Lewis Namier, *The Structure of Politics at the Accession of George III* (2nd edn. rev., Lon-

endemic to politics, but it was prevalent to an unusual degree in this particular period of British history, not because politicians were especially depraved but because the game required some new rules after the accession of George III.

These then are offered as the keys to an understanding of British political background for the formulation of American colonial military policy between 1760 and 1775: the traditional English attitude toward an army in peacetime; the incessant pressure to economize; ignorance and apathy on the part of almost all politicians concerning colonial problems; the personality, prestige, and potential power of William Pitt; the fear of a costly Indian war; and the need to use issues as a justification for political factionalism.

The Rationale of an American Garrison

As mentioned earlier, there was a general, tacit agreement to break with the past and keep an army in the North American colonies after the war. The subsequent decision to support that army by colonial taxation was a natural consequence. Despite its obvious importance, historians have not scrutinized the prior military decision with the care that they have given to most other events of the American Revolution. Exactly what was the British government doing when it assigned 15 infantry battalions to North America in 1763?

One historian has argued that, in terms of past experience and imperial defense, the decision was foolish, for in 1763 the British colonies were far more secure from foreign attack than they had ever been before, because now there were thousands of square miles between them and any po-

---

don, 1957), 1. It was Namier who awakened historians to the bewildering political complexity of these years, and we all stand deeply in his debt. As for the basic agreement which underlay the political controversy over American policy, Thomas Pownall's successive revisions of *Administration of the Colonies* (London, five editions 1764-1774) suggest how difficult it was for one articulate "liberal" to formulate any real alternative to the policy of the government.

tential aggressor.[8] An older, standard account states that no one gave the decision much thought, and that the Secretary at War simply issued the necessary orders as if it were a matter of routine rather than a decision far above his province to consider, much less to make.[9] More recently, one historian has suggested that the principal motive of the government was to keep unruly Americans in check.[10] There is some merit in all these views, but the full truth is buried much too deeply to be revealed by such simple explanations.

The most recent attempt to answer the question is also the most thoroughly researched and carefully considered. Bernhard Knollenberg has concluded in his *Origin of the American Revolution: 1759-1766* that British motives remain somewhat fuzzy and largely unrecorded, that neither the desire to coerce American colonists nor the desire to increase the military patronage of the Crown was the chief reason, but that the "classic explanation" of George Louis Beer in particular does not bear examination.

Beer stated that the "Indian question," exacerbated by the acquisition of Canada, gave the British government "no alternative" but to maintain an American army, and that the Indian uprising of 1763 would not have permitted the withdrawal of troops in any case. Knollenberg takes sharp issue with Beer: "So far as this explanation is based on 'the formidable Indian rebellion that Pontiac had organized,' it is clearly fallacious. The rebellion did not begin until after the addition to the British standing army in America had been voted, and there is no evidence of the rebellion having been foreseen in England." Knollenberg goes on to question the remainder of Beer's attempt to con-

[8] John R. Alden, *The South in the Revolution, 1763-1789*, Vol. III of *A History of the South* (Baton Rouge, 1957), 45, 51-55. Because of his studies of John Stuart and Thomas Gage, Professor Alden's opinion on this subject carries considerable weight.

[9] Clarence W. Alvord, *The Mississippi Valley in British Politics* (Cleveland, 1917), I, 129-130.

[10] Dora Mae Clark, "George Grenville as First Lord of the Treasury and Chancellor of the Exchequer, 1763-1765," *Huntington Library Quarterly*, XIII (1950), 393.

nect the army to the Indian problem by noting that the ranger and light-infantry units best fitted for Indian fighting were disbanded; that colonial agents Richard Jackson and Benjamin Franklin, and Indian superintendent Sir William Johnson, all agreed that small, scattered garrisons could not effectively protect the frontier against Indian raids, an opinion confirmed by the British experience in 1763; and that the Commander in Chief in America, Sir Jeffery Amherst, was not consulted until after the decision to maintain a garrison had been made in London.[11] Assuming that this is a fair statement of the argument, then who is right?

Before one enters into this controversy, it must be recognized that the British choice in 1763 was not between keeping and not keeping a large military force in North America. The fortunes of war had reduced the range of available alternatives, so that the question had become "where and how large?" As late as April 1762 the Earl of Hardwicke could express doubts about the wisdom of retaining Canada: "If you don't remove the French inhabitants," he wrote his colleague and confidant the Duke of Newcastle, "they will never become half Subjects, and this Country must maintain an army there to keep them in Subjection."[12] Hardwicke was right in seeing that the retention of Canada, with its potentially hostile French population, required a sizeable regular garrison. No one had forgotten the difficulty of controlling one-tenth as many Acadians before the war. But amphibious operations then under way in the Caribbean, operations made possible by the achievement of British command of the sea lines of communication, were to drop both Guadeloupe and Cuba into the laps of British peacemakers. To return Canada to France then became unthinkable.

The Bute ministry faced a difficult problem in the latter part of 1762: in an era of carefully limited warfare, Great Britain had been so careless as to win a war decisively.

[11] Bernhard Knollenberg, *Origin of the American Revolution: 1759-1766* (N.Y., 1960), 89-91; also, 27-28 and 87-98.

[12] 2 April 1762, BM Add. MSS. 32936, folios 310-312.

Caught between the need to recreate a stable international order and the demand of the British public for gains at the peace table commensurate with the outlay of British blood and treasure, the government seemed doomed to satisfy neither requirement. As might have been expected, it largely capitulated to the immediate pressures of domestic politics, and even then could not please a few men like Pitt. In the event, the government accepted the inevitability of future conflict with France and Spain, and so let military considerations determine its selection of Canada and Florida.[13]

Several battalions to watch over 80,000 Frenchmen in the St. Lawrence Valley were thus essential, as were several more to garrison the key harbors of the strategically important but almost deserted southern coast—St. Augustine, Pensacola, and Mobile. Granted these needs, it seemed to require only a small increment of troops and effort to control the "interior," guaranteeing if nothing else that British title to this vast area would not be jeopardized by failure to carry out physical occupation.[14] One had only to push a battalion or two up the St. Lawrence into the Great Lakes toward Michigan and Wisconsin, and another up the Mississippi to Illinois. Such self-evident logic accounts for the general acquiescence of British politicians in the maintenance of an army in North America. It is true that the Treaty of Paris made British subjects in America far more secure from French, Spanish, and Indian attack, but it is

[13] On peacemaking 1762-1763, see especially Sosin, *Whitehall*, 3-26.

[14] The need to occupy in order to establish sovereignty is seldom mentioned in modern accounts of the decision. Failure could (and still can) jeopardize territorial possession in international law; a dispute, supposedly resolved in earlier treaties like that of 1763, over part of this area had precipitated the Seven Years War. Alden, *South*, 54-55, argues that the West and the Indians, and thus taxation, ought to have been left to the Americans. This seems to ignore the question of occupation, and to assume that the British government could have disregarded colonial cries for help in time of Indian war. Without the wisdom of hindsight, one cannot imagine leaving this vast area unoccupied and unpacified.

also true that the great extension of territorial control, which accounted for this new security, made the traditional system of local self-defense inapplicable.[15]

When these new requirements for about ten battalions are added to the three battalions stationed in Nova Scotia and Newfoundland before the war, it appears that the structure of the peace settlement largely determined not only the existence of a British army in postwar America, but its approximate size and deployment as well. In view of the constraints imposed on them by the British military victories won between 1759 and 1762, it may seem that the decision makers in Whitehall had no room for choice at all, and that Knollenberg is quite right to dismiss Beer's concern with the Indian problem. To accept such a conclusion would be a mistake, however: it explains too little and ignores too much. Why was an extra battalion or two stationed in America? Were there other, reinforcing motives behind the establishment of an American army? If so, to what extent did these motives affect the exact location and the assigned missions of the army?

The year 1754 had been a time of crisis in British colonial affairs. Just as officials on both sides of the Atlantic despaired of blocking French military pressure in the Ohio Valley without a large-scale commitment of British regulars, so disaffection among Indian tribes traditionally friendly to the Anglo-Americans led to an intercolonial congress at Albany. The problems were obviously related to one another, and the British response to them was similarly linked. Two new offices were created: American commander in

---

[15] In an amazing letter to the Earl of Bute, Governor Dinwiddie of Virginia argued that considerations of strategy and security, not commerce, ought to guide postwar arrangements. He urged an army, a stamp act, and centralizing the management of the Indian trade. His views, it seems to me, are typical of those widely held at this time. 17 January 1763, BM Add. MSS. 38334. See Jack P. Greene, "The Flight from Determinism: A Review of Recent Literature on the Coming of the American Revolution," *South Atlantic Quarterly*, LXI (1962), 235-259, for an excellent discussion of how the Seven Years War was related to the Revolution, especially his comments on Knollenberg on p. 244.

chief, and imperial Indian superintendent. For a time, there was some thought of combining both functions in a single commission. In the end, the Indian superintendency was made separate and itself divided into northern and southern offices, with the Ohio River and Pennsylvania-Maryland line as boundary, and the commander in chief acting as nominal supervisor of Indian affairs.[16]

An important share of the responsibility for both measures belonged to the President of the Board of Trade, George Montagu Dunk, Earl of Halifax. Neglected by historians and biographers, Halifax had more direct and indirect influence on colonial policy in the two decades before the American Revolution than any other man. Richard Cumberland, the playwright and secretary to Halifax for a time, described him as "extremely brilliant . . . a scholar much above the common mark. . . . He was formed to be a good man; he might also have been a great one. His mind was large, his spirit active. . . ."[17] Halifax not only had an unusual knowledge of and interest in colonial affairs, but he had strong views on colonial policy and, until he left the Board of Trade in 1761, carried the political weight to make them effective.[18]

From his actions and words, it is evident that Halifax saw the political, military, fiscal, and Indian aspects of American policy as intimately related to one another, and that he favored comprehensive changes to improve efficiency and tighten British control. He was a Secretary of State from 1762 to 1765, and then went into political and personal decline until his death in 1771, shortly after he had become Secretary of State for the second time. In and out of office, his views on American policy influenced others who played important roles before 1775: George Gren-

[16] John R. Alden, "The Albany Congress and the Creation of the Indian Superintendencies," *MVHR*, xxvii (1940), 193-210. There is an agonizing reappraisal of New York Indian affairs by Thomas Pownall, before the Albany Congress met, in LO 460.

[17] Richard Cumberland, *Memoirs* (London, 1806), 71, 130.

[18] The most complete account of Halifax at the Board of Trade is in Arthur H. Bayse, *The Lords Commissioners of Trade and Plantations . . . 1748-1782* (New Haven, 1925).

ville, with whom he shared ministerial control, 1763-1765; the Earl of Egremont, Grenville's brother-in-law and Secretary of State with Halifax, 1762-1763; the Earl of Hillsborough, member of the Board of Trade, its President 1763-1765 and in 1766, and Secretary of State for America 1768-1772; John Pownall, Secretary of the Board from 1753 to 1768, when he became Undersecretary of State for America; Viscount Barrington, Secretary at War, 1755-1761 and 1765-1778; and perhaps Charles Townshend, a close friend, five years an associate on the Board, first Secretary at War and then President of the Board of Trade for a short time during the critical winter of 1762-1763, and Chancellor of the Exchequer 1766-1767.[19] Lord North was the nephew of Halifax. These men appear repeatedly when crucial decisions are taken on American affairs; it is sufficient here to indicate the concern of the Halifax Board with the Indian problem before 1763.

The imperial Indian superintendents were commissioned in 1755 to do what the colonies had failed to do; that is, maintain the British interest among the Indians by pursuing a uniform and consistent policy toward them. This new system of Indian management went into effect at about the time General Edward Braddock was marching his little army to destruction in the forest near the forks of the Ohio. Despite the new system, during the war the Iroquois Six Nations of New York, traditional allies of the British, had proved difficult to control; the Shawnee and Delaware in western Pennsylvania and Virginia had allied with the French; and, in 1760, the Cherokee in western Carolina began a "rebellion" even without active French assistance. The complaints of the Indians centered on land and trade; they were being cheated in both. Such complaints were nothing new to the colonists, for this situation had always been more or less characteristic of Anglo-American contact

---

[19] John Pownall had joined the Board as clerk in 1741, and had become its acting Secretary long before 1753. For Townshend, see Sir Lewis Namier, *Charles Townshend: His Character and Career* (Cambridge, 1959), especially 16-30.

with Indians, but at last the complaints had become matters of imperial concern.

In 1759 the superintendent for the Northern Department, Sir William Johnson, virtual lord of the Mohawk Valley and the white man of greatest influence with the Six Nations, was directed by an Order in Council to investigate reported fraudulent sales of Delaware land in western Pennsylvania.[20] The situation became worse as fighting ended on the American mainland (1760), and in 1762 the Board of Trade heard Brigadier General John Stanwix, a respected veteran of the French and Indian War, testify "that the making settlements upon the lands to the westward of the Alleghany Mountains, would infallibly irritate and provoke the Indians, and might be attended with fatal consequences."[21] Later in the year, the Board received a report from Johnson concerning the peace conference held with the western tribes at Detroit the previous summer. He had promised the Indians regulations which would protect them in the fur trade, and in his covering letter to the Board made it clear that these regulations could be effectively enforced only by military garrisons at the various posts.[22] Johnson was not alone in thinking along this line; in March 1762, Brigadier General Thomas Gage, military governor of Montreal, recommended to the Board that "to remedy the Inconveniences and abuses, which both the English and French have suffered, through the management of the Indian Trade; I know no better method, than to assign a certain Number of Posts in the distant Country, to which only, the Traders should be allowed to traffick, . . ."[23] In fact, both Johnson and Gage were resurrecting a plan of Indian management based on military garrisons that had first been adumbrated by Halifax in 1754.[24]

[20] 20 November 1759, *JBT 1759-1763*, 65.

[21] 7 April 1762, *ibid.*, 271.

[22] Johnson to the Board of Trade, 20 August 1762, *Johnson Papers*, III, 867. The promise to the Indians is on p. 496.

[23] Gage to Amherst, 20 March 1762, *DCH Canada*, 94. Amherst forwarded this letter, a general report on the state of Gage's government, to London.

[24] Alden, *MVHR*, XXVII (1940), 200.

To many of those who saw the problem at first hand, it appeared that only force could make the white fur traders obey any set of rules governing their relations with the Indians. These traders could not possibly have been as bad as numerous contemporary observers stated, but perhaps for colonial military policy the prevalent opinion is more important than the truth. One Philadelphia commercial house connected with the Indian trade characterized the traders as "a sett of the most debased banditti that ever infested a government, the greater part gaol gleanings and the refuse of Ireland."[25] A British army ensign in South Carolina wrote that they were "a Shame to Humanity, and the Disgrace of Christianity. . . . The Savages daily saw themselves cheated in Weight and Measure; their Women debauched, and their young Men corrupted."[26]

All these reports and recommendations influenced not only the Board of Trade, whose powers after the departure of Halifax became largely advisory, but the cabinet minister responsible for colonial affairs as well. Within two months after he had succeeded William Pitt as Secretary of State for the Southern Department, the Earl of Egremont reminded the North American Commander in Chief "how much His Majesty's Interests may be promoted by treating the Indians upon . . . principles of humanity," and ordered him to do what he could about "the Shamefull manner in which business is transacted between them and our Traders, the latter making no Scruple of using every Low Trick and Artifice to Overreach and Cheat these unguarded ignorant People."[27] At the same time, Egremont issued new, strict instructions to the Governor of New York not to approve any grants of land purchased from the Indians without first referring the matter to the Board of Trade.[28] Egremont was, if anything, even more concerned about the Indian situation in the South; immediately after the peace

[25] Nicholas Wainwright, *George Croghan, Wilderness Diplomat* (Chapel Hill, 1959), 67.
[26] Quoted in Gipson, *British Empire*, IX, 58.
[27] Extract, 12 December 1761, *Johnson Papers*, III, 588.
[28] 9 December 1761, *ibid.*, X, 340-342.

settlement in early 1763 he ordered the southern governors and the southern Indian agent to convene an Indian congress. As the removal of French and Spanish power from the area between Georgia and the Mississippi River "will undoubtedly alarm and increase the Jealousy of the Neighbouring Indians, the King judges it to be indispensably necessary to take the earliest Steps for preventing their receiving any Impressions of this kind, and for gaining their Confidence and Good-Will." That Egremont was not thinking about troops and forts for *defensive* purposes is shown by his order to the Commander in Chief to destroy three small southern forts that could not be used for trade control, and which would only anger the Indians if occupied in peacetime.[29]

Despite this well-documented anxiety over Indian affairs, it has been contended that "there is no evidence of the [great Indian] rebellion [of 1763] having been foreseen in England."[30] Without doubt, this is literally correct. But in May 1762, Sir William Johnson informed Egremont "that the Indians are not only very uneasy, but Jealous of our growing power." He said that garrisoned forts in the backcountry were of little use in stopping surprise attacks on the frontier. "If this mischief can be the Consequence of a breach with the Indians I humbly submit it to your Lordship whether it will not be tend more [*sic*] to the interest of the Crown, and the good of the Publick, to prevent it from taking effect, and that at a much less expence than one Expedition will be to endeavor at quelling them."[31] Johnson was, of course, alluding to his previous recommendations concerning Indian diplomacy and a policed fur trade. In August 1762, he warned the Board of Trade that the Six Nations, disgusted with encroachments on their lands, might well "fall upon our Settlements; and it is not improbable, that other Nations, not knowing how soon

[29] Circular letter, 16 March 1763, PRO 30/47 (Egremont MSS., LC microfilm), XIV, 61; Egremont to Amherst, 16 March 1763, Amherst-Gage MSS., I. There is a full discussion of this matter in Sosin, *Whitehall*, 27-33, 39ff.
[30] Knollenberg, *Origin*, 89. [31] *Johnson Papers*, x, 460-465.

they may meet with the like treatment, will unite with them, as in a Common Cause, and thereby involve the American colonies in an Indian War."[32] Johnson's letters may not qualify as predictions of Pontiac's rebellion, but, on the other hand, neither they nor the actions of the Earl of Egremont and the Board of Trade offer any support for the argument that key officials on both sides of the Atlantic were out of touch with the realities of the Indian question.

In short, the principal missions of those British troops in the "interior" would be to garrison the posts at which the Indians traded, and to prevent unauthorized white settlement on Indian land. One then may safely conclude: (1) the security of Nova Scotia, Canada, and Florida made the presence of a considerable force of regulars in America essential, and (2) once in America, a part of this force could be conveniently employed in enforcing the imperial management of Indian affairs. Most members of Parliament and the British public, if it thought about the matter, understood the first point; a small group within the administration—Halifax, Egremont, John Pownall, probably George Grenville and Charles Townshend, perhaps even the Earl of Bute and George III—understood both points. The latter group, and not the former, were important in deciding to keep an army in America.

A major question remains: in the winter 1762-1763 did this inner circle seriously think of using the army to control the older colonies? There is, in fact, impressive evidence to

[32] 1 August 1762, *ibid.*, III, 851. He reiterated his earlier warning to Egremont in a letter to the Board of Trade on 20 August, *ibid.*, 865-869. Mr. Knollenberg emphasizes Amherst's tendency to ignore the warnings from Johnson, and implies that the British ministry remained uninformed of the deteriorating Indian situation; he does not mention Johnson's direct correspondence with British officials, or the long history of growing British concern over Indian affairs. That the Earl of Egremont, who was responsible for colonial affairs, knew of the need to use troops against the frontiersmen (rather than the Indians) in defense of the line of settlement is seen by his response to trouble in Pennsylvania over people from Connecticut settling on Indian land. See below, pp. 201-204.

support an unequivocally affirmative answer to the question posed. A number of contemporary documents discuss this point in frank terms, but remain inconclusive because their influence on the decision makers cannot easily be established. A British army officer serving in America, Captain Walter Rutherford, had earlier advised Gilbert Elliot, politically connected with the Earl of Bute, that Canada should be returned to France at the peace table. Rutherford would soon leave the army, marry the sister of the future American general Lord Stirling, and sit out the war quietly on his New Jersey estate. In 1759, however, he wanted to use a French Canada as a "pretext to oblige each Colony to support a certain quota of troops, apparently for their defence, but also to keep them in proper subjection to the Mother Country."[33]

Near the end of the Seven Years War, one Nathaniel Ware, Comptroller of the Customs in the New England district, sent a complete plan for colonial reorganization to an unnamed nobleman, perhaps the Earl of Bute. Above all, Ware argued, the true interest of both England and America required that the colonies be "digested into the state of subordination and improvement." He continued: "For which happy purpose never could a more favourable opportunity than the present have offered, and if an effectual reformation be not introduced before those troops are withdrawn which could have been thrown in [to the colonies] upon no less occasion [than the war] without giving a general alarm, one may venture to pronounce it impossible afterwards, . . ."[34]

[33] 14 December 1759, quoted in Sir Lewis Namier, *England in the Age of the American Revolution* (2nd edn. rev., London, 1961), 281.
[34] Comptroller Weare to the Earl of ———, n.d., 1 *MHSC* I, 66-84. This was Nathaniel Ware (Weare), grandfather of Mesech Weare, Revolutionary leader from New Hampshire. The original document is not in the Massachusetts Historical Society, but its provenance is described in a letter from Paine Wingate to Jeremy Belknap, 23 October 1775, 6 *MHSC* IV, 93. Ware may have been writing to the Earl of Bute, because he corresponded with Bute on other matters (North Papers a.6, folio 238, Bodleian Library, Oxford).

A third such document appears in the papers of the Earl of Shelburne, usually considered one of the leading advocates of a liberal policy toward the colonies. An anonymous advisor analyzed the American problem in 1763 for Shelburne in the following terms: "The provinces being now surrounded by an army, a navy, and by hostile tribes of Indians . . . it may be time (not to oppress or injure them in any shape) but to exact a due deference to the just and equitable demands of a British parliament."[35] But Shelburne did not become head of the Board of Trade until April 1763, weeks after the decision had been made.

The Shelburne manuscripts do, however, contain more interesting papers: a series of undated memoranda entitled "Hints" discuss the whole range of American problems at the end of the Seven Years War. A nearly identical set of "Hints" in the papers of Charles Jenkinson, Bute's protégé and at this time Secretary to the Treasury, enhances the importance of these documents. The memoranda in the Jenkinson collection are dated February 1763, before the final decision on the army, and there is good reason to believe that they are the work of William Knox. Knox had served for a time in the government of Georgia, later became well known for his conservative views on the American question, and was Undersecretary of State for America from 1768 through the Revolutionary War. In 1762-1763, he was being consulted by both John Pownall, the key permanent official at the Board of Trade, and Knox's personal friend Henry Ellis, former governor of Georgia, who himself was the principal colonial advisor to the Earl of Egremont, Secretary of State responsible for American

[35] Plan for securing the future Dependence of the Provinces on the Continent of America, in Shelburne MSS., LXVI, 107-110, and discussed by R. A. Humphreys, "Lord Shelburne and the Proclamation of 1763," *EHR*, XLIX (1934), 247-248.

[36] There are "Hints" respecting "our Acquisitions," "the Settlement," "the Civil Establishments," and "the Military Establishments" in America. The two sets are in BM Add. MSS. 38335 and Shelburne MSS., XLVIII, though the latter does not contain a copy of Hints respecting our Acquisitions in America, which unlike the others is dated 2 February 1763. Many years later, Knox recalled

affairs.[36] Knox later established a close relationship with George Grenville.

In Knox's view, there was a logical connection among Indians, troops, and control of Americans. "The apprehension which the People have of those savages, will always induce them to look on the Station of Troops amongst them as necessary for their safety. And Troops, and Fortifications will be very necessary for Great Britain to keep up in her Colonys, if she intends to secure their Dependence on Her."[37] Knox wanted most of the American army deployed so as to protect and command the principal seaports, but he did not want it stationed within the major cities themselves because there the colonists would greatly outnumber the soldiers. The port garrisons should instead be able to threaten trade and property from secure places, presumably forts in the harbors, and thereby fulfill "the main purpose of Stationing a large Body of Troops in America . . . to secure the Dependance of the Colonys on Great Britain." Once the seacoast was manned, the remaining soldiers could be located at posts in the backcountry where the Indian trade would be centered, and where redcoats might keep Indians and settlers from killing one another.

It is difficult to estimate accurately the importance of the "Hints." As will be seen, most of the British army in America was not stationed on the seaboard, but there were good reasons, among them the Indian rebellion and British political instability, why this extreme proposal was not adopted. Its rejection certainly does not indicate that its assumption and logic were rejected. Knox's political con-

---

that both Ellis and John Pownall had been consulting him in 1763, and that he had drawn up long memoranda on the colonies which he transmitted through Lord Grosvenor to Bute. This would explain the initial "G" on the set in BM Add. MSS. 38335. Knox may have erred in stating that the original set was done for Shelburne (who did not yet hold office in the government, since the copies in BM Add. MSS. 38335 are indorsed 25 February 1763). On Knox, see *HMC Various Collections*, vi (*Knox MSS.*), 282.

[37] Hints respecting the Settlement of our American Provinces, Shelburne MSS., xlviii, 475-487, and BM Add. MSS. 38335, 14-18.

nections at this time, and the fact that someone thought the "Hints" worth copying and sending on to Shelburne, indicate at least that they were carefully considered. Finally, one more document suggests that Knox's reasoning carried weight.

When the Earl of Egremont formally directed the Board of Trade in May 1763 to prepare a report on postwar policy for North America (a directive that would lead to the issuance of the Proclamation of 1763 in October), one of many enclosures was an anonymous "Plan" for the disposition of troops in the colonies.[38] The "Plan" did not propose to concentrate troops on the seaboard as did the "Hints," but in most other respects there is definite similarity between these documents. According to the "Plan," an army was in America: "1st To Keep His Majesty's New Subjects in Canada and Louisiana in due Subjection. 2ndly To retain the Inhabitants of our antient Provinces in a State of Constitutional Dependance upon Great Britain. 3d To create a proper Respect for us and establish necessary Authority among the Indians." The "Plan" goes on to list the prevention of French encroachment, and colonial defense in case of foreign war. One may reasonably suppose that the author set down his proposed missions for the army in their order of importance. Moreover, there are several specific references in the plan to the use of regulars to control the Americans. The retention of a garrison at Crown Point would be "usefull in guarding against any Disobedience or Disaffection amongst the Inhabitants of the Maritime Provinces [New England], who already begin to entertain Some extraordinary Opinions, concerning their Relations and Dependance on their Mother Country." Two good reasons for stationing a full regiment in the South were "that Fort Johnston commanding the Port of Charles Town may be in possession of His Majesty's Troops," and "that the Civil Power in Georgia, where it

[38] Plan of Forts and Garrisons, printed in *IHC,* x, 5-11, where it is attributed to Amherst; there is a copy in HL, Stowe MSS., Miscellaneous (Papers of George Grenville). Its transmission to the Board of Trade is recorded in *JBT 1759-1763,* 363.

has not been long introduced may be properly supported."

As with the "Hints," the effect of the "Plan" is difficult to assess. For many years, it was thought to be the work of Amherst, but both internal and external criticism have established that Amherst did not write it.[39] The "Plan" seems too crude in both style and content to be the work of Knox himself; the obsolete French name "du Quesne" is used for Fort Pitt, little knowledge is shown of the structure of the peacetime army which was worked out in January and February 1763, and a curious dual system of military command is recommended that would have divided the office of American commander in chief into northern and southern districts. On the other hand, the "Plan" clearly reveals a greater knowledge of and interest in the southern colonies than in the northern (which fits Knox's experience), its recommendations accurately foreshadow the establishment of two new posts on the lower Mississippi, and it did acquire official status by being transmitted to the Board of Trade. There is another copy of the "Plan" in the papers of George Grenville. Whatever its exact influence, the "Plan," together with the "Hints," establishes beyond question that the ministry, before making their decision, considered how the army might be used against rebellious Americans. To expect fuller documentation of a point as politically delicate as this one is to expect too much.

In conclusion, there is no authoritative expression of the reasons for keeping an army in peacetime America. But a sifting of the available evidence yields a fairly coherent picture: a large force was needed to occupy and defend the uncolonized and non-English rim of the expanded North American empire; because this force had to be there in any case, a part of it could be conveniently employed in managing Indian affairs; finally, an American garrison had the added attraction of putting some teeth in the imperial system. All three elements of this rationale are to be found

[39] Charles S. Grant, "Pontiac's Rebellion and the British Troop Moves of 1763," *MVHR*, XL (1954), 75-88, though Grant called it the " 'doodling' of a clerk," an opinion with which I strongly disagree.

neatly tucked into a traditional mercantilist setting in a memorandum written by Henry Ellis for his patron, the Earl of Egremont. Ellis was explaining the advantages of the peace treaty of 1763: "First. All Canada, which unites our settlements in Hudsons Bay to our other Provinces; besides upwards of 70,000 French settlers. Dominion over the Numerous Tribes of Indians inhabiting that vast Country. The whole Furr Trade. A new market for our manufactures. An Inland navigation behind our ancient Provinces, which as it were gives them another Front. A convenience thereby of exporting the products of the Country to the sea Coasts. A facility of securing the Kings Subjects there in their obedience by their being accessible to us on both sides. A general security to those Colonies from Foreign attacks; a deliverance from the calamities attending Indian wars."[40]

The Decision and Its Acceptance

To understand the rationale for keeping a large army in America in 1763 is not, however, to understand fully the process of deciding. Though the rationale itself was never completely clear, composed as it was of three unequal parts somewhat hazily related to one another, the decision by the King and cabinet, and its acceptance by the House of Commons, were far more complex. It is no exaggeration to say that the process of deciding added to the rationale a confusion of petty, extraneous, and accidental factors.

"I have been some days drawing up a state of the troops for the Peace," George III wrote to the Earl of Bute in mid-September 1762, "and hope to send it this evening, by which the ten regiments raised at the beginning of the war remain, and yet the expense will be some hundred pounds cheaper than . . . in 1749."[41] Between the lines of this letter lie clues to the riddle of how the British government took what might be called its first step toward Lexing-

[40] PRO 30/47 (Egremont MSS.), XIV, 248.
[41] ?13 September 1762, *Letters from George III to Lord Bute, 1756-1766*, ed. Romney Sedgwick (London, 1939), #186.

ton. Note that the King himself, not a minister or secretary, was drafting the army organization plan, and that he had been at work on it "for some days." He was still drafting and redrafting four months later. The intense personal interest of George III in his army indicates two things: first, however much he may have tried to reverse the political habits of his predecessors, he remained a typical Hanoverian warrior-king, delighting in the mastery of military minutiae; and, second, the reorganization of the army was a matter of considerable political importance.[42]

The number of regiments in the British army had approximately doubled during the war, with an even greater increase in the number of officers. Unlike 1945 in the United States, when the main task of demobilization was somehow to retain a bare skeleton of career soldiers, the problem in 1762-1763 was to provide for a host of officers who were "deserving," whether for military or political reasons, and who wanted to keep their commissions, their full pay, their rank, their companies and regiments. The army officer corps was a source of profit and prestige as well as a way of life attractive to many more British subjects than could possibly be accommodated. It also represented royal power; it was a set of offices more nearly than any other set at the personal disposal of the Crown. Not only did colonelcies and seats in Parliament usually go together, but the regimental hierarchy of offices gave the King a great body of lesser patronage and a lever to keep the colonels in line.[43]

In that last winter of war, as peace drew visibly closer, the reduction of the army to a peacetime footing became complicated and painful. Colonels of regiments threatened with disbandment, and their business agents who cleared about £200 annually for each regiment they served and who were often M.P.'s themselves, brought heavy pressure

[42] Namier, *Structure of Politics*, 28; and James Hayes, "The Royal House of Hanover and the British Army, 1714-1760," *Bulletin of the John Rylands Library*, XL (1958), 328-357.

[43] Rex Whitworth, *Field Marshal Lord Ligonier* (London, 1958), 373-376, and Knollenberg, *Origin*, 94-95.

to bear on the government.[44] Two examples are enough to indicate what form this pressure took.

George Bowles, a younger son of a Protestant gentleman in County Cork, realized sometime in 1761 that he was not meant for the clergy, and so decided to follow the other path open to younger sons, the army. For 300 guineas "Mr. Ross, a Commission broker" bought him an ensigncy in the 100th Regiment. The 100th was one of the junior regiments certain to be disbanded at the end of the war, and many officers in these units were eager to sell out at the first hint of peace rather than be retired on half-pay. When George joined his regiment at York in September, he persuaded his lieutenant colonel to recommend him for a vacant lieutenancy to Charles Townshend, then Secretary at War. Townshend already knew that the Lord Lieutenant of Ireland had promised the Bowles family to do what he could to further George's career. In October, Ensign Bowles learned that he had been promoted. Lieutenant Bowles noted in his diary that the other junior officers, most of them "excessively proud" Scots and presumably too poor to purchase a step in rank, were envious. A month later, Ross notified George that he was now cornet (second lieutenant) of dragoons in a regiment that was "sure of standing" after the war. The "exchange" was a bargain at 200 guineas. The cornetcy was worth perhaps £1,000, but the man who was trading commissions with George was Sir Robert Laurie, who had become "very obnoxious" to his colonel and brother officers. Laurie had had to get

[44] The sort of pressure exerted is illustrated by a letter from Lord Harcourt to Charles Jenkinson, Bute's private secretary, 5 November 1762: "Colonel Evelyn who came here last Tuesday tells me that General Acourt who is Lieutenant Colonel of the Coldstream Regiment is supposed to be so much displeased and disappointed in not getting the Regiment that Gansell had, that it is thought he will go into Opposition." *The Jenkinson Papers 1760-1766*, ed. Ninetta S. Jucker (London, 1949), 80. Gansell's regiment (the 55th) was at that moment in North America, scattered among Crown Point, Albany, Schenectady, and Oswego. That an agent could expect to clear at least £200 per regiment is stated by Tom Ramsden to Jenkinson, 11 December 1763, *ibid.*, 228.

out of the regiment quickly, and apparently was happy to go on half-pay with the rank of lieutenant and 200 guineas to boot.

Three months later, the Secretary at War asked George to join his regiment in Germany. Cornet Bowles reluctantly departed for the war, but on the way met one Cornet Kirwan of the Royal Dragoons. Kirwan was willing to go to Germany, so George negotiated an exchange with him. Whether money changed hands is unknown, but it almost certainly did. George made it through both war and peace, unshot at but still on active duty, secure on his horse in a fashionable regiment.[45] Such antics were stimulated by the way Britain had hung on the brink of peace for almost two years; they were made possible by the kind of political connections that George had through Dublin to the War Office. Dozens of men like Bowles, Laurie, Kirwan, and the ensign who sold out in the 100th had had time to scurry about, trying to secure their futures.

Quite different but no less typical was the case of James Robertson; he had accomplished the rare feat of entering the officer corps through the enlisted ranks. The very model of the canny Scot, Robertson had—by talent, hard work, and an ability to walk the tightrope of headquarters politics—made himself an almost indispensable staff officer in North America. He had compiled an excellent record by 1762; his future, however, depended neither on that record nor on the money and influence available to a George Bowles, but simply on how he came through the impending reduction of the military establishment. From New York he begged his former Commander in Chief "to be keeped on the Staff, to get a little government . . . anything of this kind would Satisfy my Ambition." He added: "I'm told that Mr. Calcrafts freind is again in powr, perhaps he may help me."[46] In the end, Robertson stayed on the staff and played an important part in the later history of the Ameri-

---

[45] "George Bowles Diary 1761-2," *Antiquary*, XXXVI (1900), 344-345, 367.
[46] To Loudoun, 28 January 1763, LO 6330.

can garrison; he rose to the rank of major general during the Revolutionary War.

"Mr. Calcraft's friend" was Henry Fox, government leader in the House of Commons. Calcraft himself might more accurately be described as Fox's political lieutenant in the House and the acknowledged prince of army agents. Calcraft at one time represented almost half the regiments in the army.[47] In December 1762 another protégé of Fox, Welbore Ellis, succeeded Townshend at the War Office.[48] Under these circumstances, the pressure generated by the Bowleses and the Robertsons, not to mention all the colonels, bore directly on the springs of power. King George and his ministers were thus delighted to find some way to retain ten of the wartime regiments. Edmund Burke accused the King twelve years later of having deliberately enlarged his military influence in Parliament, but in fairness to George it ought to be seen that it was a question of keeping rather than creating regiments in early 1763, and that a political price had to be paid for every one disbanded.[49]

Reorganization of the army was not the center of political attention as Parliament convened in December 1762; rather, the principal issue was the way in which the government had ended the war. On December 9 Pitt made a long and equivocal speech criticizing the peace preliminaries, which had been laid before the House of Commons, and Newcastle helped to muster almost a hundred votes against them.[50] From that day all government measures, including the army estimates, were threatened by the opposition of Pitt and Newcastle. But the personal antagonism of the two men toward one another made cooperation impossible, and the ministry had weapons to use in further re-

[47] *DNB*, VIII, 236-237; John Brooke, *The Chatham Administration, 1766-1768* (London, 1956), 251; James Hayes, "The Military Papers of Colonel Samuel Bagshawe (1713-1762)," *Bulletin of the John Rylands Library*, XXXIX (1957), 374-378.

[48] *DNB*, VI, 710-712. Pitt called him "that clerk of Fox," quoted in Alvord, *Mississippi Valley*, I. 129n.

[49] Mentioned in Knollenberg, *Origin*, 94.

[50] Namier, *England*, 395ff.

ducing the danger. The remains of Newcastle's political machine were swept away by firing every one of his appointees who would not support the government. The Duke himself was terrorized by talk of a Parliamentary investigation of his management of the Treasury. The extent to which the government actually sponsored such an investigation is not clear, because Army Paymaster Henry Fox had acted as frightened as Newcastle, but until the end of February it did little to head off the economy minded country gentlemen who were bent on looking into wartime expenditures.[51] These country gentlemen were also the key to controlling William Pitt. The ministry could not silence him, but it had been able to pull most of his fangs by detaching his Tory following in the House of Commons.[52] The King's boast that he had found a way to keep ten additional regiments *at less than the cost of the army in 1749* was directly related to the notorious dislike of these Tory gentlemen for spending public money.

The Earl of Halifax, then Lord Lieutenant of Ireland, had a plan to meet both the Tory demand for economy and the military demand for more regiments. He proposed increasing the Irish establishment of the army from 12,000 men, set by law in the reign of William III to 18,000 or 20,000. The financial burden would fall on Ireland, and Halifax was at first confident about getting the increased appropriation through the Irish House of Commons. There may have been other motives behind the scheme. It could have been intended to avoid taxing America for her garrison, though this seems doubtful. It was said that Halifax thought he would soon move to a new post and would not have to suffer the political consequences in Ireland, so he proposed the increase to serve his friends in the army. It was also said that the Primate of the Established (Anglican) Church was behind the plan, desirous of turning the Irish House of Commons into a bear garden, thus making his own services more necessary to the British government.

[51] The Newcastle correspondence, BM Add. MSS. 32946-7, is filled with this subject in early 1763.
[52] Ritcheson, *British Politics*, 6-8.

Whatever the truth of these charges, the plan had an obvious appeal for the King.[53]

Most politicians knew by the time Parliament convened that the proposal had been made and favorably received. Despite a discouraging opinion from the Attorney General that an Act of Parliament would be needed to raise the ceiling of 12,000 men, Edmund Burke reported at the end of the year that the cabinet had decided to go ahead.[54] The King continued to juggle regiments and colonelcies throughout January, while Newcastle was hearing rumors of growing opposition to the government's "favourite plan for the army."[55] There was no doubt in Newcastle's mind about what was behind the plan; it was meant "to keep up as Many Men, as they please, without being an Immediate Expence to this Country."[56] Halifax's Secretary himself admitted that the plan would "ingratiate us exceedingly with all the country gentlemen."[57]

But if the country gentlemen liked economy, they, more than any other part of Britain's political community, disliked a standing army as a matter of habit and principle. Their dislike was not simply the chronic fear of what a Whig ministry might do with a large armed force, it was also a more realistic distaste for enlarging the power of the Crown. Even with a King who seemed to like them, giving them honors and offices, it seemed to many of them that a lifetime of Tory consistency was being jeopardized by the siren song of the Court. Young Edward Gibbon, after a visit to the Cocoa-Tree Club, the heart of Toryism in London, remarked on how the tension between their

[53] William Gerard Hamilton to John Hely Hutchinson, 4 December 1762 and 12 March 1763, 12 *HMC* IX, 242, 245; Newcastle to Hardwicke, 31 January, and Hardwicke to Newcastle, 2 February 1763, BM Add. MSS. 32946, 263, 296.

[54] Edmund Burke to Charles O'Hara, 30 December 1762, *The Correspondence of Edmund Burke*, ed. Thomas W. Copeland (Cambridge and Chicago, 1958), I, 161.

[55] Thomas Walpole to Newcastle, 24 January 1763, BM Add. MSS. 32946, 199.

[56] Newcastle to Hardwicke, 31 January 1763, *ibid.*, 264.

[57] Hamilton to Hutchinson [c. 15 February 1763] 12 *HMC* IX, 243.

traditional and their current attitudes toward government was causing a number of independent Members a good deal of discomfort.[58] This discomfort was responsible for most of the growing opposition to the army plan that Newcastle had been hearing about.

The record of events leading to March 4, when the House of Commons considered and approved the army estimates, is susceptible of more than one interpretation. In outline, the record is simple: the plan to increase the army in Ireland was dropped at a meeting held on February 24, and Secretary at War Ellis laid the estimates before the House on the following day; the debates were set for a week later. The meeting of February 24, however, had been unusual. "Promiscuous," Horace Walpole called it, while a follower of Newcastle described it as "an Extraordinary Step."[59] Advertised as a meeting of "the principal people of the House of Commons" with the Chancellor of the Exchequer, it was in fact attended by Fox, Ellis, Charles Townshend (recently appointed President of the Board of Trade), the Chancellor of the Exchequer, Sir Francis Dashwood (a well-known Tory), most of the Tory M.P.'s, "and scarcely any Body else."[60] Ostensibly, Tory opposition at the meeting forced the government to back down. Even Townshend seconded the objections of Sir Charles Mordaunt to the Irish augmentation, according to Horace Walpole.[61] But

[58] David M. Low (ed.), *Gibbon's Journal to January 28th, 1763* (N.Y., 1930), 185.

[59] Horace Walpole, *Memoirs of the Reign of King George the Third,* ed. G. F. R. Barker (London, 1894), I, 193; Journal [of George Bussy], BM Add. MSS. 47584, 6.

[60] Richard Rigby to the Duke of Bedford, 23 February 1763, *Bedford Corr.,* III, 210; Bussy Journal, BM Add. MSS. 47584, 6. "Tory" is used as it was used at the time—to describe those independent country gentlemen who had traditionally disliked the Whig aristocracy, who had followed Pitt, and who were now flocking to support George III.

[61] Walpole, *Memoirs of George III,* I, 194. Other accounts of this meeting, from the Whig, Tory, and Court points of view, respectively, are in BM Add. MSS. 32947, 92-93; Diary of Sir Roger Newdigate, quoted in Sir Lewis Namier, *Crossroads of Power*

there is evidence to suggest that the government had neatly conned the country gentlemen.

The King's desire for an enlarged military establishment of 85 regiments received wide publicity during February; for Americans, the *Pennsylvania Gazette* carried the news.[62] Newcastle told the Duke of Cumberland on the 19th that the government would introduce a bill immediately to raise the Irish establishment, and that the Tories were going to oppose the whole plan for the army.[63] But a letter from London to the *Pennsylvania Gazette* dated the 22nd said that the King would lower his request by 15 regiments.[64] A day later Bute assured the Tory leader, Sir John Phillips, that the original plan would be "greatly reduced."[65] The Whig who called the meeting of the 24th "an Extraordinary Step," thought as he did because "it was known that the Measure was given up and the Army was to stand upon the Establishment of 67 Regiments."[66] William Gerard Hamilton, Secretary to Lord Halifax, said later that Halifax had withdrawn his offer to secure a larger military appropriation in Ireland, thereby displeasing the King very much.[67] All evidence thus indicates that the government had decided at least two days before the meeting of February 24 not to proceed with the plan for a larger force in Ireland, perhaps for reasons that concerned Irish as much as British politics.

And still the meeting was held. Why? It may be that the King was simply making one last effort to get the Tories to go along with him. On the other hand, it is more likely that the government intentionally dramatized a concession in order to protect the remainder of the plan. If that was not the intention, it certainly was the effect. The King was not unhappy about the objections of Mordaunt and Phillips to the Irish part of the plan; on the contrary, he

---

(London, 1962), 41-42; and the King to Bute, 24 February 1763, *George III-Bute Letters*, ed. Sedgwick, #270.

[62] 28 April 1763.   [63] BM Add. MSS. 32947, 41-47.
[64] 28 April 1763.   [65] Knollenberg, *Origin*, 27.
[66] Bussy Journal, BM Add. MSS. 47584, 6.
[67] Hamilton to Hutchinson, 12 March 1863, 12 *HMC* IX, 245.

was pleased that they had "in the handsomest manner yielded" to the rest of it.[68] Henry Legge, who was probably at the meeting, thought that Mordaunt had acted as bellwether, leading the Tories—intoxicated by the magnanimity of His Majesty—where they did not mean to go.[69] A two-part pamphlet soon appeared, entitled *An Address to the Cocoa-Tree from a Whig; And a Consultation on the Subject of a Standing Army*, which satirized the Tories for their failure to resist the blandishments of the Court.[70] Mordaunt appeared in it as the shade of Sir Robert Filmer who at last had found the doctrine of passive obedience applicable, and who urged his colleagues to do likewise; "We have overthrown the Whigs, by personating Whigs," but now was the time to act like Tories. Legge thought that many of the country gentlemen were "sick" about what they had done.[71]

Whether by design or accident, the plan of a garrison for North America had been lost in the concern for what seemed of greater importance—15 regiments in Ireland.

[68] To Bute, 24 February 1763, *George III-Bute Letters*, ed. Sedgwick #270. For the continuing interest of the King in the army question through January, February, and March, see *ibid.*, pp. 181-200.

[69] To Newcastle, 26 February 1763, BM Add. MSS. 32947, 98.

[70] *An Address to the Cocoa-Tree from a Whig; And a Consultation on the Subject of a Standing-Army, Held at the King's Arms Tavern, on the Twenty-eighth Day of February, 1763* (London, 1763). The latter part (on a standing army) is marked second edition in the copy which I used in the British Museum. The date of the meeting was February 24, not 28, but clearly it is the same meeting. For the Tory club, the "Cocoa Tree," see John Timbs, *Clubs and Club Life in London* (London, 1872), 69-71.

[71] To Newcastle, 26 February 1763, BM Add. MSS. 32947, 98. Another aspect to the plan of augmenting the army establishment in Ireland was the legal problem. The crown lawyers thought it could not be done except by Act of Parliament (see the Attorney General's report, 27 December 1762, in *CHOP*, 1 #725), and this made it considerably less attractive to the government (Hardwicke to Newcastle, 2 February 1763, BM Add. MSS. 32946, 296). It is one more circumstance suggesting that the government had given up the plan earlier, but used it as material for negotiation with the Tories.

Newcastle thought the army estimates, even as reduced, were "amazing . . . an Extensive Plan of Power, and Military Influence . . . never thought of before, in this Country."[72] But Newcastle knew, as did all those Tories who may have been having second thoughts, that everything now depended on the line taken by William Pitt in the House of Commons. Only Pitt could perhaps tap the emotional content of the issue to win the Tory votes that the Newcastle Whigs had to have if they were to make more than a pitiful display of opposition.

Newcastle hoped that Pitt would either oppose the "Court Plan for the Army" or stay away during the debates so that Legge—known as a Tory but cooperating with Newcastle—could "expose at least, the American Part."[73] But Pitt was playing his own game. Contemptuous of the man who had betrayed him in 1761, too proud to work with the demoralized and discredited Whigs, Pitt used the army issue to needle the government he could not topple, and to remind the nation of his own illustrious services. He came into the House of Commons on March 4, "with all His Eloquence, and *Vehemence*," to support the army estimates on the ground that the peace treaty was a botch, no more than an armed truce.[74] Then he added, invoking the rosy glow of victory still clinging to the army, that for a mere £27,000 more not one of the "bravest men the world ever saw" would have to go on half-pay.[75] The great war leader had spoken. Newcastle and his followers kept silent, consoling themselves that "we have avoided giving Him any Disgust, or Cause of Discontent."[76] If the Tories were unhappy, they gave little sign of it; more likely they were relieved not to be

[72] To Hardwicke, 3 March 1763, BM Add. MSS. 32947, 163-165.

[73] *Ibid.* See also Hardwicke to Newcastle, 3 March, and Legge to Newcastle, 4 March 1763, *ibid.*, 168-169, 172.

[74] Newcastle to Devonshire, 5 March 1763, *ibid.*, 182-183.

[75] Whitworth, *Ligonier,* 375-376. See also Rigby to Bedford, 10 March 1763, *Bedford Corr.*, III, 218; and Bussy Journal, BM Add. MSS. 47584, 6.

[76] Newcastle to Devonshire, 5 March 1763, BM Add. MSS. 32947, 182-183.

forced to choose between the King and Pitt. Only the City Radical William Beckford objected to the enlargement of Crown patronage, and even that was smoothed over when, three days later, the House resolved that half-pay officers should get first call to any vacancies in the army.[77]

The decision to maintain a garrison in North America had been accepted without scrutiny or criticism, primarily for reasons that had nothing to do with North America. In retrospect, a number of points stand out. The House of Commons passively accepted the decision because the government had adroitly played on the Pitt-Newcastle-Tory triangle. The government had let the Tories frighten Newcastle with the threat of an investigation of wartime expenditures, so that he dared not openly disagree with all those who could hurt or help him: Pitt, the Tories, and the Court. The government had let the Irish part of the army plan serve as a buffer for the remainder of the plan, including its American part. The government had counted on Pitt's romantic view of the military services to lend support in the House for a larger military establishment. Perhaps the government had not planned it all this way, for there is little in the letters between the King and Bute to suggest a plot, but such tactical skill would have done credit to the talents of Henry Fox.

The American part of the plan hardly appears in the story, except for the single reference to it by Newcastle. With a London dateline of February 3, the *Pennsylvania Gazette* accurately reported that the government meant to keep 20 regiments in America and the West Indies.[78] Nine days later, the Secretary at War officially notified the Commander in Chief in America of the fact.[79] Ellis, in naming the regiments for General Amherst, revealed that the government had still been serious about the Irish augmentation as late as February 12, because his American troop list included the 80th Regiment, the one light infantry corps in the army, subsequently disbanded. The failure to

[77] Bussy Journal, BM Add. MSS. 47584, 8.
[78] 28 April 1763.
[79] Ellis to Amherst, 12 February 1763, WO 4/987, 3-6.

maintain light infantry in North America, which has been used as evidence that the Indian problem had no relation to the decision, in fact proves nothing except that in the intricate and rapid maneuvers of late February and early March, when 15 regiments had to be cut from the establishment, seniority was the only safe criterion of selection; the 73rd was the last regiment to survive the reduction.[80]

On February 19, as Tory opposition to the army plan seems to have reached a peak, the first hint appears that the colonies were to pay for their own garrison after 1763.[81] This hint became a public promise in the House on February 25; it was clearly a further sop to the Tories.[82] It is also clear that the 20-regiment figure for the colonies was determined by considerations other than those that inspired the proposal to increase the army in Ireland; during the events of the three weeks following February 12, there is never a hint of changing the size of the American garrison.

The last step in the process took place seven months later, and provides the only public link with the private proposals for using troops in America to control the long-settled seaboard. William Pitt had been angered by evidence of American trading with the French enemy as

[80] The shifting in regiments that went on while the final establishment was still in doubt may be traced in WO 4/987, in the correspondence between Amherst and Calcraft in WO 34/99 (Amherst MSS.), and in Egremont to the Lord Lieutenant of Ireland, 30 March 1763, *CHOP*, I, #845. Knollenberg, *Origin*, 89, makes the point about light infantry. If the question had been raised in 1763, the answer would have been, 1) these troops were not intended primarily to *fight* Indians, and 2) any commander in America could train his troops to meet the conditions under which they were serving. In fact, the 80th Light Infantry had not enjoyed unusual success, and the Rangers were even less suitable for peacetime garrison duty than militia.

[81] Inclosure in Newcastle to Cumberland, 19 February 1763, BM Add. MSS. 32947, 47. See also Rigby to Bedford, 23 February 1763, *Bedford Corr.*, III, 210.

[82] Knollenberg, *Origin,* 28. See also *Pennsylvania Gazette,* 12 May 1763.

early as 1758 and had ordered the governors to put a stop to it. Finally, in 1762, when the focus of British military effort in the Western Hemisphere had shifted to the Caribbean, Amherst intercepted letters proving that American merchants were supplying the very West Indian islands which British and American troops were about to attack. Amherst not only urged colonial governors and customs officials to stop this illegal trade, he also reported to London on the matter in strong language.[83] As the late Professor Richard Pares has pointed out, one simply cannot judge the wartime "smuggling" of the eighteenth century by twentieth-century standards.[84] But it is also true that a number of Crown officials on both sides of the Atlantic had become thoroughly outraged by this activity. One result was that on the same day (October 5) in which the Proclamation of 1763 was under consideration, the Privy Council responded to a Treasury memorial on the subject of the American customs service by issuing an order that "all Military [Officers] are strictly commanded to give their assistance . . . in protecting the Officers of the Revenue . . . in the same manner as is practiced in England."[85]

In attempting to arrive at a satisfactory general explanation of the decision to maintain an American army, one must distinguish between the active minority who were in a position to make the decision, and the passive majority who accepted it. One can be sure that those members of the latter group who gave the matter any thought were influenced by the "common sense" need for an army in the colonies, and the convenience with which it could be used

[83] *Colden Papers, 1761-1764,* 146ff; extracts of thirteen letters concerning illicit trade referred to in Amherst to Egremont, 12 May 1762, WO 34/72 (Amherst MSS.), #40.

[84] Pares, *War and Trade,* 395-468.

[85] *APCC,* IV, #520. Robert Hunter Morris, perhaps while in London during the war, had drafted a long letter to Pitt dealing with this and other problems. He wrote: "Such are the inclinations of the people in favour of that trade [smuggling] that it is next to impossible without a standing force to carry the Laws into Execution." CL, Miscellaneous MSS.

against Frenchmen or Americans, as circumstances might require. Available evidence indicates, however, that the small policymaking circle was moved by more specific and immediate considerations. King George was thinking primarily of the size and composition of his army. The Board of Trade, the one governmental agency continuously and exclusively concerned with colonial affairs, and especially its influential Secretary, John Pownall, who had served at the Board for so long and who was keenly aware of the Indian problem, had repeatedly gone on record as favoring imperial control of both trade with the Indians and acquisition of their lands. Bute and his successor at the Treasury were attracted by the long-run economy of pacifying the Indians rather than fighting or exterminating them, especially if the colonists could be made to pay part of the cost. Both Grenville and the Board of Trade also saw, apparently as an afterthought, that troops in the colonies might improve the effectiveness of the customs service as well.

The Earl of Egremont provided a convenient summary of informed British thought on the relationship between an American garrison and the Indian problem in his last letter to Amherst; he said that the interior forts and garrisons were "kept up, for the security of the Indian Trade," and he implied that diplomacy rather than military force was the only way to restrain the Indians.[86] If there is any doubt that Egremont accurately expressed the thinking of the ministry, his successor, Lord Halifax, an "old American hand" at the Board of Trade, spelled out the peacetime missions of the military in his first letter to the Commander in Chief in America: to prevent illegal settlement on Indian land, to regulate the fur trade, and to assist the customs officers.[87]

Although external defense against Indian or foreign attack was an implicit mission, the American army was explicitly ordered to act as a police force, and historians who have assumed that imperial military action on the

[86] Egremont to Amherst, 13 August 1763, *NYCD*, VII, 540.
[87] 11 October 1763, *Gage Corr.*, II, 2.

Indian question meant only or even primarily defense of the frontier line have obscured this point. On the other hand, the police role of the army should not be read as proof of the Grenville ministry's anxiety to keep the often contentious Americans under its thumb. The men that counted were thinking at this time in more discreet categories: the army would act against only the "banditti" who cheated in the fur trade, against the "squatters" who provoked the Indians by settling on their land, and against the "smugglers" who undermined the mercantilist basis of Anglo-American prosperity. In this policy there was little of either altruism or oppression, but the American Revolution would lead politicians and has continued to lead historians toward viewing the decision in these terms. In fact, the North American army was not originally established either to defend colonial society or to control it. In time, to be sure, it was called upon to do both.

III · The End of War in America

THE title selected by Francis Parkman for his narrative of the Seven Years War in America was *Montcalm and Wolfe*. The mortal combat of these two young generals, symbolizing the culmination of the struggle for hegemony in the Western Hemisphere, has a human appeal that is difficult to resist. It is not surprising then that the glorious, and conveniently simultaneous, deaths of Montcalm and Wolfe before the gates of Quebec in 1759 have tended to obscure what the British army in America was doing for the following three years. To understand how the politics of demobilization affected the army in 1763 it is first necessary to look again at those last years of the war.

If the history of the French and Indian War is to be seen with an eye to the future rather than the past, two other generals come into sharper focus while James Wolfe and his adversary fade away on the Plains of Abraham. Jeffery Amherst and Thomas Gage had none of the imagination, boldness, and instability that Wolfe displayed. Both Amherst and Gage were several hundred miles from Quebec when the city fell, and both might have faced official displeasure for their own actions had Wolfe failed. But Amherst and Gage were the men who would remain to work out the consequences of Wolfe's victory. They, more than Wolfe who played only a brief two scenes on the American stage, reflected in their careers as well as affected by their actions the nature of the war and its conclusion. The capture of Quebec made British victory in the fight for North America certain, but the less dramatic story of how the war was finished is equally important in explaining the role of the British army in the coming of the American Revolution.

The Nature of the French and Indian War

The romantic view of the French and Indian War is part of American folklore. This view is briefly summarized: the haughty and irascible Major General Edward

Braddock, spurning the advice of young Colonel Washington, destroyed his army and himself south of modern Pittsburgh in 1755. His heir to military command, William Shirley, Governor of Massachusetts, was prevented by political factionalism and his own lack of military experience from carrying out a promising strategic plan in 1756. Shirley's successors arrived from England just in time to confuse matters, thus preventing effective counteraction to Montcalm's seizure of Oswego; they then failed, in 1757, to recoup this loss, for while Lord Loudoun debated and finally did nothing with the main attack force aimed at Louisbourg, Loudoun's grossly incompetent subordinate, Brigadier General Daniel Webb, not only lost Fort William Henry at the head of Lake George but fled in panic to New York. Perhaps the lowest point in military leadership came in the following year when Major General James Abercromby (Pitt had appointed him because of political considerations) succeeded in shattering the largest army yet assembled in North America in a series of frontal attacks against the French position around Ticonderoga, manned by a force no larger than a quarter of his own. Braddock, Loudoun, Webb, and Abercromby—these were the military offspring of the sort of politics practiced by the Duke of Newcastle, and of the sort of war waged by the Duke of Cumberland, British Commander in Chief and corpulent son of King George II. It was, of course, Pitt who brought new life to a moribund political and military structure. The promotion of Jeffery Amherst over the heads of senior officers to the command of the independent expedition against Louisbourg in 1758 was Pitt's first important act in the American war. But his greatest achievements were to recognize and utilize the genius of James Wolfe, and to formulate and execute the global strategy that left Great Britain actually embarrassed in 1762 by the extent of her military victories. So the tradition.

Obviously the tradition is not all wrong. In fact, it is largely right: British generals could not seem to do anything correctly for almost four years; British regulars were not very good at irregular warfare; and British political and administrative confusion impaired the waging of war in America until Pitt began to cut red tape and to inspire or frighten his subordinates to do likewise. Historians of the last generation have refined the tradition, however. For one thing, they have been kinder to the British professional officer, thereby reducing Pitt's part in the war to life size. Of Wolfe's predecessors only Webb still appears to have been hopeless, and a new look at the achievements of some of the generals—Ligonier, Monckton, Forbes, and Bouquet—suggests that the Newcastle-Cumberland era was not as militarily bankrupt as it once was believed to be. There is renewed emphasis on the fact that British regulars won the war, and that it would not have been won otherwise. There are even hints that the war might have been won more quickly if Pitt had dabbled a little less in the details of strategy.[1]

The greater significance of modern research is not in the reapportionment of praise and blame, but in changing the categories within which the war is considered. The aptitude of a few individuals for strategy and tactics is no longer a satisfactory explanation of success and failure. The traditional emphasis on battles won and lost, on military blunders and brilliant strokes, had clouded some elementary truths about the nature of the war in America. In writing of another war, one much closer to us in time, but nearer to the French and Indian War in the conditions under which it was fought, Charlton Ogburn paints an eloquent word picture of fighting in Burma during World War II: "It was all either side could do to make a military effort here at all. One has the impression of two Goliaths fully extended and barely able to reach each other on this remote sector, and constrained to grapple—albeit with undiminished ferocity—with their fingers alone."[2]

---

[1] Among revisionist works may be mentioned Pargellis, *Loudoun*; Whitworth, *Ligonier*; Gipson, *British Empire*, vi-viii; and Eric McDermott, "The Elder Pitt and His Admirals and Generals," *Military Affairs*, xx (1956), 65-71.

[2] *The Marauders* (N.Y., 1956), 89.

The French and Indian War was something like that, a war in which geography created problems of communications and supply so great that the principal task of generalship was in simply moving a force of moderate size into contact with the enemy. The great Anglo-American superiority in people and resources was evident to all, but the French had strategic advantages which neutralized, at least for a number of years, those of their enemies.[3]

First, the French fought on the strategic defensive; it was the British and Americans who had to penetrate tens or hundreds of miles of trackless and unsettled country. Even if the law and conventions of eighteenth-century warfare had not forbidden it, there was no way in which the attacker could supply himself from the countryside as he moved through it. Under the circumstances, it was necessary to use waterways as highways wherever possible, to build roads to the waterways whenever necessary, to find wagons to move on the roads and animals to pull the wagons, to make boats that could move on the shallow waterways with a worthwhile load and yet could be carried on the roads, to find men who could build the boats and others who could man them, to find contractors who could furnish food when and where it was needed and in a condition to survive rain and heat and dirt for months and still remain edible, and, finally and most important, to do all this on the scale required for thousands of troops. As if these were not obstacles enough, there was the war to be considered. Every supply column had to be escorted, not by a few guards, but by a task force. Every supply dump had to be a fort with a garrison and guns large enough to hold out against strong raiding parties.

The French also had the advantage of basing their operations on the continuous waterway between Louisbourg and Niagara. Although it was over a thousand miles in length, it gave the French comparative ease of movement which allowed them to threaten and to respond to threats more quickly than could their enemies. This ad-

[3] Pargellis, *Loudoun*, emphasizes the problems of administration and logistics throughout.

vantage was actually multiplied by the great distances necessarily traversed by war in North America, and by the size of the forces engaged. These armies, although huge in terms of logistical effort, were small by European standards and miniscule in terms of the ratio of forces to space. Map strategy was fairly simple, as it usually is: Mohawk River-Lake Ontario, Hudson River-Lake Champlain, and the St. Lawrence were the corridors that clearly mattered, while Halifax and Louisbourg, Fort Edward and Crown Point, Oswego and Niagara, and the Allegheny Front Range roughly defined both the limits of firm control and the no-man's-land between. But the great difficulty of moving even the small armies involved over these enormous distances made strategy a hostage to the imponderables—timing, weather, and accident.[4]

Logistics and luck, system and its antithesis, were the poles of strategy. The forces of nature were so nearly overwhelming that the French and Indian War had to be a war of organization and administration. It was siege on a grand scale. The approaches and parallels of British supply lines and bases inched forward, occasionally smashed back by a French sortie, but eventually permitting seizure of the outworks at Louisbourg and DuQuesne in 1758 and a breach of the bastion at Quebec in 1759. American con-

---

[4] This analysis draws heavily on the introduction to Stanley M. Pargellis (ed.), *Military Affairs in North America, 1748-1765: Selected Documents from the Cumberland Papers in Windsor Castle* (N.Y., 1936). British officers saw Braddock's defeat as largely a failure to reconcile logistical and tactical considerations: "Braddocks march was delayed by the preparation of Carriages, He was retarded on his march by their Numbers at last obliged to divide his force to lesson his train And the emberras occasioned by the great Number that he had Still with him, was one of the principal causes of his distruction." Lt. Col. James Robertson to Lt. Col. Frederick Haldimand [February 1758], BM Add. MSS. 21666. The commander of the 1758 campaign against Fort Du Quesne reported to his Commander in Chief: "I am ruined and undone by Rain, So pray God send us a few fair days—At present cannot move one yard . . ." Brigadier John Forbes to Maj. Gen. James Abercromby, 16 October 1758, *The Writings of General John Forbes*, ed. A. P. James (Menasha, Wisconsin, 1938), 234.

ditions weighted the classic tension of warfare—boldness versus caution, surprise versus security—in favor of the cautious approach. Only bad luck could nullify the natural English superiority, and only rashness or faulty logistics could enhance the possibility of bad luck. Braddock had been crippled by his supply problems, and then had lost his battle through a single careless act. Shirley had guaranteed the loss of Oswego by his mismanagement of supply. Loudoun failed to calculate correctly the risk of exposing New York while attacking Cape Breton, but he succeeded during 1756-1757 in creating the logistical system that was the basis of ultimate victory. By 1758, the lessons of North American warfare were clear: leave nothing to chance, and take no chances.

The Rise and Fall of Jeffery Amherst

When Jeffery Amherst joined the fleet off Cape Breton Island in 1758 to lead the attack on Louisbourg, he was reaping the benefit of three years of the labor and mistakes of other men. Brigadier General John Forbes, who commanded the expedition against Fort DuQuesne and who would finally share the laurels of the year with Amherst, expressed this thought in a bitter letter written to General Abercromby in the middle of the campaign: "I am sorry to hear you have your own share of difficulties, and cant help thinking that Mr. Amherst has come to lick the butter off both our breads, No manner of trouble; every thing ready to his hand, a weak Garrison to oppose him, and a great name to be acquired by the surrender of the place, . . This you will allow is very good luck."[5] A year later, with Forbes dead and Abercromby recalled, Amherst had taken command of the army in America, a military organization built on the ruined reputations of his predecessors. If Pitt had been seeking someone who could keep a going concern in operation, and who would do nothing to make good luck turn bad, he could not have picked a better man.

[5] [15 June 1758], *Forbes Writings*, 113.

Born in 1717 into a respected but impecunious family of lawyers and clergymen, his path into the army had been smoothed by the patronage of the powerful neighbor of the Amhersts, the Duke of Dorset.[6] Once in the army, young Amherst had the good fortune to be associated with both of the principal military figures of the day, the Duke of Cumberland and John Ligonier, a Huguenot who had made his name as a Major General under Marlborough. Amherst became known as a zealous officer, but these connections proved decisive. As he himself put it later when advising his younger brother about a career: "For a man who intends to be military nothing so pretty as an aide de camp in service with an intelligent general."[7] He moved up quickly under Cumberland to colonel and aide-de-camp, but when Cumberland fell in disgrace after his humiliating defeat in Hanover in 1757, the friendship of Ligonier helped to save Amherst. Ligonier was by then the chief military advisor to William Pitt, and successfully recommended Amherst for the command of the Louis-bourg expedition.

To the historians who know most about the Seven Years War, Amherst has been a minor mystery.[8] He succeeded in conquering Canada, and then failed to prevent a war with the Indians. During the American Revolution, he became Commander in Chief in Britain and acquired great unpopularity for his handling of the Gordon Riots in 1780. He lived until 1797, letting the British army decay to an unusual extent before the French Revolution. It has been difficult to reconcile his early success with the later events of his life. Horace Walpole, biased but candid, explained Amherst this way: "When men shine but once, it is probable that fortune has the chief merit in their success."[9] Walpole was unfair. Amherst had no flair for

[6] John C. Long, *Lord Jeffery Amherst, A Soldier of the King* (N.Y., 1933), is the standard biography.

[7] *Ibid.*, 41.

[8] See Rex Whitworth, "Field Marshal Lord Amherst," *History Today*, IX (February, 1959), 132-137.

[9] *Memoirs of the Reign of King George, The Second*, ed. Lord Holland (2nd edn., London, 1847), III, 285-287n. In the text, Wal-

the special kind of combat possible only in the American wilderness, but he had virtues that were more important. His talents were managerial, not inspirational or tactical. His experience as quartermaster in Germany had revealed and developed the qualities of care and method so essential to the North American theater, and his personality matched his talents.

A close friend could describe Amherst as "so quick in taking everything right, so resolute in all he designs, and at the same time so mild, so good and considerate to every creature under his command." A loving sister saw him as a "good humored, patient cheerful man; . . hardly ever in a passion . . . generous, humane and modest, rather to a fault . . . steady, cheerful and alert when other hearts fail."[10] Those who knew Amherst well, but in an official capacity, gave a slightly different emphasis to their descriptions of him. They conceded his self-control and resolution, but sometimes used other names for these qualities— lethargy and stubbornness. Wolfe thought Amherst "slow" and was irritated by the General's refusal to confide in him.[11] Dr. Richard Huck, an army surgeon who could use his pen like a scalpel, saw Amherst at close range in

---

pole is eulogistic; the note is clearly an opinion formed much later. On the use of Walpole's writings, see Carl Becker, "Horace Walpole's Memoirs of the Reign of George the Third," *AHR*, xvi (1911), 255-272, 496-507.

[10] Quoted from the letters of Amherst's sister in the Bodleian Library, Oxford, in Whitworth, "Amherst," *History Today*, ix, 132-137.

[11] *Watts Letter Book*, 194, 306; *Johnson Papers*, iii, 825 (in which Amherst is a stickler over a brass cannon Johnson was using to defend his home), 547, 553; iv, 341; Charles Jenkinson to George Grenville, 19 June 1760, *Grenville Papers*, i, 344. Ezra Stiles accused Amherst of making a fortune during the war (*Extracts from the Itineraries . . . of Ezra Stiles,* ed. F. B. Dexter [New Haven, 1916], 61), but John Watts, an army provision contractor, knew Amherst intimately and had reason to attack him at the time that he described him as completely honest. In the correspondence of junior officers, I have found a number who expressed a strong personal dislike for Amherst. A few admire him as a soldier, but there are no expressions of personal affection as one finds later concerning General Gage.

1759 and confirmed Wolfe's judgment: "The General is humane, polite and easy. His words or Actions never discover his Liking or Dislike of any Man; equally civil to those that have done Nothing, done amiss, or executed an hardy Enterprize, I do not know that he ever disgusted by saying an harsh Thing. He is silent secret or misterious in his Conversation."[12] Years later associates found Amherst "so D——d Dry" that it was difficult to talk to him.[13] Sitting in the cabinet as chief military officer during the American Revolution, Amherst refused to do more than agree or disagree with any measure, never disclosing the reasons for his opinion. Nathaniel Wraxall, biographer of an era, said he had never known a man with more "stoical apathy."[14]

Walpole suspected there was nothing at all behind the mask of silence: "Whether being conscious of his own defects and of being incompetent to converse with men whom he knew enlightened, he seemed determined to bury his deficiency in obstinate silence; or else his pride and vanity, of which he had a tolerable share, made him disdain to communicate his paucity of ideas."[15] Dr. Huck agreed: "His Taciturnity and Secrecy impose upon many for Wisdom and Project. I think him just and honest, and have a better Opinion of his Heart than his Head."[16] Suspicion that Amherst's mind was neither broad nor deep is borne out by the sympathetic Wraxall: "His judgment was sound and his understanding solid, but neither cultivated by education nor expanded by elegant thought."[17]

Amherst's own journal, a dull document, adds a few touches to the picture of a narrow mind taking refuge in silent cautiousness. No British officer failed to be ex-

[12] Dr. Richard Huck-Saunders to Loudoun, 3 December 1759, LO 6153.

[13] Adjutant General Edward Harvey to Alexander Mackay, 4 December 1775, WO 3/5, 106.

[14] *The Historical and Posthumous Memoirs of Sir Nathaniel William Wraxall,* ed. Henry B. Wheatley (N.Y., 1884), I, 406-407.

[15] *Memoirs of George II,* ed. Holland, III, 285-287n.

[16] Huck to Loudoun, 3 December 1759, LO 6153.

[17] *Wraxall Memoirs,* ed. Wheatley, I, 406-407.

asperated from time to time by his American allies: the Rangers, the provincial volunteers, and the Indians. But Amherst's opinions are unusually harsh, and show no appreciation of the importance of these people to his own operations. The provincials "if left to themselves would eat fryed Pork and lay in their tents all day long." As for the Rangers, who were the eyes of the army, "There is very little to be depended on all they say as they generally make out a story to come back with." Indians were worst of all, "A most idle worthless sett. . . . If I send them on a Scout they all come back in twelve Hours, and here they will do nothing but eat and drink, except forced to it."[18] An old comrade, a Swiss officer who owed a good deal to Amherst, described him years later as fussy, occasionally deceitful, and hostile to foreigners.[19] There is no doubt that Amherst disliked America and longed to return to England. Only grave silence and correctly formal manners kept Amherst from revealing himself as the stereotype British general of American folklore. Instead, the grateful colonists of New Hampshire, Massachusetts, and Virginia named three towns in his honor.

Amherst took one great risk during his five years in North America, and he took it less than a fortnight after his arrival. Following a personal reconnaissance, he had changed the plan of attack and ordered an assault landing through the surf and onto the rocks of Gabarus Bay, east of Louisbourg. Even James Wolfe, who led the landing force and got most of the credit for its success, could not recall the affair without a shudder: "Amongst ourselves be it said, that our attempt to land where we did was rash and injudicious, our success unexpected (by me) and undeserved."[20] In retrospect, it may have been a scare for Amherst too. A month later, General Abercromby had

[18] *The Journal of Jeffery Amherst*, ed. J. C. Webster (Toronto, 1930), 167, 158, 173.
[19] The Diary of Frederick Haldimand, *PAC Report, 1889*, 163, 167, 185, 187, 209.
[20] Wolfe to Lord George Sackville, 30 July 1758, in Beckles Willson, *The Life and Letters of James Wolfe* (London, 1909), 390.

taken a similar risk when he ordered his army to storm the French entrenchments at Ticonderoga, only to lose 1,500 men and end his career. In any case, Amherst behaved ever after as if he wanted to avoid any setback that would shade his first victory.

In 1759, he renewed the attack on Ticonderoga with painful slowness. According to Dr. Huck and others, he stood mute while bickering staff officers delayed matters, and weeks were spent at Albany and Lake George doing the work of days.[21] His luck held, however. The garrison of Ticonderoga fled soon after British troops had encamped before the fortress. A secondary attack that Amherst had launched against Niagara in obedience to orders from Pitt—a superfluous operation some thought—also succeeded without the completion of a regular siege.[22] Then, with Wolfe stymied before Quebec, Amherst stopped and built a huge fort at Crown Point. He reasoned that the army could not move down Lake Champlain until the French naval force on the lake had been neutralized, and that it would take weeks to build the necessary vessels.

In a question of judgment such as this one, historians are prone to ratify any decision, so long as it does not lead to disaster. Dr. Huck, however, minced no words; to him, the failure to exert pressure in support of Wolfe was inexcusable and the whole campaign had been "the most ignominious and scandalous one this War." He called the French naval force "trifling sloops," and reported that interrogation of prisoners indicated a British advance would have produced a French withdrawal.[23] Major James Abercrombie (nephew to General Abercromby) also condemned the building of Crown Point as an unwise diversion of time and energy, and doubted the French ships would have put up much of a fight against any British

[21] Lt. Col. James Abercrombie to Loudoun, 27 July 1759, LO 6128; Huck to Loudoun, 13 October and 3 December 1759, LO 6145 and 6153.

[22] *Military Affairs*, ed. Pargellis, xix.

[23] Huck to Loudoun, 3 December 1759, LO 6153.

movement in force down the lake.[24] Even James Robertson, always careful of criticizing men whose favor he enjoyed, hinted that the campaign might have been conducted more expeditiously.[25] It should be said that all these opinions come from letters sent to Lord Loudoun, the former commander in America. But earlier letters from Huck, Abercrombie, and Robertson do not support the view that they were simply backbiting to please their old chief. Amherst did not move his army down the lake until October, and then turned back when he learned Quebec had fallen the previous month. Abercrombie, sure that Montreal could have been taken, was disgusted.[26] Huck believed Wolfe's death a fortunate event for Amherst, else there would have been a "noise."[27] Many years later, Wolfe's closest comrade confirmed the doctor's opinion.[28] The behavior of Jeffery Amherst in 1759 makes sense, granted one assumption: he expected Wolfe to fail, and did not mean to have himself deeply committed in Canada when it happened.[29]

During the winter of 1760, Amherst seemed to be hoping that a general peace would make another campaign unnecessary.[30] He again learned the penalty of rashness when the British garrison of Quebec, besieged by a larger French force, sallied out in April and was repulsed with severe losses. Amherst's luck remained good and the defeat had no consequences because British ships were first up to the

[24] Abercrombie to Loudoun, 24 November 1759, LO 6149.

[25] Robertson to Loudoun, 21 October 1759, LO 6146.

[26] Abercrombie to Loudoun, 24 November 1759, LO 6149. French accounts bear out the criticism of Amherst; see *NYCD*, x, 1042-1043, 1054-1056.

[27] Huck to Loudoun, 3 December 1759, LO 6153.

[28] Willson, *Wolfe*, 475.

[29] Years later, a former officer of Marines who had served during the Seven Years War wrote of Amherst's notorious cautiousness: "Amhersts advice to his officers at Table, and upon all occasions was never to lose an inch of ground gained, . . . He mov'd so slow and cautiously, that he never lost an Inch, or met with a check by which he acquir'd the name of snail. . . ." Trevor Newland of Freehold, N.J., to Benjamin Franklin, 5 February 1776, *NYHSC for 1871* (N.Y., 1872), 291.

[30] Huck to Loudoun, 19 February 1760, LO 6221.

city after the St. Lawrence had thawed. The final continental campaign, once under way with three powerful forces converging on Montreal, has all the appearance of three sledgehammers being used to drive a single nail. But again luck and logistics played their part. Amherst led the main attack force up the Mohawk to Oswego, across Lake Ontario, and down the St. Lawrence; Huck said that without a quick success half the army would be needed to keep the other half supplied, and Abercrombie thought that a more resolute delaying action by the French commander would have forced the expedition to turn back for lack of provisions.[31] Whatever the part played by accident, the campaign of 1760 epitomized Amherst's methodical caution when faced by French regulars.

With the capitulation of Canada, the task of the Commander in Chief ceased to be the simple and direct one of defeating French regulars, but became less self-defining and more diffuse, less strenuous but more difficult. The problems he faced concerned money, manpower, the Caribbean, the Indians, and his position at home. None of them promised any glory for a satisfactory solution; all promised trouble if fumbled. As Amherst tried to solve them, he found that each affected the others in some way, and so, drawing on his own experience and beliefs, he sought the simplest approach possible.

As winter closed in around the army in 1760, and Amherst prepared to shift his headquarters back to New York, he might well have viewed these troops with some martial pride. Seventeen battalions of them stretched down the river from Oswegatchie at the foot of Lake Ontario to Quebec and beyond. The 44th and 48th, those two pitiful regiments from Ireland that had marched with Braddock, were there, no longer pitiful but now senior in point of active service, with their hardened core of survivors of 1755. There was the 42nd, the Highland regiment that had earned the suffix "Royal" just before losing half its strength in a few hours at Ticonderoga in 1758. But now it

[31] Huck to Loudoun, 6 August, and Abercrombie to Loudoun, 17 October 1760, LO 6258 and 6270.

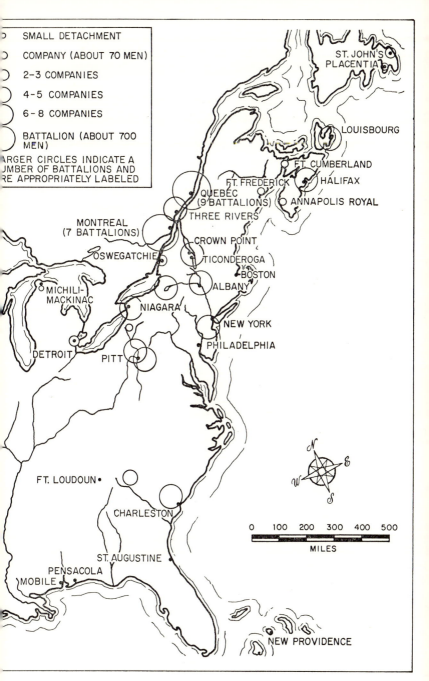

	SMALL DETACHMENT
	COMPANY (ABOUT 70 MEN)
	2-3 COMPANIES
	4-5 COMPANIES
	6-8 COMPANIES
	BATTALION (ABOUT 700 MEN)

ARGER CIRCLES INDICATE A
UMBER OF BATTALIONS AND
RE APPROPRIATELY LABELED

ST. JOHN'S
PLACENTIA

LOUISBOURG

FT. CUMBERLAND

FT. FREDERICK   HALIFAX

QUEBEC
(9 BATTALIONS)   ANNAPOLIS ROYAL

THREE RIVERS

MONTREAL
(7 BATTALIONS)

CROWN POINT

OSWEGATCHIE   TICONDEROGA

BOSTON

ALBANY

MICHILI-
MACKINAC

NIAGARA

NEW YORK

DETROIT

PHILADELPHIA

PITT

N
W   E
S

FT. LOUDOUN

0   100   200   300   400   500

MILES

CHARLESTON

ST. AUGUSTINE

PENSACOLA
MOBILE

NEW PROVIDENCE

*The Army in late 1760, after the fall of Canada and before
the complete occupation of the West.*

was grown from the usual single battalion to two, and would be better known as the Black Watch.[32] There were three battalions of the four-battalion 60th or Royal Americans, the oddest corps in the army and the closest the British ever came to adapting military organization to the circumstances of colonial society. Conceived by a Swiss soldier of fortune, approved by a doubting Duke of New-castle, the 60th had been organized in 1756 to allow mer-cenary officers from the European continent to recruit among the German-speaking population of the Pennsyl-vania hinterland. Only the urgency induced by a sense that the war was almost lost had permitted anything so un-orthodox, but the Royal Americans, while never the re-cruiting success that had been hoped, had given good service.

The fourth battalion of the 60th had gone off to Niagara and the post at Presque Isle, which served to link the Great Lakes with Fort Pitt at the head of the Ohio. One company of that battalion had even accompanied Major Robert Rogers and two companies of his hardy, undis-ciplined Rangers in a race against winter to accept the surrender of Detroit. Other regular battalions held the inevitable lines of communications and supply: one at Crown Point and Ticonderoga, another along the Mohawk River, and a third from Lake Oneida to Oswego—the supply line to Niagara. Three more battalions garrisoned Nova Scotia and neighboring Cape Breton Island.[33]

This was a veteran army, about 16,000 men in all. Its 1,000-man battalions, however, were about 30 per cent below their nominal strength.[34] Units in America were perenially short of men. Early in the war, regiments had

---

[32] The words "regiment" and "battalion" were often used inter-changeably, but, properly speaking, the former was the administra-tive echelon, and the latter the tactical unit. The terms could be interchanged because in the Seven Years War most regiments con-sisted of a single battalion of about one thousand men.

[33] Disposition of His Majesty's Forces in North America, Janu-ary 1761, WO 34/74 (Amherst MSS.).

[34] *Ibid.*; Amherst to Pitt, 18 October 1760, *The Correspondence of William Pitt*, ed. Gertrude S. Kimball (N.Y., 1906), II, 342.

recruited directly in the colonies with considerable success. But ruthless methods, legal disputes, and the consequent extension of the recruiting provisions of the British Mutiny Act to America had helped to dry up this source by 1757. The most important reason, however, for the inability of the British army to recruit successfully among the Americans after 1757 was Pitt's promise to reimburse the provinces for their military expenses. Each colony could then offer large enlistment bounties to its annually raised volunteer force. This situation, combined with the certainty of longer and more hazardous service in the regulars, made it difficult for British recruiting parties to compete. In fact, the high provincial bounties increased desertion from the regulars.[35]

The steady drain of death, desertion, and discharge for age or disability meant a continuing need for replacements. Numbers of Americans recruited early in the war had enlisted for limited service—three years or the duration. As early as 1759, one battalion of the 60th had had to discharge some 18 sergeants and 80 men whose enlistments had expired.[36] Only a small proportion of these men could be replaced by recruiting in America, and little help was available from England. Sir John Ligonier, British Commander in Chief, was scraping the barrel. At first, he had commissioned wealthy and well-connected gentlemen to raise personal regiments in their home territories. Amherst already had one of these units at Fort Pitt—Vaughan's Royal Welsh Volunteers. But there was a fairly low limit on the number of gentlemen with both the will and the capacity to recruit whole regiments, and Ligonier had had to resort to the raising of so-called independent companies, like those that had been stationed in New York and South Carolina before the war. The only attraction for their officers was perpetual half-pay after the peace, and good junior officers would not join them. Although Ligonier grouped the independent companies into provisional battalions, they

[35] Amherst to Pitt, 5 October 1761, *ibid.*, 476.
[36] Amherst to Haldimand, 31 October 1759, BM Add. MSS. 21661.

were obviously not effective units. Amherst had two of these provisional battalions wintering in New Jersey.[37]

The continent was generally at peace at the end of 1760, but the war itself was not over and Amherst knew that further operations, on the Gulf Coast or in the Caribbean, were in the offing. Amherst asked the colonies to raise two-thirds as many volunteers in both 1761 and 1762 as he had requisitioned in 1760, when fighting was still going on.[38] It was difficult, however, to arouse much enthusiasm among the Americans for such undertakings. During the latter years of the war, the quality of these provincial units seems to have declined steadily.[39] Consequently provincials were employed more and more as pioneer and service troops, freeing regulars for combat duty. This trend surely was one of the reasons for the decline in quality itself. The British view of the American soldier in 1760 was rather innocently expressed by one regular officer: "the Provincials," he wrote, are "sufficient to work our Boats, drive our Waggons, to fell Trees, and do the Works that in inhabited Countrys are performed by Peasants."[40] After the surrender of Canada, even the pretense of being soldiers was dropped and most Americans were used as coolies to work on fortifications or haul provisions. The British army now occupied a great network of posts that had to be kept repaired and supplied, but Amherst received orders in the spring of 1761 to send every available regular for service in the West Indies; never before had he needed colonial manpower so badly. To Americans, sure that the war was won and sick of the great annual encampments that killed without firing a shot, it had never before all seemed so unnecessary.

And yet, most of the provincial assemblies voted and raised something close to the number of volunteers demanded. Perhaps the legislators were anxious to persuade

[37] Whitworth, *Ligonier*, 345-346, 367-368.

[38] *Amherst Journal*, 327-330.

[39] "The provincial Troops this Year have been raised late, are very bad, worse than Usual, . . ." Lt. Col. James Robertson to John Calcraft, 22 June 1760 (Extract), LO 6251.

[40] *Ibid.*

Whitehall by their good behavior not to return any of Canada to France in the peace negotiations.[41] Perhaps they were exhilarated by news of victories throughout the empire, or excited by the declaration of war against Spain in 1762. In any case, their response was surprisingly good under the circumstances, although Amherst never failed to register an objection when his demands were not met exactly.[42] The troops themselves, however, had lost any zest they may have had for the service; on July 15, 1761, not one of the 1,637 men allotted from Massachusetts for summer duty at Crown Point had yet arrived.[43]

But Amherst needed more than volunteer coolies; he needed fillers for the regular battalions. He sent 2,000 regulars under Lord Rollo to occupy Dominica in May 1761, 11 more battalions of about 7,000 under General Robert Monckton to attack Martinique in November, and every man he could spare to join the expedition against Cuba in the summer of 1762. Immediately after the surrender of Canada, Amherst had asked Pitt to take the unprecedented step of calling on each of the provinces to raise a quota of regular recruits.[44] Pitt had demurred because he saw no way of enforcing such a requisition, and "a Failure therein might be attended with Consequences disadvantageous to the King's Service."[45] Instead, he had sent Vaughan's Volunteers and two of Ligonier's provisional battalions to Amherst. After Pitt's fall and the levies for

[41] Namier, *England,* 273ff., argues that Canada versus Guadaloupe has been exaggerated as an issue debated by the British government, 1760-1761. He is undoubtedly correct, but Americans *thought* it was a major issue because of the pamphlet controversy which it produced.

[42] *Amherst Journal,* 327-330, lists the number of provincial troops voted and the number actually raised. Most troublesome were Pennsylvania and the southern colonies. See Amherst to Governor Fitch of Connecticut, 15 April 1761, for an example of his response to colonial failure to meet his demands; *Connecticut Historical Society Collections,* XVIII, 109-119.

[43] Amherst to Pitt, 13 August 1761, *Pitt Corr.,* ed. Kimball, II, 462-463.

[44] Amherst to Pitt, 18 October 1760, *ibid.,* 342.

[45] To Amherst, 15 July 1761, *ibid.,* 453-454.

the West Indian campaigns began to be felt, Amherst repeated his proposal.[46] Egremont, facing the prospect of war with Spain and without any alternative source of recruits, agreed; in early 1762 the colonies were asked to raise, in addition to about 14,000 volunteers, 4,000 recruits for the regulars, to serve during the duration of the war.[47]

This was asking too much. The New Jersey Assembly said men were so scarce that even to make the attempt would be "trifling with the King's general."[48] The New York Assembly was afraid, so it said, to create a precedent for recruiting any regular forces that might be left in America during peacetime.[49] When Amherst asked Governor Fitch of Connecticut to complete that colony's quota by a draft from the militia, Fitch replied that the Assembly would "by no means" agree to such a step.[50] Under pressure, seven colonies finally voted money for 2,982 recruits, but only 788 were ever enlisted. Most of these arrived too late to have any effect on the Havana campaign. It is a fact worth noting, however significant it may be, that the most rebellious colonies after 1765 had the best recruiting records in 1762: Massachusetts raised 213 of her quota of 893; Rhode Island, 64 of 178; and Virginia, all of her 268.[51]

The Indian problem put an additional and unexpected

[46] On the manpower problem throughout the empire at this time, see Whitworth, *Ligonier*, 345-346.

[47] Egremont told Amherst, 12 December 1761, that Britain was "drained, by the great numbers of men furnished for the various services. . . . Not a man can be got to supply deficiencies." Quoted in Gipson, *British Empire*, VIII, 261.

[48] Quoted in Edgar J. Fisher, *New Jersey as a Royal Province, 1738-1776* (N.Y., 1911), 357.

[49] Lt. Gov. Colden to Board of Trade, 7 April 1762, *Colden Letter Book*, I, 186-187.

[50] Gov. Fitch to Amherst, 20 July 1762 (Extract), in Amherst to Egremont, 15 June 1762, WO 34/74 (Amherst MSS.).

[51] There are two sets of figures extant. One is in *Amherst Journal*, 331; the other is in WO 34/74 (Amherst MSS.), 176. The latter, dated 1 November 1762, seems to be an interim report, but the former seems to be in error, perhaps through transcription. I arrived at 788 by using the latter to correct the former. In any case, the figures are approximately correct.

strain on Amherst's shrinking resources. Before the northern campaign had gotten under way in 1760, Amherst received a call for help from Governor Lyttleton of South
Carolina. Most of the Cherokee Indian nation had taken
up the hatchet against the English as a long-deteriorating
situation finally produced an uprising. The Cherokee, wartime allies of the British, were disgusted about a number
of things, among them the lack of adequate trade, British
failure to protect them from their enemies, and bad treatment at the hands of individual white men. Inept diplomacy
on Lyttleton's part, and the impetuous massacre of Cherokee hostages by the British garrison at Fort Prince George
brought on open warfare.[52] Amherst, at New York, quickly
responded by stripping two regiments close at hand of their
best troops, 1,300 in all, and sending them to Charleston.
He ordered their commander, Colonel Archibald Montgomery, to punish the Cherokees and to return to the northward as quickly as possible for the campaign against Montreal; under no circumstances was Montgomery to engage
in defending the Carolina frontier.[53] Montgomery's force,
although hampered by a lack of logistical support from the
province of South Carolina, penetrated deeply into the
rugged Cherokee country, just south of present day Great
Smoky Mountains National Park. But a lack of time and
of fortified supply points made it difficult for Montgomery
to relieve besieged Fort Loudoun on the headwaters of the
Tennessee River; without bringing the Cherokee to a
formal submission, he decided to return to Charleston. Despite Amherst's orders, acting Governor William Bull was
able to persuade Montgomery to leave four of his regular
companies for the defense of the province.[54]

As it turned out, Montgomery's force did not get back
to New York in time to help Amherst in the conquest of

[52] John R. Alden, *John Stuart and the Southern Colonial Fron-
tier* (Ann Arbor, 1944), 74-88, 101-106; and David H. Corkran,
The Cherokee Frontier: Conflict and Survival, 1740-62 (Norman,
Oklahoma, 1962).

[53] Amherst to Pitt, 8 March 1760, *Pitt Corr.*, ed. Kimball, II,
263.

[54] Alden, *Stuart*, 106-113.

Canada. Although the garrison of Fort Loudoun—a mixed force of 200 regulars and provincials—was starved into surrender in August 1760, and Amherst decided to fulfill Governor Bull's request by sending a second expedition to Charleston in 1761, the back of the Cherokee uprising appears to have been broken by Montgomery's destruction of Indian crops and towns in 1760. Nevertheless, Lieutenant Colonel James Grant, who had been second in command to Montgomery the previous year, arrived at Charleston in early January 1761, at the head of about 1,200 regulars. This time, however, about half of them came from Ligonier's provisional battalions.[55] With almost as many more provincials joined to his force, he completed the work begun by Montgomery. By December, South Carolina and the Cherokee were at peace.

Jeffery Amherst had never liked Indians; now he hated and despised them. They had proved themselves treacherous, but they had also proved they were no match for good regular officers like Montgomery and Grant. As he saw it, the fall of Fort Loudoun demonstrated only that Indians were not to be trusted and the commandant was a fool: "I had conceived no idea, that one of the King's Forts could yield to a parcel of miscreants, without artillery or apparatus capable to reduce it, if properly defended; the little Carpenter [the Cherokee chieftain], in whom Col. Bird [of Virginia] seems to put so much confidence, was, I am afraid, a great instrument in advising the commanding officer to this inconsiderate step."[56] In 1761 there was another Indian alarm. The commandant of Detroit had gotten wind of a conspiracy; an Oneida had killed a settler in the Mohawk Valley; the Shawnee were behaving badly around Fort Pitt.[57] The evidence suggests that a general

[55] Disposition of troops, January 1761, WO 34/74 (Amherst MSS.). Grant thought that the Cherokee were more sinned against than sinners, and that the Cherokee "war party" existed primarily in the minds of a few Carolina officers, merchants, and planters who found continuance of the war profitable. Corkran, *Cherokee Frontier*, 245.

[56] Amherst to Monckton, 3 November 1760, 4 *MHSC* ix, 347.

[57] Capt. Donald Campbell to William Walters, 17 June 1761;

uprising in the North, such as took place two years later, was imminent. When warned about the danger by Sir William Johnson, Amherst revealed what he had learned from the Cherokee rebellion: "I am Sorry to find, that you are Apprehensive, that the Indians are Brewing something privately amongst them; If it is Mischief, it will fall on their own Heads, with a Powerfull and Heavy Hand . . . I am hopefull they are not so Blind."[58]

Amherst had other problems which became more pressing in 1762. His position at home was increasingly shaky. Neither of his powerful friends was in a position to give him much support in the future; Cumberland was no longer in disgrace but was still in the shadows, while Ligonier was obviously at the end of a long and distinguished career. Pitt, to whom Amherst owed his elevation to high command, was out of office and his appointees under a cloud. The new regime seemed unwilling to keep Pitt's promise to Amherst of leave to come home as soon as the war was over. When Amherst gave several half-pay army officers permission to build a settlement around Niagara, the Privy Council—with the Board of Trade prodding it to action—overruled him. The Board of Trade was also unimpressed by Amherst's support of a similar venture near Crown Point. The Board, more concerned with Indian relations than with the military convenience of agricultural settlements around the backcountry forts, seemed to be harking to Sir William Johnson's fears that such settlements would stir up the Six Nations.[59] Even Amherst's laurels as the conqueror of Canada had faded, because the military idol of Britain in 1762 was Lord Granby, a dashing and hard-drinking cavalry leader.

Amherst's military position was also weakening in 1762.

Conrad Frank to Sir William Johnson, 17 June 1761, *Johnson Papers*, III, 405-407; "Journal of James Kenny, 1761-1763," *PMHB*, XXXVII (1913), 8, 15; George Croghan to Johnson, 5 October 1762, *Johnson Papers*, III, 889-890.

[58] Amherst to Johnson, 24 June 1761, *Johnson Papers*, III, 421.

[59] *APCC*, IV #483; Amherst to William Sharpe, 20 October 1762, *NYCD*, VII, 509-510.

The failure of his recruiting scheme forced him to strip the continent for the West Indian expeditions of every regular he dared spare. "The Troops are so draind," wrote a New York merchant, "that General Amherst has not so much as a Centinel."[60] And if the General assumed that his replacement problem was only a temporary one because most of the troops would return after the fall of Havana, he was mistaken. Just before the last transports caught a fair wind for Cuba off Sandy Hook, Amherst and the people of New York got an inkling of what West Indian service would do to this army. The first load of sick and wounded arrived from Martinique on June 17, 1762. Of 605 men, Amherst sent 269 to the barracks at Elizabeth, New Jersey, to recuperate; 101 to the general army hospital at New York for treatment; and 101 of the worst cases to Kennedy's Island, presumably to die. He ordered the remaining 134 to return to the West Indies without disembarking, noting that "if they landed they would half desert."[61] At about the same time, the Earl of Albemarle, the commander-designate for the attack on Cuba, reported that he had just taken over from Monckton at Martinique "the remains" of what had once been "a very fine army."[62] It was not battle casualties that had transformed Monckton's "very fine army" into "remains," for French resistance had not been heavy; rather, it was disease—the beginning of the great yellow fever epidemic of 1762.[63]

The British high command knew the lessons of West Indian warfare and Pitt had planned accordingly that the expeditions of both Lord Rollo and Monckton should take place in the winter months, and then be withdrawn before the onset of the "sickly season." But a combination of circumstances—the fall of Pitt in October 1761, the Spanish entry into the war in February 1762, and the consequent

[60] John Watts to Sir William Baker, 13 January 1762, *Watts Letter Book*, 9.

[61] *Amherst Journal*, 285.

[62] To Egremont, 27 May 1762, quoted in Sir John Fortescue, *History of the British Army* (London, 1902-20), II, 550.

[63] John Duffy, *Epidemics in Colonial American* (Baton Rouge, 1953), 161 and *passim*.

need to expand British operations in the Caribbean—had led to the change of plan. Even if Pitt had remained in office, it is doubtful if he could or would have resisted the obvious military necessity for a summer attack on the Spanish possessions. It should also be noted, however, that the very dispute which brought about his resignation stemmed from his desire for (what would be called 200 years later) a "preemptive strike" against Spain, which would have given British soldiers and sailors the benefit of cooler weather in the Caribbean. As amphibious warfare, the Cuban campaign was a masterpiece of planning and execution; in terms of human lives, it was a catastrophe.[64]

Unfortunately, the French decided at this moment to add to the already great strain on British military energy and resources in North America. In a move intended to strengthen their position at the peace table and perhaps to divert British attention from the Caribbean, a French expedition seized St. John's, Newfoundland, from its depleted garrison in June. In the long run, the security of the Newfoundland fisheries depended on the British navy, but the imminence of peace made quick recapture essential, and the navy was busy elsewhere. Without orders from England, Amherst organized a scratch force, put it under the command of his capable brother, Colonel William Amherst, and sent it northward under convoy of a warship borrowed from the province of Massachusetts. Young Amherst succeeded quickly, with only light casualties, and his accomplishment is all the more impressive when one considers how his brother had found the troops for the expedition: he had taken most of the able-bodied men from the garrisons of Louisbourg and Halifax, added 500 Massachusetts provincials who were at the latter post, and then scoured the hospitals of New York for enough regulars to form two more companies that eventually contained men from 17 British regiments.[65]

After the fall of Havana on August 12, 1762, the army began to trickle back to North America. When the first

<hr/>

[64] Whitworth, *Ligonier*, 364-367.
[65] Gipson, *British Empire*, VIII, 269-273; *Amherst Journal*, 291.

brigade arrived at New York in early September, Amherst sent all of the surgeons on board the transports and converted all of the barracks around New York City into hospitals. The only word he could find to describe the condition of the men was "deplorable"; he used it again and again.[66] John Watts, a prominent New York merchant and army contractor, has given us a more graphic and poignant account of what these shiploads of redcoats looked like: "The Conquest of The Havanna ought to procure us a peace for it has quite broke the heart of the American Army. . . . Four Battalions of the Victors just arriv'd are an Epitome of the Resurrection. . . . They Bury'd Allmost one half at Sea in a Passage of Sixteen Days and of those that survive not a hundred men it's said are fit for Duty. . . . Never did I see such a Spectable. One Ship took on board at the Havanna One hundred and ten Royal Highlanders and . . . landed here hardly alive thirty odd, the rest I beleive did not suffer quite so much."[67] Amherst expected a second brigade of four battalions in early October, but it was decided to let them die or recover in Cuba rather than kill them with the sea voyage to a healthier climate.[68] Apparently the American provincials were surviving the West Indies better than British regulars, but even about the Americans there were horror stories to tell.[69] The *Pennsylvania Gazette* reported that of eighteen men from Hebron, Connecticut, fifteen were dead, two were in the New York hospital, and only one had returned to Hebron.[70] Moreover, the provincials were losing about one-quarter of their men

[66] *Amherst Journal*, 292-293; Amherst to Calcraft, 21 September 1762, WO 34/99 (Amherst MSS.), 192; Amherst to Haldimand, 30 September 1762, BM Add. MSS. 21661.

[67] To Smith and Nutt, 9 September; to Isaac Barré, 21 September; and to Sir William Baker, 22 September 1762. *Watts Letter Book*, 82, 84-85. I have rearranged the extracted quotations for emphasis.

[68] Lt. James Dow to Col. Henry Bouquet, 26 November 1762, *Bouquet Papers*, BM Add. MSS. 21648, 168.

[69] Whitworth, *Ligonier*, 367. But Amherst reported that half the provincials would not come back; to Calcraft, 30 November 1762, WO 34/99 (Amherst MSS.), 193.

[70] 13 January 1763.

during the passage home, and, noted Amherst, "many who arrive, I fear, will not live."[71] For a time, regulars and provincials alike continued to die daily by the dozen in the barrack-hospitals around New York and in the towns of New Jersey and Long Island where they were cantoned.[72]

Jeffery Amherst was not a sentimental man. But as he settled down in New York for what would be his last winter in North America, he may have mused on what he had seen during the past year—the destruction of the army he had led to victory in Canada. More likely he thought about other things: the apparent decay of his political position, the condition of his ailing and mentally unstable wife, and the government's incessant demand to cut expenses.[73] Earlier in the year, he had heard how Bute forced Newcastle out of office using the cost of the war in Germany as the issue. Scarce labor, great distances, and bad roads had made the cost of the war in America seem even more exorbitant; to most British politicians, large military expenses when there was no fighting were inexcusable. Perhaps Amherst also thought how much he disliked America and Americans. When he had learned in 1761 that colonial merchants were smuggling provisions to the very West Indian islands that were the targets of British expeditions, his icy reserve was for once melted by the heat of his anger, and he had denounced American officials and merchants, to their faces and to Whitehall.[74] Only in Canada, where the military government was running with unexpected smoothness, were there no problems. Undoubtedly this was the result of a gentle policy toward the inhabitants, and of

[71] Amherst to Haldimand, 28 November 1762, BM Add. MSS. 21661.

[72] State of brigade returned from Havana, 24 November 1762, WO 34/74 (Amherst MSS.); William Plumsted and David Franks to Bouquet, *Bouquet Papers*, BM Add. MSS. 21648, 111; Surgeon James Adair to Amherst, 18 September 1762, quoted in E. A. H. Webb, *The History of the Services of the 17th (The Leicestershire) Regiment* (2nd edn., London, 1912), 57.

[73] Long, *Amherst*, 189.

[74] See above, pp. 80-81; and William Smith, *History of the Late Province of New York* (N.Y., 1830), II, 350-351.

five regular battalions ready to put down any insurrection in a moment.

As Amherst saw it, money was the key to most of his troubles. If he could rigorously economize, then the government might be impressed and even grateful. In February 1762, he had recommended to the Treasury that, once the war was over, the traditional "ration stoppage"—a deduction from a soldier's pay for his rations—might be established in America.[75] In wartime, troops received rations free in return for their arduous service; in peacetime, duty was lighter and there was often time to earn extra money in nearby communities, so the men were expected to pay for at least part of the cost of their food. Benighted as this practice seems by modern standards, it was generally accepted in the British army. Amherst apparently did not believe at this time that the special conditions of American service rendered the custom inapplicable. A year later, when he received news of the signing of the preliminary peace treaty, he immediately stopped all recruiting "that every expense which is not absolutely necessary may be avoided."[76] The shortage of regular troops no longer worried him, because the only possible danger was from the Indians, and there again money seemed to be the key. It was simple: cut Indian expenses to the bone.

Amherst's correspondence furnishes ample evidence of his pattern of thought on the Indian question: if Indians were kept short of weapons, especially during this period when the army was weakened by disease and a lack of replacements, then the Indians would be less dangerous. On the other hand, if Sir William Johnson had his way, he and the other shady members of his department would spend Amherst right out of office, giving the Indians scalping knives, hatchets, guns, powder, and lead to make them happy. So far, Johnson had not much to show for the Crown's largesse, because Amherst knew how little help the Indians had been to the Anglo-American war effort.

[75] Amherst to James West, 11 February 1762, WO 34/74 (Amherst MSS.).

[76] *Amherst Journal*, 301.

Johnson (another slippery American) was probably taking a percentage of these presents, and it was in his own interest to pretend that the Indians were more powerful and more threatening than they really were. Actually, a handful of regulars could keep any number of Indians in awe— the comparative combat records of the two showed that. Like all men without moral fiber, the Indians understood nothing but force or the threat of it, and would become, truly dangerous only if the present weak policy of treating them like semisovereigns were continued, especially if the policy included large gifts of weapons. Deny the Indians these gifts and they would work for the white man's weapons, trapping furs and trading for British manufactures, keeping too busy to hatch any silly savage plots against the small detachments of redcoats who watched over them.[77]

Given these premises, Amherst's plan to handle both Indian and fiscal problems was logical and realistic. Given his temperament and experience, it was understandable, almost predictable. There were, however, flaws in the premises. Perhaps he did not understand how utterly dependent the Indians had become on firearms and especially on repairs, replacements, and ammunition for them. Indians in contact with white men had given up the use of the bow and arrow in the seventeenth century, and by the eighteenth it was a skill that could not be easily resurrected. Perhaps Amherst did understand, but did not care; after all, they were animals who just happened to look like men. But if they were animals, then Sir Jeffery should have been more careful about imputing to these animals a man-like rationality that would deter them from attacking an unbeatable opponent.

In May 1763, the Indians struck. Detroit was attacked,

[77] He had written to Johnson, 18 August 1761, that Indians "upon the first Hostilities they May be Guilty of, . . . Must not only Expect the Severest Retaliation, but an Entire Destruction of all their Nations, for I am firmly Resolved, Whenever they give me an Occasion, to Extirpate them Root and branch, . . ." *Johnson Papers,* III, 520. Knollenberg, *Origin,* 106-115, is a harsh but accurate indictment of Amherst's Indian policy, which errs only in attributing Amherst's views to the whole of British officialdom.

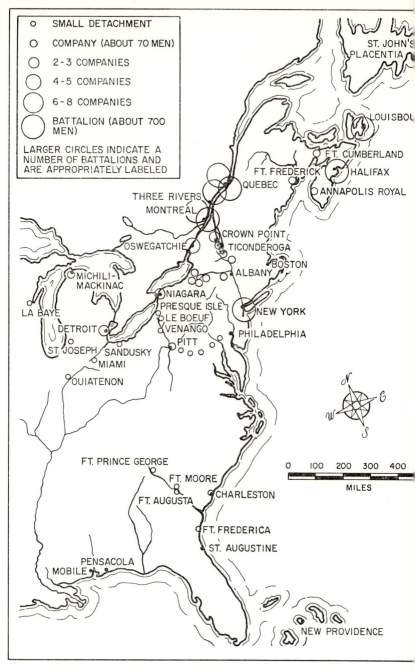

The Army in early 1763, on the eve of the great Indian uprising.

and Fort Pitt besieged. The small garrisons at Sandusky (Ohio), St. Joseph and Michilimackinac (Michigan), Miami and Ouiatenon (guarding the Maumee-Wabash portage in Indiana), Presque Isle, La Boeuf, and Venango (linking Fort Pitt to Lake Erie) were wiped out with the loss of about 225 men.[78] By the end of June, when news of the worst reached New York, it was clear to Amherst that his luck had at last turned bad. With a few months at most remaining of his time in America, everything had exploded in his face without warning.

The Response to Indian Rebellion

It has been argued that regular troop movements in North America during the spring and summer of 1763 provide strong circumstantial evidence that no high British official on either side of the Atlantic took the great Indian uprising, which began in late May, at all seriously. According to this argument, Amherst did not bother to use many of the regular troops at his disposal, while the reaction of the British government to the rebellion can be characterized as a yawn. The argument is mistaken.[79]

Applied to Amherst, it is a gratuitous charge against a man who had already done quite enough to merit the censure of contemporaries and historians alike. If the argument were valid, it would also force a reappraisal of Amherst's character, since he was neither a careless nor a casual officer. These are minor points compared to the serious misunderstanding of British policy and policymakers that the argument entails. As discussed previously, the government had been concerned with the Indian problem for almost a decade. It had not regarded Amherst's views on the problem as of any great weight, because the General, despite his high office, had relatively little experience in Indian affairs. And when Amherst made a mess of the problem, the government promptly recalled him; nothing in its behavior bespoke indifference.

[78] Howard H. Peckham, *Pontiac and the Indian Uprising* (Princeton, 1947), 156-170.
[79] Grant, *MVHR*, xl (1954), 79-82.

At the beginning of 1763, Amherst had about 8,000 men under his command: 3,650 in Canada; 1,700 in Nova Scotia, Cape Breton Island, and Newfoundland; 1,250 in the upper New York posts; 400 in western Pennsylvania; 350 in Michigan; 450 in South Carolina and Georgia; and the remaining several hundred in and around New York City.[80] He received no substantial reinforcements during the winter and spring. The first news of Indian trouble to reach Amherst came from Fort Pitt in early June, and he immediately prepared the light infantry companies of the 17th, 42nd, and 77th Regiments at New York for action.[81] Although he thought at this time that three companies would be sufficient to quell any disturbances, it would have been difficult for him to have done more even if he had believed it to be necessary. The three regiments were those that had returned from Havana the previous fall. Not only were their numbers sadly depleted by disease (all together only 535 enlisted men present for duty), but Amherst also noted that "some of the officers as well as the men have frequent relapses of their disorder."[82] Within a week, Amherst sent two of the companies to relieve Fort Pitt, and the third to Albany. He still doubted the unconfirmed reports from the West, and it was inconvenient to be sending units into the backcountry when final disposition instructions were due from England at any moment, but he was taking necessary precautions: "If the Indians have really Cutt off any of our Garrisons, no time must be Lost in Retaking the Posts, and Securing them, so that We may keep Entire Possession of them."[83] By June 19, he had sent what was left of the 42nd to Philadelphia, "but the Small Remains of the 77th which Scarce Amount to One Company are so feeble and Weak, with the West India Distemper that I Fear they will not be able to go on Service."[84] As the news became still

[80] Return, December 1762, WO 34/74 (Amherst MSS.).

[81] Amherst to Bouquet, 6 June 1763, *Bouquet Papers*, BM Add. MSS. 21634, 182.

[82] *Amherst Journal*, 304-305.

[83] Amherst to Bouquet, 12 June 1763, *Bouquet Papers*, BM Add. MSS. 21634, 185-186.

[84] *Ibid.*, 19 June, 192.

worse, he changed his mind and sent these "feeble and weak" Highlanders to Philadelphia in spite of his earlier doubts. In the Great Lakes area, the commander at Niagara was reinforcing Detroit on his own initiative, and the "small Remains of the 17th Regiment" from New York were moving up the Mohawk River. When the 17th arrived at Oswego, the 55th Regiment already there would then be able to reinforce threatened Niagara.[85]

In a letter to Lord Loudoun, James Robertson summarized the military problem facing Amherst: upon the outbreak of the rebellion, "The only troops in this country was three regiments which Lord Albemarle sent from the Havanna to save the trouble of burying them there . . . all properly Speaking but convalescents"; thus, able-bodied men could not be freed for offensive operations until the backcountry garrisons had been replaced by "convalescents and bad marchers."[86]

Those battalions that had wintered in Cuba and had been designated for service in North America should have provided a welcome reinforcement. Of about 4,000 men still alive at Havana, the Secretary at War had told Amherst he could expect five battalions at New York.[87] But in early July, General Keppel in Cuba notified Amherst that he could in fact expect little more than the officers of these battalions, because Keppel had discharged all men who were debilitated by illness or whose enlistments had expired, and had drafted others into other regiments; Keppel, of course, had heard nothing of the Indian rebellion.[88] When these weak battalions arrived at New York in late July, Amherst sent the 46th—apparently the healthiest of the five units—to Niagara, so that the Niagara garrison could then move westward to the aid of Detroit.[89] Several weeks later, Sir William Johnson reported from his home in the Mohawk valley that "the 46th, amounting in all to

[85] *Ibid.*, 23 June 197-199.   [86] 25 June 1763, LO 6337.
[87] Ellis to Egremont, 17 March 1763, WO 4/987.
[88] *Amherst Journal*, 311.
[89] Amherst to Bouquet, 7 August 1763, *Bouquet Papers*, BM Add. MSS. 21634, 232.

something less than 200, and of them many sick, passed by a few days ago. . . ."[90]

According to the peacetime organization plan, which had recently arrived from England, two of the regiments in Canada and Nova Scotia were to embark for home, and two others were to be "reduced"—disbanded immediately. Consequently, Amherst sent the other four Cuban battalions to Canada and Nova Scotia. This is one of the actions that has been used to indict him for indifference toward the Indian rebellion.[91] In fact, these Cuban "battalions" were hardly more than skeletons. Amherst sent them northward in order to replenish their strength by drafting every able-bodied man from the departing regiments. Under direct orders from the War Office and anxious to return home, the latter could not be expected to delay their embarkation, perhaps until the following spring. Moreover, the nature of military administration in the eighteenth century made it almost essential that regiments receiving drafts be on the spot to inspect and pay for them. Finally, the three military governors in Canada feared an insurrection, especially if the garrison were further reduced. Most British officials believed that the French government had played some part in the outbreak of war with the Indians, and they thought it might simultaneously foment a rebellion among its former subjects in the British rear. Preyed upon by such fears, the governors showed themselves reluctant to obey Amherst's order that Niagara be reinforced by thinning out the troops stationed in the St. Lawrence Valley.[92] In short, not only was the movement of the Cuban battalions northward meant to catch as many of the scarce regulars as possible before they left America with their units, it was also intended to keep the Canadian garrison at what all agreed was a bare minimum.

As might be imagined, the aftermath of its service in Cuba

[90] Johnson to Thomas Gage, 25 August 1763, *Johnson Papers*, x, 803.

[91] Grant, *MVHR*, xl (1954), 81-82.

[92] Haldimand-Murray correspondence from 15 November 1763 to 8 January 1764, BM Add. MSS. 21666.

continued to plague the army. After Colonel Henry Bouquet, commanding the relief expedition to Fort Pitt, had beaten off a two-day Indian attack on his column and had finally arrived at his destination, he reported to the Commander in Chief that so many of his Highlanders were sick again that he could not carry out orders to push on to Presque Isle.[93] Later in the year, the commander at Montreal complained that his men were still suffering recurrences of illness contracted at Havana.[94] A survey of the location, movement, and condition of the North American army in the summer and autumn of 1763 offers no support for the contention that General Amherst was lackadaisical in his response to the Indian uprising, once he became fully informed as to its extent. Nominally, there were 18 battalions under his control in August. Eight of those battalions had lost a great proportion of their numerical and physical strength in the West Indies; nevertheless, Amherst, by transferring men from one to another, hurled four of them against the enemy as soon as he possibly could, and sent what was left of the other four northward where two battalions were departing for home and two more were disbanding. A thirteenth battalion (the 55th, at Oswego and Niagara) was under orders to return to Europe, and a fourteenth (the 80th Light Infantry, at Fort William Augustus at the head of the St. Lawrence) was to be disbanded; Amherst kept both of them in service on his own initiative and moved them westward as soon as they could be replaced by troops from New York and Montreal, respectively. Of the remaining four battalions, one garrisoned Louisbourg and Newfoundland, part of one was besieged at Detroit and the remainder of it was under orders to march to its relief by way of Fort Pitt, and the other two were the healthy backbone of an otherwise sickly Canadian garrison at Montreal and Quebec.[95] The

[93] Bouquet to Amherst, 26 August 1763, *Bouquet Papers*, BM Add. MSS. 21643, 249.

[94] James Murray to Ralph Burton, 25 December 1763, BM Add. MSS. 21666.

[95] All "supernumaries" in Canada were organized into platoons and sent toward Niagara.

Indians had unintentionally timed their attack to hit the army at its weakest moment; not only was it understrength and in poor physical condition, but the peacetime reduction voted by Parliament reduced its effectiveness in several other ways.

Before the outbreak of the Indian rebellion, the Secretary at War had informed Amherst that the 15 battalions designated to remain on the North American continent were to be reduced to a strength of 500 men. Under the proprietorial system of eighteenth-century military organization, the regiment was the key administrative echelon, with any field commander, like Amherst, exercising at most an ill-defined supervisory role. This meant that in 1763 each regiment received a royal warrant for its reduced, peacetime establishment directly from the War Office. Traditionally, this was the time to discharge men who were too old or unfit for further service, and, legally, it was time to discharge men who had enlisted only for the duration. Before Amherst could intervene, regiments everywhere began to get rid of their weaklings and undesirables, on the assumption that it would be possible to replace them with good, sturdy men from home. Still more serious, the need to discharge men whose time had expired affected the only three battalions whose status as well as health was sound—the 44th and two battalions of the 60th. The 44th, at Montreal, was one of the first two regiments sent to North America, in 1755. As early as 1758 a majority of its men were native-born Americans, due to losses and vigorous recruiting activity.[96] Of the two battalions belonging to the 60th or Royal American Regiment, one was at Quebec and the other at Fort Pitt and Detroit. It is not certain how many Americans recruited by the British Army before 1759 had enlisted for short service. It is known that Americans were very reluctant to enlist for the usual term, that is "for life" (in actuality twenty years more or less). Presumably, most recruits after 1759 took advantage of the law passed that year which authorized three-year-or-duration enlistments.[97]

[96] Pargellis, *Loudoun*, 104.
[97] Whitworth, *Ligonier*, 293. For evidence that any Americans

In any case, in August 1763, just as the Indian threat seemed gravest, considerable numbers of the 44th and of the 1st and 2nd Battalions of the 60th demanded their discharges.[98] The situation was most embarrassing for Colonel Bouquet at Fort Pitt; he reported to Amherst "a Spirit of discontent and desertion which discovers itself among the Royal Americans at this Post: I had the honor to inform you at different times that a number of them claimed their Discharges; having Served the time they had inlisted for, The necessity of the Service has not permitted hitherto to grant them their request, and occasions those bad dispositions. . . ."[99] Other battalions had the same problem, if to a lesser degree. Lieutenant Colonel John Tulleken, commanding the 45th at Louisbourg, reported: "I find a great many more of my men entitled to their discharge than ever I imagined, however I am reinlisting them with Success, and I hope I shall be able to keep up our number, tho' the greatest part will be very bad recruits."[100]

There was mutinous behavior elsewhere that autumn, and not only because terms of enlistment had expired. At the worst moment, in mid-July, the Treasury directed Amherst to put a fourpence ration stoppage into effect. It will be recalled that Amherst had himself agreed to this measure early in 1762, but to deduct fourpence from the soldier's daily eightpence was to take no account of the special difficulties of service in America.[101] Amherst, however, transmitted the order; whenever money was involved, any British public servant at this time always ran the risk of being held pecuniarily liable if he exercised his own discretion. But he also remonstrated with the Treasury that a fourpence stoppage was unduly severe.[102] The reaction of

---

enlisted were assumed to have been enlisted for limited service, see Gage to Lt. Col. Elliott, 15 April 1764, Gage MSS.

[98] Presumably the only non-Americans in the 60th were occasional drafts from other regiments and some men recruited in Europe.

[99] 26 August 1763, *Bouquet Papers*, BM Add. MSS. 21634, 249.

[100] To Amherst, 12 September 1763, Amherst-Gage MSS.

[101] Ellis to Amherst, 20 May 1763, WO 4/987.

[102] To Charles Jenkinson, 23 July 1763, Amherst-Gage MSS., I.

the soldiers themselves quickly confirmed his judgment. He had already given the commanders in proximity to the enemy permission to suspend any reduction of their forces to the peacetime establishment until "you think the Service will Permit, and not before," and the ration deduction was effective only upon the reduction in strength.[103] But elsewhere there was trouble: from Newfoundland, Louisbourg, Halifax, Quebec, Montreal, Fort William Augustus, and Crown Point came reports of uneasiness and of near mutiny.[104] The soldiers at Halifax were among the most recalcitrant, and they were certainly the most articulate. When notified of the stoppage, they threw down their arms and declared "that it was impossible for them to Serve in this Country upon these Terms, the small remainder of Pay, not being Sufficient to aford them clean Linnen, far less the Supply of Necessarys required in this Cold Climate. . . .[105] At Quebec, officers were struck and muskets fired, though no one was hurt.[106] The situation became so serious throughout the army, and the justice of the soldiers' case so plain, that Amherst finally lowered the deduction on his own initiative to twopence-halfpenny. This mollified the men at least enough to keep committees of soldiers from calling on their commanders in the future. The Treasury later ratified Amherst's action.[107]

Despite these difficulties, Amherst pushed troops west-

[103] Amherst to Bouquet, 7 August 1763, *Bouquet Papers*, BM Add. MSS. 21634, 234.

[104] Capt. Gualy to Amherst, St. John's, Newfoundland, 17 August; Lt. Col. Tulleken to Amherst, Louisbourg, 19 September; Col. Forster to Amherst, Halifax, 5 September; Murray to Gage, Quebec, 21 September 1763, Amherst-Gage MSS., ii-iii. Capt. Dunbar to Gage, Fort William Augustus, 11 September; Col. Beckwith to Gage, Crown Point, 29 September; Gage to Col. Burton, 19 November 1763, Gage MSS. Daniel Claus to Johnson, Montreal, 24 September 1763, *Johnson Papers*, iii, 207.

[105] Council of War, inclosed in Forster to Amherst, 3 September 1763, Amherst-Gage MSS., ii.

[106] *Annual Register* for 1763, 159-160.

[107] Amherst to commanders in Florida, 11 October 1763, Amherst-Gage MSS., i; Gage to Tulleken, 26 November 1763; Gage MSS.

ward along three lines: Philadelphia-Fort Pitt-Sandusky, Albany-Oswego-Niagara, Montreal-Fort William Augustus-Niagara. All lines converged on Detroit. It is easy to look at the map dispositions and assume that Amherst was not responding strongly to the uprising. In fact, he was displacing all available troops forward along his supply lines and maintaining only minimum garrisons for the security of the Canadian rear area. As in the past, the need to man and to protect long lines of communications determined the rapidity and strength with which force could be exerted at the ends of those lines.

The British government reacted as strongly as did Amherst to the rebellion. News of the outbreak of a major Indian war in America reached London in July 1763. As the details began to come in, the ministry learned that all of the small posts in the Great Lakes area and the Ohio valley, except Niagara and Oswego, had been lost to surprise attacks, and that Detroit and Fort Pitt were isolated. There never was any question of sending reinforcements to Amherst, for how could Indians possibly resist the 8,000-man army already there, small by European standards, but huge when compared to both the numbers and the effectiveness of Indian warriors seen in the past war? An order from the Earl of Egremont to the Lord Lieutenant of Ireland to alert three regiments for immediate embarkation has been mistaken as the first, panicky reaction of a "timid, senile" minister to the rebellion, only to be countermanded quickly by an order from the Earl of Halifax, who was more knowledgeable about American affairs and thus more representative of the government's view.[108] The truth is that Egremont's original order had nothing to do with the Indian uprising; rather, it concerned the apparent failure of the Earl of Albemarle to receive instructions to send four regiments from Havana to Florida before he sailed for England. If the ship carrying the instructions had missed Albemarle, Egremont believed it would be necessary

---

[108] The documents are in *CHOP*, I, #971 and #973; the interpretation is in Grant, *MVHR*, XL (1954), 90.

to send regiments from Ireland directly to Florida. A week later Egremont was dead of apoplexy and news arrived that the original instructions had reached Albemarle after all.[109] These events explain both the countermanding of Egremont's order to the Lord Lieutenant, and the fact that it was Halifax who did the countermanding. This is a minor point, of course, but one which has been misinterpreted to show that British officialdom, with one "timid, senile" exception, was not impressed by the Indian uprising.

Egremont was neither timid nor senile—apoplectic he certainly was—and one of his first acts after hearing of the uprising was to give Amherst the leave to come home that the General had sought for so long.[110] The routine words of praise in the letter of recall should not be taken as an accurate measure of the government's attitude toward Amherst; that can better be found in other documents. First, the Commander in Chief in America lost some of his authority over Indian affairs when a regular correspondence with the Indian superintendents was reinstituted by the Board of Trade.[111] Then, when the Board received a report from Sir William Johnson in which he strongly condemned Amherst's cheese-paring policy toward the Indians, it stated its view of the General's conduct in clear terms: "We do entirely agree with you in Opinion as to the causes of this unhappy defection of the Indians and are convinced that nothing but the speedy establishment of some well digested and general plan for the regulation of our Commercial and political concerns with them can effectually reconcile their esteem and affections. His majesty's ministers are intirely of the same opinion. . . ."[112] In a private letter to the Governor of Pennsylvania, Thomas Penn reported from Lon-

[109] Ellis to the King [16 August 1763], *Geo. III Corr.*, I, #24; Lewis Namier, *Additions and Corrections to the Correspondence of George III* (Manchester, 1937), 13.
[110] Egremont to Amherst, 13 August 1763, *NYCD*, VII, 538-541.
[111] Board of Trade to Johnson, 5 August 1763, *NYCD*, VII, 535-536.
[112] Johnson to the Board of Trade and reply, 1 July and 29 September 1763, *NYCD*, VII, 525-527, 567.

don that "Sir Jeffery Amherst's conduct is extreamly in-
jurious to the Colonys, and his Schemes not approved of
here. . . . I saw Lord Hilsborough [President of the Board
of Trade] to Day, and find they intend to confide much in
Sir William Johnson. . . ."[113]

There is abundant evidence that the Indian rebellion
caused a stir in the community of British politics, and that
Amherst was the target of considerable criticism. Both
John Calcraft and Thomas Hutchinson, Chief Justice of
Massachusetts and shrewd observer of the Anglo-American scene, remarked on how the Indian war had alarmed
London.[114] Colonel Bouquet heard from a fellow officer
that Sir Jeffery was ordered home "and a violent clamour
. . . began against him. . . ."[115] After Amherst had returned
to England, Sir William Johnson received a firsthand report from his brilliant but semiliterate lieutenant, George
Croghan; it deserves to be quoted if only for its prose:
"Gineral Amhirsts Conduct is Condemned by Everybody
and has been pelted away in the papers. The army Curse
him in publick as well as the Merchants. Colonel Lee [the
future American general] who was Captain in the 44th is
Now Writeing apices against him which I will Send you
Next Week with the other papers Wrote on his Conduct,
in Short he is No body heer nor has he been askt aqustion
with Respect to the affairs of amerrica Sence he Came over
which a gentelman might nott ask his footman."[116] The
general interest of Great Britain in the Indian problem
during the years before the Stamp Act troubles is attested
by a survey of the English press, which concludes: "Information concerning the American Indian was greater

---

[113] Penn to Hamilton, 9 December 1763, *The Susquehanna Company Papers,* ed. Julian P. Boyd (Wilkes-Barre, 1930-33), II, 284.
See also *Johnson Papers,* XI, 127.

[114] Calcraft to Gage, 12 November 1763, BM Add. MSS. 17496;
Hutchinson to Mr. Wilson, 15 December 1763, Massachusetts
Archives, XXVI (Hutchinson MSS.).

[115] Capt. Basset to Bouquet [10 December 1763], *Bouquet Papers,*
BM Add. MSS. 21649, II, 171.

[116] 24 February 1764, *Johnson Papers,* IV, 341.

in volume than any other news coming from across the Atlantic."[117]

The official reflection of this excitement is in the letters from the Secretary of State to the American Commander in Chief. In October, the Earl of Halifax approved a call for provincial troops, and in so doing stressed a point that would be repeated many times in the coming years: prevention of land encroachments and trade abuses is the only true security against Indian attack.[118] As soon as he was certain that Amherst had departed, Halifax became still more explicit: "Many Persons of Consideration, as well in America, as here, are of Opinion that the Indians have of late years been too much neglected, and that the Commencement, and Continuation, of Their present Hostilities, have been in a great Measure owing to an apparent Contempt of their Consequnce, either as Friends, or Foes."[119] The reference to Amherst is unmistakable. In other words, the uprising appeared to confirm one of the basic premises behind the establishment of garrisons in the North American interior; only after two years of expensive and difficult warfare were the warriors of present day Ohio, Michigan, and western Pennsylvania and New York to be pacified. As will be seen, another result would be the blocking of eastern access to the Mississippi River, and consequent inability of the British army to take possession of the Illinois country until the end of 1765. From 1763 until the outbreak of the American Revolution, neither the men in London concerned with colonial matters nor the Commander in Chief in America dared risk provoking another uprising; they would pay close attention,

[117] Fred J. Hinkhouse, *The Preliminaries of the American Revolution as Seen in the English Press, 1763-1775* (N.Y., 1926), 37-38.

[118] Halifax to Gage, 11, 18, 19, and 22 October 1763, *Gage Corr.*, II, 1-6.

[119] 14 January 1764, "Private," *ibid.*, 10. Further evidence that the Indian uprising shook the British political world appears in the *Virginia Gazette*, 4 November 1763: "The ministry are greatly embarrassed by the Indian war, which engages the publick attention at present more than any other object."

perhaps too much attention considering the seriousness of other problems, to Indian affairs.

The Advent of Thomas Gage

During the late summer and early autumn of 1763, before he learned of his recall, Amherst was striving to extract some credit from the debacle. But after hearing of the failure of a sortie at Detroit in August with the loss of about 60 men, an ambush at the Niagara portage with the massacre of 70 more, and the inability of Bouquet's force to move west of Fort Pitt, Amherst realized that winter would stop the army before he could bring its true strength to bear against the Indians. He wrote plaintively and accurately to Sir William Johnson: "You know I have not a Man but what I have already pushed forwards to Niagara etc.; But, I Trust we shall be able Early in the Spring to put in Execution a proper Plan for Reducing and Punishing the Barbarians as they Deserve."[120]

It would not be Amherst, however, who would execute the plan. In the past three years, he had presided over the dissolution of an army: from the big, tough, competent force at Montreal in 1760, it had withered to a sickly, mutinous, scattered garrison, beaten and harassed by despised Indians. And that was the way Amherst would leave it. Reputation tarnished by his inept handling of Indian policy, and then by failure to cope with the consequent uprising, Sir Jeffery sailed for England in the sloop of war *Weasel* on the evening of November 17, leaving the military problems of peacetime North America in the hands of his successor, Thomas Gage. As with Amherst, it is worth while retracing his wartime experience.

Thomas Gage was a younger son of Sussex nobility, and thus had been less dependent, in his military career, than had Amherst on assistance outside the social ties of his own family.[121] But if more self-sufficient in the cross-currents of army politics, he had little of Amherst's reputa-

[120] 16 October 1763, *Johnson Papers*, x, 883.
[121] John R. Alden, *General Gage in America* (Baton Rouge, 1947), is an excellent biography.

tion for military prowess which awed the Americans. In a sense, both Amherst and Gage were men on the make; the former a squire's son whose advance depended on the favors of great men—the Sackvilles, the Duke of Cumberland, John Ligonier, William Pitt; the latter a noble's son who inherited status and influence, but who also had somehow to find a substitute for the patrimony only his elder brother would enjoy. Amherst was only two years older than Gage, but he had been first a page to the Duke of Dorset and then an ensign in the Guards while Gage was still a schoolboy at Westminster. Amherst had to move forward if he were not to slip back, and needed both martial honors and the pecuniary advantages which went with them; Gage sought, more than anything else, a comfortable niche.

Gage had been lieutenant colonel of the 44th Regiment in Ireland when orders came to embark with Braddock for Virginia. Behind him were the usual services as aide-de-camp to a general officer (for him, the Earl of Albemarle), at Culloden in the Scottish rising of 1745, and in Flanders during the War of the Austrian Succession. Currently of concern to him was an unsuccessful contest for a Sussex borough seat in the House of Commons. Ahead of him loomed either opportunity or death in North America. Opportunity came when Braddock gave him command of the advance guard during the march through the forest; death might easily have followed when the advance guard failed to flush out and to protect the column from the French and Indian ambush which all but destroyed the British force. Primary responsibility for defeat undoubtedly belonged to Braddock, but the best that can be said for Gage is that he did not show cowardice and that his handling of the situation might have been worse.[122]

The new Commander in Chief sent from England in 1756, the Earl of Loudoun, singled out the commander of the 44th as one of the few men he could rely upon: "Lt Col Gage is a good Officer and keeps up Discipline Strictly;

[122] Stanley M. Pargellis, "Braddock's Defeat," *AHR*, xli (1936), 253-269.

the Regt is in Rags but look like Soldiers."[123] Gage did not distinguish himself in the dreary campaign of 1757, but then neither did anyone else, and he had the good sense to avoid the violent squabbling within general headquarters which grew out of the abortive attack on Louisbourg. As the Army went into winter quarters and commanders began to plan for the spring, Gage saw his chance, not so much for glory as for security. Lieutenant colonels, especially sons of nobility, could not live on their army pay. A regimental colonelcy, on the other hand, was usually a position of profit as well as prestige, entailed little active service in peacetime, and made its holder readily available for important and often remunerative general commands in time of war. Gage had used all of his moderate political influence to secure a permanent colonelcy from 1755 to 1757; he had failed. In the autumn of the latter year, he tried a new approach, an approach that exploited the army's most vulnerable spot.

Perhaps the most important legacy of Braddock's fiasco was the fear it bred among redcoats of fighting in the forest. Whether the British common soldiers actually panicked on that summer's day and thus were the principal cause of the ensuing debacle is still a matter of some controversy. There was, in fact, no reason why a well-trained regular force employing accepted European doctrine for fighting in close terrain should not have been able to defend itself against ambush. But the casualty lists of 1755 and the tales of the survivors seem to have affected every new British regiment soon after it disembarked. Even the American recruits were not immune.

Ten campaigns, through 1764, worked surprisingly little change. As it schooled itself through the years in amphibious, siege, and open-field warfare, the army in America never wholly mastered its fear of the wilderness. In 1758, moving through the woods toward Ticonderoga, eight battalions of regulars with 9,000 American provincials bumped into a 300-man French outpost trying to

[123] To Cumberland, 2 October 1756, *Military Affairs,* ed. Pargellis, 235.

scuttle back to safety. In a few minutes of confused combat, the French force was wiped out, but a British major
was not pleased by what he had seen: "I am more than
ever convinced that numbers of our People cannot hear
a great deal of firing round them cooly. I mean when they
hear and do not See."[124] Jittery as darkness came on, the
troops began firing again as the columns crossed a small
valley, and the front "gave Way immediately in the
greatest Disorder, and it ran down for two or three
hundred yards along each Column." Eventually the firing
ceased. There had been no enemy. It had been one of
those ghastly jokes of war that more than one inexperienced
army has played on itself when faced with unseen foes.[125]

But the army could hardly plead inexperience in 1763.
As Colonel Henry Bouquet prepared to push his weary
veterans through the Pennsylvania backwoods to the relief
of Fort Pitt, his Swiss countryman and colleague, Colonel
Frederick Haldimand, addressed himself to the perennial
problem: "I am afraid that our troops have still not gotten
over the panic which infected them some years ago. It is
necessary to work on this point unremittingly. For if they
are still susceptible to it, it will be impossible to move,
without being exposed to the consequences and blame
which usually fall on those commanders who fail in even
the best planned defenses."[126] Bouquet himself wrote that
"I labour under a great Disadvantage for want of men used
to the woods, as I cannot send a Highlander out of my
Sight without running the Risk of losing the Man; which
exposes me to a Surprise from the sculking Villains I
have to deal with. . . ."[127] Amherst had noted the same
problem in 1759, but without drawing the logical conclusion.[128]

[124] Maj. Eyre to Robert Napier, 10 July 1758, *ibid.*, 418-419.
[125] Maj. Gen. Abercromby to Gov. DeLancey of New York, 18
July 1758, AB 445, HL.
[126] 23 July 1763 (in French, my translation), BM Add. MSS.
21666.
[127] To Lt. Col. Robertson, 26 July 1763, *Bouquet Papers,* BM
Add. MSS. 21634, 225.
[128] *Amherst Journal,* 120-121.

Blind and frightened whenever it found itself surrounded by trees, the British army, as early as 1756, depended heavily on Indians and Rangers for reconnaissance
and march security. Rangers were Americans, but must
not be confused with the provincial regiments, who were
just as bewildered and even less effective in the forest
than regulars. There never were more than a few hundred
true Rangers, and a number of them came from the
"Christianized" Indian settlements like Stockbridge. They
were hard to find, they were expensive by eighteenth-
century standards, and they were hard to control. Their
performance was seldom all that could be desired. It
is fairly clear that only the extraordinary talents of
their organizer, Robert Rogers, former frontiersman and
counterfeiter, made them worth keeping in service.[129] Most
important, there seemed to be no available alternative.
Loudoun wrote in late 1756 that "it is impossible for an
Army to Act in this Country, without Rangers." This
letter crossed one from the Duke of Cumberland advising
Loudoun to "teach your Troops to go out upon Scouting
Parties: for, 'till *Regular* Officers with men that they can
trust, learn to beat the woods, and to act as *Irregulars*, you
never will gain any certain Intelligence of the Enemy."[130]
This was advice that gave Gage his chance.

Lieutenant Colonel Gage offered in December 1757 to
raise a regiment of light infantry, at his own expense
pending final approval from home, with himself, of course,
to be colonel. The Rangers encamped near Fort Edward,
New York, had mutinied on December 6. Gage's letter
was dated December 18.[131] Gage did not mention that the
proposed regular light infantry might eventually replace
the rowdy Rangers, but Major General James Aber-

[129] Rogers has received his scholarly due in the sympathetic but
sound biography of John R. Cuneo, *Robert Rogers* (N.Y., 1959).
Rogers did not command all the Rangers, but he commanded most
of them, and those the best.

[130] Loudoun to Cumberland, 22 November-26 December 1756;
Cumberland to Loudoun, 2 December 1756, "Private," *Military
Affairs,* ed. Pargellis, 255-256, 269.

[131] Cuneo, *Rogers,* 62-65; Gipson, *British Empire,* VII, 156.

cromby, destined to succeed Loudoun within a few months, was more open in his support of the plan: "The present Rangers . . . might be reduced or brought down to reasonable terms [of pay if a light infantry] Corps was established which I am confident would discharge all the functions of Rangers in a short time, better than those in your present pay." At the same time, Abercromby had to admit that Rogers himself was "so necessary and Usefull a man, that I should be extremely Sorry to part with him, and rather than that, to give him some Encouragement to Continue diligent and hearty in the service. Without him these four [Ranger] Companies would be good for nothing."[132] Gage got his light infantry regiment, but Rogers stayed—a new major with a regular commission— as did the Rangers, brave and drunken as ever. Whether this bit of by-play permanently affected the relations between Gage and Rogers is unknown, but those relations would have consequences a decade later.[133]

Gage had an opportunity to make up for 1755 in the campaign of 1758. Promoted to brevet brigadier general, he was third in command of the British force assigned to attack north through the Lake George-Champlain Valley. The second in command, the brilliant Lord Howe, was himself determined to avoid any repetition of 1755 by personally leading the advance guard. Howe was killed for his pains in the skirmish described above. The following three days, when the army approached, reconnoitered, and unsuccessfully attacked Montcalm's fortified line across the Ticonderoga peninsula, should have seen Thomas Gage, as Howe's successor, in the forefront of activity. Perhaps he was, but no document records it. Instead, Colonel John Bradstreet, army quartermaster and a man not unlike Robert Rogers in many ways, took up the slack left by the death of Howe. Gage's light infantry performed passably, but they had been divided and put under the control of the regular colonels commanding brigades. Thus Gage

[132] Quoted in Burt G. Loescher, *The History of Rogers Rangers* (San Francisco, 1946), I, 213-214, 217.

[133] Compare Alden, *Gage,* 41-43, with Cuneo, *Rogers,* 60-69.

should have been free to assist the lethargic Abercromby, but for the inquiring historian, Thomas Gage was the invisible man.[134]

In the campaign that followed in 1759, under his new chief Amherst, Gage could hardly remain invisible because he was given his third military opportunity—an independent command. While Wolfe knocked at the gates of Quebec, and Amherst organized his way down Lake Champlain, Brigadier General Gage was ordered to unite the British forces at Niagara and Oswego and to seize the fortified island of La Galette at the head of the St. Lawrence. From the beginning, Gage was in an agony of indecision. His orders were explicit, but all intelligence reports indicated that the French outnumbered his own forces. Moreover, it would be difficult to gain control of Lake Ontario for the movement and supply of the army. Sir William Johnson, who was with him at the time and was destined to cooperate closely with him on Indian policy in the years before 1775, painted a picture of vacillation that would be amusing had the alternatives not been so grim.[135] Finally, Gage informed Amherst that he could not do it. The Commander in Chief angrily recorded "his great concern that he [Gage] had given up la Galette which the Enemy could not have hindered him from taking and which he had my positive orders for doing; he may not have such an opportunity as long as he lives. . . . They have found out difficulties where there are none. . . ."[136] Amherst was unfair in minimizing the obstacles, for Gage had been correct in his intelligence estimate of French troop strength. Recent scholars have tended to justify Gage's decision by noting this fact as well as Amherst's own lack of progress down Lake Champlain, and the un-

[134] Gipson, *British Empire,* VII, 225. The negative conclusion concerning Gage was reached in John Shy, "James Abercromby and the Campaign of 1758" (unpublished M.A. thesis, U. of Vermont, 1957).

[135] James T. Flexner, *Mohawk Baronet: Sir William Johnson of New York* (N.Y., 1959), 212-214.

[136] *Amherst Journal,* 171.

certainty over Wolfe's situation at Quebec.[137] But, in judging Gage, one needs to remember that making war is bloody business, and that especially in such a three-pronged operation as Amherst was conducting, every excuse that Gage found for inaction was an argument for obeying orders. Outnumbered?—then this secondary attack might pin down a disproportionate number of French troops. Amherst held up?—all the more reason to exert pressure elsewhere. Wolfe doubtful?—perhaps this minor operation, even if unsuccessful, could tip the balance in Wolfe's favor.[138] It is instructive to note that Pitt was no less sour in his reaction to Gage's decision than Amherst, sourer in fact than the great war leader had been to news of Abercromby's shocking defeat at Ticonderoga the year before.[139] The picture painted by the friendly Johnson reveals Gage as a man who lacked the quality needed to lead in war, the quality so inadequately described by the phrase "moral courage."[140]

Amherst did not give Gage another chance. After the failure at La Galette, relations between the two men were cool. Amherst ordered him to bring up the rear in 1760, an important task, but one which required good sense and attention to detail rather than determination and sound

[137] Gipson, *British Empire*, VII, 357-360; Alden, *Gage*, 49-52.

[138] Sir William Johnson described Gage's state of mind just after Gage had written to Amherst that an attack was not possible: "I told the General [Gage] that our going and destroying La-Galette, would be the means of drawing all the Swegatchie Indians away from the French, and that if we did not attempt it now, it might be the means of riveting them more firmly in it. Besides that, our destroying LaGalette, might make us masters of the French vessels. . . . All he said was, that it all depended on General Wolfe." Johnson's journal in William L. Stone, *The Life and Times of Sir William Johnson* (Albany, 1865), II, 418. Both Johnson and Lt. Col. Eyre Massey favored at least a reconnaissance in force.

[139] Pitt to Amherst, 11 December 1759, *Pitt Corr.,* ed. Kimball, II, 216-217; Pitt to Abercromby, 18 September 1758, *ibid.,* I, 353-354.

[140] To be perfectly fair, it is doubtful if James Wolfe had a full share of it either; see C. P. Stacey, *Quebec, 1759* (N.Y., 1959).

judgment under pressure. Dr. Huck, who liked Gage, was sorry that he would not have an opportunity to redeem himself, as "He has suffered very undeservedly for his Conduct in the last Campaign."[141] More expert witnesses were not so sure; Lieutenant Colonel Robertson had suspected before the event that Gage might find an excuse for not taking La Galette, and Captain Abercrombie had made a similar prediction: "I dont imagine G—e will try much for the wrenching the laurels of Montreal from us."[142] Abercrombie had also noticed that Gage was in no hurry to take over his command at Niagara; even Huck admitted that Gage had "too much Nonchalance."[143]

Whatever handicap nonchalance may have been to Gage in wartime, it was a quality better suited to the tasks of peace. For three years after the fall of Canada, Gage sensibly and gently governed the Montreal district. The French Canadians liked him well enough to pun, in an address to the Commander in Chief, that he was "*un Gage précieux*" of Amherst's goodness to them. The comment of Daniel Claus, deputy Indian agent at Montreal, that "General Gage has lost a good deal of his lenity," is better evidence of Gage's usually relaxed demeanor than it is of any newly acquired severity.[144]

The mildness of his rule contrasted with his dislike of the harsh Canadian climate, but the loneliness of long winters was eased by a growing family. After his first campaign as Colonel of the 80th Light Infantry, Gage had married into the New Jersey aristocracy. Perhaps the Kemble family would rank as no more than wealthly gentry in Sussex, but the marriage of Gage to young Margaret

[141] Huck to Loudoun, 22 June 1759, LO 6250. On poor relations between Gage and Amherst, see Huck to Loudoun, 19 February 1759, LO 6223.

[142] Robertson to Loudoun, 4 August, and Abercrombie to Loudoun, 13 August 1759, LO 6133 and 6137.

[143] Abercrombie to Loudoun, 5 August, and Huck to Loudoun, 3 December 1759, LO 6135 and 6153.

[144] To Johnson, 21 May 1761, *Johnson Papers*, III, 383. After the specific misunderstanding which gave rise to this remark was resolved, Claus did not again make such a judgment.

Kemble provided, like the colonelcy, a security he badly needed, and, more important, gave him a tie to America that Amherst never had.

To compare him with Amherst is useful in other ways. Unlike Amherst, Gage had been in America during the years of defeat, and had learned through bitter experience some of the lessons that Amherst had missed. Indians and Rangers may have been disgusting species of soldiers to the British regular, but Gage knew what could happen to the regular when they were not present. In 1755 he had composed an official report, which concluded that "the want of Indians or of other irregulars to give timely notice of the enemy's approach" was a major cause of Braddock's defeat.[145] A year later he had learned how low regulars could sink under the pressures of the American environment; after seeing a detachment of the 51st "in a filthy condition covered with vermin, . . . legs mortified thro dirt cold and want of change," unpaid for a considerable time, and ready to mutiny, it was difficult to share Amherst's illusions about the inherent superiority of the redcoat.[146] Gage himself had been quick enough to capitalize on the special demands of American warfare when he formed his light infantry regiment in 1758. In the same year, Amherst arrived at Louisbourg to find a light infantry corps already organized. Both personally and professionally, Gage was far better prepared than his predecessor to understand the environment in which he was destined to serve the next twelve years.

On the other hand, nothing about Gage's wartime service suggests a talent for independent command, even in peacetime. In fact, it is difficult to imagine a more undistinguished record that does not contain any major failure. So far as one could tell in 1763, Gage was no more than a pleasant mediocrity. He had made no mistakes large enough to disqualify him for high command, and his social and political position was both adequate and noncontroversial (not being a Scot in the autumn of 1763 was an

[145] Quoted in Freeman, *Washington*, II, 92.
[146] Gage to Maj. Craven, 19 June 1759 (Copy), LO 6114.

asset) ; the seniority system did the rest. He was known to be sober, sensible, and accessible. One wondered if he would prove forceful and honest. The job was obviously bigger than the man.

When Amherst departed, he left Gage with complete instructions for the campaign of 1764. Gage, by his own orders from Egremont, was obliged to obey them, but was thus relieved of the responsibility for hastily formulating a strategy of his own for the pacification of the Indians. In any case, the strategy was fairly simple. Amherst had already asked Virginia, Pennsylvania, New Jersey, and New York for 3,800 men. Fifteen hundred of these from the former two provinces were to assist Colonel Henry Bouquet and his small command—less than two battalions of regulars—in pushing from Fort Pitt into Ohio and chastising the Delaware and Shawnee. The 2,000 men from New York and New Jersey were to do the same for Colonel John Bradstreet, who, based at Albany with an understrength regular battalion, was to strike the rebellious Seneca in western New York and then relieve Detroit. Any peace overtures from the Indians were to be referred to Sir William Johnson. As can be seen, this plan was no more than a reinforced continuation of the operations of the previous year.[147]

While the main attacks were to come from the middle colonies, the outermost flanks of the new North American empire were to play supporting roles. In August 1763, Amherst had ordered the trusted staff officer, Lieutenant Colonel James Robertson, to inspect the regiments and newly acquired posts at St. Augustine, Pensacola, and Mobile, and to send a battalion up the Mississippi to take possession of the Illinois country as soon as possible.[148] Of course Illinois would have to be occupied in any case, but rapid movement to the area would surely discourage any support, French or Indian, for Pontiac's rebellion com-

[147] Egremont to Gage, 13 August 1763, and reply, 17 November 1763, *Gage Corr.,* II, 1, and I, 1-2; Amherst to Gage, 17 November 1763, *ibid.,* II, 209-214.

[148] 24 August 1763, Amherst-Gage MSS., I.

ing from that quarter. The northern wing was called into action when Gage, soon after taking command, directed the newly conquered Canadians to furnish 300 men to assist Bradstreet. Gage reasoned that nothing would more quickly discourage Indian hopes for French support than to see Canadians in arms acting with British and American forces against them.[149]

Militarily, the campaign of 1764 was a success. Moreover, it was almost bloodless. There were, of course, some delays and difficulties. All the provinces were unwilling to raise the number of volunteers requested. Some of their reluctance was due to the lack of any promise of reimbursement by Parliament as had become customary during the war. Some provincial foot-dragging resulted from a distaste for doing more than their share—the New England colonies, more remote from the danger, had not been levied.[150] But old Cadwallader Colden, acting Governor of New York, had another explanation: "Between ourselves," he wrote to Gage, "I suspect the true reason of the backwardness in all the Assemblies is owing to a doubt that Sir Jeffery Amherst's plan will be pursued now he is gone."[151] He advised Gage to wait for the next packet from England before pressing the issue. The next packet from home did support Gage, but the incident is indicative of the decline in effective political power of the Commander in Chief upon the departure of Amherst.

Gage also felt compelled to ask the four New England colonies for 1,600 men, most of whom could not possibly be raised and reach the scene of action in time, but a necessary gesture if the middle colonies were to cooperate. Later snags were the failure of Major Arthur Loftus and the 22nd Regiment to reach Illinois from Mobile, and an unauthorized armistice which Colonel Bradstreet made directly with several Delaware and Shawnee "ambassadors" he met near Presque Isle. But none of these hitches materially affected the military outcome of the campaign.

[149] Gage to Halifax, 13 February 1764, *Gage Corr.*, I, 17.
[150] 9 December 1763, *ibid.*, 2-4.
[151] 26 February 1764, *Colden Letter Books*, I, 309-310.

The Seneca and most of the western tribes sued for peace to Sir William Johnson when Bradstreet's motley army reached Niagara in July. In late August, shortly after his blunder at Presque Isle, Bradstreet relieved Detroit, where a truce had been in effect since the previous winter. To the southward, Bouquet, ignoring Bradstreet's "armistice," drove to the Muskingum River and brought the Delaware and Shawnee to heel without a battle.[152]

One historian has concluded that the campaign represents a British military failure because Johnson and the army accepted Indian submission on very mild terms after the Indians had wiped out at least 400 soldiers and several times that number of frontier people.[153] It is true the soldiers did not come with fire and sword as they had during the Cherokee uprising in 1760-1761, and, if one means by failure that bloody reprisals and a draconian peace were not a viable policy for an area as big as this one (with as many Indians and as few soldiers as were to be located in it), then, in this sense, the campaign did fail. But the point apparently was lost on Lancaster, Pennsylvania, where there was little doubt that Bouquet and his soldiers had ended the Indian War. "You can hardly imagine," reported Captain George Etherington in a letter to his chief several months after the campaign was over, "how this place rings with the News of your promotion, for the Towns Men, and Boors stop us in the streets, to ask If it is true that the King has made Colonel Bouquet a General and when they are told it is true; they march off with great Joy. . . . sure I am that all the people here are more pleased with the news of your promotion than they would be if the Government would take off all the Stamp Dutys."[154] Both the Pennsylvania and Virginia Assemblies voted Bouquet their thanks for his services in 1764.[155]

[152] Gipson, *British Empire,* IX, 114-126.
[153] Knollenberg, *Origin,* Chapter IX, "Failure of the British Army."
[154] 19 April 1765, *Bouquet Papers,* BM Add. MSS. 21651, 194.
[155] Knollenberg, *Origin,* 126, but which also stresses that there

Three factors were indispensable components of success in 1764: the refusal of the French officials in Illinois and Louisiana to aid Pontiac, the diplomatic skill of Johnson in bringing the powerful Seneca back into the Iroquois Confederation and then in turning the Confederation against the rebels, and the movement of strong military forces into the Lake Erie-Ohio Valley region. Few would seriously argue that force alone could or did put down the uprising. Johnson was "convinced that those Posts cannot be maintained even with 10 times the Numbers of the late garrisons unless the Indians are perfectly contented and approve of them."[156] But even Johnson, who never underestimated the crucial role of his own diplomatic services, admitted that only force paved the way for worth-while negotiations: "The sooner some Troops move will certainly be the better, as it will greatly encourage our Friends, and Confound our Enemys, who will be at a loss how to guard all quarters, and unable to collect in a body."[157] The regular army obviously could not *defend* the frontier, but it would help to *deter* future uprisings by its patent ability to gather large numbers of soldiers, to organize and supply retaliatory expeditions that could penetrate deeply into Indian country, and to do what neither Indians nor provincial volunteers cared to do— to take heavy losses and yet keep coming.

The greatest significance of the campaign of 1764 is not to be found, however, in Indian pacification. Like the Cherokee uprising, the rebellion had dissipated itself in its first year when the Indians found they could not take Detroit and Fort Pitt as they had taken Michilimackinac and Sandusky, and could not successfully ambush Bouquet's column of regulars at Bushy Run as they had ambushed Braddock's on the Monongahela eight years before.

---

were more American provincials than British regulars under Bradstreet and Bouquet. Of course the same had been true in most campaigns of the Seven Years War in America, but few would contend that the Americans had therefore won the war.

[156] To Colden, 9 June 1764, *Johnson Papers*, IV, 443.

[157] To Gage, 16 March 1764, *ibid.*, 370; see also pp. 389-392.

The Indians failed in 1763; Bouquet, Bradstreet, and Johnson simply registered the fact of failure in the campaign of 1764. The greater importance of those military operations is that, unintentionally, they raised serious questions about the legal position of a standing army in peacetime colonial America, questions which, in one form or another, were never satisfactorily answered before 1775. To see these questions as they first arose, one must look again at the events of the year 1764.

IV · The Problems of Peace

IN cataloguing those crimes of George III that justified the American Declaration of Independence in 1776, Thomas Jefferson did not neglect the decision to maintain British regulars in the colonies: "He has kept among us, in times of peace, standing Armies without the Consent of our legislatures. He has affected to render the Military Independent of and superior to the Civil Power."[1] If put to the test of historical accuracy, these sentences appear hypocritical. Until early 1774, most Americans would have been happy to have the services of British regulars without the "Consent," that is, the appropriation of funds, of their provincial assemblies. The second specification to the charge—that the King "affected" to render the military politically dominant—appears even more implausible in the context of Anglo-American history. Were Jefferson and his colleagues simply dragging a red herring of Whig tradition across the face of the Declaration? Or were they seeing the twelve years before 1775 through the distorting glass of the year of warfare that immediately preceded the Declaration? Or do these sentences have a specific historical content that is not readily apparent?

How Americans Saw the Army

The earliest explicit objections to a large peacetime garrison for North America are to be found where one would expect to find them, in the papers of Benjamin Franklin, the writings of James Otis, and the records of the Massachusetts Assembly. In an exchange of letters during 1763-1764 with Richard Jackson, agent for Penn-

[1] *The Papers of Thomas Jefferson*, ed. Julian P. Boyd (Princeton, 1950—), I, 430-431. See also the sections on the military in "A Summary View" (*ibid.*, 133-134), and "Declaration of the Causes and Necessity for Taking Up Arms" (*ibid.*, 187-219). In drafting the latter document, Jefferson did not include a complaint against quartering troops; this was added by John Dickinson; neither included a complaint against a standing army as such, though "A Summary View" does.

sylvania in London, Franklin said he thought the plan to have the colonies support an army of 10,000 "not worth your while." Jackson replied that it was no use protesting, though "how far it is necessary to keep any considerable Number [of troops in America] I will not say, but I have long argued that those kept there are for the most part maintained for the Interests of G. Britain only."[2] Later in 1764, the Massachusetts House of Representatives reprimanded the colony's agent, Jasper Mauduit, for his failure to protest recent steps taken by the Grenville ministry. "We conceive," said the House in a letter that the Privy Council would eventually lay before Parliament, "nothing could restrain your liberty of opposing so burthensome a Scheme as that of obliging the Colonies to maintain an army. What merit could there be in a Submission to such an unconstitutional Measure?" The House went on to remind Mauduit "that these Colonies Subsisted for more than a Century and defended themselves against the French and Indians with very little assistance from England."[3] In its letter, the House enclosed the famous pamphlet of James Otis, *The Rights of the British Colonies Asserted and Proved*. When Otis discussed the army, he argued from history, which was "full of examples, that armies, stationed as guards over provinces, have seized the prey for their generals. . . . The danger of a standing army in remote provinces is much greater to the metropolis, than at home."[4]

After the passage of the Quartering and Stamp Acts in the spring of 1765, some Americans became more vehement, at least in private correspondence, about the evils of a standing army. Denys DeBerdt, Mauduit's successor, listed the grievances of America for the Earl of Dartmouth; among them was "sending Troops to defend America,

[2] Franklin to Jackson, 10 June 1763, and Jackson to Franklin 26 January 1764, *Letters and Papers of Benjamin Franklin and Richard Jackson, 1753-1785*, ed. Carl Van Doren (Philadelphia, 1947), 108, 123.

[3] 13 June 1764, HM 2587.

[4] (Boston, 1764), 51-52.

which has great appearance of care over them, but really is as absurd as it is needless." Americans can defend themselves, argued DeBerdt, so that a regular army means "creating a large expence to carry and support an useless, nay I am sorry to say, a dissolute sett of Men to live in Idleness among them, and deprave the manners of the People, . . ."[5] Cortlandt Skinner, Treasurer of New Jersey, asked Governor Thomas Boone of Georgia "What occasion is there for garrisons and forts hundreds of miles in the Indian country. These are so far from protecting that they are the very cause of our Indian wars, and the monstrous expenses attending them." Remove these garrisons, said Skinner, and "we shall live in all the security we have heretofore enjoyed, when a few independent companies were sufficient for the continent."[6] Charles Thomson of Philadelphia echoed Skinner: "While we were surrounded by the French, we had no army to defend us: but now they are removed, and the English in quiet possession of the northern Continent of America we are burthened with a standing army and subjected to insufferable Insults from any petty officer. . . ."[7] John Watts of New York was provoked to sarcasm by new proposals for quartering the army. "If Administration, as you call it," he wrote to a business partner in London, "put the Troops by Act of Parliament into private Houses, it will be extremely kind and Constitutional in the Bargain. . . ."[8]

Similar remarks could be quoted, but these are sufficient to illustrate the one point all of them have in common: none is an objection to the army as such. Almost all date

[5] 5 September 1765, "Letters of Denys De Berdt, 1757-1770," *CSMP,* XIII (1910-11), 435-436.

[6] 5 October 1765, quoted in William A. Whitehead, *Contributions to the Early History of Perth Amboy* (N.Y., 1856), 103n.

[7] To Messrs. Cook, Lawrence & Co., 9 November 1765, *NYHSC for 1878* (N.Y., 1879), 7.

[8] To Moses Franks, 1 June 1765, *Watts Letter Book,* 354. In a letter to James Napier, same date, Watts used stronger language: "People say they had rather part with their Money, tho' rather unconstitutionally than to have a parcel of Military Masters put by Act of Parliament a bed to their Wifes and Daughters." *Ibid.*

many months *after* the decision to keep a garrison in America was made known; and they all appear in a context that makes it clear that the basic complaint is against taxation, with the army simply recognized as the source of this difficulty. A letter written from London in March 1763, and reprinted in the *New York Gazette* had expressed the point perfectly: "The Inutility of these Troops in Time of Peace, tho' evidently apparent, might not be complained of by the People of America, was the Charge defrayed by England."[9] Otis goes further than the others, and even he must allude to antiquity rather than object to the army as a peril and a grievance in 1764. He concedes everything but the point of taxation when he writes: "If an army must be kept in America, at the expense of the colonies," then let it be done by the traditional method of requisition.[10] The well-known public protests of 1764-1765 by the several colonies and the Stamp Act Congress do not go so far as Otis and the others, because their petitions barely mention the army as the cause of controversy over taxation.

These conclusions should not be surprising. In 1763 British and American soldiers had just won the most impressive military victory of modern times. During the early years of the war, there had been civil-military friction sufficient to explain an American rebellion if one had occurred. But the last five years had been a time of triumph, educative and euphoric in effect. About 8,000 Americans had enlisted as redcoats, and British soldiers in turn had adapted themselves to their American environment.[11] A letter of Ezra Stiles, Congregational minister and future president of Yale, exemplifies the process: "From the conduct of the officers of the Army you entertain an expectation favourable to virtue," he wrote to the Reverend Jared Eliot in 1759. "Far from this I imagine the American morals and religion were never in so much danger as from our commerce with the Europeans in the present war.

---

[9] 30 May 1763.
[10] *The Rights of the Colonies*, 43.
[11] Pargellis, *Loudoun*, 104.

. . . The religion of the army is infidelity and gratification of the appetites. . . . [Here] the British officers put on the mask and profession of sobriety and regularity, as they conceived they were among the strict Presbyterians whose public morals were not debauched by the polite national vices, except at New York and a few other places. . . . I look upon it that our officers are in danger of being corrupted with vicious principles, and many of them I doubt not will in the end of the war come home minute philosophers initiated in the polite mysteries and vitiated morals of Deism."[12] Other authors have cited this letter to indicate Stiles' fear and dislike of the British army, but his complaint of its officers as Deist debauchees seems feeble beside his admission that they had learned to "put on the mask" so as not to offend, at least not too grossly, Puritan sensibilities.

In the same year, the *annus mirabilis* of British victories, a younger Puritan had recorded in his diary an anecdote that said the same thing in a homelier way: John Adams liked the story he had heard of the huge, fierce Highland sergeant whose anger at the crowd pressing in on the troops at a review on Boston Common was softened to politeness by the sight of several genteel American spectators of the softer sex.[13] Something similar happened further up the social scale; though his earlier criticisms of American soldiery still stuck in the craws of his colonial acquaintances, Captain James Cunningham, rakehell aide-de-camp to Loudoun and Abercromby, did his best to make amends by first praising the provincial troops in an interview with William Pitt, then writing to America about what he had done.[14]

As the initial disputes over the recruitment of indentured servants, the rank of provincial officers, the supply and pay

[12] To Jared Eliot, 24 September 1759, quoted in Namier, *England*, 301, where it is interpreted in the opposite sense from that used here.

[13] *Diary and Autobiography of John Adams,* eds. Lyman H. Butterfield, *et al.* (Cambridge, Mass., 1961), 1, 76.

[14] Lt. Col. Abercrombie to Loudoun, 27 February 1759, LO 6046.

of provincial forces, and the quartering of regulars in private houses were resolved or adjusted, Americans could more readily participate in that emotional experience known as winning the war. After eight springs of recruiting, and eight summers of hard campaigning, Massachusetts seemed to Thomas Hutchinson not so much war-weary as perfectly adjusted to wartime existence. When Amherst had asked the colonies for regular recruits as well as several thousand volunteers in 1762, Hutchinson recalled that, though the Assembly had been somewhat reluctant, "Men were raised with greater ease than ever. By habit they became fond of the life of a soldier. The number, now required, being not half what had been required in former years, there was not room for many who inclined to serve, and who, thus, were obliged to remain at home."[15] Again John Adams can confirm a generalization with a personal note; in 1759, young Oxenbridge Thacher had shocked Adams with a confession: "I wish my self a soldier. I look upon these private soldiers with their Guns upon their shoulders, as superior to me."[16]

By the last campaign, when Amherst's battalions helped pick up, one by one, the West Indian pearls of the French and Spanish empires, colonists like John Watts had learned to identify these regulars as American. Watts was a shrewd and slightly cynical merchant, a rich man with a sense of humor but not much sentimentality; but Watts called them "the stoutest little Army in the world." The sense of identification with America came through clearly when he added: "Your Hyde Park Generals it's said treated them with great contempt, because they were not high dressed, they had been too long away from St. James' to be fashionable, hard labour, in the Woods and Batteaus had soild their Cloths and discomposed the smart Cock, yet without such Troops . . . the Conquest had never been made, . . ."[17]

[15] Thomas Hutchinson, *The History of the Colony and Province of Massachusetts Bay,* ed. L. S. Mayo (Cambridge, Mass., 1936), III, 70.

[16] *Adams Diary,* ed. Butterfield, 110.

[17] Watts to Moses Franks, 27 October 1762, *Watts Letter Book,*

The dissenting clergy, many of whom would later lead colonial resistance to British measures, expressed better than anyone else the effect of the war on the American attitude toward the British army. Like Stiles, they were disposed to view any regular army with distaste, for moral as well as political reasons. But they were also bound by their theology to see the outcome of battle as the judgment of the Lord, and His judgment had been favorable for five years running. When time came to preach thanksgiving sermons for military victories, ministers who called "The Art of War, The Gift of God" logically translated such a theory of war into rhetoric.[18] The capture of Louisbourg, the fall of Quebec, the surrender of Canada, the capture of Havana, and the signing of the peace treaty each brought forth a wave of these sermons. In a number of them, the years after 1757 were treated as the glorious culmination of the Reformation, with Catholic France, Spain, and Austria going down before the inspired forces of Protestant Britain and Prussia. The preachers drew little distinction between England and America, and still less between regular and provincial troops. Victory was "British" or "English," the troops "ours" and "God's." John Treat intoned at the Presbyterian Church in New York City, "Havannah the rich, the strong, is fallen, is fallen. And this is British property. Sing aloud unto God, and exalt the right hand of his power."[19] At the same time in Shrewsbury, Massachusetts, Samuel Frink proclaimed that "the God of the English Israel . . . has shewed himself to be Lord of our Hosts, and the God of our Armies."[20]

---

92. Carl Bridenbaugh, *Cities in Revolt* (N.Y., 1955), 311, misconstrues this passage by incomplete quotation and by interpolation, thus: " 'Your Hyde Parke Generals' treated the provincial troops. . . ." Provincial troops were only a small part of the total force sent from America against the West Indies in 1762.

[18] Preached on 6 April 1759, Sylvanus Conant, *The Art of War, The Gift of God* (Boston, 1759).

[19] *A Thanksgiving Sermon* (N.Y., 1762), 9.

[20] *The Marvellous Works of Creation and Providence, Illustrated* (Boston, 1763), 36.

A few of the sermons are so fulsomely personal that they flirt with blasphemy. Eli Forbes, who had served as chaplain to a Massachusetts regiment and had seen British regulars at first hand, apotheosized Amherst after the fall of Canada: "How divine did he appear when he stood at the Head of his impregnable Battalions." Forbes believed Wolfe was surely among the Princes of Heaven.[21] When the regulars were singled out, it was to praise and not to criticize them. Thomas Balch, preaching the annual sermon to The Ancient and Honourable Artillery Company at Boston in 1763, admonished the militiamen to take a lesson from the regulars: "Skilful and brave Soldiers are ever the Beauty and Glory, and under God, the Safety and Defence of a People."[22] For a time at least, the dogmatic dislike of the Puritan clergy for professional soldiers was overwhelmed by the aura of Grace that the British army had acquired in crushing the papist enemy.

It is no wonder then that Americans were slow to object as a matter of principle to the retention in Canada, Florida, and the backcountry of a part of that army to whom they felt a certain gratitude, with whom they shared a sense of mutual accomplishment. Friction had never altogether disappeared, but the elation that came with victory was a balm that healed sore points. Even the Indian war of 1763-1764, not an impressive display of British arms, served to prolong the wartime attitude. Pennsylvania frontiersmen, in the course of criticizing the conduct of their own provincial government, spoke "of the almost despaired of Success of his Majesty's little Army, whose Valour the whole Frontiers with Gratitude acknowledge, as the happy Means of having saved from Ruin great part of the Province."[23] The Massachusetts Representatives, when they protested to Mauduit against paying for regulars stationed in America, had admitted, perhaps inadvertently, that troops were there

[21] *God the Strength and Salvation of His People* (Boston, 1761), 32.
[22] *A Sermon Preached to the Ancient and Honourable Artillery Company at Boston, June 6, 1763* (Boston, 1763), 33.
[23] 17 February 1764, 8 *Pa. Arch.* VII, 5550-5551.

"to protect them."[24] James Otis, while asserting and proving the rights of the British colonies, felt constrained to "grant our regular troops are the best in the world, and that the experience of the present officers shews that they are capable of every species of American service." Otis could only add, "yet we should guard against the worst"; then he fled again into Roman history to seek warnings for the present.[25]

The Problem of Governors

Because Americans would not directly denounce "His Majesty's little army," however indefinite or superfluous its peacetime mission might seem to some of them, it was left to an Englishman to register the first clear, reasoned protest. In retrospect, Thomas Pownall appears to have put his case against the army on a somewhat abstract and insignificant basis; nevertheless, it also rested on his own wartime experience. He was the brother of John Pownall, Secretary to the Board of Trade, and had, with the patronage of the Earl of Halifax, been secretary to the Governor of New York, then to the Earl of Loudoun, at last Governor of New Jersey and Massachusetts in turn. While Governor of Massachusetts, he had found himself in violent conflict with his old chief, Loudoun, over the quartering of troops and other military matters, and Pownall never forgot it.[26]

In England after the war, Pownall was attended to as an American "expert." He secured his title by the publication of a treatise on the *Administration of the Colonies*, a book that would be in its fifth edition by 1774. In the first edition of 1764, Pownall is liberal in tone (Americans are brother "free-born Englishmen,") if occasionally making suggestions that Americans would recognize as dangerous ("let a revision be made of the . . . governments of the colonies."). He utterly fails, like Benjamin Franklin, to antici-

[24] HM 2587.
[25] *Rights of the Colonies*, 64.
[26] A brief account is in Gipson, *British Empire*, VII, 160-162. For a full treatment, see Pargellis, *Loudoun*.

pate serious resistance to taxation.[27] In general, the book is a mixture of vague ideas and specific proposals, perceptiveness and obtuseness; prolix in style, it is saved by the obvious open-mindedness of the author.

On one point, however, Pownall had made up his mind: the creation of a peacetime Commander in Chief for America was a mistake. As Governor of Massachusetts, with a war on and military necessity overriding all fine points of law or policy, Pownall had been unable to do more than protest the diminution of civil authority which was a consequence of a unified military command. After the recall of Loudoun, Abercromby and Amherst in turn had held the same broad, ill-defined powers of Commander in Chief, although they were careful to use them with more discretion. But the peace of 1763, as Pownall saw it, should have led to a reexamination of this constitutional question. "Where the office and power, as now exercised, of a military commander in chief, are not absolutely necessary; neither prudence, justice, nor sound policy can justify such an establishment. In time of peace, it cannot be necessary. . . . If there be, in time of peace, in the civil governors, and other officers of the crown, the least subordination to this military commander in chief; it will be found a dangerous thing to have given so much of civil power out of the King's hands, and to have done so little to maintain those, into whose hands it is entrusted."[28] Thus Pownall did not object to a colonial garrison ("Regular troops are in the same manner and degree necessary in North America, as in Britain or Ireland"),[29] but only to the organization that made them independent of civil governors.

In view of the size of the new American military establishment, and in order to correct the appalling deficiencies in colonial military administration described previously, it had seemed only sensible to continue the wartime office of Commander in Chief. Like the decision to maintain the

[27] (London, 1764), 66. This edition was anonymous. On Franklin, see Carl Van Doren, *Benjamin Franklin* (N.Y., 1938), 322.

[28] Pownall, *Administration* (1764 ed.), 64-65.

[29] *Ibid.* (1765 ed.), 69.

army itself, the retention of a Commander in Chief appears to have been so reasonable as to be taken for granted; thus, the consequences were not carefully considered. The decision to keep an army in the colonies ultimately raised the fundamental question of the power of Parliament to tax colonists. But the decision to centralize the control of that army under a military officer and to divorce its administration from colonial politics also raised a parallel, if less acute, set of questions. For anyone who would see American revolutionary resistance to British colonial policy after 1763 either as stingy provincials sacrificing the imperial weal in order to defend their pocketbooks, or as liberty-loving Americans refusing to accept the arbitrary dictates of a corrupt King and Parliament, then these secondary constitutional questions—those arising from an independent military establishment under the control of a single general officer—offer interesting insights into the nature of the Revolution.

The issue of military officers versus royal governors in peacetime first arose during the execution of the supporting missions assigned to the flanks of the North American Empire in the suppression of Indian rebellion in 1764; that is, the occupation of Illinois by way of the Mississippi from Florida and the reinforcement of the Great Lakes from Canada. While the Earl of Bute had still dominated British government in 1762-1763, four Scots received appointments to govern the four new American provinces: the Ceded Islands in the West Indies, Canada (to be renamed Quebec), and East and West Florida. All were military men and all were to end their governorships under a cloud of some sort. Two of these governors, James Murray of Quebec and George Johnstone of West Florida, had become involved in serious disputes with local military commanders by the end of 1764.

West Florida was a miserable place. Consisting primarily of Pensacola and Mobile (previously Spanish and French, respectively), West Florida provoked great hopes as an entrepôt for the fur and skin trade, and as a producer of valuable and exotic crops. But, like East Florida, it had been valued at the peace table primarily as a means of securing the rest of British North America. To expel French and Spanish governments from the southeastern coastal plain would mean an end to their influence among the great Indian nations of the South, always a grave threat to Anglo-American security.[30] The hopes for Florida were an afterthought.

The troops that first occupied the Floridas came directly from Cuba. Because of a delay in the transmission of orders from England, they were woefully understrength. After suffering the horrors of Havana in the previous year, the sight of Pensacola and Mobile must have been unbearably discouraging in the autumn of 1763. Soon after Major Robert Farmar took possession of Mobile and its 350 inhabitants, he reported that aggressive Indians daily swarmed in and out of his headquarters demanding presents of food and rum, the fort was so badly designed that it could not protect its own provision storehouse in the event of an Indian war, the inhabitants claimed everything outside the fort as private property, there was not sufficient room in the dilapidated barracks for his two depleted battalions, and his men spent most of their time scrounging firewood, "for when the Northerly winds prevail, it is so cold as to freeze in one night to such a degree that the Ice will be of a great substance."[31] But at least Mobile had barracks. Major William Forbes with a regiment at Pensacola reported "nothing more than miserable bark hutts, without any sort of Fire places, or windows void of every utencil." The fort at Pensacola was "a rotten stockade without a ditch, so defenceless that any one can step in at pleasure," and it appeared "fifty times better upon paper then it really is." Major Forbes also noted the rumor that a governor had been appointed for West Florida, and prophetically

[30] See, for example, the anonymous "Thoughts concerning Florida [1762-1763]," PRO 30/47 (Egremont MSS.), xiv, 88-89.
[31] Farmar to the Secretary at War, 24 January 1764, *Mississippi Provincial Archives, 1763-1766,* ed. Dunbar Rowland (Nashville, 1911), 7-17.

observed: "Untill the Country is greatly improved, I know of nothing he has to govern."[32]

A governor had indeed been appointed, and if anything was certain about him it was that George Johnstone would find something in West Florida to govern. A naval officer, his record was speckled with gallantry in action, courts-martial, and duels. Of equal importance, he was a member of Parliament and leader of a "remarkable and ferocious" faction of the stockholders of the politically important East India Company.[33] Although the fall of Bute in April 1763 had compromised his position even before he arrived in West Florida, Johnstone was powerful enough in his own right to protect himself from a political purge.[34]

Had Major Arthur Loftus been able to get the 22nd Regiment up the Mississippi to Illinois in March 1764, Johnstone's arrival would not have been as consequential as it turned out. But even before they set out from Mobile, Loftus and his battalion appear to have been demoralized, either by their service in Cuba or by the magnitude of their assigned mission, or perhaps by both. It soon became evident that the provision of the peace treaty which fixed the boundary of Florida at the easternmost "channel" of the Mississippi, permitting the French to retain the "island" of New Orleans, was a gross error. The Iberville River "channel" connecting the Mississippi to Lake Maurepas was found to be clogged with "fallen trees and rubbish so as to be impassable even by Canoes," and Loftus had to take ship up the main channel and to ask the French governor for permission to establish an advanced base at New Orleans.[35] Loftus departed New Orleans on February 27, 1764, with two pirogues, ten bateaux, 320 soldiers, 30 women, and

[32] Forbes to the Secretary at War, 29 January 1764, *ibid.*, 141-143.
[33] Lucy S. Sutherland, *The East India Company in Eighteenth Century Politics* (Oxford, 1952), 213.
[34] Johnstone to Bute, 16 June 1763, *Jenkinson Papers*, 157-159, suggests that something of the sort was attempted. See also James Murray to Amherst, 25 October 1763, *PAC Report, 1912*, 87.
[35] Report of Lt. Col. James Robertson, 8 March 1764, *IHC*, x, 216.

17 children, and with warnings of Indian trouble ringing in his ears.[36] Ten men deserted the first day, and, despite strict precautionary measures and at least one summary execution, several more disappeared into the brush every night after that.[37] His hands full with simply trying to hold the expedition together, Loftus did nothing to prepare the Indians for his coming. On March 20, when Indians opened fire on the leading pirogues some two hundred miles from New Orleans, just above the mouth of the Red River, Loftus had the excuse he needed and ordered his remaining men to paddle back to New Orleans.[38] It was in the midst of preparations for a second, reinforced expedition that Governor George Johnstone arrived in West Florida.

Johnstone had not been there a fortnight when he put the case bluntly and in writing to Captain Robert Mackinen, acting Commander of the 35th Regiment at Pensacola: "Imperium in Imperio cannot exist in a Common wealth, much less within the Fortifications of a Garrison; either you must have the Command of the Fort or I; this is indubitable."[39] Johnstone also asserted his right to control the troops in West Florida; if he did not have such a right, then "it is the first Settlement of any Colony since the beginning of the

[36] Variant figures are in *IHC*, x, 173 and 227. The French governor, d'Abbadie, noted that the British soldiers "are frightened at the difficulties of the passage and are afraid of the savages; some of the officers are not much more reassured." Betting at New Orleans was that they would never make it to Illinois "on account of the difficulty of the route, the few precautions which they have taken, and the impediment due to their boats as from the savages." *Ibid.*, 172-173.

[37] Capt. Christopher French, "Journal of the Proceedings of His Majesty's 22d Regiment up the River Mississippi," LC MS.

[38] In his report to Gage, 19 April 1764, Loftus said that there were at least two hundred Indians, "which was Enough to Stop Two Thousand Men in open Boats." *IHC*, x, 238 (Misdated 9 April 1764). A French account, however, doubts if there were more than thirty Indians, and is highly critical of Loftus for not trying to shoot his way through to Natchez about fifty miles up river; "We have had many example of French convoys which have suffered more severe attacks and gone on in spite of them." *Ibid.*, 235, 230.

[39] 3 November 1764, *Miss. Prov. Arch.*, 158.

world, where somebody on the Spot had not the general Command of the whole military force within the Province."[40] He soon dropped Mackinen for bigger game, as his claim to command all the troops in the colony brought him into conflict with Major Robert Farmar.

Farmar had orders from General Gage to lead his regiment, the 34th, in the second attempt to occupy Illinois. Trouble with Johnstone was inevitable, but it was multiplied by Farmar's evident need to make extensive preparations and to spend considerable sums of money for the expedition. In January 1765, Johnstone accused Farmar of, among other things, embezzling public property and funds, and demanded a court-martial.[41] Farmar also demanded a court-martial, in order to clear himself, and charged Johnstone and his Council with obstructing the movement of the 34th Regiment to Illinois. The specific accusations seem incredible: Johnstone had refused to permit the transfer of provisions to New Orleans because they were going out of the province and the provision contract was for West Florida only; Johnstone, with intent to dishearten the troops, had published hearsay accounts that the Indians would never let the 34th reach Illinois; the provincial Secretary had demanded that each officer and man procure a passport (with a fee to the Secretary for this service) before leaving West Florida.[42]

Lieutenant Colonel David Wedderburn, who had recently arrived, was a fellow Scot and the senior military officer in the province, but he kept out of trouble with Johnstone by not claiming to command any more than his

40 To Mackinen, 7 November 1764, *ibid.*, 165.

41 Johnstone to Gage, 3 January 1765, Gage MSS. Farmar drew bills for at least £13,883 Sterling in 1765 (*Commons Journal*, xxx, 554ff.) and £4,683 the following year (*Commons Journal*, xxxi, 124ff.).

42 Farmar to Gage, 11 March 1765, *IHC*, x, 464-466. The provincial secretary was James Macpherson, a talented author who had just published his "translation" of the spurious third-century Gaelic poet Ossian. For intimate glimpses of Macpherson before he departed for West Florida, see *Boswell's London Journal, 1762-1763*, ed. Frederick A. Pottle (N.Y., 1950), 32 and *passim*.

own 22nd Regiment, mercifully no longer under orders to go anywhere or do anything. Wedderburn thought Farmar had behaved badly, and wrote of the Governor as "the meek, moderate, patient, ill-treated Johnston."[43] But Wedderburn's attitude soon embroiled him with Gage, who first gave him "*Specific, Absolute,* and *Supreme*" orders to assist Farmar in getting up the Mississippi, and then, when Wedderburn did not appear to be getting the message, severely reprimanded him.[44] Though Wedderburn sympathized with Johnstone, even he admitted that the Governor had claimed more power than his commission gave him, and that probably no military commander could avoid a quarrel with him over this question.[45]

The guilt or innocence of Johnstone and Farmar, however interesting, is not the most important aspect of the dispute. Johnstone was surely rash, behaving at times like a lunatic, but his basic arguments were not frivolous. West Florida had almost no civilian population. According to the Royal Proclamation of October 5, 1763, it was British policy to encourage settlement in Canada, Nova Scotia, and the Floridas. West Florida had to be able to offer military protection and internal police if it were to attract immigrants in competition with the older colonies, but it also could not hope to compete with them if it had a military government. The situation contained an unavoidable dilemma. The British government wanted to centralize military command and administration in North America, but it also wanted effective and attractive civil government in colonies like West Florida. The dilemma illustrates two institutional flaws that made imperial expansion and rationalization difficult. How could a Commander in Chief in New York City exercise effective command of troops in Pensacola and Mobile when it often took months to communicate with those troops?

[43] To Alexander Wedderburn (his brother and later British Solicitor General), 14 April 1765, Wedderburn MSS., I, CL.
[44] Wedderburn to Gage, 7 May 1765, Gage MSS. Johnstone's favorable opinion of Wedderburn is in a letter to Halifax, 14 September 1765, *Miss. Prov. Arch.*, 288. Wedderburn's reprimand from Gage, 31 July 1765, is in *ibid.*, 392-395.
[45] Wedderburn MSS., CL.

How could one expect civil governors and military officers of even the best judgment and will to work together smoothly in such a situation when effective authority depended less on commissions and explanatory instructions than on precedents?

The commissions of the Commander in Chief and of the royal governors were plainly incompatible with one another, and it was left to the officeholders themselves to work (or fight) out a rough delineation of function and power that would serve as a precedent to the future, taking on with time the character of law. If Johnstone on the one side and most army officers on the other appear to have displayed a picayune scrupulosity over who was to receive military status reports, when military escorts were to be provided, who was to issue the daily sign and countersign, who was to convene a court to inventory the effects of a dead officer, who was to assign quarters, who was to appoint the garrison staff, ad infinitum, ad nauseam, it was not just the human failure that one expects in hot, remote, and primitive places. The real power of either Johnstone or Gage in West Florida could have been reduced to virtually nothing by an accumulation of precedents which could be used to support the position of the other. The British habit of mind which made possible an unwritten constitution and a common law exacted a discouraging price in situations, like West Florida, that required flexibility, initiative, and good temper.

To be sure, West Florida was in a sense unique. Not only was Johnstone in many ways the worst possible man for the job of Governor, but his own description of the troops in the colony during the first two years would be unbelievable were it not amply corroborated by other evidence. In his first dispatch home, he reported "that the two Regiments could not now turn out 250 Men; most of the officers are absent; when they are ordered to their Corps, not one has taken effectual means to come out; those who are here— the Debris of an Havannah Regiment—are really excellent Officers, but fairly worn out and debilitated. Their barracks are in the most miserable Situation. A Disorder has been prevalent at Mobile, something in effect like a Plague. The Officers here were summoned to a general Court Martial at Mobile; all who went have been seized with the Disease; three have died and the rest continue ill."[46] In June 1765, he told Secretary of State Halifax that "An Account of the Spectacles which I have seen would shock men of less Humanity than Your Lordship."[47] In September, he reported that a quarter of the soldiers and a fifth of the inhabitants had died in an epidemic at Pensacola.[48] Wedderburn had written of widespread scurvy that kept even the smallest cuts from healing, often resulting in the amputation of fingers, arms, and legs.[49] Under such conditions, the wonder is that anything at all was accomplished.

West Florida, however, if in some ways uniquely terrible, was also the most visible instance of a common problem. In fact, there was friction between the royal governor and the local troop commander sometime during 1763-1765 in almost every North American province where regular troops were employed. The basic trouble was always the same as that revealed in West Florida, although the outward form varied according to circumstances. Because the governor of Newfoundland was traditionally a nonresident naval officer, Captain Stephen Gualy's refusal to let Governor Thomas Graves, a captain in the navy, shift troops northward from St. John's could be treated as inter-service conflict, to be suppressed at all costs.[50] The Governors of Nova Scotia

[46] To John Pownall, 31 October 1764, *Miss. Prov. Arch.*, 169. I have altered the punctuation slightly for clarity.

[47] 11 June 1765, *ibid.*, 257.

[48] To Halifax, 19 September 1765, *ibid.*, 289.

[49] To Alexander Wedderburn, 14 April 1765, Wedderburn MSS., I, CL.

[50] Egremont to Amherst, 12 March 1763, Amherst-Gage MSS., I; Gualy to Amherst, 23 June 1763, and reply, 15 September 1763, *ibid.*, III. Amherst told him to "avoid everything on your part that can give the least Room to Suspect that a Jealousy should Arise between the Land and Sea Officers: the Good of the Service is at all times to be Studied: and I know Nothing that can Obstruct it so much as Disputes between the two Departments: I would at any time give up Matters of Form, or Punctilio. . . ." The recently learned lessons of amphibious warfare appear to have been still fresh in his mind.

and East Florida, Colonel Montague Wilmot and Lieutenant Colonel James Grant, respectively, had recently
been comrades of Gage and his army so that conflict was
muted in these provinces. But Wilmot did insist upon and
succeeded in obtaining the military command at Halifax
until his own regiment was disbanded and he retired to
half-pay in 1765, and Grant quietly cajoled the local commander into letting him run the regiment at St. Augustine
while Johnstone at Pensacola was noisily fighting for similar power.[51] In South Carolina, Governor Thomas Boone
attempted to give orders to the three companies of Royal
Americans stationed in that province and in Georgia. These
troops had replaced the three independent regular companies which had previously been under provincial control
but which were disbanded in 1763. Boone claimed to be
acting with the unanimous advice of his Council and agree-
able to the orders of the Commander in Chief; when re-
buffed, he did not press the issue.[52] Governor James Wright
of Georgia asked the Secretary of State, concerning the
regular detachments within that province, "in what manner
he should act on an emergency, the commanding officer
being in Carolina?"[53] The Governor of Pennsylvania never
claimed military power, probably because his status at the
head of a proprietary colony was weaker than that of his
colleagues.[54] The location of general headquarters in New
York either prevented or concealed friction in that province for the time being.[55] There were no regulars in either

[51] Halifax to Gage, 14 July 1764, "Private," and reply, 21 September 1764, *Gage Corr.*, II, 15, and I, 35; Gage to Halifax, 10
August 1765, *ibid.*, I, 65. Alexander Fraser to Haldimand, 21 April
1768, BM Add. MSS. 21728.

[52] Capt. James Mark Prevost to Bouquet [January 1764], *Bouquet
Papers*, BM Add. MSS. 21650, 19-22. Boone's letter to Prevost, 2
April 1764, is in Gage MSS.

[53] Capt. Cochrane to Gage, 27 November 1764, Gage MSS.

[54] In a "Warrant for Settling the Rank and Precedence in North
America, 17 Dec. 1760," Amherst-Gage MSS., I, governors (that
is, lieutenant-governors) of proprietary colonies rank eighth, below
colonels in the army, while governors of royal colonies rank second,
behind the commander in chief.

[55] There was similar trouble in the Ceded Islands, in which Gage

the Chesapeake or the New England colonies. In Quebec, however, a violent conflict occurred and its consequences were even more profound and longer-lasting than those of the West Florida dispute.

Trouble in Canada came into the open with the order from Gage to raise 300 Canadians for service against the Indians in early 1764. After the fall of Canada in 1760, Amherst had divided it into three military districts and appointed a military governor for each. Gage was in charge at Montreal, his old friend Lieutenant Colonel Ralph Burton at Three Rivers, and James Murray at Quebec. Murray had been one of Wolfe's three brigadiers in 1759. He had commanded at Quebec during the winter 1759-1760, and had come near losing the city in a rash and badly managed sortie in April.[56] Murray's brother was a Scottish peer, Lord Elibank, and his nephew none other than Governor George Johnstone of West Florida. Like Johnstone, Murray was promised the civil governorship at a time when the Earl of Bute rode high in British councils. Murray received notice of his appointment in the early autumn of 1763, but did not receive his commission until almost one year later.[57] It was in the interim, when Murray was in limbo between the military governorship of the district of Quebec and the civil governorship of all Canada (also styled "Quebec"), that trouble began.

Before the order to enlist the Canadians arrived, Murray had clashed briefly with Lieutenant Colonel Frederick Haldimand, Burton's successor at Three Rivers.[58] While Haldimand was effusive in tendering his congratulations

---

played no part because his command did not extend to the West Indies. Barrington to Lt. Col. Johnstone, 8 May 1766, WO 4/988.

[56] Stacey, *Quebec, 1759*, 163-164.

[57] His commission was dated 28 November 1763, but it did not arrive until the following August.

[58] Earlier, in 1762, there were hints that military governors of Montreal and Three Rivers disliked Murray's tendency to assume that the Quebec military governor was primus inter pares. See Murray to Haldimand, 13 June and 2 July 1762, and Haldimand to Murray, 28 June 1762, BM Add. MSS. 21666.

to Murray on being appointed governor, he was at the same
time politely adamant in refusing to let Murray move troops
from Three Rivers to reinforce Montreal.[59] Then, when
Murray received the order from Gage to recruit 300 Canadians, he officiously informed Haldimand, Burton at Montreal, and the Commander in Chief that the recruits would
have to be volunteers, because to draft men from the militia
would violate the term of the peace treaty granting French
Canadians eighteen months in which to decide to stay in
Canada as British subjects or to emigrate.[60] The upshot
must have been humiliating to Murray, for after promising
the Secretary of State that he would try to keep Burton and
Haldimand from drafting any men, and after a good deal
of wrangling with Haldimand on the subject, it was Murray himself who drafted ten men to fill the Quebec quota.[61]
The 300 Canadians were finally sent off to serve under
Bradstreet, but civil-military harmony in Canada had been
permanently destroyed.

In a letter to Burton, Murray called Gage's handling of
the recruiting affair ill-considered, precipitate, and per-
emptory.[62] To Gage and others during the summer of 1764,
Murray made it clear that he believed his powers as governor would include control of the troops at Montreal and
Three Rivers as well as at Quebec, the capital.[63] By September, he was writing to his brother, Lord Elibank, of
"the Plot of Divesting me of my Military Command, as

[59] Haldimand to Murray, 1 November (incorrectly dated 11 October in the Haldimand calendar, *PAC Report, 1884*, 88) and 15
November 1763, *ibid.*

[60] To Gage, 5 February [March?] 1764, and to Haldimand, 9
March 1764, *ibid.*

[61] Murray to Halifax, 5 March 1764, "Calendar of State Papers,"
PAC Report, 1890, 7-8. See especially Murray to Haldimand, 11
March 1764, in which he clucked insincerely over the reluctance of
Canadians in Three Rivers to enlist, and said that he had a thousand
more volunteers than he needed at Quebec, and same to same, 2
April 1764, in which he admitted that he had had to resort to a
draft, BM Add. MSS. 21666.

[62] 2 April 1764, *PAC Report, 1912*, 93.

[63] To Burton, 18 April 1764, and to Gage, 20 August 1764, *ibid.*,
95-96.

being now pretty evident."[64] When Burton, who by this time was clearly supporting Gage in the quarrel, received an appointment as Brigadier General to command all troops in the "Northern District," the plot appeared to Murray to have borne fruit.

Open conflict thereafter between Murray and Burton put a match to the inflammable politics of Canada.[65] Murray's paternalistic approach to his task as governor had made him popular with the French, but had been anathema to the few hundred British subjects in the province. With almost all of the population disfranchised by its Catholicism, these few Scots and Englishmen expected to control the government. Most of them were traders who had moved into Canada in the train of the army, and the military garrison was unable to forget how recently this aspiring aristocracy had been camp-followers. On the other hand, if the French were content under Murray, they also had few grievances against the army which had ruled with a comparatively light rein for the three years past. Additional complications were created by the obvious weakness of Murray's position in England after the fall of Bute, by the nearly autonomous operation of Sir William Johnson's deputy Indian agent at Montreal, and by the fact that a few of the new British subjects were *not* camp-followers but men with powerful mercantile and political connections in London. When Murray instituted civil government in August 1764, however, he could appoint none but British subjects to the magistracy, and it was this that precipitated violence.

The new civil magistrates, who had intensely disliked the former system of military courts, used their power to pay off scores against the army. The troops at Montreal had no barracks, and had quartered themselves in private houses. But with the advent of civil government the British merchant-magistracy began to make life as miserable as

[64] 16 September 1764, *ibid.*, 97.
[65] A. L. Burt, *The Old Province of Quebec* (Minneapolis, 1933), 74-127, is an excellent account, and, except where indicated otherwise, is the main source of information on Canadian affairs.

they could for the army, and the evident split between the Governor and the military officers made it easier for them to do so. Matters came to a head with the imprisonment of Captain Benjamin Payne of the 28th Regiment for occupying quarters illegally. Thomas Walker, the justice who had made the arrest, soon paid for his action when masked men, undoubtedly soldiers of the 28th, beat him and removed a piece of his left ear. The army believed that Murray, by his appointments, had incited the magistracy to persecute it, and the magistrates, when the culprits in the attack on Walker were not brought to justice, accused Murray of screening the army. Murray and Burton resolved their personal differences long enough to agree to transfer the unruly 28th to Quebec, but that hardly improved the situation. Murray continued to assert his right to military command, not only in the garrison of Quebec but throughout the province; Burton resisted this assertion by all available means. Murray tried to split the army by cultivating a faction of his own among the officers and regiments; Burton worked actively to undermine the Governor's control of the civilian population. Caught between Murray and Burton, several officers were brought to court-martial for disobedience. The issue in Canada was never clear cut, and civil-military friction there cannot be explained solely in terms of ambiguous organization. Murray, like his nephew Johnstone, was a difficult person, and he seems to have enjoyed scoring points against his old comrades and rivals, Burton and Gage, whenever an opportunity to do so presented itself. But, whatever the root causes, friction between the Governor and the military command had by 1765 produced a full-blown crisis in Canadian civil-military relations.[66]

Thomas Pownall, in the second edition of his book, sharpened his attack on the military unification of the colonies. The office of Commander in Chief was worse than impolitic, it was illegal; moreover, dealing with the colonies

[66] Murray to Haldimand, 21 April 1766, BM Add. MSS. 21666; Major Brown (commander of the 28th) to Gage, and Carleton to Gage, 23 March 1767, Gage MSS.

as a single unit was bound to have important, perhaps dangerous, political implications.[67] Pownall wrote just before the Stamp Act troubles, and his fears for the future seem exaggerated and misplaced in the light of what was about to occur. Serious conflict between governors and military officers was concentrated in West Florida and Canada, where it could be explained largely in terms of personalities and the vagaries of British politics. Elsewhere, there were only flickers of trouble. But trouble, however localized, had its effect. Daniel Dulany, author of the most influential pamphlet written against the Stamp Act, did not make the army a major issue, but—unlike James Otis the year before —he did not feel called upon to praise it. The "affair of Walker's ear," as it was generally known, had soured Dulany on British regulars. He could not resist asking why Americans should support soldiers who "are to be employed in the national Service of Cropping the Ears, and Slitting the Nostrils of the Civil Magistrates, as Marks of Distinction. . . ."[68] Pownall's argument, however, transcended incidents like the loss of Walker's ear. He was right when he stated that military centralization reduced the prestige and power of all royal governors. As matters stood in 1765, the extent of this reduction and its meaning for the future would depend on particular circumstances. It was the proper task of the British government to consider the probable effects of a centralized military organization on a decentralized political organization, and to decide whether the consequences were acceptable.

The Problem of the Mutiny Act

In early 1765, it appeared that another problem of civil-military relations had reached critical proportions during the Indian campaign of the previous year. "The Difficultys in Carrying on the Service in North America, increase very fast," Gage reported to the Secretary of State in January. "It is declared generaly, that the Mutiny Act, does not

[67] *Administration of the Colonies* (1765 edn.), 54-64.
[68] *Considerations on the Propriety of Imposing Taxes in the Colonies* (London, 1766), 59.

extend to America, but in such Clauses only where it is particularly Specified. . . . Soldiers are seduced from the King's Service, Deserters protected and Secreted, . . . Quarters and Carriages refused, without incurring any Penalty. . . . People in general begin to be Sensible, that they are not obliged to do, what they submitted to, in Times of Danger."[69] Gage went on to recommend a number of amendments to the Mutiny Act, the comprehensive military law passed annually by Parliament. The direct result of Gage's report and recommendations was, of course, the famous Quartering Act of 1765. This law became a major source of conflict and, as amended in 1774, was one of the Intolerable Acts that led to war. But before considering these effects, one might well examine the causes.

What were the specific instances that General Gage had in mind when he said that Americans were beginning to claim exemption from the Mutiny Act? The first Act for Punishing Officers or Soldiers Who Shall Mutiny or Desert Their Majesties' Service, passed in 1689, was brief; but successive amendments had expanded it by the mid-eighteenth century to a comprehensive statute covering the discipline, recruitment, housing, and movement of the army. Whether or not the Act applied to the American colonies was a question constantly agitated and never wholly resolved during the Seven Years War. Certainly in the back of Gage's mind was the recollection of this legal struggle of the decade just passed. It was not, however, a struggle over the legality of courts-martial, for Parliament earlier had extended the disciplinary portions of the Act to the colonies. In 1756, the recruiting provisions were likewise extended, as has been mentioned, with the intent to protect both recruiting parties and colonists from abuses that had previously plagued the system.[70] The real fight during the war had come over the portions of the Mutiny Act which pertained to quarters and the requisition of civilian transport for troop movements.

[69] To Halifax, 23 January 1765, *Gage Corr.*, II, 49.
[70] Pargellis, *Loudoun*, 189.

If one reads the Petition of Right of 1628, the Bill of Rights of 1689, and the Mutiny Act itself, quartering soldiers in private houses without the owners' consent violated an undoubted right of Englishmen. Unfortunately, "public houses" in America were far too few and small to accommodate the influx of British regulars which began in 1755, and the necessities of war forced Americans to follow the practice not of England, but of Ireland and Scotland, where soldiers were billeted in private houses when necessary. Understandably, Americans had disliked quartering soldiers. In part, this dislike was a political habit acquired during the previous century of English history. But even without the special English sensitivity to all matters involving soldiers, there was a good deal of personal hardship when thousands of men had to be sheltered in a sparsely settled country.

The people of New Jersey, sandwiched between two major ports, suffered as much as any. A widow in Perth Amboy, who had a house and garden and kept a tenant to eke out her income, was ruined when her house suddenly became a hospital for soldiers down with smallpox. The tenant fled, while the soldiers ravaged the garden and used fences, doors, floors, and fruit trees for firewood.[71] A petition from the residents of Princeton, on the march route between Philadelphia and New York, tells a similar if less dramatic story: "Although many of your Petitioners are poor, have small houses and numerous families, with not more than one room, they have yet been obliged to entertain sometimes ten, twelve, or fifteen Soldiers for a night. . . . During the two winters last past, they have been obliged to quarter in their houses, some two, some three, others four of his majesty's troops, . . ."[72] There were at least 39 similar petitions from New Jersey towns.[73] Soon afterward, the New Jersey Assembly voted funds to con-

[71] Historical Records Survey, *Calendar of the New Jersey State Library Manuscript Collection* (Newark, 1939), 7.

[72] Quoted in John F. Hageman, *History of Princeton* (2nd edn., Philadelphia, 1879), I, 63-64.

[73] Edwin R. Walker, *et al., A History of Trenton* (Princeton, 1929), I, 299-300.

struct five barracks between Elizabeth and Burlington.[74] At about the same time, South Carolina, Pennsylvania, and New York also built barracks. But before the several provincial governments in effect took the burden of billeting off the private citizen and into their own hands, serious trouble had occurred at Albany.[75]

Albany in the middle of the eighteenth century was a rough town. It was the entrepôt of the western fur trade, channeled down the Mohawk Valley. It had also been the center of smuggling to French Canada. Split by racial and religious conflict between Dutch and English, between Dutch and Irish, between Dutch and Germans, Albany was the assembly area for military operations in the northern theater. Every spring, the few hundred soldiers normally in and around the town increased to thousands, and British officers scoured the countryside for wagons, horses, oxen, "artificers," and teamsters. As often happens in such situations, bitter resentment and huge profits went hand in hand.[76] Before barracks could be built (which only eased but did not solve the problem) Lord Loudoun had actually used force to quarter some of his men in 1757, and had cited the *British* Mutiny Act as his authority.[77] When similar action threatened New York City somewhat later in the year, the provincial Assembly hastily, if reluctantly, made a virtue of necessity and passed a billeting act permitting the use of private houses when absolutely necessary.[78]

The problem of transport was at least as critical in the Albany area as was that of billeting, and the continual im-

[74] Fisher, *New Jersey*, 346-347. On trouble over quartering in Bordentown, see *NYHSC for 1881* (N.Y., 1882), 122.

[75] For a complete discussion of the quartering problem in these years, see Pargellis, *Loudoun*, 187-210.

[76] Anne Grant, *Memoirs of an American Lady*, ed. James G. Wilson (N.Y., 1903), I, 282, and II, 86. Mrs. Grant was recalling her girlhood in Albany. For a contemporary letter which conveys the raw, frontier-town character of Albany, see William Corry to Sir William Johnson, 2 May 1761, *Johnson Papers*, III, 385.

[77] Pargellis, *Loudoun*, 195-196.

[78] Sir Charles Hardy to Lords of Trade, 2 [December] 1756, *NYCD*, VII, 204.

pressment of horses and wagons for the movement of units and individual officers through this communications bottleneck gave rise to constant friction and harassment. In 1760, a British captain was thrown in jail for letting the King's cattle stray into a wheatfield.[79] In 1761, Amherst forced the acting Governor of New York to appoint Harmanus Schuyler sheriff of Albany in order to get more effective enforcement of the impressment law.[80] Nevertheless, in 1762 the Albany district quartermaster complained that he was being refused horses and wagons by the country people on the ground that the provincial quartering and impressment act had expired, while the Mayor of Albany accused the quartermaster of flagrantly illegal action in using two or three private soldiers as a press gang, without the supervision of a civil magistrate or even a military officer.[81] Lieutenant Governor Cadwallader Colden advised Amherst not to let this dispute get before the Assembly.[82]

Amherst did not take Colden's advice, and urged the new Governor of New York, Major General Robert Monckton, to obtain quartering and impressment acts from the Assembly. The House refused to permit impressment on the innocuous ground that "his Majesty hath a great Number of Horses, Oxen, and Carriages for carrying on his Service in this Colony."[83] It did, however, pass a new act for quartering in private houses. The preamble merits full quotation as an expression of the New York, if not the American, stand on the matter: "Whereas it is the undoubted Right of all his Majesty's Subjects in this Colony to be free from the Burthen of, having Soldiers Quartered upon them against their wills, Yet the General Assembly

[79] Cadwallader Colden to Amherst and to Sybrant Van Schaick (Mayor of Albany), 11 August 1760, *Colden Letter Book*, I, 6-8.
[80] Colden to Johnson, 2 June 1761, *Johnson Papers*, X, 276. See also *ibid.*, III, 404, 408.
[81] Amherst to Colden, 9 and 10 May 1762, with inclosures, *Colden Papers, 1761-1764*, 163-165, 168-169.
[82] Colden to Amherst, 9 May 1762, *Colden Letter Book*, I, 202-203.
[83] *NY Assembly Journal, 1762-1763* (Jenkins microfilms, A.lb, reel 3), 85, 98, 100.

of this Colony considering that there may be Occasion during the Continuance of this Act to Quarter Soldiers in Places where there are no Barracks, or where the Barracks cannot contain a sufficient Number, particularly such Soldiers as are lately recovered from Distempers contracted during their Service in the West Indies and remain still weak and Feeble, and being willing to promote his Majesty's Service as far lies in their Power in this and every thing they conceive conducive thereto, . . ."[84] In other words, New Yorkers did not want to be unreasonable, but neither did they intend to give up what they took to be a sound constitutional position. The act expired January 1, 1764; before that month was out, the Schenectady grand jury had indicted John Glen and other justices for quartering regulars on Tobias Ten Eyck.[85] During the war, the British government and army command had tacitly conceded the right of colonial assemblies to legislate on quartering and impressment; obviously the leaders of Albany County did not intend to give up that right with the advent of peace.

But aside from this incident, there seems to have been little trouble over quartering in the campaign of 1764, perhaps because the few hundred regulars could be sheltered without further resort to private houses. There continued to be, however, a good deal of other kinds of civil-military friction at Albany. In March, a riot occurred between soldiers and civilians.[86] Later, as the campaign got under way, the Albany quartermaster and others condemned the county's failure to support military operations.[87] Then, in October, a roistering group of inhabitants beat a British sentry almost to death.[88] On the surface these events would seem

[84] *The Colonial Laws of New York* (Albany, 1894), IV, 637-639.

[85] *Calendar of the Sir William Johnson Manuscripts*, comp. R. E. Day (Albany, 1909), 201; *New York Historical Manuscripts*, II, 746.

[86] Henry Van Schaick and Dirk Van Der Heyden to Sir William Johnson, 14 and 15 March 1764, *Johnson Calendar*, 211.

[87] Daniel Claus to Johnson, 10 April 1764, and James Phyn to Johnson, 23 April 1764, *ibid.*, 216, 218.

[88] Ensign Thomas Bell to Gage, 8 October 1764, Gage MSS.

to support Gage's report to London that something had to
be done to extend the Mutiny Act to America, and it may
be that the old, unresolved question of the legality of impressment underlay most of the trouble. But one misses
the mark if, in explaining the trouble at Albany, one ignores
the personality of the Albany quartermaster, Lieutenant
Colonel John Bradstreet.

Bradstreet was among those remarkable people who
firmly grasped the nettle of opportunity during the Seven
Years War.[89] Any list of these men would include such
diverse characters as Robert Rogers, Benjamin Franklin,
Robert Clive, and William Pitt. Bradstreet was a Nova
Scotian who had begun his career with a commission in
the regular regiment stationed at Halifax, and had acquired moderately good connections in the world of English politics. He had shot to the fore during the war by
his ability to get "bateaux" built quickly and in huge numbers,
and by his knack for leading the irregulars, the "bateau-
men," who navigated these delicate, flat-bottomed craft in
the waters of northern New York. Not only had he become
a master of the art of military transportation and supply
in the American wilderness, but he had shown a talent for
daring tactical operations when he destroyed Fort Frontenac with a small force in 1758. After that, even the Duke
of Newcastle, not noted for his knowledge of American affairs, had called Bradstreet "one of our alert fellows."[90]

The same drives, however, that made Bradstreet work
with demonic energy to move supplies, or made him beg
commanders to approve this or that risky scheme, also
made him a hotly ambitious person who could not bear to
be opposed or thwarted. He quarrelled incessantly with
fellow staff officers, so that Amherst kept him away from
headquarters in 1759 because of his "untractable Disposition."[91] As a task force commander in 1764, Bradstreet

[89] The only biography of Bradstreet is by Stanley M. Pargellis,
DAB, ii, 578-579. There is additional information in Pargellis, *Loudoun*, and Gipson, *British Empire*, vi, vii, and ix, *passim*.
[90] Quoted in Whitworth, *Ligonier*, 275n.
[91] Huck to Loudoun, 19 May 1760, LO 6246.

disobeyed orders and tried to negotiate a peace with the Indians on his own.[92] If he had brought off this coup, his stock would have stood high on both sides of the Atlantic. But the Indians duped him, and thereby insured that Bradstreet's career would never regain the peak it had reached in 1758 at Frontenac; instead, after 1764 the way led gently down.

Bradstreet deserves no pity, however, because by the end of the war he had created an impressive cushion for himself at Albany. He had lived there almost a decade, had married a Rensselaer, had controlled the expenditure of tens of thousands of pounds Sterling in the area, and had become virtually a member of the powerful Schuyler family by making young Philip, the future general of the Revolution, his principal lieutenant. It was Bradstreet who, behind the scene, had picked another Schuyler for sheriff of Albany in 1761, overriding the opposition of the city Council and Sir William Johnson.[93] And in the course of becoming a magnate of upper New York, Bradstreet had learned neither tact nor caution; civil-military friction at Albany was in large part Bradstreet's own handiwork.

He had a host of enemies and, until his death in 1774, never ceased fighting them. During this long campaign, the distinction between his private interest and that of the government was submerged. His official letters describe these battles as attacks by town against Crown, but it is difficult to read the correspondence without sensing something more behind, for example, his insistence that certain pasture lands near Albany be enclosed, although they were no longer needed for military purposes and the Crown title to them was admittedly flimsy.[94] His carelessness in keep-

[92] Peckham, *Pontiac*, 255-264; Gipson, *British Empire*, ix, 117-123.

[93] Henry Van Schaick to Johnson, 17 June, and Johnson to Colden, 18 June 1761, *Johnson Papers*, iii, 404, 408.

[94] See the legal opinion of William Smith on this matter, 23 February 1762, and Amherst to Bradstreet, 30 May 1763, "Private," WO 34/56 (Amherst MSS.). This bundle is full of Bradstreet's troubles. Two years later, Bradstreet boasted that he would act with "the greatest violence" against both the Dutch Church and the

ing and paying accounts was responsible for much of the local resistance to the requisition of horses, oxen, wagons, and labor.[95] He wrote of the "nest of Harpies" forever making trouble at Albany, but Amherst, who valued his services, felt constrained to warn Bradstreet not to start trouble himself.[96]

After Gage replaced Amherst, Bradstreet found the atmosphere at headquarters more hostile. The new Commander in Chief had a score with his Albany quartermaster that went back to 1759, when Gage had been accused of timidity by Amherst, but had excused himself by blaming Bradstreet for his failure to provide adequate logistical support.[97] When Bradstreet disobeyed Gage's instructions in 1764, and then publicly defended his conduct, Gage wrote privately to Sir William Johnson: "Colonel Bradstreet's usual strain of talking is very high. . . . Had the Interest of the Publick, and a real sincere desire to use the most zealous Efforts for Her Service, outweighed Jealousy, envy, and above all an immoderate vanity and self-opinion, and the pleasure to puff and bluster away a sort of Reputation amongst the Vulgar; these matters could never have happened."[98] Gage knew his man, and surely must have known that Albany did not provide the clear-cut case of American resistance to British law and the British army that it appeared to.

The significance of chronic trouble at Albany is further exposed by comparing it with the similar case of Colonel Bouquet and his operations in Pennsylvania, where there was almost no trouble over either quartering or impressment. What can be seen clearly in Bouquet's experience is

Albany city charter; to John Tabor Kempe (Attorney General of New York), 20 May 1765, Sedgwick MSS., II, box no. 2, Massachusetts Historical Society.

[95] Bradstreet's mishandling of accounts in 1764 was especially flagrant. See Alden, *Gage*, 72-73.

[96] Amherst to Bradstreet, 14 March and 12 September 1762, WO 34/56.

[97] Lt. Col. Robertson to Loudoun, 21 October 1759, LO 6146.

[98] 22 November 1764, *Johnson Papers*, IV, 605.

that, although Pennsylvania had legalized the impressment of transport, a fair price had to be paid for it if wagoners and packhorse men were to appear in sufficient numbers.[99] There was little of the French corvée about the assembling of Bouquet's supply train; rather, it was primarily a business transaction and Bouquet treated it that way. He authorized his agents each to contract for a certain number of wagons or horses, disinterested parties set rates and appraised values, and agreements were signed.[100] To be sure, there were claims and complaints after the campaign as there had been after every previous campaign, but Bouquet dealt with them promptly and fairly, so that the primary incentive to be an army teamster was not fear of punishment but desire for profit.[101] A similar situation obtained at Albany, and if Bradstreet had had Bouquet's tact and good judgment (and perhaps his honesty), the long wrangle over impressment could largely have been avoided.

Apparently there was no need in Pennsylvania, with its chain of small forts stretching westward to Pittsburgh, to quarter troops in private houses. The province supplied the Philadelphia barracks as it had in the past.[102] The settlement at Bedford, simply upon request of the local commander, furnished its garrison with firewood during the cold winter of 1764-1765, and was pleased by Bouquet's public thanks.[103] The major problem in Pennsylvania was desertion.

[99] Press warrant from Governor James Hamilton [28 June 1763], and Slough and Simon to Bouquet, 30 June 1763 (2 letters), *Bouquet Papers* BM Add. MSS. 21649, II, 179, 184-185.

[100] See especially "Memorandum" [29 June 1763], *Bouquet Papers* BM Add. MSS. 21653, 181-182, and Matthias Slough to Bouquet, 19 June 1764, *ibid.*, BM Add. MSS. 21650, I, 187.

[101] Ironically, Bouquet was disgusted at the way in which frontiersmen were volunteering as packhorse drivers and wagoners instead of as soldiers. To John Harris, 19 July 1764, *ibid.*, II, 32-33. For the profit motive, see, for example, Jacob Kern to Bouquet [13 May 1764], *ibid.*, I, 134.

[102] Capt. William Grant to Bouquet [24 July 1764], *ibid.*, II, 40-41.

[103] Lt. Nathaniel McCulloch to Bouquet, 4 February 1765, and reply, 28 March 1765, *ibid.*, 122, 178.

As mentioned previously, most of the men of the 60th or Royal American Regiment had enlisted for limited service, many of them claimed their discharges at the end of the war, and the departure of some and the mutinous attitude of the others had weakened Amherst's ability to respond to the Indian attack in 1763. Most of Bouquet's regulars were Royal Americans, and Amherst would not let him grant more than a few discharges until the Indians were put down, especially since the only other regulars in Pennsylvania were Highlanders still weak from service in Cuba.[104] In fact, Bouquet knew that the Royal American battalion itself was near the limit of its endurance. Despite the danger of increased desertion, he wanted the battalion to winter in the settled areas, away from the frontier zone; he reminded Gage that these men had been in the woods six years, "and their spirits so much cast down, I would hope a little rest would recruit them."[105] But the unit was beyond saving by such limited measures.

Many Royal Americans were Germans, recruited either in Pennsylvania or Europe, and so they were among countrymen, friends, and relations between Carlisle and Fort Pitt. To desert was simply to go home for some of them, and that is what they did during the winter of 1763-1764. The personnel leak of the previous summer became a flood, while discipline and morale collapsed among those who remained. A wagon-escort commander reported nothing "but the Greatest Mutiny and Disobedience of Orders. Some of the R. Americans threatened to Shute their officers."[106] From Fort Pitt came similar news: "I have served over 22 years," wrote Captain Simeon Ecuyer, "but I have never seen such a tribe of rebels, bandits and hamstringers. . . . I have been obliged, after all imaginable patience, to have two of them horsewhipped on the spot and without court-martial. One wanted to kill the sergeant and the other

[104] Amherst to Bouquet, 7 August, and Bouquet to Amherst, 1 December 1763, BM Add. MSS. 21634.

[105] Bouquet to Gage, 24 October 1763, BM Add. MSS. 21637.

[106] Capt. John Stewart to Bouquet, 11 November 1763, *ibid.*, BM Add. MSS. 21649, II, 138.

wanted to kill me. I was on the point of blowing his brains out. . . . What a disagreeable thing!"[107] When three more companies of the 60th arrived during the winter from Niagara, where they had been kept since the capture of that fort in 1759, over one-third of the men had deserted by May; by July, these three companies had all but vanished.[108]

During the spring, Bouquet began to hear that three other companies of the 60th, sent to South Carolina to relieve the disbanded independent companies, were suffering from the same problem. As was usual when units were disbanded, most of the soldiers of the South Carolina independent companies—"old, drunken, dirty, insolent soldiers . . . worse in drilling than recruits"—were drafted into the 60th.[109] Within a month, 15 had deserted. The commander at Charleston reported: "Few boats leave which do not take away some of our men. Some time ago, I wished to seize one of them who was working four or five miles from here; he escaped into a house, and in a few minutes he had more than a hundred men to defend him."[110] Each subsequent letter from South Carolina mentioned further desertion, both of drafted "independents" and of veteran Royal Americans who demanded to be discharged.[111] Bouquet was a sensible officer, not given to tantrums or panic, who had adapted himself unusually well to American conditions, but in May 1764 he was convinced that "The Encouragement given every where in this Country to deserters, Skreened almost by every Person, must in Time ruin the Army."[112] Here certainly was justification for Gage's demand that the clause of the Mu-

[107] Capt. Ecuyer to Bouquet, 13 November 1763, *ibid.*, 144-147.
[108] Bouquet to Gage, 20 May 1764, BM Add. MSS. 21637; Capt. Schlosser to Bouquet, 23 July 1764, *Bouquet Papers*, BM Add. MSS. 21650, II, 39.
[109] Capt. James Mark Prevost to Bouquet, [January 1764], *ibid.*, I, 19-22.
[110] Prevost to Bouquet, 20 March 1764, *ibid.*, 63-64.
[111] Capt. Cochrane to Bouquet, 25 May and 22 July 1763, *ibid.*, 152-153, and II, 36-37.
[112] Bouquet to Gage, 20 May 1764, BM Add. MSS. 21637.

tiny Act against harboring deserters be extended to America. But was it?

It has been noted that the 60th was an unusual regiment, composed mainly of Americans who had enlisted for no more than the duration of the war. No regiment in America, except perhaps the Black Watch and the 44th, had seen service so long and arduous. The conditions of the years 1763-1764 were also unusual: men who had, or dared claim, short enlistments wanted to be released, but the Indian rebellion kept them in, and they were further embittered by the deduction from their pay for rations. To make the problem of this regiment in these years typical of the whole army in America was to generalize on the basis of a localized, short-term phenomenon. Moreover, desertion rates from eighteenth-century armies were high everywhere.[113] Bouquet, as the commander on the spot who had been charged with crushing the Delaware and Shawnee, may be excused for giving way to despair as his troops disappeared. But if Gage seriously believed at this time that a stringent law against harboring deserters could materially decrease desertion, he had learned little about colonial society from his ten years of service in North America. Residents of Lancaster, Pennsylvania, could simultaneously express their thanks to Bouquet for defeating the Indians, and express their affection for his redcoats in somewhat different form: "It begins now to be true, what I always feared," wrote a company commander stationed at Lancaster, "that we would have Desertion when we Should march from here, everybody debauches and conceels our Men, it is impossible to hinder it, if the

[113] For example, the British regiments stationed in Ireland, somewhat less than 12,000 men, had about 500 deserters in one peacetime year. Lord Lieutenant Townshend to Secretary of State, 16 October 1768, *CHOP*, II, #1012. The average annual loss of the French army (about 180,000 men) through desertion *and sickness* was estimated at 20,000. Albert Duruy, *L'armée royale en 1789* (Paris, 1888), 34. From 1713 to 1740, when the Prussian army was increasing from 38,000 to 80,000, there were 30,216 desertions. Penfield Roberts, *The Quest for Security, 1715-1740* (N.Y., 1947), 64; Walter Dorn, *Competition for Empire, 1740-1763* (N.Y., 1940), 98n.

Men are not willing themselves to Stay, they are easily persuaded, in telling them, that at any Rate they could winn more then they have as Soldiers, . . ."[114]

Gage, however, could cite some other cases in support of his general contention that portions of the Mutiny Act needed extension to the colonies. In South Carolina, Governor Boone and the Assembly had refused to furnish the customary transportation of provisions to the frontier posts after 1764. Their argument was that when the governor had controlled the independent companies in South Carolina, then the province had helped support them, but now that someone else had the command, the duty to support the companies should likewise shift. The argument might appear frivolous, but the original arrangement had been peculiar to South Carolina, and the loss of provincial control of the regular independent companies meant not only some decline in power and prestige but also an important loss of income for the royal governor.[115] The governor of New York, who had suffered in a similar way by the disbandment of the four New York independent companies, was said to have lost an annual sum "of more value than all . . . [his] other perquisites and emoluments put together."[116] In this respect, at least, the problem raised by the Mutiny Act in 1764 harks back to the problem raised by military centralization.

The event which probably was the trigger to Gage's letter home was the refusal of New York City to provide firewood for the barracks when the remnants of the 80th and 55th Regiments moved into them in late November; the Mayor also pointed out in passing that there was no law for quartering in public houses as in England.[117] It is difficult to be sure of what lay behind this action: the New

[114] Capt. Schlosser to Bouquet, 18 April 1765, *Bouquet Papers*, BM Add. MSS. 21651, 193.

[115] Capt. Prevost to Governor Boone, 3 April 1764, and reply, 4 April 1764, Gage MSS. Capt. Cochrane to Bouquet, 22 July 1764, *Bouquet Papers*, BM Add. MSS. 21650, II, 36-37.

[116] Colden to Pitt, 23 November 1761, *Colden Letter Book*, I, 134.

[117] Gage to Colden, 27 November 1764, *Colden Papers, 1761-1764*, 389-390.

York Assembly, a little more than a month before, had formally protested against the idea of taxing the colonies; Lieutenant Governor Colden was deep in a dispute with most of the province over the right of appeal from the Supreme Court to the Governor and Council; Mayor John Cruger had never forgotten how Lord Loudoun had cursed him and forced the City to quarter troops during the war; and, in January 1764, a party of regular soldiers had forced the City jail, wounded the jailer, and freed the popular Major Robert Rogers, imprisoned for debt.[118] The most likely cause, however, would appear to be a wave of belt-tightening that swept the province at just this time. New York, like the other colonies, was in an economic recession, and a group of the principal inhabitants of the City (including half-pay British officers and future Tories) announced the organization of the "Society for Promotion of Arts, Agriculture and Oeconomy," whose aim was to make New York more self-sufficient. It was a forerunner of both the Chamber of Commerce and the nonimportation agreements, and Mayor Cruger, wealthy merchant and member of the Society's Committee of Arts, doubtless was in no mood to spend City money he did not have.[119] One or all of these events, in some combination, must have provoked Cruger to act as he did. Perhaps Gage, known around New York City by this time as "mild and well temper'd" with "a diffidence of himself . . . his greatest weakness," appeared to be an easier mark than any of his predecessors.[120] It should be noted, however, that Cruger

[118] Edmund S. and Helen M. Morgan, *The Stamp Act Crisis* (Chapel Hill, 1953), 36-37; Milton M. Klein, "Prelude to Revolution in New York," 3 *WMQ*, XVII (1960), 439-462; Martha J. Lamb, *History of the City of New York* (N.Y., 1887-1880), I, 662-663; William Dunlap, *History of . . . New York* (N.Y., 1839-1840), II, cxci.

[119] *New York Gazette*, December 10 and 24, 1764. The announcement refers to "the vast Luxury introduced during the late war." See also Morgan, *Stamp Act*, 32, which describes the Society as primarily a protest against the Sugar Act of 1764.

[120] John Watts to Moses Franks, 24 February 1764 and 6 November 1763 (quoted in that order), *Watts Letter Book*, 335, 306.

was simply refusing to furnish fuel to the barracks on the ground that funds were unavailable; no soldier was without shelter, nor was the Crown denied the hope of future reimbursement if one of its officers had to buy a few cords of wood.

The case for the Quartering Act, so impressive at first glance, does not stand up very well under close scrutiny. Each instance has peculiarities that weaken its justificatory force. Neither Bradstreet at Albany, desertion from the 6oth Regiment, parsimony in New York City, nor resentment in South Carolina provided a sound basis for generalization. Gage himself put the harboring of deserters at the head of his list of problems, but when his principal staff officer, Lieutenant Colonel James Robertson, drew up the memorandum on billeting and impressment, Robertson unintentionally admitted that headquarters was *anticipating* rather than *experiencing* difficulty.[121] His proposals, which Gage sent to Whitehall, reveal a philosophy of colonial administration that one may recognize as either the "military mind" or "enlightened despotism" in action.

So far, wrote Robertson in his memorandum, there have been only a few, scattered incidents; force of habit on the part of American civilians, tactful conduct on the part of British officers, and the small numbers of troops marched through the settled area of the colonies have all served to prevent conflict. But these few incidents are straws in the wind, he continued, because reputable lawyers are sure that the army does not have a legal leg to stand on if it forces the colonists to furnish quarters and transportation, or even to give up deserters. Some factious Americans will surely refuse to do these things as a matter of principle; when this begins to occur "the people" will applaud and follow the example of these few, and all the restraints imposed by habit and authority will collapse. If Parliament enacted "a law confirming a practise that has never been abused," Robertson concluded, it "would be received without a murmur," but once let the public mind

[121] Inclosure in Gage to Ellis, 22 January 1765, *Gage Corr.*, II, 264.

become inflamed on this issue, and the most moderate law will be considered a great grievance. Robertson assumed that "a general and effectual Law" was a necessity, and that such a law could never be obtained from the various colonial governments.

To understand the genesis of the Quartering Act of 1765 it is necessary to understand Gage and Robertson themselves. Gage had been in his new job little more than a year. He had moved up from a field command, still lacked some of the self-assurance that was expected of a Commander in Chief, and had neither the experience nor the temperament to resist informed advice. Robertson, the apparently indispensable staff officer to be found in almost any headquarters, the man who seems to be running the organization by sheer energy and factual knowledge of every problem, was just the person to give advice. No document records what would only have been a conversation, but the men and the circumstances indicate that Robertson had a major part in getting Gage to act.

If Robertson pushed Gage on this matter, and it is difficult to believe otherwise, then it is not difficult to discern the direction in which he was pushing. Robertson was a Scot. Contemporary Anglo-American opinion identified Scots with most of the vices, especially harshness of spirit and lack of sympathy for English ideas of liberty. It was a grossly distorted view, but it was not wholly false. Its very prevalence did lead some, like James Boswell, to apologize for their origins, but seems to have driven other, tougher men, like Cadwallader Colden of New York, to act as if it were true. James Robertson was an unmistakable Scot, a man of low birth who had climbed high with the help of fellow Scots, and he could not hide.[122] But perhaps it was only coincidental that he had, long before 1764, reached some harsh conclusions about America and Americans, conclusions that undoubtedly helped shape the Quartering Act of 1765.

In a letter of early 1759 to his former chief and Scottish patron, the Earl of Loudoun, Robertson expressed his

[122] See the brief, unflattering sketch in *DNB*, xlviii, 409.

feelings with a candor missing in his official papers. General Amherst, he wrote, "is an amiable man, but vainly fancys he can govern these provinces by yielding and the Arts of complyance. Alderman Scot lately sent me notice that he woud prosecute for pressing a Slay for the publick Service, and the General in place of punishing the fellow bowed and flatter'd and adored him. . . . In a country where no man will hire a house boat or any thing else to the crown without double the worth, and where the magistrates threaten and prosecute the Quarter Master General for pressing for the publick service with the Governors warrant, fear will prove a more effective motive to action than flattery."[123]

It is useless to argue that Gage and Robertson were wrong, for the argument would have to rest on might-have-beens, but one may reasonably question their good judgment as of early 1765. Their picture of the future was hazy. If only small numbers of troops had marched through the settled areas in the past, why should there be more when the army was reduced to a fraction of its wartime strength? Under peacetime conditions, why could not the barracks in Boston (at Castle William), Albany, New York City, New Jersey, Philadelphia, and Charleston house the few regiments stationed on the seaboard, and troop movements be scheduled for seasons when units could encamp overnight? As a rule, why could horses and wagons not be procured on a contract basis, as Bouquet had procured them in 1764? Because the troops would not be evenly distributed among the colonies (in early 1765, there was no prospect that regulars would be stationed in the Chesapeake or New England colonies), why should each colony supply its own barracks, especially if America was to be taxed? Would a law against harboring deserters yield results commensurate with the animosity it would surely arouse, whether enforced or not? If support from colonial governments was occasionally needed, why not *negotiate* for that support, using the real if intangible power of the office of Commander in Chief,

[123] 3 February 1759, LO 6039.

the mutual interest of civilian and military (troops put money into the economy, as Albany well knew), and the reservoir of British tact and American good will built up in the later years of the war? For example, both Pennsylvania and New Jersey, as a matter of course, supported the march of troops from Lancaster to New York City three months *after* Gage had submitted his proposal.[124] Moreover, why was "a general and effectual Law" needed, because only four of the older colonies—New York, New Jersey, Pennsylvania, and South Carolina—were of major importance in the deployment and movement of the army?

To have reasoned in this way would have required no knowledge of what came later, although, in fact, what came later reveals Americans willing to compromise about as often as they were determined to resist. Gage's mind, with Robertson's help, was tending in another direction, however; he was confusing what he would like to have with what he had to have, what would be irritating with what would be crippling. An examination of the specific cases— Albany, the Pennsylvania backcountry, South Carolina, and New York City—on which Gage erected a general argument suggests that his own conception of the situation more than any compelling necessity led him to his conclusions. On a small scale, he appears to have been trying to tighten and clarify the lines of authority in much the same way that the Grenville government was attempting for the empire as a whole. But by trying to codify a delicate modus vivendi, Gage destroyed it. By assuming the inevitability of American resistance, he helped to make it inevitable. Both his analysis and his recommendations were probably faulty. It was left to the British government to compound the error.

Proffered Solutions and Problems Unsolved

Whitehall began to grapple with these two peacetime problems—the military authority of the royal governors, and the application of the Mutiny Act to the colonies—

[124] Gage to Franklin and Penn, 24 April 1765, and Franklin to Gage, 29 April 1765, Gage MSS.

at the same time, in early 1765. Secretary at War Welbore Ellis did most of the grappling. Once again, as in the decision of 1763 to keep an army in America, Ellis is found acting outside the normal area of War Office responsibility, which historically had been confined to military administration. Unfortunately, Ellis had few qualifications for even the administrative task, much less that of making military and colonial policy. He owed his appointment in 1762 to Henry Fox, and even Fox would later say "that Ellis had by my friendship and accident got into a place much above his pretensions," adding that Ellis "was the only man in England who did not think so." Pitt, in the autumn of 1763, had spoken bluntly to the King about Ellis: "Your army is in the utmost confusion, and must no longer be governed by a Secretary at War ignorant of all military affairs."[125] The ability of almost every important British official in the era of the American Revolution has been questioned by historians at one time or another, but in the case of Welbore Ellis there can be little argument; he was genuinely incompetent.[126]

In May 1764, Lieutenant Colonel Edward Maxwell of the 21st Foot, under orders to join his regiment in West Florida, had a conversation with Ellis, in which Maxwell first raised the question of the power of the royal governor over regular troops in his province. Ellis, in answering, simply referred to the words of any governor's commission: "To be sure the Governor is Captain General and Commander in Chief."[127] If there was any thought at all behind this oracular reply, it must have been Ellis's intent

[125] Fox's remark is in *The Life and Letters of Lady Sarah Lennox*, eds. Countess of Ilchester and Lord Stavordale (London, 1902), 15; Pitt's is in Sir Henry Erskine to Andrew Mitchell, 27 September 1763, *Original Letters Illustrative of English History*, ed. Henry Ellis, 2nd series (London, 1827), IV, 470.

[126] The opinions of Horace Walpole must be treated with caution, especially because they are easily available and always witty; but see Walpole's utter contempt for Ellis in letters to George Montagu, 16 June 1763, and Lady Mary Coke, 15 October 1765, *Walpole Corr.*, ed. Toynbee, V, 343, and VI, 325.

[127] Alexander Fraser to Haldimand, 21 April 1768, BM Add. MSS. 21728.

either to conceal his ignorance of the subject or to avoid becoming involved in what promised to be a ticklish problem. A little research would have told him that the question had not arisen in serious form during the war, but that there existed a royal warrant of 1760, which had set the respective ranks of civil and military officers in America.[128] According to the warrant, the Commander in Chief was to take first place, royal governors when in their provinces second, and other general officers third.

When, in Canada and West Florida, this question ceased to be hypothetical, Ellis collaborated with Secretary of State Halifax in working out a verbal formula that seemed to contradict or ignore the warrant of 1760. At the end of the Indian rebellion, Northern and Southern Military Districts had been created, each commanded by a brigadier general directly under Gage. Ralph Burton was at Montreal, and Henry Bouquet was to be at Pensacola. Henceforth, said Ellis and Halifax, the orders of the Commander in Chief *and* of departmental brigadiers were to be supreme in military matters. If the brigadier were out of the province, however, a governor with the consent of his council might give directions to regular troops when "for the benefit of his Government," though in no case was a governor to interfere with regimental administration.[129] These vague phrases, as might be imagined, only added fuel to the fires in Canada and West Florida.

It is reasonable to assume that the decision appeared to be a victory for the military point of view because both Johnstone and Murray were Bute's nominees, while Halifax was one of the triumvirate, with Grenville and Egremont, that had forced Bute away from the throne.

---

[128] "Warrant for Settling the Rank and Precedence in North America," 17 December 1760, Gage-Amherst MSS., I. Amherst's instructions to Capt. Gualy in Newfoundland, 15 September 1763, and to Lt. Col. Robertson on mission to Florida, 14 October 1763, *ibid.*, III, can be interpreted as evidence that Amherst thought his local commanders in remote stations were under command of the governors.

[129] Ellis to Halifax, 7 February 1765, WO 4/987; Halifax to Gage, 9 February 1765, *Gage Corr.*, II, 23.

Perhaps the creation of Military Districts was, at least in part, an earlier gambit in this same game of curbing the influence of Bute.[130] Halifax, in transmitting the decision to Gage, referred to Johnstone's "violent and tyrannical Behaviour."[131] But Ellis, who had not broken openly with Bute and seemed as yet unsure which way to jump in the political melee, interpreted the decision for Gage in opposite fashion; he blamed all trouble on military officers who did not know their constitutional place.[132] Probably Gage understood what was happening in Whitehall, and was not as confused by these contradictory opinions as he might reasonably have been, but neither had he received a clear statement of policy.

In any case, Ellis and Halifax begged the important questions. How could a military command, which was in no sense responsible to civil authority, exist without seriously diminishing that authority, especially in nonrepresentative governments like Canada and the Floridas? If the brigadier general were absent, and he had to be absent from one of the Floridas or the other, how could the officer left in charge decide whether to obey the orders of the governor in case an unexpected situation arose, or to remain bound by the standing orders of his military superior, weeks or perhaps months away? On the other hand, if the governors made their extreme claims good, Gage would have lost effective control of all regular forces outside of New York. In terms of eighteenth-century communications and without drastic political consolidation of the colonies, the problem could not be wholly solved, but it might at least have been faced squarely.

The problem of the Mutiny Act was far more complex. The government responded to Gage's recommendation with unusual haste; his letters arrived March 1, and the next day Halifax asked Ellis for his opinion as soon as possible, because he wanted to act "without Loss of Time, in a matter of so much Importance."[133] On the 7th, Ellis replied

---

[130] See p. 161, above.
[131] 13 April 1765, *Gage Corr.*, II, 25.
[132] 9 February 1765, WO 4/987.
[133] SP 41/25.

equivocally: "It will certainly be useful and necessary for the magistrates there to have power given them to quarter upon private houses," he wrote, but already there had been some opposition to this, and he thought "the principal Objections are well founded."[134] The King had heard of it by the 9th, and that afternoon sent all the papers to Grenville, asking his advice, since Halifax "appears to disregard the noise that may be made here in Parliament," while Ellis "seems to decline approving the mode proposed for rectifying" the quartering problem in America.[135] By midnight Grenville had perused them and, though he would see the King the next day, had returned an opinion. He agreed that the quartering clause was "by far the most likely to create difficulties and uneasiness . . . especially as the quartering of soldiers upon the people against their wills is declared by the petition of right to be contrary to law." Because the cases of America and Scotland were similar, Grenville thought "perhaps some general words of the like nature referring to the former usage may be the properest precedent to follow. . . ."[136] The American Stamp bill had survived its crucial second reading not long before, despite some opposition in the House of Commons; Grenville now seemed ready to be gentler in a matter involving the military in the colonies.

The annual Mutiny Act had already passed, so it could not easily be amended, as Robertson had suggested. Instead a supplementary bill had to be drafted, which rejected Robertson's explicit language in favor of Grenville's more moderate, if vaguer, proposal: when neither barracks nor public houses could shelter the troops, then any two magistrates might "billet the residue of such Troops and Forces in such manner as hath hitherto been Practiced to billet His Majesty's Troops in His Majesty's Dominions in America."[137] But this was not moderate enough for the

---

[134] *Ibid.* See also *CHOP*, I, #1661.

[135] *Grenville Papers*, III, 11-12.

[136] *Ibid.*, 12-14.

[137] PRO 30/8 (Chatham MSS.), xcvii, 42-44, indicates words removed and words added in committee.

agents representing the American colonies in London, or for many of the merchants with American connections. They had missed the boat on the Stamp bill, and did not mean to be caught again. Charles Garth, agent for South Carolina, reported to Charleston on April 5 that the bill "has been twice the subject of four or five hours debate already."[138] Garth and Richard Glover, both M.P.'s, aroused and organized the merchants trading to America, who in turn bombarded Grenville with letters about the natural rights of Englishmen and the danger of a military coup d'état in the colonies. In a two-hour meeting with Garth and Glover, Grenville promised to do what he could to meet the objections of the friends of America.[139] Pitt himself had expressed strong objections "against the American Mutiny Bill, as an oppression they ought not to be subjected to, and in a great measure unnecessary."[140] On April 19 the bill got its second reading and was sent to committee, but several days earlier Grenville had accepted the offer of Thomas Pownall to draft a palatable substitute.[141]

Grenville and his lieutenant, Charles Jenkinson, were suspicious of Pownall's self-advertised expertise in American affairs, but they had little choice.[142] Pownall claimed that as Governor of Massachusetts in 1758 he had solved the quartering problem, and now could do the same trick for all the colonies. In collaboration with Benjamin Franklin, he drew up a new quartering clause; instead of billeting troops in private houses or "as hath hitherto been Prac-

---

[138] To committee of South Carolina Assembly, 5 April 1765, quoted in Namier, *England*, 294-295.

[139] *Ibid.* For the pressure brought against the bill, see *Grenville Papers,* 11-12n.; *Connecticut Historical Society Collections,* XVIII, 343-344; Grenville to Ellis, 27 April 1765, Stowe 7, II, HL MSS.; *The Correspondence of the Colonial Governors of Rhode Island, 1723-1775,* ed. G. S. Kimball (Providence, 1902-1903), II, 363-364.

[140] Calcraft to Shelburne, 15 April 1765, *Life of . . . Shelburne,* comp. Lord Fitzmaurice (London, 1875-76), I, 225.

[141] *Commons Journals,* XXX, 350.

[142] Charles Jenkinson to Grenville, 11 and 13 April 1765, *Jenkinson Papers,* 358-360. See also Grenville to Jenkinson, 13 April 1765, Stowe MSS. 7, II, HL MSS.

ticed," royal governors with the advice of their councils were to hire vacant buildings and fit them up as temporary barracks. Because barracks, whether permanent or improvised, were being provided in lieu of billets, Pownall incorporated Robertson's requirement that the provinces furnish firewood, bedding, candles, salt, vinegar, cooking utensils, and a daily ration of small beer, cider, or diluted rum.[143] In other words, the barracks were to be made as much like public houses as possible, at provincial expense. The revised bill also provided for the impressment of wagons and drivers at seven pence per twelve hundredweight per mile (not an unfair rate), for the payment of inn-keepers for victuals but not accommodations furnished to soldiers, and for half-fare passage on ferries for troops on the march. Because the clause against harboring deserters had always been part of the British Mutiny Act, its extension to the colonies went by without a murmur from the friends of America, although a better informed Secretary at War might have questioned its value. In this amended form, the bill passed on May 3.[144]

[143] PRO 30/8 (Chatham MSS.) XCVII, 42-44.

[144] The statute is cited as 5 Geo. III, c. 33. Most of it is printed in William MacDonald (ed.), *Select Charters and Other Documents Illustrative of American History, 1606-1775* (N.Y., 1899), 306-313. For some reason, a number of recent scholarly accounts of the period incorrectly state that the Act was either passed or substantially amended in 1766, and that the amendment of 1774 permitted quartering in private houses. To set the record straight at this point gets ahead of the narrative, but it needs doing: the Acts of 1766, 1767, and 1768 (6 c.18, 7 c.55, and 8 c.19, respectively) merely extended the basic Act of 1765, cited above. The Act of 1769 (9 c.18) authorized "local option"—the substitution of a satisfactory provincial law or arrangement for the Act of Parliament. The Acts of 1770, 1771, 1772, 1773, and 1774 (10 c.15, 11 c.11, 12 c.12, 13 c.24, and 14 c.6, respectively) extended the amended Act, but a second Act of 1774 (14 c.54), one of the Coercive Acts, gave the troop commander the right to locate his troops *geographically*; the Act was designed to prevent magistrates from housing troops on Castle Island in Boston harbor and calling it "Boston"; it did *not*, despite its vague language, authorize quartering in private houses, nor did the Act of 1775 (15 c.15), though doubtless this was done during the war whenever necessary.

What Thomas Pownall forgot, or at least forgot to mention, was the difference between his experience in 1758
and the needs of 1765. In 1758 there had been a war going
on. The Massachusetts Assembly itself had passed the
law, had done so with every prospect of being reimbursed
for its expenses, and even then had enacted it for periods
as short as three months in order to guard against
abuses.[145] Pownall implied that Americans would quietly
accept his revision in 1765, and the agents and friends of
the colonies in England, including Franklin, as well as the
government, were so out of touch with American conditions that they believed him. John Watts of New York,
no radical but an army contractor and future Tory, gave
an early hint of how Americans would in fact respond:
"The Colonists have no doubt of the Billeting Bills passing or anything else that is brought in. . . . They seem
convinc'd that not only doing the thing itself is meant at
home, but an air of both severity and contempt is design'd
to go along with it, and it has its *effect* to full—I could
wish to see Squire Pownall's performance. . . . He is said
here to affect being the patron of the Billeting Bill from
his great acquaintance with and experience of America, I
believe there are many such, who make America by falling
into the humor of the times, the handle for their own dirty
purposes, not caring one farthing so they do but succeed,
what is the consequence either to the mother country or
the Colonies."[146] Benjamin Franklin modestly claimed
credit, in 1765, for Pownall's revision; in 1767, when
Franklin wrote on the subject again, he had learned it was
not wise to make that claim.[147]

The Quartering Act was an abortion, especially from the
military point of view. Previously, local officials had
usually quartered and supplied the troops as necessity dic-
tated, including putting them in private houses when un-

[145] *The Acts and Resolves, Public and Private, of the Province
of Massachusetts Bay*, IV, 71-72, 165, 199.
[146] To Monckton, 1 June 1765, 4 *MHSC* X, 572-573.
[147] Franklin to Lord Kames, 11 April 1767, *The Writings of
Benjamin Franklin*, ed. A. H. Smyth (N.Y., 1905-1907), V, 18.

avoidable. It was a loose arrangement, and there occasionally had been resistance, as at Albany, but seldom if ever without provocation. Under the new law, however, the very omission of private houses made it illegal to put soldiers in them under any circumstances. In fact, its provisions were largely inapplicable to the problem which had been uppermost in Gage's mind—troops on the march—and instead required the colonies to help support troops on *station*, a burden borne largely by the Crown in the past. Moreover, the law required the action of provincial legislatures; no local magistrate would dare make a move to furnish firewood or the other supplies if his legislature had not acted.

Americans did not immediately and vigorously protest the Quartering Act, as they protested the Stamp Act. They were not happy about it, but some of them must have seen that it represented a slight but perceptible improvement in their legal position vis á vis regular troops. Moreover, the Quartering Act offered political opportunity. To thwart it was absurdly easy; a legislature had only to neglect to appropriate funds. This ease of resistance would provide a convenient weapon against imperial authority. Compliance could be an equally convenient concession. The desire of the Grenville ministry to tighten the imperial machinery, and to pinch pounds and pence in particular, made it receptive to those proposals in Gage's plan which promised to save a little money. British sensitivity to all matters pertaining to civil-military relations, and Thomas Pownall's "expertise" worked a modification of these proposals that made them something worse than useless. The British government was attempting to act directly on provincial governments, rather than on individuals. Americans themselves would try the same device less than two decades later under the Articles of Confederation, and they too would find it impracticable.

Perhaps Jefferson exaggerated. Certainly George III and his ministers had rendered "the Military independent of . . . the Civil Power," but they had not intended, nor would they have dared, to make it "superior to" that power. Unfortunately, the logic (or illogic) of the imperial structure led them in a direction they did not mean to go. It required no armed clashes, no bashing of American heads by arrogant redcoats to raise the first crisis in pre-Revolutionary civil-military relations. There was only a small, scattered, sickly, mutinous army, commanded by a mild, sober, sensible man, an army to whom most Americans were vaguely grateful for its hard work against Frenchmen, Spaniards, and Indians. But the very presence of that army under a single commander in peacetime North America raised unexpected legal difficulties. When the British government attempted to resolve those difficulties within the framework of the decision of 1763 it inevitably tried to cut into the power of colonial civil authority, whether royally appointed governor or popularly elected assembly. Better men in Quebec, Mobile, Albany, New York, and London might have used better judgment, and resolved the matter quietly among themselves. They could have succeeded, however, only so long as the army was not required to carry out its assigned mission—to act as imperial police.

V · Soldiers Against Civilians

THE only one of Gage's proposed amendments to the Mutiny Act that might have been truly vital to the missions of the army was the one that never received serious consideration. In addition to his other requests, Gage had asked that courts-martial be given jurisdiction over all crimes committed in areas outside any provincial government. The effect would have been to put the American interior under martial law.

When confronted with this recommendation, Welbore Ellis gave additional proof of his unfitness to be Secretary at War. He displayed ignorance of basic facts about the disposition of the army in America. In a letter to Halifax, his lack of interest and knowledge shines through: "The addition proposed to the 60th clause [of the Mutiny Act] being new, and an extension of military jurisdiction over crimes and persons not military, [I] can give no opinion relative thereto. All the posts within North America are within some civil jurisdiction."[1] One may reasonably suppose that Halifax shuddered and swore as he read the last sentence, because he sent a copy of the Proclamation of 1763 to Ellis for his perusal with the comment that the Secretary at War should note that there were indeed a number of army posts in Indian country, beyond the bounds of any civil authority. Halifax also referred him to the Crown lawyers on the legal questions involved in extending courts-martial to civilians.[2] At this, Ellis appears to have bogged down. The quartering clause for the colonial version of the Mutiny Act was beginning to excite the resistance described in Chapter IV, and Ellis decided against (or perhaps forgot) to do anything about the 60th clause, probably because it was politically delicate and because he could shelve it without incurring any immediate financial loss to the Crown. But the result was to end all hope that the army would get the power to carry out its assigned task of policing the interior.

[1] 7 March 1765, *CHOP*, I, #1661.
[2] 11 March 1765, *ibid.,* #1671.

It would be wrong simply to blame Ellis for his failure to provide the tools needed for the execution of policy. The truth is that not until the Stamp Act troubles, later in 1765, were civil and military officials fully aware that this army was in all its multifarious missions, both explicit and implicit, primarily a police force. Ellis was but a little more numb than his colleagues to this fact. Perhaps numbness seems strange in view of the peacetime missions originally given to Gage, but of course armies are not usually regarded, by themselves or by others, as police, and it took more than two years for the implications of the decision of 1763 to sink into the British consciousness. During those years, however, there were some straws in the wind, some incidents which seemed minor at the time, but which become more significant when seen in the perspective of later events. Parts of the army early found themselves involved in trying to maintain order and enforce law, not only in the crude rough-and-tumble of Pensacola or Quebec, but in the older and more sophisticated societies of Pennsylvania and New York.

Perception of the Problem

Policing the fur trade had been second on the list of missions for the army, as enumerated by Halifax for Gage, but it was first in immediacy and difficulty, and perhaps first in importance as well. Trade abuses had played a large part in Indian discontent, and pressure was mounting from merchants at Philadelphia, Albany, and Quebec to reopen the trade which had been closed by the war. The "trading post" was as old as colonial history, but now it was to be more than a convenient place for protected commerce with the Indians; it was to become an instrument of imperial control. All trade would be confined to designated posts or towns, agents of Sir William Johnson and John Stuart would supervise the trade, and fort commanders would use regular troops to keep order and enforce the trade regulations. No longer would Indian country be the lawless breeding ground of costly war; peace and business would march hand in hand. It was an appealing concept, for which Halifax and Johnson deserve about equal credit, and there was a good deal of unjustified optimism about its feasibility.

It was in the drafting of the Royal Proclamation of October 7, 1763, that the first difficulties appeared. As is well known, the Proclamation made no provision for law enforcement in the area beyond provincial frontiers. But the question had indeed arisen, provoking a brief struggle in which personalities and politics overwhelmed considerations of policy. The struggle was somewhat petty, even now not altogether clear, but worth recounting both for its outcome and as an instance of how fortuitous factors once again made a simple problem complicated.

Secretary of State Egremont at the time was being advised by an "expert," the able ex-Governor of Georgia, Henry Ellis.[3] John Pownall, long-time secretary to the Board of Trade, clearly resented Ellis's recently acquired influence and urged the Earl of Shelburne, the new president of the Board of Trade, to stand up to Egremont, who apparently was attempting to make the Board of Trade a rubber stamp for his plan of colonial organization.[4] Shelburne had his own political reasons for seeking to embarrass Egremont and the government, because if the Grenville ministry could be weakened, Pitt—Shelburne's new leader —conceivably could be brought into office.[5]

Henry Ellis had recommended to Egremont that Canada

[3] On Ellis, see W. W. Abbot, *The Royal Governors of Georgia, 1754-1775* (Chapel Hill, 1959), 57-83.

[4] The "rubber-stamp" interpretation is convincingly developed in Sosin, *Whitehall*, 52-65.

[5] The Earl of Sandwich wrote to Lord Holland (Henry Fox) that if there should be any Parliamentary inquiry as to the cause of the delay in issuing the Proclamation of 1763, "it will appear that it was chiefly owing to your friend Shelburne's [Shelburne had broken with Fox earlier] intriguing disposition, when he was at the head of the board, who chose rather to draw up representations that might occasion contest and difference of opinion with Lord Egremont and the rest of the Administration, to whom he wished no good, than to attend plainly and simply to the business of his office and the dispatch of the great affairs under his direction." 26 September 1763, *Letters to Henry Fox*, ed. Earl of Ilchester (London, 1915), 175.

be divided into two governments, and that the Indian country "be put under the immediate Protection and Care of the Officers commanding at the distant posts. But . . . all Matters cognizable by Law should be reserved to the Civil Power in any of the Neighboring Provinces."[6] Egremont forwarded this suggestion to the Board, where Pownall strongly objected, in a report for Shelburne, to "the idea of some person that it might be adviseable to establish two governments upon the river St. Lawrence."[7] Pownall, whether through neglect or for some other reason, did not mention the problem of law in the Indian country, nor was it mentioned in the Board's formal report to Egremont. Egremont noticed this and recommended to the Board that the boundary of Canada be extended to include most of the Ohio and Mississippi valleys.[8] Shelburne and Pownall disliked the idea: to extend the boundary would seem to make the British title to the Indian country depend on the conquest of New France, give Canada an unfair advantage in the fur trade, and make a clash between the Governor of Canada and the American Commander in Chief inevitable. They suggested instead that the Commander in Chief be given a commission to govern the interior, but they asked that action be delayed until the Board could investigate and report on the subject.[9]

By this time news of the Indian war had made the need for a proclamation pressing; moreover, Egremont died within a fortnight and Shelburne resigned two weeks later. Halifax, Egremont's successor, ordered the Board simply to authorize military officers in the interior to apprehend fugitives and suspected criminals and send them to a civil

[6] "Hints Relative to the Division and Government of the Conquered and Newly Acquired Countries in America," ed. Verner W. Crane, *MVHR*, viii (1922), 370-373. There is a copy of this document in HL, Stowe MSS., 103(c).

[7] Humphreys, *EHR*, xlix, 261.

[8] Egremont to Board of Trade, 14 July 1763, *DCH Canada*, 147-148. The Board of Trade report is in *ibid.*, 131-147.

[9] Board of Trade to Egremont, 5 August 1763, *ibid.*, 151-152. Sosin, *Whitehall*, 62, incorrectly says that the proposed commission was merely to send alleged criminals east for trial.

jurisdiction for trial, and to prepare a commission for the Commander in Chief to govern there if it appeared practicable.[10] So the matter ended, about where Henry Ellis had started it. Nothing was done about the commission (it was possibly no more than Shelburne's idea for enhancing James Murray's position), and the crucial months when some arrangement for law enforcement in the interior could have been worked out were instead consumed by controversy.[11]

Although the Proclamation of 1763 failed to provide for the enforcement of law in the interior, it did sketch the system of trade regulation that eventually would have to be enforced by someone, somehow. Trade with the Indians, according to the Proclamation, was to be "free and open to all our Subjects whatever," provided that the trader was licensed by a provincial governor or the Commander in Chief, and obeyed "such regulations as we shall think proper to prescribe." Halifax had already instructed the Board of Trade to work out these regulations as soon as possible.[12]

[10] Halifax to Board of Trade, 19 September 1763, *ibid.*, 154-155.

[11] On 11 August the Duke of Newcastle wrote the Duke of Devonshire that: "Our friend Mellish brought me a piece of news from London. . . . That my Lord Shelburne, at the head of the board of trade, intends to propose the making General Murray, who is now Governor of Canada only (as I understood it), to be general governor in those parts, as M. de Vaudreil the French governor was," quoted in Humphreys, *EHR*, XLIX, 251n. Humphreys dismisses this as typical Newcastle garbling of *Egremont's* proposal, but it seems likely that Newcastle had it right. On about the same day the decision was made to give Amherst "leave," and Murray was next in line for the position of Commander in Chief; see Alden, *Gage*, 60. Shelburne, anxious to bring Pitt, Bute, and George III together, might have seen this as a way of turning Egremont's proposal into a political boomerang; that is, by making a man supported by both Bute and Pitt into a virtual American viceroy. Note that Murray would have had commissions as Governor of Canada, of the Indian country, and as Commander in Chief; and that both Egremont's requirement and the Board's objections to it would have been answered. It is difficult to believe that even Newcastle could have garbled such fresh information.

[12] *DCH Canada,* 154-155, 168.

In July 1764, when Bradstreet and Bouquet were just beginning their military advance to the westward, the Board of Trade submitted its plan for the management of Indian affairs. With Hillsborough, a protégé of Halifax, replacing Shelburne as President, it was only to be expected that the Board would follow the repeated recommendations of Sir William Johnson, Thomas Gage, and John Stuart. Accordingly, the plan proposed to regulate the fur trade by confining it to certain fixed locations—the principal towns of the Indian nations of the South, and the military garrisons of the North. Commissaries were to be appointed to oversee the trade at these locations under the general supervision of Johnson and Stuart, and were to be given commissions as justices of the peace. Like magistrates anywhere, they would be able to invoke military support when necessary, but the army was to have no routine role in regulating the trade. Johnson and Stuart were to receive appellate judicial powers equivalent to that of the normal colonial courts of common pleas. In short, the Indian department was to become autonomous rather than remain a branch of the military as was currently the case.[13]

Obviously such a plan required Parliamentary approval, not only for the funds needed to effect it, but for the legal jurisdiction as well. For a variety of reasons—the press of other business, the novelty of the proposals, the requirement for legislative action, political instability, and bureaucratic inertia—the plan officially remained no more than a plan, although both Johnson and Stuart took the chance of putting as much of it as they dared or desired into effect.[14] Gage was reasonably cooperative, permitting Johnson to assume full control of Indian affairs wherever he already had deputies, as at Montreal and Fort Pitt, but he balked at the appointment of an Indian staff for each post on the grounds that the Treasury had forbade all unauthorized expenditures. It was in this context that Gage requested an extension of the Mutiny Act to cover civil offenses com-

---

[13] The Plan is reprinted in *NYCD,* VII, 634-641.
[14] Flexner, *Johnson,* 312ff.; Alden, *Stuart,* 247ff.

mitted in the interior, a request to which the government did not respond.

There was, however, a bare possibility that Gage could enforce law in the interior on his own initiative. Since 1717, a clause in the Articles of War had said that "where there is no Form of Our Civil Judicature in Force, the Generals or Governors, or Commanders respectively are to appoint General Courts Martial to be held, who are to try all persons guilty of Wilfull Murders, Theft, Robbery, Rapes, Coining or Clipping the Coin of Great Britain . . . and all other Capital Crimes, or other offences, and Punish Offenders according to the known Laws of the Land, or as the nature of their Crimes shall deserve."[15] Like so much of British law and practice, this clause was ambiguous. Did it apply only to soldiers, who would normally be tried by civil courts for any violations of civil law, or to "all persons," as the clause stated?

The weight of legal opinion and precedent was on the side of a narrow interpretation of "all persons," but the clause originally had been drafted to cover the cases of Gibraltar, Minorca, and Newfoundland, which were without civil government.[16] If civilians broke the law in those places, by whom could they be practicably tried? Even if the clause applied only to the army, its scope was less than clear, because there was a general belief that anyone who had "an immediate relation to, or connection with the military" was subject to the Articles of War.[17] In other words, campfollowers—women, sutlers, teamsters, commissaries,

[15] The quotation is from Section 20, Article 2, of the manuscript copy of the Articles of War for 1749 in WO 72/2. The practice obviously antedates 1717, because in those articles the phrasing is: "The Governors or Commanders, respectively, are to hold General Courts Martial, and to punish Criminals by their Sentence, as has been practised heretofore, and authorized by former Articles of War." *Commons Journal*, XVIII, 713.

[16] The places are mentioned in the Article itself. In 1734 and in 1750, the Attorney General had given an opinion against any but the narrowest definition of this Article. BM Add. MSS. 36226, 89-90; and Shelburne MSS., LXI, 585-586.

[17] These were the words of the Solicitor General, spoken in debate in the House of Commons in 1754 over the extension of

perhaps Indian traders residing at army posts—might be tried by military tribunals in the absence of civil courts. But the legal question was further clouded by the fact that the Articles of War, under which courts-martial were constituted, were not laws at all; they were Royal regulations authorized, but not enacted, by Parliament.[18]

During the war, the British army had governed Canada by martial law. It was with some surprise, then, that Amherst and Murray in the autumn of 1763 read the opinion of Charles Gould, acting Judge-Advocate General, that civilians could never be tried by military courts.[19] There may have been some obscure personal or political motive behind Gould's action, but it seems more likely that Gould, in his own small sphere, was responding to the general impulse after the Seven Years War to tidy up procedures that had too long been in doubt.[20] When Gage inquired about this matter in 1764, Gould referred it to Halifax, who replied that there was no longer any problem because Murray had received a commission as Governor of Canada, with full power to constitute civil courts.[21] This of course was not an answer but an excuse for not answering.

Ellis's failure to deal effectively with important questions

---

the Mutiny Act to the forces of the East India Company. *Parliamentary History,* xv, 263.

[18] *Considerations on the Act for Punishing Mutiny and Desertion; and the Rules and Articles for the Government of His Majesty's Land Forces* (London, 1772), a pamphlet which demanded a reform of military justice, clearly sets forth the legal status of the Articles. Both this pamphlet, 35ff., and Stephen Payne Adye, *A Treatise on Courts Martial* (N.Y., 1769), 7, interpret the "no civil judicature" as applicable to crimes committed by civilians, thus illustrating the confusion over this point. Adye was an Acting Judge Advocate under Gage's command.

[19] Gould to Murray, 11 August, and reply, 12 November 1763, WO 72/5. An earlier opinion to the same effect is in Gould to Welbore Ellis, 2 June 1763, WO 81/10, 169-171.

[20] Gould had somehow become closely connected to Bradstreet, and so might be suspected of trying to impair the position of Bradstreet's superiors (and rivals). But he was consistent in his narrow interpretation of the Article, even for Minorca. See Gould to Halifax, 7 March 1765, WO 81/11, 66-67.

[21] Gould to Gage, 7 June 1764, *ibid.,* 14.

of legal, colonial, and military policy can easily be understood, but what of Halifax, who had consistently urged that the empire be reformed along rational, centralized lines? At last in a position to shape policy, he seemed to be continuing the tradition of Sir Robert Walpole of letting sleeping dogs lie. The answer is to be found in the vicissitudes of British politics. When Gage asked in 1764 about martial law in Canada, Halifax had just acquired great notoriety as the principal oppressor of John Wilkes. When Gage suggested in 1765 that the Mutiny Act be extended to the American interior, Halifax was about to play his tortuous part in the affair of the Regency Bill, which would topple the Grenville government by July. Halifax probably had no time, and he certainly did not have the political capital, to become involved in any controversial measures for the colonies; his relations with his royal master, not to mention the whole political community, were already bad enough.

Gage, for his part, was not the sort of man to risk using power he did not clearly have by right. It is obvious, though largely unrecorded, that post commanders kept some sort of order among the traders and Indians at the forts, even without the formal authority to do so.[22] But the only authorized action against lawbreakers, whether red or white, was to ship them—along with all witnesses, depositions, and other evidence—to the nearest provincial government. In short, the legal basis for the systematic regulation of Indian trade did not exist.

On the surface at least, the other task of interior police —patrolling the frontier boundary—seemed easier to accomplish.

The concept of a boundary line between Indian and white man had had a long history before 1763, and the exact meaning of the concept has provoked disagreement among historians.[23] Only a few reference points need be

[22] See, for example, the "Journal of James Kenny, 1761-1763," *PMHB,* xxxvii (1913), 1-47, 151-201.
[23] See Max Farrand, "The Indian Boundary Line," *AHR,* x

established here: by the beginning of the Seven Years War, a boundary had become less a means to establish what white men and their governments could legally claim than to make clear to both Indians and speculators what the whites could *not* claim. The distinction is a subtle but important one. The primary emphasis had shifted from the acquisition of land—as in the notorious "Walking Purchase" in Pennsylvania—to the limitation of acquisition. In the same report which urged the appointment of Sir William Johnson as interprovincial Indian agent, the members of the Albany Congress in 1754 recommended "that the Bounds of those Colonies which extend to the South Sea, be contracted, and limited by the Allegheny or Apalachian Mountains."[24] The Pennsylvania proprietors took the first concrete step to carry out the recommendation in 1758, when, at the Treaty of Easton, they returned to the Delaware and Shawnee all those lands west of the Alleghenies which the Penns had acquired from a few Iroquois—nominal suzerains of the Delaware and Shawnee—in 1754. The Easton Treaty was a diplomatic coup, detaching as it did these latter tribes from their French allies. The judgment of Lawrence H. Gipson is accurate: "The treaty, solemnly ratified by His Majesty in Council, became, in fact, with the end of hostilities in this area, the basis for trans-Appalachian British policy."[25]

By 1761, however, frontiersmen were beginning to move onto the Indian land in western Pennsylvania in spite of the Easton Treaty, and the Indians complained that they were "penned up like Hogs."[26] In order to protect their interests and to prevent trouble, Colonel Bouquet, then commanding at Fort Pitt, broadly interpreted the royal confirmation of the Easton Treaty and proclaimed that white men could settle or hunt to the west of the mountains

---

(1905), 782-791. Craven, 3 *WMQ*, I, 76, describes perhaps the first case of an Indian boundary or pale. The works previously cited by Alvord, Sosin, and Humphreys explore the boundary concept as it developed in the 1760's.

[24] Report of 9 July 1754, *The Documentary History of the State of New York*, ed. E. B. O'Callaghan (Albany, 1850-51), II, 356.
[25] *British Empire*, VII, 279.   [26] Quoted in *ibid.*, IX, 89.

only with written authorization from the Commander in Chief or from a colonial governor.[27] Later in the same year, the Privy Council further defined frontier policy by issuing instructions to the royal governors that forbade any settlement on land claimed by the Indians and required approval by the Board of Trade for any request to purchase Indian land.[28]

When the Indian war erupted in 1763, officials on both sides of the Atlantic concluded that a definite, comprehensive boundary was an immediate necessity. Both Johnson and Stuart begged permission to negotiate such a boundary; the ships carrying their letters passed the one carrying the Royal Proclamation of October 7th, which forbade "for the present . . . all our loving subjects from making any purchases or settlements Whatsoever . . . [of] any lands beyond the heads or sources of any of the rivers which fall into the Atlantic Ocean from the West or North-West, or upon any lands whatever, which not having been ceded to or purchased by us . . . are reserved to the said Indians."[29]

But one of Thomas Hobbes' "lewd principles" would have it that "covenants, without the sword, are but words," and if a boundary was to have more than a verbal existence it had to be enforced. In the months before the outbreak of the Indian war in 1763, the most flagrant violations of the boundary policy seemed to be occurring far to the east of Fort Pitt, on the East Branch of the Susquehannah River in Pennsylvania. There a land company, claiming to hold title from Connecticut on the basis of that colony's sea-to-sea charter clause, had begun to occupy the area around modern Wilkes-Barre, which was part of Delaware country.[30] When, however, Governor James Hamilton of Penn-

[27] The documents concerning Bouquet's action are printed in *PAC Report, 1889,* 72-80.

[28] 12 December 1761, Labaree, *Royal Instructions,* II, #687.

[29] The watershed line was an emergency measure. It was intended that the line should be more carefully delineated after the return of peace.

[30] For a history of this Connecticut venture, see the editor's introduction in *Susquehannah Company Papers.*

sylvania requested the assistance of General Amherst in eliminating this menace to good relations with the Indians, Amherst declined to interfere in what he regarded as an intercolonial boundary quarrel.[31] In any case, Amherst never worried very much about Indian relations; but Whitehall did. Moreover, the friends of Thomas Penn, especially the Earl of Halifax and John Pownall, were in power, and Penn continually pushed for imperial military intervention.

At about the same time, Sir William Johnson was negotiating a settlement of Delaware complaints in a congress at Lancaster, and he naturally supported Hamilton and Penn in their demand for action against the Connecticut immigrants. Thomas Penn, in London, wrote Hamilton in December 1762: "I suppose orders are sent to Sir Jeffery Amhurst to send a Military Force."[32] But Secretary of State Egremont, while deeply concerned about the Indian question, could not bring himself to go so far. After the Privy Council approved a strongly worded report by the Board of Trade on the matter in January 1763, Egremont instructed Amherst to "employ every legal means in your Power" against the Susquehannah Company settlers, and asked for more information "that His Majesty may be able to judge, what farther Orders, it may be expedient to give."[33] The emphasis was thus on "legal" measures, which, for a military commander acting alone, meant moral suasion at most. Amherst, with problems of his own as the shattered army dribbled back from Havana, was reluctant to become involved in what might prove to be a messy business and found an excuse for his inaction in the qualified orders from Egremont; he persisted in regarding the problem variously as unimportant, solved, and unsolvable.[34]

As 1763 wore on, Thomas Penn was outraged by his shilly-shallying; he had expected to hear "that Sir Jeffery

[31] 10 and 17 May 1761, inclosed in Amherst to Pitt, 13 August 1761, WO 34/74.

[32] 10 December 1762, *Susquehannah Company Papers,* II, #141.

[33] 27 January 1763, *ibid.,* #145.

[34] See especially Amherst to Johnson, 17 October 1762, *Johnson Papers,* III, 904-905.

Amhurst has in pursuance of his orders, issued a proclamation for them to remove, or threatned them with an
armed force, it is indeed amazing that he should not have
. . . received orders to remove that settlement."[35] Amherst
had indeed received stronger orders. When Egremont heard
of additional settlers on their way from Connecticut to the
Wyoming Valley, he ordered the Commander in Chief in
May 1763, to "use every Means in Your Power to prevent
any further Attempts of this Nature."[36] The adjective
"legal" was missing, and the clear sense of the order con-
jures up a picture of troops blocking the road and turning
the caravan back toward Connecticut. Moreover, an Order-
in-Council followed a month later which rejected outright
the claims of the settlers.[37] The picture never materialized,
however, for Amherst had his hands full with the Indian
war by the time he received the order, and the Delaware
temporarily solved the problem for him by swooping down
on the Wyoming settlement and killing, capturing, and
scattering its inhabitants.[38]

And so, the army never acted to enforce the line of
settlement before the Indian rebellion, and one might therefore conclude that the story of the Susquehannah Company
from 1761 to 1763 scarcely merits telling. Several aspects
of it were portentous, however. One is the reluctance of
authority, civil as well as military, to act quickly whenever
there was any question of legal title to property. Certainly
the Connecticut claim was shadowy to the point of absurdity, but one never knew what lawyers and courts might
do, so one dared not act rashly. A second aspect is the
need of the military commander for *local* political guidance
if he was to stay safely on the right side of the law; but
the Indian boundary was imperial in dimension, and inevitably involved conflicts of local interest. A third aspect
was the tough line eventually taken, apparently inducing a

[35] To Hamilton, 10 August 1763, *Susquehannah Company Papers*, #198.
[36] 21 May 1763, Amherst-Gage MSS., I.
[37] 15 June 1763, *Susquehannah Company Papers*, II, #189.
[38] See *ibid.*, #211, 212, 230, 232.

certain optimism on all hands about enforcing the boundary in the future, coupled with the fact that this tough line did not have to be made effective at the time, thus not dampening optimism with any unpleasant experience.

Gage himself seemed to share this optimism, and had shown himself readier than Amherst to keep white men off unoccupied land. While still military governor of Montreal, he had directed local commanders to arrest squatters in the Lake Champlain area, using force if necessary, and to send them to Canada for trial.[39] Soon after the Indians had laid down their arms in 1764, he sent similar orders to the commander at Fort Prince George concerning squatters in South Carolina and Georgia.[40] Like almost every British official who had any first-hand experience with the problem, Gage was convinced that, in the constant friction along the frontier, the Indian was the victim, not the villain.[41]

Policing the Settled Areas

In the first months after assuming the supreme command, General Gage had faced another kind of civil disorder, a kind hardly foreseen before it occurred. Inhabitants of western Pennsylvania, maddened in late 1763 both by the atrocities of Indian raiders and by the failure of the Quaker-dominated Assembly to take effective military action, descended on a small settlement of Christianized Indians at Conestoga, near Lancaster, and butchered all twenty of them in two successive sorties.[42] It so happened

[39] Gage to Lt. Samuel McKay, 1 July 1763, CL, Gage Letter Book IV; Gage to the Commanding Officer at Crown Point, 30 September 1763, Gage MSS.

[40] Gage to Halifax, 10 August 1764, *Gage Corr., I,* 33-35.

[41] For example, Bouquet to Gage, 22 December 1764: "The Licenciousness of the Frontier Inhabitants in general is carried to a high Degree, and unless Severe Measures are taken to restrain them within proper Bounds, and hunting beyond the Allegheny Mountains expressly forbid to them, it will be impossible to preserve Peace with the Indians." BM Add. MSS. 21637.

[42] Brook Hindle, "The March of the Paxton Boys," 3 *WMQ* III, 461-486, includes an interesting contemporary picture of the troops drawn up to defend the Indians at Philadelphia.

that there were regular troops in Lancaster on December 27, when the "Paxton boys" struck the second time. On this raid, they killed the remaining fourteen members of the settlement, who were thought to be secure in the Lancaster workhouse. There are a number of conflicting accounts as to why Captain James Robertson did not use his detachment of Highlanders to save the Indians, but one senses from them all that neither the magistrates nor Robertson were anxious to intervene.[43] Probably most important on the military side is the fact that Robertson was simply passing through Lancaster on his way to New York with the "remains" of the companies of the 77th Regiment, which Amherst had sent to Bouquet earlier in the year. Bouquet had drafted the able-bodied men of the 77th Highlanders into the Black Watch, and had ordered Robertson to march what was left of the former unit to New York for embarkation.[44] The 77th was one of the regiments, it will be recalled, that had suffered through the Cuban campaign and Bouquet's march to Fort Pitt, and it is not difficult to imagine how willing or able the human dregs of these experiences must have been to stop a hundred armed and bloodthirsty farmers.[45]

Governor John Penn immediately applied to Gage for military assistance in protecting 140 more domesticated Indians who had been put in the pesthouse on Province Island (at the mouth of the Schuylkill River) for their own safety.[46] In response, Gage directed the march of three companies of Royal Americans, on their way down to New York from Albany, toward Philadelphia, and told Penn that, if necessary, he could also employ three companies of

[43] See the discussion by the editor in *The Paxton Papers*, ed. J. R. Dunbar (The Hague, 1957), 28-33. Following contemporary accounts, Dunbar refers to "Colonel Robinson," but the officer could have been only Capt. James Robertson of the 77th Regiment, not to be confused with Gage's staff officer of the same name.

[44] Amherst to Bouquet, 7 August 1763; Bouquet to Amherst, 1 December 1763, *Bouquet Papers*, BM Add. MSS. 21634, 238, 294.

[45] See the address to Penn from Cumberland County, 5 February 1768, 8 *Pa. Arch.*, VII, 6137.

[46] 31 December 1763, *Pa. Col. Rec.*, IX, 104-105.

the 42nd quartered at Carlisle.[47] But before Penn received the reply, he had become sufficiently alarmed to tell Captain Robertson (who had reached Philadelphia by this time) to escort the Indians northward, where Sir William Johnson could take them under his wing.[48] Penn had expressed a fear that provincial troops, even if available, "could not be brought to act vigorously against their Friends, Neighbours, and relations."[49] Acting Governor Colden of New York, however, wanted no part of any Indians, Christianized or otherwise, and refused to allow them to enter Richmond County.[50] The three companies of Royal Americans, commanded by Captain John Schlosser, then escorted the poor souls back to Philadelphia across frozen New Jersey.

When it became evident that the Paxton boys planned to march into Philadelphia to finish the job begun at Conestoga, Governor Penn put the Indians in the barracks in the northern part of Philadelphia along with their military escort, and asked the provincial Assembly to pass a riot act. In his message, he noted the great difficulty under the English constitution in framing proper orders to the commander of regular troops, and doubted whether any order of his could excuse bloodshed "till the civil power has first been called in, and in vain endeavored to suppress the Tumult."[51] Joseph Galloway and John Dickinson brought in a bill which in effect extended the British Riot Act to Pennsylvania for one year; it was passed the same day.[52] Primarily because the people of the city, especially the Quakers, stood firmly behind the regulars in their defense of the Indians, the Paxton boys apparently lost heart when they reached Germantown, and Benjamin Franklin was able to persuade them to return home without testing either

[47] 6 January 1764, *ibid.*, 118.   [48] 5 January 1764, *ibid.*, 110-111.
[49] 31 December 1763, *ibid.*, 104-105.
[50] Colden to Penn, 10 January 1764, *ibid.*, 120.
[51] 2 February 1764, *ibid.*, 129.
[52] 8 *Pa. Arch.*, VII, 5537; *Pa. Statutes at Large*, VII, 325-328. The act does not mention military forces, but simply gives the magistrates the power to call for the assistance of "such other person or persons," including any of the King's subjects.

Captain Schlosser's detachment or the new provincial riot act.[53]

The act had just expired when the unruly farmers of Cumberland County again clashed with the military arm of the law. When a packhorse train passed near Fort Loudoun in March 1765, on its way with Indian trade goods to Johnson's deputy George Croghan at Fort Pitt, some hundred disguised backwoodsmen stopped the train, drove off its attendants, and destroyed most of the cargo. The raiders pretended to be Virginia militiamen, still unpaid from the campaign of the previous year, and out to collect their pay by fair means or foul. The disguise fooled no one, however, for they were evidently the Paxton boys bent on blocking the movement of supplies to their blood enemies, the Indians. Lieutenant Charles Grant, in command of the Highlander detachment at Fort Loudoun, immediately supported one Justice Maxwell and Robert Callendar— army provision subcontractor, also a justice of the peace, and in charge of the train—by giving them a sergeant and twelve soldiers. This small force managed to catch six of the raiders and deposited them in the fort.[54] But, fearful lest the rest of his goods be destroyed in retaliation by the country people, Callendar soon accepted bail and let the six men go.[55]

For the next few months, Grant and his men were highly unpopular with their neighbors. The Paxton boys effectively blockaded Fort Loudoun. They plundered and flogged a sutler who attempted to enter the fort, and, when Grant refused to return muskets taken from rioters in the March encounter, they struck back by kidnapping Grant himself and forcing him to sign a bond that he would return the weapons.[56] When he did not do this after being

[53] Note that this was the same detachment which began to desert en masse later in the spring. See Schlosser to Bouquet, 4 March 1764, *Bouquet Papers,* BM Add. MSS. 21650, 41.

[54] Grant to Bouquet, 9 March 1765, *Bouquet Papers,* BM Add. MSS. 21651.

[55] Callendar to Bouquet, 11 March 1765, *ibid.,* 156-157.

[56] Lt. Col. John Reid to Gage, 1 and 4 June 1765, *Pa. Col. Rec.,* IX, 268-270.

released, the Paxton boys spent a day and a night pumping musket balls into the fort while Grant and his men cowered inside. Fortunately, the troops did not return the fire and no one was hurt.[57] But when Gage heard of this "insult" to the King's garrison, he was livid. "If he had returned the Fire of those Ruffians," Gage wrote to Penn, "and killed as many as he was able, I conceive he would have acted consistent with the Laws of his own and of every other civilized Country."[58] For purposes of comparison, it is interesting to note that the commandant at Bedford (40 miles to the westward) reported at about the same time: "The Inhabitants have used me and the Troops under my Command extreamly well, and upon every Occasion show their readiness in Serving us."[59]

Governor Penn, upon receipt of the news of the March affair, had set out for Carlisle in order to investigate and to restore order in Cumberland County. Captain Schlosser and his three companies of Royal Americans were once again in the line of fire, for they were stationed at Lancaster and thus available if Penn should call for military support. Schlosser had had experience with civil disorder in 1764, and, as he awaited Penn's arrival, he reflected on that experience: "It is a very disagreeable Bussiness to be employd against the Kings Subjects as bad as they may be, particularly as the Law of that Country to which we have the honour to Serve, keeps allways our hands tied, in the execution of our Duty in Such Cases."[60] Schlosser begged Bouquet that, if he and his men should be directed to put down the Paxton boys, their orders be accompanied "with Sufficient Civil Power."

Penn found, in fact, little to put down. The grand jury at Carlisle had failed, as might be expected, to indict any of Grant's six prisoners.[61] Penn learned that Callendar had

[57] Gage to Conway, 6 May 1766, *Gage Corr.*, I, 91.
[58] 13 December 1765, *Pa. Col. Rec.*, IX, 292.
[59] Lt. Nathaniel McCulloch to Bouquet, 28 March 1765, *Bouquet Papers*, BM Add. MSS. 21651, 178.
[60] 16 March 1765, *ibid.*, 167-168.
[61] Penn to Johnson, 23 May 1765, *Johnson Papers*, XI, 746.

been paying the soldiers for their assistance, and he heard accusations that Grant had accepted bribes to let the pack-horse train pass the fort without the required inspection.[62] Obviously the train itself had been much too large to have contained only "presents" for Croghan's use in diplomatic dealings with the Indians at Fort Pitt and in the Illinois country; it had, in fact, been mainly an unauthorized shipment of trade goods from the Philadelphia firm of Baynton, Wharton, and Morgan, who intended to be first in the market when Gage, the Indian department, and the governors agreed to reopen the Indian trade. Moreover, the nasty rumors persisted that Croghan himself was a heavy investor in the shipment, and that some of the kegs had contained not rum but scalping knives.[63] One could hardly blame the Paxton boys.

As for the army, the two incidents involving the Paxton boys suggested that rural disorder could not be handled by regulars unless they had both political and popular support, as they had had in 1764 from the Pennsylvania Assembly and the Philadelphia Quakers. Without it, their task was impossible, as it had been at Lancaster in 1763 and at Fort Loudoun in 1765. Even with it, Gage and his army could still not be certain that, if it came to open violence, armed and angry American farmers could be controlled by comparatively small bodies of regulars. By August 1765, however, Gage's attention was no longer on Pennsylvania farmers, for the Stamp Act had raised problems closer at hand.

In July 1765, Gage had ordered a company of Royal Americans from Crown Point into Fort George in New York City upon the request of Governor Colden, who thought a guard was needed there "to secure it against the Negroes or a Mob."[64] Colden was obviously anticipating

[62] Grant to Gage, 16 September 1765, Gage MSS.

[63] Wainwright, *Croghan*, 212-218. Even Bouquet sympathized with the country people against Croghan; Bouquet to Gage, 10 April 1765, BM Add. MSS. 21637, 105.

[64] Colden to Gage, 8 July 1765, *Colden Letter Book*, II, 23; Gage to Colden, 8 July 1765, *Colden Papers*, VII, 46.

trouble, and Gage noted in his report to the Secretary of State that the customs officers in New York had also asked for military assistance in the performance of their duty.[65]

The first disorder over the Stamp Act occurred where there were no troops: Boston (August 14 and 26), Newport (August 27), and Annapolis (September 2).[66] Immediately Colden requested a battalion of regulars for New York City: "The only method in my opinion to prevent mischief is to have such a military force present as may effectually discourage all opposition to the Laws. A weak force which the Seditious can have any hopes of overcoming may be productive of great mischiefs."[67] Five days later, however, the Governor's Council officially advised Colden "that the Number of Troops at present in Garrison is sufficient for the Defence of the Fort; and that it will be more safe for the Government to shew a Confidence in the People, then to discover its distrust of them by Calling in any assistance to the Civil Power."[68] The question was somewhat academic in any case, because Gage had no battalions to spare, and even company-size reinforcements were located several weeks away in the Champlain Valley.

There was another question, also academic at the time, but which could not be answered simply by having more troops available. When Gage had first mentioned the reinforcement of New York to Colden, he reminded him in writing "that the Military can do nothing by themselves; but must act wholy and solely in obedience to the Civil Power . . . and when Troops are granted . . . , they are no longer under my Command, or can the officers do any thing with their Men, but what the Civil Magistrate shall command. This must be the situation of Military Force, and ought to be so, in every Country of Liberty."[69] Colden, in turn, reminded Gage of what they both could expect from the New York city officials: "In case the civil Magis-

[65] Gage to Conway, 10 August 1765, *Gage Corr.,* I, 64.
[66] For the best general account, see Morgan, *Stamp Act.*
[67] To Gage, 2 September 1765, *Colden Letter Book,* II, 30-31.
[68] 27 September 1765, *Colden Papers,* VII, 61.
[69] 31 August 1765, *ibid.,* 58.

trates cannot or are not willing to do their duty, you must Judge what is incumbent on you as well as on me in such case, when all civil Authority is at an end."[70] Clearly each was trying to shift the responsibility for using force to the other.

While Gage could not reasonably hope to control the city with a handful of men, he prepared to hold Fort George at the southern tip of Manhattan; at the same time he looked beyond Manhattan. To Governors Bernard of Massachusetts, Franklin of New Jersey, and Sharpe of Maryland, he offered 100 men each if they thought such a force would be useful.[71] But the troops for Boston would have to come from Halifax, those for New Jersey from Crown Point, and those for Annapolis from Fort Pitt; moreover, 100 men was a number which might be provocative without being effective. Franklin, however, thought at first that a force of that size would be sufficient, but, as in New York, his Council opined that he "ought not to have Recourse to the Aid of the Military till the last Necessity."[72] Neither Bernard nor Sharpe accepted the offer.

On October 23, the vessel carrying the stamps arrived at New York, escorted by two frigates. A crowd of 2,000 waited in vain for the stamps to be landed; instead, the stamps were secretly slipped into Fort George that night.[73] A company of artillery, fortuitously arrived from England, brought the garrison up to about 130 men. As the effective date of the Stamp Act (November 1) drew near, Major Thomas James, artillery officer and commander of the garrison, did what he could to strengthen the fort but did little to weaken the threat. An officious man by his own admission, he shooed "Ladies and Gentlemen" off the ramparts that they might not peek at the new defenses; he publicly

[70] 2 September 1765, *Colden Letter Book,* II, 30-31.

[71] Gage to Conway, 23 September 1765, *Gage Corr.,* I, 68; Gage to Franklin, 16 September 1765, Gage MSS.

[72] 25 September 1765. Relevant correspondence from the Gage MSS. is printed in *New Jersey Historical Society Proceedings,* LVI (1938), 220-225.

[73] *The Montresor Journals,* ed. G. D. Scull (*NYHSC for 1881*), 336.

threatened to ram stamps down New York throats with his sword, and—if the city should "rise"—to chase the rascals out of town with two dozen regulars.[74] John Ketcham, shoemaker, replied by openly threatening to bury Major James alive if he caught him outside the fort.[75] Ketcham and his friends warmed up on Hallowe'en, roaming the streets, crying "Liberty," and breaking a number of windows. Major James reaped what he had sown the following night. As a huge mob swirled before the fort gate, "with the grossest ribaldry" hanging old Colden's effigy, burning his carriage, and taunting the troops to fire, it also found time to sack the Major's house.[76] By this time, the situation had lost whatever light-hearted quality it had previously had. Reinforced by Marines from His Majesty's ships, the garrison now numbered 183 of all ranks. The engineers built earth and wood "lodgements" on the ramparts and bastions for squads of musketeers, distributed hand grenades, spiked the guns of the Battery, erected *chevaux de frise* and scattered the ugly "crows' feet" behind the gates and sally ports, covered them with artillery, and sited the remaining artillery and anchored the two frigates so as to obtain raking, interlocking fire along the faces of the fort. Their only unsolvable problem was the way in which rising ground to the northward and the houses built on it "commanded" the fort.[77] The zealous Major James, already under orders from the Board of Ordnance to return to England, found it expedient to obey them, perhaps on Gage's suggestion.[78] Gage himself sent secret orders to Bradstreet on November 4 to move the companies at Fort Stanwix and at Lake George, and three of the four companies at Crown Point, to Albany with all possible speed.[79] The rumor ran that the mob would storm the fort on the night of Guy Fawke's day, and that day passed in hectic

[74] James to Colden [early 1766?], *Colden Papers*, VII, 99.
[75] Colden to John Cruger, 31 October 1765, *Colden Letter Book*, II, 53.
[76] Colden to Conway, 5 November 1765, *ibid.*, 54-56.
[77] *Montresor Journals*, 336-339; *Colden Papers*, VII, 87-88.
[78] *Montresor Journals*, 339.
[79] Gage MSS.

negotiations among Colden, the Council, the city government, and Gage. Gage refused to take any initiative, but,
when formally queried by the Governor and Council, replied "that tho a fire from the Fort might disperse the
Mob, it would not quell them," and that to fire would start
"a Civil War, at a time when there's nothing prepared or
can timely be so, to make opposition to it."[80] This of course
was the way out that everyone sought, and, with Gage's
opinion to support him, Colden in effect capitulated by
turning the stamps over to the city government and allowing them to be "escorted" to the city hall by a large crowd.[81]

From this affair, Gage gained a reputation for moderation. As George Croghan, who had been passing through
New York at the time after his return from the Illinois
country, put it, Colden was thought to have acted "with
Great Sperrett and Resolution . . . [and] was Determined
to Support the perrogatife of the house of Comons," but
"he and the General Did Nott agree in Sentiments the
Later Indeavering to plase the pople."[82] There were at
least two important reasons for Gage's moderation. One
was the fact that while Colden and his house were inside
Fort George, Gage lived outside and was reluctant to take
the drastic and humiliating step of seeking refuge with
the garrison. Although Gage remained unmolested on October 31 and November 1, there was a rumor current on
November 5 that the mob planned to "collect" him and
some other "friends to the Government," and to march
them in front when they assaulted the fort.[83] A more available justification for moderation was the location of the
ordnance storehouses: containing great quantities of arms
and ammunition left over from the war, they were outside
the fort, on the East River.[84] Although Gage was fairly
certain the fort could be held against any initial assault,

[80] To Colden, 5 November 1765, *Colden Papers*, VII, 70.
[81] Gage to Conway, 4 and 8 November 1765, *Gage Corr.*, I, 70-73.
[82] To Johnson, 18 November 1765, *Johnson Papers*, XI, 969-970.
[83] *Montresor Journals*, 339.
[84] *Ibid.*, 352.

the resulting loss of the ordnance stores would provide the mob with what they needed to wage war.

Events at most other places where troops were stationed never reached the pitch of New York in early November. Both Philadelphia and Albany had their Stamp Act "riots," forcing the local stamp distributors to resign, but at neither place was the use of the regular garrison ever a question. News of more serious disorders elsewhere—at Boston and New York—seems to have been decisive in weakening the will of either magistrates or stamp distributors to make a fight of it. From Charleston came a different story, however. There Governor Bull put up some resistance. In early October, he had asked the local commander to delay plans for reinforcing Fort Charlotte in the backcountry because "he expected an atempt would be made to resque some of the prisoners now in Goal here [at Charleston] to stand their Trials."[85] When the stamps arrived, Bull, like Colden, put them in Fort Johnson in Charleston harbor, and requested a sergeant and 12 men of the 60th to guard them.[86] This left but five regulars in the town, hardly an impressive police force.[87]

But Governor James Wright of Georgia had no regulars at all in Savannah (although there were small detachments of the 60th at Forts Augusta and Frederica), and he, alone of all the governors of the older colonies, executed the Stamp Act. Moreover, he did it by using military force. During the war, Georgia had raised several troops of mounted rangers, and these rangers had been placed, somewhat informally, on the British military establishment. They were under the Governor's rather than Gage's command, and, perhaps through oversight, had not been disbanded with the New York and South Carolina independent companies in 1763. Wright used these troops, not by requisitioning their support, but by putting on his sword and leading them himself, first in awing the local Sons

[85] Capt.-Lt. Ralph Phillips to Gage, 9 October 1765, Gage MSS.
[86] Bull to Gage, 22 March 1766, *ibid.*
[87] 16 November 1765, SC Council Journal, 1763-1766, folio 655.

of Liberty, then in facing down several hundred armed men from the backcountry.[88] Eventually, he too had to transfer the stamps to a warship, but his greatest setback came from South Carolina. There, Bull had secured the stamps, but had done nothing to distribute them or to curb disorder in Charleston. Finally, Bull permitted unstamped ship clearances when Governor James Grant of East Florida said that regular troops at Saint Augustine were in danger of starvation if the provision contractors could not replenish their stores from South Carolina.[89]

After the first serious riot in New York, Gage, for all his reputed moderation, was convinced that never again should he or provincial governments be caught without the forces necessary to control disorder. His orders to Bradstreet were not simply an ad-hoc response to turbulence in New York City, but were also the first step in a contemplated change of colonial military policy. Before the frost set in, Gage had moved 200 Royal Americans southward into Albany, and 100 Highlanders from Fort Pitt to Lancaster.[90] In orders to the commander at Charleston, he told him to give Bull all possible support; the backcountry would have to take its chances until the seaboard returned to obedience, and, if disturbances continued, the outposts must be given up.[91]

In post-mortem reports to the Secretary of State, Gage made clear his premises and conclusions. "During these Commotions in North-America," he confessed in January 1766, "I have never been more at a Loss how to Act, to perform the Duty which I owe to my King and Country, and at the same Time prevent any Cause of Clamor against Military Power and Influence, being well aware that the bitterest Invectives would have been thrown out against the Army had I given them an opening." Although the governors had been afraid to employ the small forces

[88] Abbot, *Georgia Governors,* 103-125.
[89] SC Council Journal, 1763-1766, folios 664-667. This incident has the smell of collusion about it.
[90] Gage to Conway, 21 December 1765, *Gage Corr.,* I, 77.
[91] To Capt.-Lt. Phillips, 19 January 1766, Gage MSS.

available, and the magistrates—at least in New York—had sided with the Sons of Liberty, "I thought Myself justified in ordering by my own Authority, Such Troops as could be got at, to March into the inhabited Country."[92] A month later, he went further by asserting that it was his "Duty when I See the King's Affairs in such a Situation, to do everything which depends on me for the Support of his Service, and I must take my own Resolution; which is to draw all the Force I can, and as soon as it can be done, into these Provinces. . . . A New Disposition must be made of the troops to answer the Purposes intended."[93] Perhaps Gage believed that a recent Order-in-Council, directing governors to apply for military and naval assistance if all legal means failed to keep order, would stiffen future resistance.[94]

The Secretary of State was Henry Seymour Conway, military hero and one of the followers of the Marquis of Rockingham who had succeeded in overthrowing the government of Grenville, Halifax, and the Duke of Bedford. The stand of the Rockinghamites on questions of policy was initially vague, claiming as they did to represent the thinking of William Pitt who had refused to take office. At first Conway praised Gage for his initiative in concentrating troops toward the seaboard, and expressed doubt only concerning the defeatist advice given to Colden on November 5.[95] Although the evidence is thin, it appears that the Rockingham ministry even toyed for a time with the idea of enforcing the Stamp Act.[96] But their felt need to oppose everything associated with the Grenville ministry, along

[92] To Conway, 16 January 1766, *Gage Corr.*, I, 80-83.
[93] 22 February 1766, *ibid.*, 83-85.
[94] 6 September-23 October 1765, *APCC*, IV, #621.
[95] Conway to Gage, 15 December 1765, *Gage Corr.*, II, 29-31.
[96] See Tom Ramsden to Charles Jenkinson, 30 November 1765, *Jenkinson Papers*, 393; Lord Northington to the King, 12 December 1765, *Geo. III Corr.*, 428-429; Edmund Burke to Charles O'Hara, 31 December 1765, *Burke Corr.*, ed. Copeland, I, 229; Horace Walpole to Horace Mann, 29 February [1 March] 1766, *Walpole Corr.*, ed., Lewis, XXII, 400-401; and Conway to Bernard, 24 October 1765, in HL, Temple Correspondence.

with their assessment of the mind of Pitt and the general
political situation, led them to move for repeal. Consequently, in May 1766, Conway informed Gage that "bringing any
considerable number of Troops into the Interior of those
Provinces, . . . will probably be looked upon as an object
of Jealousy and may occasion Difficulties. . . . The Number, You mention, of near three Regiments in New York
County only will scarce be found necessary or advisable in
the present Situation."[97] This expression of opinion con-
stitutes one of the clearest guides to policy Gage received
between the Stamp Act and the Tea Act of 1773. But the
Rockingham ministry was weak and Gage, if he did not
violate this instruction, could never bring himself to accept its spirit of conciliation rather than coercion. And even
before Conway's letter reached America, the situation was
being complicated by several new factors as the focus of
military police action once again shifted, from the town
back to the countryside.

Comparative peace returned to New York City after November 5, but some friction continued as the Sons of Liberty pressed home their victory and awaited news from
England. On a Sunday in December, an artilleryman bayo-
neted a Liberty boy; several months later, an officer of the
Royal Americans received a beating on the Common at
dusk from five Sons of Liberty, who also broke his sword
for him when he tried to use it. There was some talk among
the inhabitants of fighting up to their knees in blood if the
British government should try to enforce the Stamp Act.
When the Sons of Liberty held a procession in February,
they stopped by British army headquarters and gave three
cheers. But Gage, who was standing outside with several
officers, did not join "in the Huzza," and the Liberty boys
"told them—that they would have their Hats off yet before they were done with them."[98]

A few months later, no hats had come off, but the shoe
was on the other foot. During the winter, apparently encouraged by the Stamp Act disorders, tenant farmers in

[97] 20 May 1766, *Gage Corr.*, II, 37-38.
[98] *Montresor Journals*, 352.

Westchester, Dutchess, and Albany Counties began to take the law of land titles into their own hands. In every case, one of the Hudson River manor lords—Cortlandt, Philipse, Van Rensselaer, or Livingston—laid claim to land also claimed by others, namely, Massachusetts and Connecticut. The tenants held title from the latter provinces, and were either being evicted by the former or asked to meet exorbitant demands in order to retain their land. The dispute was not a new one, having its origins in the previous century, and its history had been punctuated by violent outbreaks.[99]

When three of the Westchester rioters were arrested and brought to the New York jail in April, their compatriots threatened to march on the city and forcibly release them. Governor Henry Moore, who had arrived at his new post a week after the Stamp Act riots the previous November, called on General Gage for support. Gage complied, and kept the city garrison on alert. When 500 of the rioters entered the city limits, Moore published a proclamation offering a reward for the ringleaders, and requested military aid; the rioters quickly dispersed.[100] Engineer John Montresor typified the military awakening to certain facts. On April 25, he had noted in his diary: "Levelling esteemed to be of service and moved by many of the Sons of Liberty"; but on May 1 he wrote: "Sons of Liberty great opposers to these Rioters as they are of opinion no one is entitled to Riot but themselves."[101] It could hardly have been otherwise, for not only were the sponsors of the Sons of Liberty lawyers like William Smith, Jr., and John Morin Scott who had associated themselves closely with the great landed families like the Livingstons, but their recent rallying cry had been "Liberty and Property."

[99] Oscar Handlin, "The Eastern Frontier of New York," *New York History*, xviii (1937), 50-75. An excellent account of the trouble in Dutchess County is in Staughton Lynd, *Anti-Federalism in Dutchess County, New York* (Chicago, 1962), 37-54.

[100] *Montresor Journals*, 360-363; Moore to Conway, 30 April 1766, *NYCD*, vii, 825-826.

[101] *Montresor Journals*, 361-363.

Disorder was not so easily quelled in Dutchess County. The 28th Regiment happened to be en route from Quebec to New York, and Gage ordered the commander to put his troops at the disposal of the sheriff or other magistrates.[102] Late in June Major Arthur Brown led his 330 men into action under direction of the sheriff against the squatters on the Philipse estate, and, after three soldiers had been wounded, one mortally, Brown's force captured 60 of them. He described them as "a Sett of Miserable, harden'd Wretches, who don't seem to understand what they are about."[103] The 28th left two companies in Dutchess County to guard the prison and Governor Moore informed the Secretary of State of the "greatest commendations" given to the regiment by the county officials "not only for the exact discipline they maintained but for their great readiness in going on any service required by which means the rioters were so soon reduced."[104] One should recall that this was the regiment which had cut off Thomas Walker's ear twenty months earlier.

The 28th was marching to New York when Moore again asked Gage for help, this time in Albany County where Robert Noble and his friends from Massachusetts had been raising hell on Livingston Manor and around Claverack for more than a decade, and had just routed a sheriff's posse. Gage immediately sent Captain John Clarke and 100 men of the 46th Regiment up the Hudson; his orders to them mixed toughness with caution. He told Clarke, in accordance with the stereotyped instructions issued by the War Office for handling riots, to act only under the direction of the civil authorities, which included the ambiguous warning "not to repell Force by Force, unless in Case of absolute Necessity, and being thereunto required by the Civil Magistrate."[105] At the same time, however, Clarke was to use "all means" to capture proclaimed traitors (as

[102] Gage to the commanding officer, 28th Regiment, and to Moore, 19 June 1766, Gage MSS.
[103] To Gage, 30 June 1766, *ibid.*
[104] To Conway, 14 July 1766, *NYCD,* VII, 846.
[105] Christopher D'Oyley to Gage, 24 October 1765, WO 4/988.

distinct from mere rioters), and was to use artillery in case the enemy barricaded themselves and the magistrates approved.[106] But in a subsequent letter, Gage warned Clarke not to go into Massachusetts without a magistrate from that province; he found it necessary to mention this, "as you are just upon the borders of two Governments, who I find seem to think very differently upon the present Subject of Dispute."[107]

Clarke and his men landed at Livingston Manor, marched to its western edge, pulled down the houses of the principal rioters at "Nobletown," and drove Noble's followers before them. But Noble kept his men together as a body in the field, and Clarke, who had served in Indian country before coming to New York, found that, instead of dispersing a mob, he was engaged in fighting a guerrilla war. Bands of rioters kept popping up in unexpected places, and Clarke responded by destroying or occupying their houses and by guarding their crops, nearly ready for harvest. Clarke successfully used feints to draw out the rioters, and always moved his detachments as if they were in Indian country. The rioters responded by using Massachusetts as a sanctuary, flitting back and forth across the border, now to threaten, now to recuperate. "They advance and retire at pleasure," wrote Clarke, "playing a Game by no means Satisfactory."[108] He found great difficulty in keeping suitable magistrates at his side: first there was only old Justice Ten Eyck, "a poor *Ignorant Man*"; then Justice Killian Rensselaer, who returned home "being *weary'd* out"; and finally two men hastily deputized by the sheriff.[109] Although surprisingly little blood was shed, the

[106] Instructions to Capt. John Clarke, 19 July 1766, Gage MSS. Gage had been angered by the casualties suffered by the 28th. He wrote to Maj. Brown: "If these Sons of Liberty fire upon You, You will not then trouble yourself about Orders, and I am to desire if they fire upon the King's Troops, and become Rebels that You will give them a good Dressing, and beat these Sons of Liberty into Loyal Subjects." 2 July 1766, *ibid.*

[107] 23 July 1766, *ibid.*

[108] 29 July 1766, *ibid.*

[109] From Clarke, 1 and 17 August 1766, *ibid.*

legal niceties tended to be lost in this exhausting and nerve-wracking work. Clarke was disgusted that he could not get permission to destroy the crops. Even Gage, who had earlier warned him about crossing the border, told him to "pursue, Kill or Apprehend" anyone who fired on the King's troops "wherever you can, without any Distinction of Government, or further aid of Magistrates."[110] Finally, after blocking the Claverack and Kinderhook roads, Clarke took up a position with his main body on the eastern slope of the intervening mountain, which he believed to be 400 yards from the Massachusetts border. The residents of Egremont, Massachusetts, did not agree; they were sure British troops had come onto Massachusetts soil, and they were genuinely afraid that they were about to be put to fire and sword. Justices Woodbridge, Williams, and Dwight, the Berkshire County sheriff, and some officials from nearby towns, backed by a 350-man "posse," called on Clarke at his camp. Clarke refused to budge or to let them serve a warrant on Colonel Robert Rensselaer, who was with him, and, in effect, called their bluff by demanding to know by whose authority the posse had been raised. Apparently unnerved by the prospect of a full-scale battle, put on the defensive by Clarke's questions, and rattled by his lofty manner, the magistrates fell to accusing one another and finally withdrew. Subsequently Clarke withdrew his troops west of the mountain, thereby agreeing with Justice Williams, "a half pay Officer of Shirleys Regiment" who had "acted with prudence."[111]

There was nothing equivocal about the outcome. Up and down the Hudson Valley, the New England claims had been smashed, never to threaten the New York manor lords again. But the New England side of the story had its effect. Perhaps the local magistrates wrote truly to Gage and Moore that the 28th Regiment had been a model of good

[110] 4 August 1766, *ibid.*

[111] From Clarke, 19 August 1766, *ibid.* An interesting account of the meeting between Clarke and the Massachusetts men is the Deposition of William Henry Ludlow, a New York merchant from Claverack, 27 August 1766, HM 1506.

behavior, "not having taken the least thing during their Stay in the Country, and even refusing to plunder the Houses of Some of the proclaimed Rioters, tho' desired to do it."[112] There was another version current, however; according to it, the troops "burnt and destroyed some of their houses, pillaged and plundered others, stove in their cyder barrels, turned their provisions out . . . into the open streets, Ript open their feather beds. It was beyond the powers of language to paint in lively images the Horror! the surprize and astonishment of this poor distressed people on that occasion . . . their habitations some pillag'd, and others of them invelloped in flames . . . deprived of all their sustenance for which they had labored, sweat and fatigue themselves all the days of their lives."[113] The accounts from Egremont of the conduct of the 46th at Nobletown found their way not only into the Boston newspapers but into the *Virginia Gazette* as well, and described looting, destruction, and the abuse of children.[114]

It can hardly be doubted that the army, despite few casualties on either side,[115] had gone too far. But much worse was the way in which Gage and his troops had been used to settle, once and for all, a dispute over property in favor of New York landlords. Those "magistrates," whom Gage was ever anxious to obey, had in this instance proved to be something less than that pristine abstraction, "Civil Authority," which so often appears in his letters. When the Earl of Shelburne, Secretary of State for colonial affairs in the new Chatham (Pitt) ministry, heard of it, he rapped the knuckles of both Gage and Moore: "Accounts from Boston give room to think that the whole of this Affair has

[112] Gage to Conway, 15 July 1766, *Gage Corr.*, I, 99.

[113] "Geographical, Historical Narrative or Summary of the Present Controversy Between Daniel Ninham . . . and . . . Colonel Frederick Philipse," 40 (Lansdowne MSS., LC transcript, vol. 707), quoted in Handlin, *New York History*, XVIII, 71.

[114] 12 and 16 September 1766.

[115] The only death I have found is that of George Henry of the 28th, killed by three men near Robeson's store in Dutchess County as he guarded provisions en route to the troops. *Pennsylvania Journal*, 14 August 1766.

not been transacted with the Temper and Prudence requisite on such an Occasion. . . . It is to be hoped that the Rights of the Parties were very well ascertained before the Military Power was called in to the aid of the Civil, for few Exigencies can justify such a kind of Decision."[116]

Policing the Interior

If Thomas Gage, by the middle of 1766, had learned that the use of soldiers against civilians, whether farmers or burghers, in the settled areas was a treacherous and frustrating business, he was also becoming more aware of the difficulties of policing Indian lands and trade. In fact, his ever-growing experience was leading him slowly to the conclusion that the problems of the Indians and the West were beyond the capacity of his army, or at least beyond the economic and political capacity of the British government to support it, and that the problems of the East, both town and country, would require a level of military force that could be drawn only from the West. This line of thought had received a nudge from home. Lord Barrington, who had succeeded Ellis as Secretary at War when Grenville and Halifax went out and Rockingham and Conway had come in, asked the question which Gage must have been asking himself: Why not withdraw from the western posts?

Barrington, an experienced Secretary at War, had returned to this office almost by accident on the fall of the Grenville ministry, but he would not leave it again until 1778.[117] In 1765, he appears to have been almost as ig-

[116] Shelburne to Gage, 11 December 1766, *Gage Corr.*, II, 47; Shelburne to Moore, 11 December 1766, *NYCD*, VII, 879.

[117] By the rules of the game, Barrington (then Treasurer of the Navy) should have gone out of office when the Duke of Newcastle, his former patron whom he had "betrayed," returned to power with Rockingham in 1765. He did not go out because the King was interested in the army and thought Barrington would be a good Secretary at War. This dumbfounded a number of politicians. See Horace Walpole and Charles James Fox to Lord Holland, 19 and [20] July [1765], *Fox Letters*, 241-242; also, Barrington to Bernard, 5 August 1765, *Barrington-Bernard Corr.*, 86-87.

norant of American affairs as his predecessor, but unlike
Welbore Ellis he was interested in the army and was anxious to know more about the sizeable part of it stationed
in the colonies. In one of the first letters of a private correspondence with Gage which was to continue until 1775,
Barrington suggested that, if the Proclamation of 1763 was
right, then forts to the west of the Indian boundary line
were wrong. "Why keep Garrisons in a Country pro-
fessedly intended to be a Desert?" he queried, but added,
"I am sensible how liable I am to error in matters of this
sort. . . ." He asked Gage's opinion and promised never to
quote him without permission. In conclusion, he suggested
that troops withdrawn from the West be concentrated in
"any convenient place near the Sea."[118] This was the opening statement in a long if not great debate on colonial military policy; although Barrington would learn much about
America from the lengthy, cautious letters of the Commander in Chief, he never receded from the basic points
in this first proposal.

Gage received the letter from Barrington at the same
time that he heard from Illinois that the war was finally
over. After a 1,000-mile journey from Fort Pitt, Captain
Thomas Stirling and his detachment of Highlanders had
accepted Fort Chartres from its French commander within
hours of the moment at which Barrington suggested the
British army be withdrawn from the West.[119]

The great difficulty, perhaps the impossibility, of regulating the northern fur trade by confining it to the western
posts was already becoming apparent. Even before the trade
was officially reopened after the Indian rebellion, it had
begun to be evident that someone was needed to keep an
eye on the police. When Bradstreet arrived in Detroit on
his expedition against the Indians in 1764, he stopped (as
he should have) all fur traders on their way from Montreal
to Michilimackinac. But Bradstreet seems to have had several thousand pounds worth of Indian trade goods with

[118] Barrington to Gage, 10 October 1765, "Private," Gage MSS.
[119] Gage to Johnson, 25 and 30 December 1765, *Johnson Papers,*
XI, 986-989.

him, labeled "King's stores," with which he, Commodore Joshua Loring of the Navy, and several others planned to make a killing. When the fur traders remonstrated with Bradstreet, he is said to have replied in his usual tactful manner: "God-Dam you All for a Parsel of Raskels, I will have some of you hanged." The traders soon learned, however, that for a bribe the officers would let them and their goods pass.[120]

If Gage did not know of Bradstreet's peculations, he was highly suspicious of George Croghan and his connection with Baynton, Wharton, and Morgan, which had caused so much trouble in the spring of 1765. Both Gage and Johnson had to depend on Croghan for information and the diplomatic handling of all those Indians on the right bank of the Ohio, from Fort Pitt to Fort Chartres and south of Detroit. Croghan was energetic, shrewd, generous, colorful, and highly intelligent in an uneducated way. Unfortunately, Croghan was also dishonest. He could be relied upon to perform brilliantly in the wild and murky atmosphere of an Indian congress; he could hardly be expected to assist in the strict and impartial enforcement of regulations governing the fur trade or the purchase of Indian land.[121]

When the Montreal fur traders arrived at Michilimackinac in the spring of 1765, they found the commandant, Captain William Howard of the 17th Regiment, bound by his instructions from Gage to confine the trade to that post and not to let the traders winter among the Indians. The traders protested, and Howard, like the other post commanders, under orders to deal directly with Sir William Johnson on all matters pertaining to Indian affairs, referred their protest to the Indian superintendent.[122] One would expect Johnson, the champion of trade regulation, to support Howard's action. Instead, Sir William wrote

---

[120] Henry Bostwick to James Beekman, 10 December 1764, *Beekman Mercantile Papers, 1746-1799*, ed. Philip L. White (N.Y., 1956), II, 952-954.

[121] Wainwright, *Croghan*.

[122] 5 and 6 July 1765, *Johnson Papers*, XI, 825-829.

a whining reply to the traders, in which he said that royal, provincial, and military desires to limit trade to the posts "are too powerful for me to take upon me the giving so favorable an answer as I could wish," but that "I shall write to the General, and do all in my power to procure your Desire." He added that he was writing to Howard that nothing definite could be done at present, but noted parenthetically, "at the same [time] admitting such few Exceptions, as his present Situation, and knowledge of Affairs will enable him to make."[123]

When Gage heard of Howard's difficulty, he wrote to Johnson that now was the time to stand firm. "Cannadians will oppose the New Regulations, as much as they can in every other Place as well as Missilimakinak. And if they Succeed, there will be an End, and a total One, of our Regulations, and the Posts and Forts will be of no more Consequence."[124] Johnson replied that "You are of the Same opinion as Myself concerning the Traders Wintering with the Indians."[125] But that was not the way Howard or the traders heard it; Johnson told Howard that restriction was the government plan, that the main problem was French traders being too tricky for the English traders when there was no supervision (Johnson and Gage did agree on this point), that he should use caution, but that, as the man on the spot, he should also use his own discretion.[126]

It is little wonder that the next news from Michigan brought a strong complaint. Howard, supposedly under heavy pressure from the Indians, had permitted several traders to pass beyond Michilimackinac to winter among them. Among those traders not accorded this privilege were the representatives of Thomas Walker of Montreal. Mr. Walker must have been delighted to lead the protest against military interference with free trade. Walker and his as-

[123] [c. 7 August 1765], misdated 2 July 1765, *Johnson Papers,* XI, 816-817.
[124] 18 August 1765, *ibid.,* 903.
[125] 8 September 1765, *ibid.,* 927.
[126] [c. 7 August 1765], misdated 2 July 1765, *ibid.,* 814-816.

sociates protested to Johnson, to Gage, to Governor James Murray, and to the Board of Trade. Walker claimed, among other things, that Howard had been bribed.[127] Johnson said that he was "inclined to suppose that Captain Howard has acted with prudence and as a Commanding Officer ought to do, in which case complaints of that nature ought not to be countenanced."[128] Governor Murray, when he issued the required licenses to the fur traders in the following spring, decided not to include the clause limiting the trade to posts "Established by His Majesty and Garrisoned by His Troops." As an excuse for ending his cooperation in the plan of trade restriction, Murray said that he had heard from Gage "that many of the Posts in the upper Country will be Evacuated."[129]

Gage himself had no illusions about the meaning of the Howard affair. When Secretary of State Conway heard of Walker's complaint, he admonished Gage in stilted but strong language: "The Fur Trade . . . was the principal Benefit in view, in the Extent of Territory in North America, made by the late Peace." This was bad history, but the meaning was plain. He continued: "If by any misconduct of those engaged in the Publick Service, Individuals are molested, or interrupted in the Pursuit of it, such a Conduct must prove a publick Detriment: I shall therefore not only recommend it to You to preserve Mr Walker unmolested in his Pursuits; but I must farther desire you to be very attentive to what may be done at the several Posts. . . ."[130] Conway sent Walker a copy of the letter, who had the pleasure of inclosing it in a letter of his own to Gage. In July 1766, the Commander in Chief glumly noted that, "The Scheme of Indians trading at the Posts seems entirely broken through."[131]

Perhaps to be certain that no trick had been left untried, Gage had agreed earlier to let Johnson appoint an Indian

[127] F. Joliette to Walker, 14 August 1765, *ibid.*, IV, 822-823.
[128] To Gage, 14 November 1765, *ibid.*, 966-967.
[129] Murray to Johnson, 31 March 1766, *ibid.*, XII, 62-63.
[130] 27 March 1766, *Gage Corr.*, II, 34.
[131] To Johnson, 7 July 1766, *Johnson Papers*, XII, 135.

staff for all posts, and to pay the expenses out of army "extraordinaries." But Johnson soon was telling Gage that unless orders were given to the commanding officers to support the commissaries, the latter would "be in a great measure useless."[132] Gage replied that he would issue the post commanders "Orders to give what support and Assistance is in their power to the Commissarys."[133] Of course, "their power" to enforce trade regulations was legally nil, and Gage knew it.

Even felonies could not be adequately handled, for the shipment of an Indian or a trader (including all witnesses and evidence) back to provincial justice was clearly impracticable. Dramatic proof of this was offered in 1768. In 1765, Major Robert Rogers had finagled an appointment in London as commandant of Michilimackinac. Rogers, who was deeply in debt, was known to display all the energy and lack of scruples when confronted with opportunity that we have encountered in John Bradstreet. And Michilimackinac—small, remote, but important—spelled opportunity. Gage and Johnson were shocked by the appointment, and attempted to tie Rogers up with instructions. They succeeded only in leading Rogers into a disaster of some sort, even now not altogether clear. Accused of treason by the military officers at the post, Rogers was kept in close arrest throughout the winter 1767-1768, brought back to Quebec the following spring in irons, and acquitted. Whether Rogers was guilty or innocent, the whole affair was a travesty of justice, not to mention its effect on trade regulation.[134]

After 1765, the other most important post for fur trade regulation was Fort Chartres in Illinois. There, too, corrupt officials, both military and civil, vitiated the plan of using army posts as instruments of Indian diplomacy.[135]

[132] 4 July 1766, *ibid.,* 131.

[133] 14 July 1766, *ibid.,* 143. John Stuart also complained of the lack of legal power, Stuart to Johnson, 30 March 1766, *ibid.,* 55.

[134] See Cuneo, *Rogers.*

[135] See Clarence E. Carter, *Great Britain in the Illinois Country, 1763-1774* (Washington, 1910), and p. 281, below.

But long before Gage knew of these events, he had given up any hope of carrying out the original plan of trade control.

At about the same time, 1766 and 1767, Gage was learning that the Proclamation line could not be enforced. In June 1766 he heard that 500 families had settled beyond the line in the Fort Pitt area, on the Cheat and Monongahela Rivers and on Redstone Creek.[136] He informed Governors Penn, Franklin, and Francis Fauquier of Virginia, and said that he feared an Indian war if these unruly people were not removed.[137] Shortly before reprimanding Gage for using military force against the New York tenants, Secretary of State Shelburne told him that, as the settlers in the Pitt area seemed to be outside the boundaries of any province, Gage should take the initiative in removing them.[138] In September, Penn proclaimed the settlements illegal, and by the end of the year, Gage was telling the Fort Pitt commander to inform the settlers not to plant corn, because, if they were not gone by spring, "they will be driven from thence by a Military Force, which will destroy their Houses, plantations &ca."[139] In the spring, Gage once again told Fauquier, from whose province most of the settlers had come, that he was ready to supply force if needed.[140] The threat itself had had a momentary effect, causing many of the settlers to leave. But by November they had all returned and more, and Gage was informing Shelburne that he had not yet used force because there seemed to be a difference of opinion as to whether the area was Pennsylvania, Virginia, or Crown land.[141] Gage did not give up the attempt, but he must have known it was hopeless.

In all of the instances in which military coercion was

[136] Capt. Harry Gordon to Gage, 4 June 1766, Gage MSS.

[137] 2 July 1766, *ibid.*

[138] 13 September 1766, *Gage Corr.,* II, 44-46.

[139] To Capt. William Murray, 29 December 1766, Gage MSS.; *Pa. Col. Rec.,* IX, 327-328.

[140] 19 April 1767, Gage MSS.

[141] To Shelburne, 11 November 1767, *Gage Corr.,* I, 142-144. See also Capt. Edmondstone to Gage, 24 November 1767, and William Allen to Gage, 28 November 1767, Gage MSS.

attempted before 1768, there was a confusion of obstacles to effective action. First, there was the question of policy. Did the British ministry really want to regulate the fur trade, enforce the Indian boundary, and maintain order in town and country? Of course it did, in general, but specific cases posed certain difficulties which could not be easily solved by reference to a general policy. One difficulty was British dislike of military force, always an available political issue for the Opposition. Another was the fear that the discretionary power, necessarily given to colonial officials who were required to use force, would be abused. A third difficulty was the conflict of provincial interests almost inevitably involved when force was employed.

This conflict of provincial interests points to the second obstacle—the legal restrictions on the use of troops. In Indian territory, on the frontier, and in the countryside, property rights or the right of due process blocked quick and effective coercion. In the city, there were also legal difficulties, but they hardly seemed insurmountable, dependent as they were on the attitude and courage of magistrates appointed by the King's representative—the governor.

Preoccupation with these first two obstacles, policy and legality, seems to have obscured the third, an obstacle that might best be described as physical. Given a firm policy commitment by the British government, and granted some means of negotiating the legal obstacle, could coercion have succeeded? Could the fur trade have been effectively policed by a few thousand troops? Could the westward movement have been dammed? One is forced to think not, and certainly Gage had begun to sense it by 1766. But the same kinds of questions, asked of the populated seaboard, had not yet suggested a similar answer. Early in that year, William Pitt had pontificated: "In a good cause, on a sound bottom, the force of this country can crush America to atoms. I know the valour of your troops. I know the skill of your officers."[142] Perhaps because too concerned with

[142] Speech of 14 January 1766, *Chatham Corr.*, II, 372n.

the impediments to action represented by the uncertainties of policy and the complexities of law, British officials on both sides of the Atlantic were blinded to the physical limitations of military power.

The Stamp Act, by its failure to raise a revenue and by the violent resistance which it aroused, seemed to call for a new look at why and where the army was in America. The original location of units had, in fact, been more the aftermath of fighting Frenchmen and Indians than of any careful coordination of available force with the demands imposed by the missions assigned in 1763. If such coordination had been attempted, it surely would have foundered on the economizing policy which forbade repairs, much less new construction, of forts and barracks. In any case, Lord Barrington prepared to give the military situation the reappraisal it required.

VI · Confusion and Indecision

THE months between mid-1766, when William Pitt led a new group of men into office, and early 1768, when that group underwent important changes, make up the strangest phase in the breakdown of relations between Great Britain and her older colonies on the American continent. It was the period of Pitt's government, or properly speaking the Chatham ministry once Pitt had accepted a peerage, and it seems to have partaken of some of the madness which we now know afflicted that brilliant man. Understood to be sympathetic toward the cause of the colonies, and assisted by a Secretary of State believed to hold similar views, Chatham saw his own government, by sponsoring the Townshend Acts in 1767, violate the tacit understanding with America of 1766; saw it obtain the harshest law enacted against a colony before 1774 in the Restraining Act of 1767, which forbade the New York Assembly from doing any business until it had complied with the Quartering Act of 1765; and, in general, saw it fail to alter the tragic equation of 1763—an army in America requires a revenue from America.

By 1768, of course, fundamental constitutional questions had come to the fore that could not be swept away by any change in military policy alone. But the army was the root of most of the trouble, and the constitutional issues could not be resolved or even rationally considered until some questions about the army had been answered. Barrington, in the memorandum he had completed by May 1766, tried to pose the right questions.[1] Shelburne, Chatham's Secretary of State responsible for American affairs, tried to answer them. Both failed.

Barrington and His Plan

It would not be difficult to make a case that William Wildman, Viscount Barrington, was of the same ilk as Welbore Ellis; that is, a master placeman who bounced

[1] Dated 10 May 1766; printed in *IHC,* xi, 234-243.

from one second-rank office to another for a lifetime, with no thought except a determination not to "go out."[2] Sitting in the House of Commons because he was of the Irish peerage, Barrington had learned his politics with the Duke of Newcastle, for whom he had become a useful and hard-working subordinate. Barrington's job had been to round up the scattered government votes in the House which could not be controlled through an "interest."[3] By 1760, Barrington had had ten years' service as an Admiralty commissioner, and five as Secretary at War. When Ligonier, the Commander in Chief, seemed to be on the point of death in 1760, the old King countered the Duke of Cumberland's feeler concerning the succession to the supreme command with the remark that there would be no Captain General and that he himself and Barrington would run the army.[4] Apparently his grandson, George III, began with somewhat different ideas. Newcastle, when he resigned in early 1762, advised Barrington to remain with the government, which he did, but already Barrington had been translated from the War Office to the Exchequer. Later in the year, Newcastle changed his mind and began to urge his friends to resign. With much epistolary anguish, Barrington refused and stayed on, pleading his loyalty to the young King.[5] The King, in turn, told Pitt in 1763 that Barrington "was amongst those, whom he would never give up."[6] When the Grenville ministry fell in 1765, Barrington moved back to the War Office. When the Rockingham ministry fell in the following year, Barrington, by this time clearly dissociated from any political connection save with the Court, remained as Secretary at War. He would continue to survive political upheaval until his resignation in 1778.

[2] A brief sketch is in *DNB*, I, 1215. Shute Barrington, *The Political Life of William Wildman, Viscount Barrington* (London, 1812), prints extracts from a number of his letters.

[3] Namier, *Structure of Politics*, 236-238.

[4] Whitworth, *Ligonier*, 332.

[5] Namier, *England*, 378-379.

[6] Barrington, *Life*, 91.

There were contemporaries indeed who seemed to see no difference between Barrington and the unctuous, untalented Ellis. Henry Fox called Barrington "a frivolous, little minded man" who "has no regard to truth," and John Almon said that he was "ignorant of military affairs" and "hated by the army."[7] But there were differences between these two courtiers, and Horace Walpole, who disliked both men and maliciously compared them, saw how they differed. Barrington and Ellis, Walpole wrote, were similar types: "the former a little brighter by better parts, the other a little more amiable by less interestedness. . . . The former did not aim at making friends, but patrons; the latter dreaded making enemies. . . . Lord Barrington made civility and attention a duty; Ellis endeavoured to persuade you that that duty was a pleasure. You saw that Lord Barrington would not have been well-bred, if he had not been interested: you saw that if Ellis had been a hermit, he would have bowed to a cock-sparrow."[8] All independent evidence confirms Walpole's analysis. At the risk of some exaggeration, Ellis might be seen as the mindless aristocrat, dedicated to living in the royal orbit; Barrington, as a small-minded bureaucrat, dedicated to serving his royal master.

To delineate the character of such a man may seem of little importance, because the Secretary at War was a comparatively minor official, with no great power according to the constitution. He was not a member of the cabinet, nor was he expected to do more than supervise the routine administration of the army.[9] But in practice he acquired power in two ways: by having a strong supporter in the House of Commons, as Ellis had had in Fox; or by having the confidence of the King, as did Barrington. The

[7] Quoted in Alvord, *Mississippi Valley*, I, 247. The full quotation from Fox in *Life and Letters of Lady Sarah Lennox*, 40, says that everyone except Newcastle disliked Barrington.

[8] *Memoirs of George II*, ed. Holland, II, 141-142.

[9] Olive Gee Anderson, "The Constitutional Position of the Secretary at War, 1642-1855," *Journal of the Society for Army Historical Research*, XXXVI (1958), 165-169, is the best discussion of the subject.

unique importance of the Secretary at War lay in the frequency with which he entered the royal closet.[10] The early
Hanoverians looked after their army more carefully than
they did their government, and a Secretary at War who
did not displease them in the constant wrangling over the
appointment and promotion of army officers soon had a
line to the throne that some cabinet members might envy.

It was more than access to the closet and congenial
manner once in it that gave Barrington power. When, at
the age of forty-three, he broke his ties to the political community outside the Court and ceased to care what anyone except the King thought of him, he appears to have
taken on the Hanoverian attitude toward the army. The
first three Georges sought, without much apparent success,
to get politics out of the army.[11] It was an impossible task,
but they persevered. Colonelcies of course remained political plums, but more important for military efficiency
were the regimental officers who actually served in the
field. All three Kings wanted to abolish the purchase system of promotion, which was un-German, and all tried
mightily to regulate it. At least they sought a policy for
promotion that would be rational, be fair to the poorer
officer, give the Crown a major voice, and have some
relation to merit. It was an uphill fight, and the Crown
seldom won a battle when even moderate political influence was brought to bear. But it was in this fight that
Barrington enlisted. When he lost interest in active politics, and then returned to the War Office which he had
occupied during most of the Seven Years War, he found
a new interest—in both modern and contemporary senses
of the word—in becoming the guardian of the army itself.

Almon was at least partially right; there were some in
the army who hated Barrington, but they hated him for
being a stickler. When violations of the leave policy by
officers became flagrant, Barrington sent off a circular

[10] Edward R. Turner and Gaudens Megaro, "The King's Closet
in the Eighteenth Century," *AHR*, xlv (1940), 766-768. See, for
example, Welbore Ellis to Gage, 8 September 1764, WO 4/987.

[11] Hayes, *Rylands Library Bulletin,* xl (1958), 328-357.

letter about it to the various colonels, almost all of whom were colonels because of their political influence or connections. It was not a politic thing to do and the colonels were offended, but it was the only way within the existing system to enforce the leave policy.[12] With respect to a vacancy that had opened in North America, and for which there was a deserving aspirant on the spot, Barrington wrote privately that he was under pressure from many influential quarters, but concluded, *"I will take care of the officer absent and doing his duty."*[13] Even when his personal interests were intimately concerned, he was surprisingly straitlaced for an eighteenth century British politician. In one case, an officer serving under Gage and whose friends were "very considerable people" among Barrington's constituents had a fairly innocuous request to make; Barrington left it to Gage, and asked his help "so far as is proper, but no farther...."[14] In another case, he sent a note to Gage that his young grand-nephew was coming to America as a subaltern in the 7th Regiment: "Tho' I am desirous he should receive any proper marks of your Excellency's protection, & friendship for his uncle; yet I wish that no notice may be taken of him by you, except such as . . . will do him real service as well as honour."[15]

In the end, in 1778, Barrington would plead with the King to let him resign because his nerves were gone, and he could no longer hold his temper while rebuffing favor-seekers. Whatever his faults or limitations, this short, irascible man seemed to feel strongly about the army, to the point of offending men of influence who threatened its integrity. It was this feeling that had prompted him to recommend a shift in policy for the North American colonies, and that would draw him still further into colonial affairs during the next decade.

Barrington was concerned in 1766 by the bad effects of

[12] Whitworth, *Ligonier*, 385. This happened in 1766.
[13] Barrington to Gage, 8 April 1768, "Private," Gage MSS.
[14] 1 September 1770, *ibid.*
[15] 4 April 1775, *ibid.*

scattering 15 understrength battalions across half a continent. It was difficult and expensive to send them supplies and recruits, but equally important to him was the deterioration of discipline and military spirit when troops "were separated into many small Bodies, seen by nobody and seeing none but Indians for Years together." Worst of all—he wrote with the Stamp Act troubles fresh in memory—"there is no possibility of immediately assembling 500 Men on any Emergency foreign or Domestic." He wanted to get the army out of the bush, except for small garrisons at Oswego, Niagara, Detroit, Michilimackinac, Chartres, Pensacola, and perhaps Augusta in Georgia. He wanted to concentrate the army at Quebec and Halifax in the North, and at St. Augustine in the South, where it would be ready for any emergency.

In order to justify his proposals, Barrington then proceeded to develop a comprehensive rationale for the change: By the Proclamation of 1763, he wrote, the American interior was meant to remain an Indian "desert." Accordingly, there was no good reason for British regulars being there. Little packets of soldiers could not defend the border, nor could they hold down the Indians, though soldiers might likely provoke them. The fur trade was not worth the cost of protecting it. In any case, the Indians could come to the traders as easily as the traders could go to them. Barrington had tried to refine his ideas by advice from Gage, Johnson, and James Robertson, who was then in England on business, but his plan for the interior emerged as a curious mixture of good sense and fundamental misconceptions.[16]

Barrington was probably correct in seeking to withdraw the army from its costly and not very useful deployment, but, by tying his specific proposal to a broad and controversial statement of imperial policy involving Indian management, western lands, and the fur trade, he raised opposition where he might have won support. The pity is, Barrington was right, but for the wrong reasons.

[16] Barrington to Gage, 8 May 1766, "Private," Gage MSS. Gage's advice to Barrington, 18 December 1765, is in *Gage Corr.,* II, 318-324.

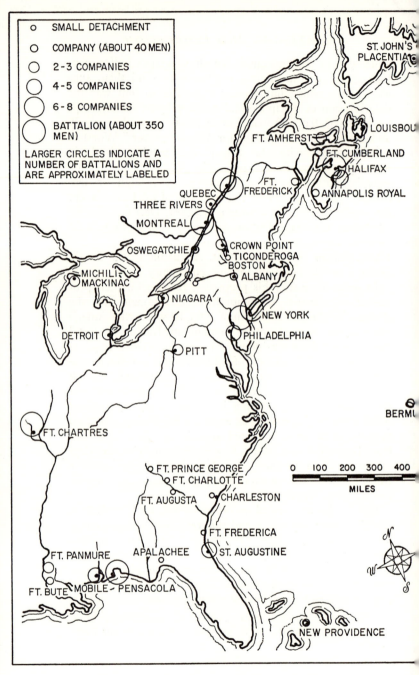

The Army in 1766, after the Stamp Act troubles and the occupation of the Illinois country.

Shelburne and the Tumultuous Session, 1766-1767

The Earl of Shelburne was the key figure in the tortuous, indecisive course on the American question followed by the Chatham ministry from mid-1766 until the end of 1767. Only thirty years old, he was disliked and mistrusted by almost all of his political associates, including the King. There were reasons for this: his personality—a mixture of hauteur and shyness; his self-conscious intellectuality; his claim to the confidence of the inscrutable Chatham; and, not the least of the reasons, his rapid swing in allegiance from Henry Fox, to the Earl of Bute, and then to William Pitt in the political melee of 1762-1763.[17] Both Shelburne and Chatham saw Barrington's plan in September 1766, and, according to Barrington, agreed with it "almost in every point."[18] Yet it took Shelburne well over a year to reach a decision of his own, and it would be more than two years before the Chatham government could decide. Why the delay, and what was its effect?

Upon becoming the Secretary of State responsible for colonial affairs, Shelburne, like Barrington, knew that something had to be done about the army. Perhaps that is why he seemed pleased by Barrington's plan, to know at least that someone else in the government was concerned. But, again like Barrington, Shelburne saw the problem largely in terms of what impinged most immediately on his own position. For the moment the general question of what to do with the army was clouded by sparse and contradictory information, and it would have to wait. The questions of the enforcement of the Quartering Act, and of the cost of the military establishment were, on the contrary, specific and pressing. They could not wait, and it was to them that Shelburne had to give his attention.

As the next session of Parliament drew closer, money was uppermost in the minds of more than a few British

[17] An excellent account of Shelburne's early career is in John Norris, *Shelburne and Reform* (London, 1963), Chaps. I-II.
[18] Barrington to Gage, 12 September 1766, "Private," Gage MSS.

politicians. The year was 1766, but fiscally the Seven Years War seemed never to have ended. The price of wheat was as high as it had been in the worst year of the war, and the King opened Parliament with an expression of fear that "a Spirit of the most daring Insurrection has in divers Parts broke forth in Violences of the most criminal Nature."[19] He was speaking of British, not American, riots. There were some who blamed it all on a dislocated economy, a result of high levels of debt and taxation. The principal source of revenue, the land tax, was still at its wartime level of four shillings per pound of income. The major reason for this situation seemed to lie in the continuation of another wartime practice.

It was the custom to vote money in the annual army estimates only for the pay and rations of the land forces. The Board of Ordnance, completely separate from either fighting service, received an annual appropriation for munitions and fortifications. In peacetime, there were few other military expenses, because clothing, medical care, and even pensions were simply deducted from the soldier's meager pay. In wartime, of course, the cost per soldier shot up, but the additional funds traditionally were voted separately, and labeled "Extraordinaries." The trouble was that by 1766 the Extraordinaries had not withered away as they were supposed to do, but instead remained, in their isolation from the army estimates, highly visible and embarrassing. In fact, Extraordinaries during the past two years had almost equalled one shilling of the land tax—roughly a half-million pounds Sterling. And a great part of those Extraordinaries had gone to support the new army in North America.[20]

To pay and feed 15 battalions in America cost roughly £200,000 according to the army estimates.[21] But in 1764

[19] *Commons Journals,* XXXI, 3.

[20] The regular estimate, the extraordinary account, and the Ordnance estimate were each published in consolidated form, so that one must know the names of regiments, garrisons, and contractors in order to disentangle the American items. See below pp. 338-340.

[21] *Commons Journals,* XXX, 470-471. The total of £197,865 is for

and 1765, troop movements, transportation of rations into the backcountry, building and repair of posts, and various expenses connected with keeping most of the army in the wilderness required an additional, "Extraordinary" outlay of well over £200,000.[22] Ordnance expenses for America, which also carried an "Extraordinary" account, were about £45,000 more.[23] There was, in truth, nothing very "extraordinary" about these expenditures, unless it was the way in which the British government handled them. Rather, they were a reasonably accurate indication of what it cost to carry out the decision of 1763. But, by voting them separately, all members of Parliament were annually reminded of that cost, and found it easy to connect it with the level of taxation. Even more disturbing was the fact that "extraordinaries" were voted only after they were spent, the disbursements having been made by the Paymaster General from his large running balance during the past year. The Treasury, and thus the House of Commons, seemed to have no real control of about 5 per cent of the annual budget. This was barely tolerable during war, not at all in time of peace.

The problem was not a new one when Shelburne and Barrington began to work on it, for George Grenville had also tried to achieve greater control of colonial expenditures. During the war, money needed by officials in North America was paid there, through resident deputy paymasters, by money contractors—great merchants and bankers of London who usually received 2 per cent for their services.[24] In late 1764 the Treasury Board under Grenville's leadership had worked out a new plan of fiscal management that eliminated the money contractors. Hence-

---

Gage's command only, and does not include five battalions in the West Indies.

[22] I have computed "Extraordinaries" *for North America only* at £208,896 for expenditures in 1764 (*Commons Journals,* xxx, 39ff.) and £265,661 in 1765 (*ibid.,* 554ff.). These sums were voted in 1765 and 1766, respectively.

[23] I have computed the estimate for 1766 at £44,026, and it changed little through the peacetime years. *Ibid.,* xxx, 482-483.

[24] Pargellis, *Loudoun,* 72-73.

forth, neither the Commander in Chief in North America nor any governor was to make expenditures which had not been approved by the Treasury, or for which money had not been granted by Parliament. If any expense was deemed necessary, an estimate was to be drawn up, and it was to be sent to the Treasury for presentation to Parliament. In case of an emergency, the Commander in Chief or governor was to draw (that is, to sell a bill of exchange) on the Lords of the Treasury and "on no other person whatever," and at the same time was to send home a full justification of his action. The Treasury warned that full accountability for these bills would be required.[25] In effect, this meant that all contingent and extraordinary expenses of the army were to be paid at home. This left only the pay of the soldiers to be disbursed in North America, and that was to be done by ordering the customs collectors and stamp commissioners to pay their money directly to the deputy paymasters.[26]

Considered theoretically, it was very neat; the Treasury would be able to control military expenditure more closely, the expensive money contractors would be eliminated, and the American Revenue and Stamp Acts would not drain the colonies of hard currency.[27] Unfortunately, the one part of the plan whereby all contingent and extraordinary expenses would be rigidly controlled was impracticable; and the other part was effectively blocked, primarily by the Paymaster General, secondarily by American reluctance to pay taxes.

[25] Treasury minute of 28 November 1764, *Gage Corr.*, ii, 269n.

[26] T 29/37, entry for 9 July 1765. Gage wrote to Brig. Gen. Burton, "From what I can learn of the present system of supplying the troops with subsistence [pay], it is to apply the revenues arising from the duties paid on the imports, and the money accruing from the stamp tax, to these purposes." 26 October 1765, Gage MSS.

[27] Jack M. Sosin, "A Postscript to the Stamp Act. George Grenville's Revenue Measures: A Drain on Colonial Specie?" *AHR*, lxiii (1958), 918-923. This article does not mention, however, that the money contractors, before they were eliminated, shipped about £100,000 in specie to North America each year.

The first part presented the Commander in Chief with three alternatives, all undesirable: he could haggle for terms with New York City merchants every time immediate expenditures were required, and then send the cash to the places where it was needed; he could transmit signed drafts on the Treasury to these places, often communities with little ready cash where such drafts could be sold only at a considerable loss or even not at all; finally, he could allow his subordinates to draw bills on him, a risky practice because he would be held responsible for what he could not control.[28] The Treasury soon saw the practical difficulties, and began to modify the system, but did it in such a way as to undermine its primary aim. On an ad hoc basis, it permitted local military commanders to sell bills directly on the Treasury.[29] The result of this could have been loss of fiscal control of the army by both Gage and the Treasury. Shortly after Barrington came back to the War Office in July 1765, he began a campaign at the Treasury to restore to the American Commander in Chief discretionary power in financial matters.[30] But not until Gage had composed and transmitted a full critique of the new system did the Treasury Board act by substantially reverting to traditional practice.[31]

[28] He wrote to Welbore Ellis that drafts were "an affair that requires management, as well to get as much benefit for the Crown, as can be had by the Exchange [rate], as to collect the money for the Bills, for even moderate Sums can't at present be raised here, under many days Notice." 1 April 1765, *Gage Corr.*, II, 274. An example of sending signed drafts to a subordinate is seen in Gage to Gov. Carleton, 3 December 1766, Gage MSS. Gage summarized his plight in a letter to Thomas Whately, one of the Treasury secretaries, 2 May 1765, *Gage Corr.*, II, 286-287.

[29] For example, see the case of Newfoundland in Ellis to Gage, 13 April 1765, WO 4/987.

[30] "General Gage is an officer of great prudence and integrity, on which account the Treasury may repose trust and confidence in him, whereby in my opinion they will better consult the real interest of the public, than if they gave directions themselves in those matters, which from their nature, a man on the spot . . . can best judge of and regulate." Barrington to William Mellish (a Treasury secretary), 7 September 1765, WO 4/988.

[31] Gage to Barrington, 10 December 1766, "Private" *Gage Corr.*,

While this was being worked out with painful slowness, the second part of the new system ran into difficulty at the Pay Office. The Treasury was informed that there was no easy way for the deputy paymasters in North America to receive the stamp and customs revenues, because there were no deputy paymasters south of Canada and Nova Scotia except at New York City, because transportation of specie was dangerous, and because inland bills of exchange were unobtainable.[32] This last assertion appears to be an outright falsehood, and it may be that Charles Townshend, Paymaster General for these few months, was angling for the patronage of three additional deputies.[33] While the Treasury was making up its mind about what to do, the troops at Montreal came near mutiny because their pay was in arrears.[34] Finally, after repeal of the Stamp Act, the attempt to tap the American revenue for military purposes was given up, and a new money contract was let.[35]

The measure of financial control sought by Grenville was clearly unattainable. "Extraordinary" expenditures were the rule in a situation as new as Gage's, and the use of Treasury bills was more cumbersome, probably more expensive, and little more effective than the old system. But the attempt to achieve greater control had forced Gage to begin collecting the kind of data required if the government were to effect any rational economies, or even were to defend itself against hostile questions in the House of Commons. As matters then stood, the government had no exact idea as to why the American army was so expensive.

The first American expense estimates began to arrive from Gage at about the time Barrington took office. They were far from complete, however. The distant posts had not

II, 392-395; and Treasury minute of 9 January 1767, inclosed in Barrington to Gage, 2 March 1767, WO 4/988.

[32] T 29/37, entries for 4 November 1765 and 18 February 1766.
[33] *Ibid.*, 23 December 1765.
[34] Lt. Col. Massey to Gage, 17 August 1766, Gage MSS.
[35] *Commons Journal*, XXXI, 515ff.

yet reported, Bradstreet had sent nothing on quartermaster expenses in the Albany district, engineer estimates for the repair and reconstruction of fortifications were missing, and Gage himself admitted he could not guess what the new plan for management of barracks was going to cost.[36] Nor were those estimates submitted satisfactory, for a year later Barrington and the Treasury were still puzzled or dubious about a number of items, and asked Gage for corrected and more detailed versions.[37] In October 1766, Gage had sixteen estimates, but there were still perhaps ten missing, and he had doubts about the accuracy of some of the others; nevertheless, he sent them on because it would take several months to get them revised again.[38] Barrington was pressing Gage to send the estimates, because only with them in hand could he hope to push through his plan during the 1766-1767 session of Parliament.

At that moment, Shelburne was less concerned about military finance than with the Quartering Act; in particular, with the failure of New York to comply with it. During the early autumn, Shelburne had been optimistic, telling the secluded Chatham that trouble in New York was only "the remains of the Storm" over the Stamp Act, "and wants a little good humour and Firmness to finish."[39] But he grew steadily more pessimistic as New York continued to refuse compliance. One of his advisors told him that the Quartering Act was unsound in conception and poor in draftsmanship, and suggested that it be repealed.[40] Chatham, however, was angry at American ingratitude, and Shelburne at this time seems to have been making a career of reflecting the attitude of his chief. Chatham was then in a state of physical and mental collapse, and in touch with events primarily through Shelburne's sycophantic letters.[41]

---

[36] Gage to Ellis, 1 April 1765, and to Barrington, 5 November 1765, *Gage Corr.*, II, 272, 310.

[37] Gage to Barrington, 15 June 1766, *ibid.*, 357.

[38] Gage to Barrington, 11 October 1766, *ibid.*, 380-381.

[39] Shelburne to Chatham, 20 September 1766, PRO 30/8 (Chatham MSS.), LVI, 60-61.

[40] Probably this was Maurice Morgann. Shelburne MSS., LXXXV, 83-84.

[41] Norris, *Shelburne*, 39.

When Parliament convened, the ministry was in no better condition than its absent leader. As support fell away in the House of Commons, the cabinet fell out among themselves. Barrington, in single-minded fashion, nagged Shelburne to reach a decision on withdrawal of the army from the West before time came to submit the army estimates.[42] But Shelburne was deeply involved in a great struggle with the East India Company for a share of its revenue, an affair which dominated the whole session.[43] What little attention he could give to America centered on the Quartering Act. Moreover, there was no rapport between the two men, for each mistrusted the other for his political ties.[44] In November, Shelburne did find time to write to Gage, asking for general advice on Indian and military policy, but it was already too late.[45]

At the end of January 1767, Barrington laid the routine army estimates before the House of Commons. At the same time, he took the unprecedented step of submitting Gage's incomplete and inadequate estimates to the House for its information.[46] It appears that there had been no more than perfunctory consideration of them beforehand by the government itself. What Barrington had done, by linking the estimates for "Extraordinaries" to the routine estimates instead of waiting until later in the session to bring in the "Extraordinaries" according to the usual practice, was to

[42] Barrington to Gage, 13 March 1767, "Private," Gage MSS. The following summer, over a year after he had submitted his plan, Barrington wrote: "I have for some time left off teasing the Ministers about a matter on which I found they would not decide." To Gage, 6 July 1767, "Private," *ibid.*

[43] Lucy S. Sutherland, *The East India Company in Eighteenth Century Politics* (Oxford, 1952), 138-176.

[44] Shelburne had earlier written about Barrington as "a bad speaker, a worse man, of no interest, no property, universally disliked and despised . . . of no consequence except that the Duke of Newcastle took him improperly up." To Lord Mansfield, 6 November 1762, quoted in Lewis M. Wiggin, *The Faction of Cousins; A Political Account of the Grenvilles, 1733-1763* (New Haven, 1958), 299.

[45] Shelburne to Gage, 11 December 1766, *Gage Corr.*, II, 47-51.
[46] *Commons Journal*, XXXI, 51.

call attention to the total cost of the American army. Perhaps he acted in naive good faith; more likely he was trying to force the ministers to reach a decision on his plan by embarrassing them in the House. Whatever his intentions, the result was trouble for the Chatham government.

Grenville, bête noire of both the King and the ministry, attacked. He moved that the colonies pay for their own troops.[47] It was in the debate on this motion that Charles Townshend, Chancellor of the Exchequer and as brilliant and unpredictable as Chatham himself, turned on his colleagues and, under persistent badgering by Grenville and Lord George Sackville, promised to find another source of revenue in America to pay for the army. On the basis of that promise, almost 200 votes would later swing against the government to reduce the land tax by one shilling.[48] Grenville's motion was lost, but he attacked again in February, when Barrington submitted the past year's "Extraordinaries." This time the former First Lord of the Treasury moved the withdrawal of the army from the interior posts because of the "boundless Expences for Extraordinaries in America."[49] The government had not yet decided what to do about the army, but it could not let George Grenville steal the initiative, and votes were again mobilized to defeat the motion.[50] It must have been some consolation to him when he heard in March that Townshend at a cabinet meeting had threatened to resign if the troops were not withdrawn.[51] The chain of events from this split to the passage of the Townshend Acts in May is clear, but no longer concerns the question of military policy.

Grenville had done more than provoke the Chancellor

[47] Conway to the King, 26 January 1767, *Geo. III Corr.*, I, #469 (See Namier, *Additions and Corrections*).

[48] On Townshend's motives and actions, see Namier, *Crossroads of Power* (London, 1962), 209-211. More generally, see Charles R. Ritcheson, *British Politics and the American Revolution* (Norman, Oklahoma, 1954), 97ff.

[49] *Commons Journal*, XXXI, 171.

[50] Conway to the King, 18 February 1767, *Geo. III Corr.*, I, #472 (See Namier, *Additions and Corrections*).

[51] Grafton to Chatham, 13 March 1767, *Chatham Corr.*, III, 232.

of the Exchequer to make a hasty and ultimately disastrous promise. He also had forced the broad issue of the American army to the fore within the government. When Chatham heard of Grenville's attack and Townshend's defection, his first thought was of the Quartering Act and how its enforcement would be made more difficult by any new attempt to tax America.[52] In short, he brought together the hitherto separate preoccupations of Shelburne and Barrington. Chatham implied that Shelburne should recommend what to do about the army, but said that in the meantime the law for the housing of the army had to be enforced. Shelburne insisted that it would take months to reach a sound decision on the first point, but neither he nor anyone else in the cabinet was disposed to disagree with the second. The rub was how to secure American obedience.

There was in Chatham's attitude toward the Quartering Act a grimness that disturbed even those who had no sympathy with American resistance.[53] When the cabinet finally began to grapple with the problem in February 1767, its members tried desperately to escape the conclusion that enforcement meant bloodshed. As Shelburne summarized it in a report to Chatham, "though everybody is strongly for enforcing, nobody chooses to suggest the mode." Shelburne even asked the King, who said he had no idea.[54] In the search for "the mode," Shelburne, as well as other ministers reputedly sympathetic to America, went down some strangely harsh paths.

In February, Shelburne was toying with the idea of sending a military officer to govern New York, who would have discretionary power "to act with Force or Gentleness as circumstances might make necessary."[55] He was con-

[52] The seriousness with which Chatham viewed the enforcement of the Quartering Act is seen in private letters to Shelburne, 3 and 7 February 1767, *ibid.*, 188-189, 193-194.

[53] See extracts from the Duke of Bedford's private journal, 24 and 31 October 1766, *Bedford Corr.*, III, 348-354.

[54] Shelburne to Chatham, 16 February 1767, *Chatham Corr.*, III, 207.

[55] Shelburne to Chatham, 16 February 1767, "Private" (1st of 2 letters of that date), PRO 30/8 (Chatham MSS.), III; Ritcheson,

sidering the same measure actually adopted in 1774, when
the North ministry made Gage governor of Massachusetts.
Shelburne went beyond the measures of 1774, however,
when he suggested that the new governor receive the power
to billet troops in private houses if the Assembly remained
obdurate.[56] By March, when the cabinet met again on the
Quartering Act, Shelburne had seen the danger, even the
illegality, of giving a governor such power, but he was still
no nearer a solution.[57]

At the final meeting, in April, Conway suggested that an
extra port duty be laid on New York, but this was rejected
as unworkable. Townshend had won support for his own
plan to block all legislation by the New York Assembly until it complied. Only Shelburne liked a third alternative,
that of letting the governor simply take the money needed
for quartering from the provincial treasury. But Shelburne
did not raise in the cabinet his own pet scheme. In his report of the meeting to Chatham, he proposed an act of Parliament that would explicitly couple the Quartering Act and
the Declaratory Act, reminding the New Yorkers that the
former was law. The act would pardon all past offenses,
but would make any future resistance on constitutional
grounds high treason. Even to write or speak against the
Quartering Act would be misprision of treason, and offenders were to be tried, if necessary, in Great Britain.[58] In one

---

British Politics, 89, gets credit for finding that both Shelburne's
biographer (Fitzmaurice) and the editors of *Chatham Corr.* omitted
this part of the Chatham-Shelburne correspondence without noting
the omission.

[56] "I see no way of enforcement except giving the Governor ["and
Council" is struck out] Power, in case of the Assemblys refuse
[*sic*] to provide the Troops as was the first Intention of the Act,
then to billet, *on Private Houses as was the Practice during the
War.*" *Ibid.*

[57] This is by inference from Grafton's brief account of the cabinet
meeting of March 12, to Chatham, 13 March 1767, *Chatham Corr.*,
III, 231.

[58] Shelburne to Chatham, [26 April 1767], PRO 30/8 (Chatham
MSS.), LVI, 86-90. This letter is not in either Fitzmaurice, *Shelburne*, or *Chatham Corr.* In fact, though the letter is a report of

act, Shelburne would have struck at both freedom of expression and trial by jury. From Grenville to North, no responsible official proposed a harder blow at what Americans called the rights of Englishmen.

In the end, Townshend's proposal won out, and Parliament suspended the New York Assembly until it had obeyed the Quartering Act. This "Restraining Act" was never applied, since the Assembly was deemed to have complied prior to the effective date of the Act. At this point, as the tumultuous Parliamentary session of 1766-1767 came to a close, it is appropriate to see what actually had happened to the Quartering Act in America.

The Quartering Act in America

Discussion of the Quartering Act invariably focuses on American resistance to its enforcement. By 1767, Massachusetts, New York, New Jersey, South Carolina, and Georgia had opposed it in some way or another. New York had gone so far as to have its Assembly suspended. But when one looks at the matter from the opposite point of view, that is, in terms of substantial compliance with the spirit of the law, it is striking to see how far most colonies were willing to go in supporting the regular troops stationed or marching within their borders.

When the Quartering Act went into effect in 1765, there were few troops near the important towns: about 100 at New York City, 50 at Albany, and 20 at Charleston. By the following spring, however, troop dispositions had taken on the pattern they would retain until 1768: a battalion or more at New York City, a battalion in New Jersey, most of a battalion at Philadelphia, together with the aforementioned Albany and Charleston detachments.[59] The

---

a cabinet meeting held April 24, Fitzmaurice says that Shelburne ceased to attend cabinet meetings after the March 12 meeting (p. 320).

[59] Distribution of troops, 24 September 1765, CO 5/83; 29 March and 10 October 1766, CO 5/84. The shift was due partly to the final liquidation of the Indian rebellion and the occupation of Illinois, partly to the Stamp Act disorders.

remaining 5,000 or so were located north, south, and west of the long-settled areas.

As might have been expected, the first trouble over the new law arose in Albany. In August 1765, Gage told Bradstreet to carry on quartering in the Albany barracks as usual because nothing could be done under the new law until the provincial government had acted; nevertheless, when six companies of the Royal Americans marched into Albany from Ticonderoga and Crown Point in November, Bradstreet submitted a requisition to the mayor of Albany for a quarters allowance for the officers and, when this was refused, stimulated a written protest to Gage from the officers themselves.[60] Although Gage ordered him not to press for the officers' allowance, which appears to have been of dubious necessity in any case, the New York Assembly resolved that the barracks at both Albany and New York were "King's barracks," and that the legislature would do nothing about quarters allowances under the new law until expenses had actually been incurred.[61] It is difficult to be certain, but it appears that Bradstreet had acted rashly, especially in egging on the officers who much preferred to live privately in snug taverns than with the troops in drafty barracks. He thus forced the Assembly to take a stand at a time—immediately after the Stamp Act riots—when it could hardly be expected to comply with a requisition made under an Act of Parliament. In fact, the existing barracks and barrack supplies at Albany apparently were sufficient to last the winter, even for the reinforced garrison.[62]

[60] Bradstreet to Gage, 25 November 1765, Gage MSS.; *Montresor Journals*, 341.

[61] Gage to Bradstreet, 2 December 1765, Gage MSS.; Gage to Conway, 21 December 1765, *Gage Corr.*, I, 76-77.

[62] I may be mistaken in implying that Gage was unhappy with Bradstreet's conduct, because Gage's letters home do not mention Bradstreet, his letters to Bradstreet do not reveal anger, and Gage himself brought the dispute at Albany to Governor Colden's attention. My surmise is that once the question had come up, Gage, uncertain of the exact situation at Albany, decided to back his subordinate and to put the best possible face on the whole affair. My interpretation rests on two points: the more or less continual fric-

Only with the annual movement of troops in the spring of 1766 did Gage begin actively to demand provincial assistance under the Quartering Act. Governor Moore of New York relayed Gage's requests to the mayors of Albany and New York, and sent a message to the Assembly for the necessary money.[63] After some hesitation, the Assembly reminded Moore of the remains of a fund appropriated in 1762 for the recruiting of regular soldiers, and authorized its use for quartering. It did limit the contingent to be stationed within the province to two infantry battalions and one artillery company, and it balked when Moore sought an additional grant for quartering the officers in public houses.[64] But the limit was not unreasonable, and Gage was pleased that the ample sum of £5,000 (N.Y.) was thus made available for quartering expenses.[65]

Earlier the New Jersey Assembly had complained that the Quartering Act was "as much an Act for laying Taxes on the Inhabitants as the Stamp Act," but had then proceeded to appropriate the necessary funds although it did not exactly conform to the terms of the British law. Governor William Franklin excused himself to the Secretary of State for assenting to the imperfect bill by noting "the Pleasure of finding the Regiment stationed in this Province perfectly satisfied with their Quarters. No Complaints whatever have been made to me, . . ."[66]

Pennsylvania did not even bother to protest the revenue-raising aspect of Gage's requisition, but simply resolved to

---

tion between Gage and Bradstreet after the 1764 campaign, and the fact that Bradstreet violated his instructions in regard to quartering. See also Mayor Volkert Van Douw to Gage, 21 November; Bradstreet to Gage, 23 November; Gage to Bradstreet, 25 November; Bradstreet to Gage, 16 December; and Gage to Bradstreet, 24 December 1765, Gage MSS.

[63] Moore to Gage, 25 May 1766, *ibid.*

[64] Enacted 3 July 1766, *Colonial Laws of New York*, IV, 901-903; *Historical Memoirs of . . . William Smith [1763-1776]*, ed. W. H. H. Sabine (N.Y., 1956), 33; *Montresor Journals*, 373-374.

[65] Gage to Bradstreet, 14 July 1766, Gage MSS.

[66] To Shelburne, 16 December 1766, 1 *N.J. Archives*, IX, 577.

make provisions for the troops as requested.[67] Philadelphia
tavern keepers complained in October about the burden of
officers quartered upon them, and the Assembly promptly
directed that rooms in the barracks be appropriately furnished to house the officers.[68] Gage expressed no dissatis-
faction in his reports to London with the £100 per barracks
granted by New Jersey, or with the £4,000 by Pennsylvania.

It has been noted previously that South Carolina had refused to continue her unique practice of transporting provisions to the frontier posts at Fort Prince George and Fort
Charlotte, but both South Carolina and Georgia continued
to furnish the small detachments stationed within their borders with some barrack supplies under the general rubric
"firewood." In fact, South Carolina continued to pay the
cost of transporting military stores *other than provisions*,
and to support soldiers' wives and children as part of her
transient poor in Charleston.[69]

Nowhere could Gage reasonably complain of resistance
to the quartering provisions of the law of 1765, and there
also appears to have been no difficulty in requisitioning
wagons, even at Albany. The repeal of the Stamp Act undoubtedly had had much to do with colonial acquiescence,
but every colony except Pennsylvania had carefully avoided
conforming to the letter of the law, usually by denying any
grant for the "liquor" mentioned in the Quartering Act.[70]

A number of minor incidents mark the apparent uncon-
cern of Americans with the "oppressive" aspect of the
Quartering Act. When James Parker, Mayor of Perth
Amboy, received a request from Gage to put up part of an
unexpected shipment of 140 recruits, Parker asked a short
delay while the barracks were refitted, "as it would be next
to Impossible to provide for that number in private quar-

[67] 11 September 1766, 8 *Pa. Archives*, VII, 5898-5899.
[68] *Ibid.*, 5944.
[69] SCCJ, XXXVIII, 188-190.
[70] Gage reported that this was the only provision of the Act he
had ever heard "complained of as a grievance." To Barrington, 21
December 1765, *Gage Corr.*, II, 328-330.

ters."[71] In other words, Parker was either unaware of the new law against billeting in private houses or was willing to conceive that military necessity might override it. Toward the end of the year 1766 an Atlantic storm blew about 70 soldiers into Boston. Although the General Court demurred at supplying them under the terms of British law, it did in fact supply them. Sam Adams asked Christopher Gadsden whether the Quartering Act "is not taxing the Colonys as effectually as the Stamp Act?" and noted that he was opposed as a matter of principle to a standing army in time of peace and therefore thought it necessary to oppose its quartering. But even Adams, so often depicted as the personification of intransigent anglophobia, added: "If a number should happen to come into a Province through Necessity and stand in Need of Supplys, as is the case at present here, is it not a Disgrace to us to suppose we should be so wanting in humanity, or in regard to our Sovereign as to refuse to grant him the aid with our free Consent?"[72] Massachusetts responded again in May 1767, by granting 14 transient recruits such supply "as has been heretofore usually made for his Majesty's Regular Troops when occasionally in this Province."[73] In January 1767, the Connecticut Assembly had agreed to billet 136 German recruits (destined for the Royal American regiment) at New Haven, Branford, and Wallingford, and had gone so far as to vote additional compensation to the innkeepers concerned.[74] Although Ezra Stiles heard that by this act of the Assembly "The Wedge has entered" and "Glut upon Glut" was sure to follow, the Germans departed Connecticut in April after paying their bills and conducting themselves with "Decency."[75]

[71] To Gage, 25 August 1766, Gage MSS.
[72] 11 December 1766, *The Writings of Samuel Adams*, ed. H. A. Cushing (N.Y., 1904), I, 110-111.
[73] 16 June 1767, *Mass. Acts and Resolves*, XVIII, 245.
[74] *Conn. Public Records*, XII, 542-543.
[75] Jonathan Devotion to Stiles, Saybrook, 6 February 1767, *Stiles Corr.*, 460; Gage to Lt. Grandidier, 19 April 1767, Gage MSS.; Governor Pitkin to Gage, 10 March 1767, *Connecticut Historical Society Collections*, XIX, 79-80.

The only clear-cut opposition to the Quartering Act appeared in early 1767, and it developed in the least "revolutionary" colony—Georgia. As the legislatures of Georgia and South Carolina convened in the winter 1766-1767, General Gage heard from the local commander that the three companies in these provinces had little more than roofs over their heads at the five posts where they were stationed. The fault lay more with the administrative slackness of previous commanders and with the long tradition of neglecting the South Carolina independent companies than it did with any deliberate evasion of the Quartering Act.[76] The Commons House of the South Carolina Assembly might have been expected to reject the new request outright. It was angry with Captain Gavin Cochrane for having done a poor job in placing Fort Charlotte, newly constructed at a cost to the province of £7,000 (S.C.), and with Ensign George Price for suspected account-padding in recent repairs done on Fort Prince George.[77] Instead, an investigating committee of the Commons House reported that the work at Fort Prince George "was compleated in a very Faithful manner, that the carrying on of the works was attended with more Labour and Trouble than was imagined," and the House voted to pay the bills incurred by Ensign Price.[78] It then proceeded to vote a per-capita money allowance which the local commander believed would be sufficient, with proper management, to meet the requirements of the Quartering Act.[79]

At the next legislative session, the local commander complained about the poor condition of the Charleston barracks, which he said had been stripped by indigent squatters who had previously occupied them, and would neither keep the soldiers in at night nor the cold out.[80] The House not only approved the necessary repairs, but also voted to give En-

[76] Capt.-Lt. Ralph Phillips to Gage, 17 December 1766, and Gage to Phillips, 14 December 1766, Gage MSS.

[77] SCCJ, xxxvii, 46, xxxviii, 138, 151, 157-159, 222-227, 236.

[78] *Ibid.*, xxxviii, 336-337, 339-340.

[79] *Ibid.*, 450, 453; Capt. L. V. Fuser to Gage, 26 August 1767, Gage MSS.

[80] SCCJ, xxxviii, 324-325.

sign Price a £400 reward for his diligence and honesty in supervising the repair work of the previous year.[81] The South Carolina Commons House continued, however, to refuse to pay for the transportation of provisions to the frontier posts. The contractors ought to pay it, provisions could be purchased locally, a large duty is raised in this province by Act of Parliament for defending the colonies, and no northern colony pays for the transportation of provisions—such were the arguments advanced in support of the Carolinian position.[82]

In Georgia, the House of the Assembly had momentarily gone the furthest of any colony when it refused as a matter of principle to provide for the regular soldiers in the province. As Governor Wright reported their stand to the Secretary of State, "Complying with the Requisition . . . would be a Violation of the Trust reposed in them by their Constituents, and founding a Precedent they by no means think themselves justifyable in introducing."[83] Before the session was over, however, it had heard of the action of South Carolina and, as often happened, decided to imitate her big sister. Because of a constitutional fight with the Governor, not until the next session (1767-1768) was the money actually made available.[84]

By the middle of 1767, just after the Chatham government had got its Restraining Act, every one of the older colonies which had regular troops quartered in it, except Georgia, had made a substantial contribution to their support.[85] At the same time, every one of these colonies except Pennsylvania had refused to make that contribution according to the letter of the Quartering Act. There is no

[81] *Ibid.*, 540, 548, 584, 606.

[82] *Ibid.*, 376.

[83] Abstract of Dispatches from the Governor of Georgia, Received the 20th May 1767, Shelburne MSS., LII, 216.

[84] There is an excellent account of the dispute between Governor James Wright and the Georgia House in Abbot, *Royal Governors of Georgia*, 126-144.

[85] For a convenient summary, see An Account of the Manner in which the several Provinces in North America yielded to the Mutiny Act [1767], Shelburne MSS., LVIII, 189-196.

reason to describe the support itself as an act of American good will or as evidence that the colonists were pleased by the presence of the British army, because, in every instance, local political factors as well as the repeal of the Stamp Act go far toward explaining the pliability of the colonial legislature. Connecticut feared an attack on her charter, New York and South Carolina had new governors, Pennsylvania wanted to overthrow her proprietor, New Jersey and Georgia sought a dispensation to issue paper money, Massachusetts wanted to ameliorate the attitude toward her held in Whitehall and Westminster as a result of the Stamp Act riots, South Carolina and Georgia not only needed the regulars to man their outposts but were increasingly uneasy over the Regulator threat to the tidewater, and all colonies valued the money which soldiers of the Crown pumped into depressed economies.[86] But such factors were always more or less operative, and had in the past provided a lubricant for the old imperial machinery. Moreover, it appears that the Quartering Act itself had proved at best irrelevant, at worst obstructive, in the gaining of colonial military assistance.

Chatham and his ministers had singled out New York for action not because soldiers were starving or freezing within its borders but because New York had protested first and most loudly. The issue was one of the letter rather than the intent of the law, and, before the Restraining Act of 1767 could go into effect, the New York Assembly had appropriated first £3,000 (N.Y.), then an additional £1,500 (N.Y.), for the support of the troops. Confronted with political instability at home and a patent willingness to compromise in New York, the Privy Council lamely accepted the offer and suspended execution of the Restraining Act.[87] Similarly, New Jersey had her quartering laws of

[86] For the threat to Connecticut's charter, see Jonathan Devotion to Ezra Stiles, 27 April 1767, *Stiles Corr.*, 463; for the Carolinian fear of the backcountry, see Capt. Fuser to Gage, 27 November 1767, Gage MSS.

[87] 12 August 1767, *APCC*, v, #66. When New York passed this act, Gage reported to the Secretary of State: "However disagree-

both 1766 and 1767 disallowed by the Privy Council because of noncompliance with the British act, and her Governor reprimanded for agreeing to them. But as late as
1771, when New Jersey again agitated the quartering issue, General Gage remarked that the colony had usually
made ample provision for the troops in the past.[88]

After the dispatch of four regiments of British regulars
to Boston in October 1768, the quartering problem of
course took on a new dimension. In that month, one im-
plication of the very presence of British troops in the
American colonies was adumbrated, later to be made shockingly clear when those troops killed five Bostonians in
March 1770.

Reappraisal, 1767-1768

Shelburne had acquired a livelier sense of the perils of
precipitancy, especially on American affairs, during the
Parliamentary session of 1766-1767. First, Barrington had
tried to get action on the deployment and cost of the army
before the government was ready to do so, even before all
the data was in hand and checked. The upshot was serious
trouble in the House, and Shelburne blamed Barrington for
most of it.[89] Likewise, Townshend's rashness had put the
government in an impossible position, leading it to sponsor
a revenue bill that almost everyone knew was worse than
the Stamp Act. And, as he and his colleagues had rushed
to find some means before the end of the session of coercing
New York, he had begun to see that American resistance
to the Quartering Act was at once more and less dangerous
than they had thought. It was becoming evident that the
military service was not being seriously impeded, that the
amount of money was small in comparison with total costs,
that the Americans had grounds for complaint the more

able this method [of disbursement] may be [in terms of the Quartering Act], . . in this manner the Troops are now supplied with
all the Necessarys directed by Act of Parliament, in the Province
of New York." To Shelburne, 31 August 1767, *Gage Corr.*, I, 150.
[88] To Hillsborough, 2 July 1771, *Gage Corr.*, I, 303.
[89] Shelburne to Chatham, 13 March 1767, *Chatham Corr.*, III,
234-235.

one looked into the matter, and that, in fact, they had gone some distance toward compliance with the intent of the law. But by the time the Restraining Act received the King's assent, Shelburne also knew that New York was not alone, that resistance was widespread, and that, in justice, the assemblies of three or four other colonies ought to be suspended as well. In all this, he must have been impressed anew, as any modern student must be, by the crippling effect of slow communications.

It was not only the time required between the dispatch and receipt of a single letter; rather, it was the inability of anyone, whether in New York or London, to gather information, to verify it, to prod laggards who failed to report, to check—in person if necessary—suspected incompetence or corruption, to make decisions, to transmit them, to clarify or modify them, to hear complaints and recommendations before they were stale, to settle disputes, to do all those things that make any group of human beings responsive to direction. This empire, which Shelburne himself had spoken of previously in the House of Lords with a glowing optimism, was impossibly sluggish.[90] The Atlantic had always been a major obstacle, but now maritime communications seemed quick and sure when compared to the difficulties of overland movement created by the postwar empire. The expense in time and money of moving men, supplies, and information over an area that reached from Newfoundland almost to New Orleans, and from the Atlantic to the Mississippi, was so great as to vitiate the attempt to draw up a rational and economical policy for the army in America.

Two years had not been enough to learn with any certainty what it cost to keep less than 7,000 men in America, or to learn exactly why the Quartering Act was not working as expected. The question now was, what should be done with the army, especially in the backcountry where it was costing more to transport rations than to purchase them? Shelburne was determined not to be rushed to a

[90] Gipson, *British Empire*, VIII, 308.

decision. When pressed to do so before Parliament adjourned in June 1767, he refused.[91]

There is little point in retracing in any detail the long struggle of 1767-1768 over a policy for the American West, because only its effect on the army and military policy concern us. In retrospect, one can see that British inability to regulate the fur trade and to raise an American revenue gravely weakened the major argument—Indian grievances over land and trade, and the cost of a resultant war—for maintaining an army in the American interior. The additional failure, then in the process of occurring, to keep white men off Indian land by military force, further weakened it. The proper course was to withdraw most of the army from the interior, to retrench military expenses as far as possible, and frankly to accept the possibility of Indian war as the lesser of evils.

Shelburne could not have recommended such a policy even if he had seen its desirability because it held too many political perils. He occupied a weakening position in a rickety, coalition government. One Indian war could be blamed on Amherst, but another would surely ruin whoever happened to be Secretary of State. Whatever he decided, it ought to improve his own position as well as the general situation in the colonies.

Barrington's plan provided the focus for Shelburne's reappraisal of Western policy. In that plan, the Secretary at War had proposed the concentration and eastward displacement of troops. He had justified his proposal by calling the West a desert reserved for the Indians; by judging small forts and garrisons as of no use in "awing, distressing, and checking the Indians"; and by describing the fur and skin trade as of little value to Great Britain.[92] It would be difficult to imagine a more impolitic and vulnerable justification of a reasonable proposal.

[91] A good account of Shelburne's "reappraisal," set in the context of British politics, is Norris, *Shelburne*, Chap. III. Shelburne's caution is evident in "Reasons for not Diminishing American Expence this year," 30 March 1767, Shelburne MSS., LXXXV, 102-110.
[92] *IHC*, XI, 236.

Shelburne sought the comments of at least four men on the plan: Gage, Amherst, Benjamin Franklin, and Richard Jackson, colonial agent and self-acknowledged expert on American affairs.[93] Amherst, Franklin, and Jackson were critical; Gage, equivocal. Franklin and Jackson were personally interested in western land speculation and colonization, and naturally were incensed by the idea that the Ohio and Mississippi valleys were a "desert" for Indians only.[94] Amherst disliked both the implied criticism of his own deployment of the army, and the view that a few regulars were ineffective against a great many Indians; Amherst had never understood, and he never would.[95] Gage refused to take any stand, insisting quite properly that the location of the army depended on decisions that were beyond the responsibility of a military commander. Instead, he explained as best he could why troops were in each of the posts currently occupied. Gage had wanted to move forces to the seaboard after the Stamp Act riots, but he also had written of the need for settlements around the interior posts in order to eliminate the costly shipment of rations to these garrisons. He seemed on both sides at once, and both sides claimed him. It appears that he was being extremely cautious, unwilling to give any official advice that might drag him down in some future disaster.[96]

Shelburne soon saw the mistakes and the crudities in Barrington's analysis. At the same time, he was being bombarded with petitions and plans for Western colonies and for the relaxation of Indian trade regulations.[97] Throughout 1767 there were rumors of imminent war filtering back

[93] Sosin, *Whitehall*, 150ff., has the best discussion of Shelburne's "advisors."

[94] *Ibid.*, 128-148, describes the pressure exerted on Shelburne by speculators in Western lands.

[95] Shelburne MSS., L, 65-76. Amherst's meddling in American policy is mentioned in Capt. Harry Gordon to Gage, 4 March 1766, *Johnson Papers*, XII, 36.

[96] Gage to Shelburne, 3, 4, and 5 April 1767, *Gage Corr.*, I, 124-132.

[97] Sosin, *Whitehall*, 148-149, discusses the desire of Canadian traders to end the system of trade regulation.

to Whitehall from the American frontier.[98] It was not clear, nor is it now, how well founded were these rumors of an Indian uprising. Johnson and Croghan were not above exaggerating the importance of their own department, and Shelburne knew this.[99] But it is doubtful if he knew that at least one land syndicate was deliberating spreading war rumors in order to speed negotiation of a final boundary with the Six Nations, by which the syndicate hoped to acquire most of modern West Virginia.[100] Gage took the rumors seriously, because migration in the Fort Pitt area was creating a situation there that seemed about to explode.[101] There were those who said that retention of the interior forts would provoke a war, and others who said that without them war was certain. Over all loomed the recollection of Pontiac's rebellion, and with that historical episode one could argue either way.

The fate of the army had come to be linked to two other issues: the future of the Indian Department, and the question of Western colonization. As the memoranda accumulated, the relation of the three became cloudier rather than clearer. The political appeal of Barrington's plan had been a quick and sizeable reduction of American expenditures, thus promising to allay discontent on both sides of the Atlantic. Even after the passage of the Townshend Acts, which no one believed would provide a substantial revenue, the appeal was a cogent one, vitiated only by delay. But by mid-summer colonization of the West and reorganization

[98] Gage to Shelburne, 13 June, 24 August, and 10 October 1767, *Gage Corr.*, I, 142-143, 147-148, 151-153.

[99] "The Substance of what passed between Ld. Shelburne and Mr. Dyson About the Superintendants," November 1767, Shelburne MSS., L, 219-226.

[100] George Croghan, Indian agent, and Samuel Wharton, Philadelphia merchant and agent for a major land company, agreed in 1767 to alarm the ministry about the threat of an Indian war in order to obtain a more westward Indian boundary. Wainwright, *Croghan*, 245; Croghan to Johnson, 2 February 1768, *Johnson Papers*, VI, 91-92.

[101] For example, see Croghan to Johnson, 18 October 1767, *Johnson Papers*, XII, 372-375; and William Allen to Gage, 28 November 1767, Gage MSS.

of the Indian Department were the principal points of discussion in Shelburne's office, and the army problem as such was neglected.[102] The assumption seemed to be that a policy for the West would dictate a military policy. In effect, the original priority of issues had been reversed. Shelburne seems never to have inquired whether deployment of the army might not be to some extent independent of Western policy.

By December 1767, Barrington was in despair. "I have beg'd them to authorize you to execute the Plan which you sent to Lord Shelburne," he wrote to Gage, "tho' far short of my Ideas: They are making references from time to time, get reports, and do nothing. I am so provoked at this unmanly conduct, that the day when the army [estimate] was voted, I advised them publickly in the House of Commons to bring the matter thither for advice to the Crown, if they could not determine on any advice themselves."[103] Chatham was still in seclusion and Barrington was certain that nothing was being done about this or any other American matter because of fear of Chatham's disapproval.[104]

It is impossible not to feel some sympathy with Barrington's exasperation, but the long delay has usually been explained by Shelburne's determination to investigate the problem thoroughly, and by his desire to secure a liberal decision favorable to America. Some other reasons for delay have already been mentioned, but there is also evi-

[102] Shelburne's approach to the problem was best expressed in a cabinet minute of mid-1767: "The present Situation of the Army being so much dependent on Indian affairs that it is impossible to consider one without the other." Shelburne MSS., L, 187. Three or four months later he revealed how little serious attention he had given to the role of the army itself: "The sole Utility arising from the several Forts which are now maintained, appears to be the forming of a certain Barrier against the Indians for the Security of the Colonies. . . ." To the Board of Trade, 5 October 1767, *ibid.*, 177.

[103] 12 December 1767, "Private," Gage MSS.

[104] Earlier he had written: "I impatiently wait for the *resurrection* of Lord Chatham . . . in the mean time we have no government." To Gage, 6 July 1767, "Private," Gage MSS.

dence that Shelburne's passion for research was not as strong as sometimes supposed, and that he was not especially sympathetic toward America or concerned with American affairs. First, the ministerial assault on the East India Company during the Parliamentary session 1766-1767, and the long, complex negotiations to reorganize the ministry in the summer and autumn of 1767, were the political cynosures during this period. American affairs were never of primary importance.[105] Second, when New York's resistance to the Quartering Act was under cabinet consideration, Shelburne's plan of action had been as harsh as any proposed by a responsible official before the outbreak of war. Third, Shelburne at times showed a surprising ignorance about the very matters under his investigation: he did not know that the Indian agents had put parts of the trade plan of 1764 into operation; he had an impossibly idealistic conception of Indian diplomacy; and he was unaware that a new boundary line with the various tribes had been under consideration for several years.[106] Finally, in early 1768, when faced with a choice between the newly created Secretaryship for the Colonies and that of the Southern Department (now divested of colonial responsibility), he chose the latter.[107]

[105] Sutherland, *East India Company*, 138-176; Brooke, *Chatham Administration*, 68-217, 295-333; Norris, *Shelburne*, 46-53.

[106] On the plan of 1764, see Shelburne to Gage, 11 December 1766, *Gage Corr.*, II, 49 (and note 35, *ibid.*, for the correspondence which, if Shelburne had read, would have informed him of the true situation). On his disapproval of playing off one Indian tribe against another, see *ibid.*, 51 (all those involved in Indian affairs agreed that such a policy was a necessity, however regrettable). On his ignorance of the status of the boundary question, see Benjamin Franklin to Joseph Galloway, 1 December 1767 (Extract), *Johnson Papers*, v, 855. For an informed opinion that saw no pro-Americanism in either Shelburne or the Chatham ministry as a whole, see William Samuel Johnson to Governor Pitkin, 12 February 1767, 5 *MHSC* IX, 215-216.

[107] The King mentioned "Lord Shelburne's having particularly of late seized every opportunity of declaring that America is a department of little business." To Grafton, 11 December 1767, *Geo. III Corr.*, I, #568. In a private letter to Chatham, "Junius" wrote: "Many circumstances have made it impossible for you to depend

Before his transfer, Shelburne had reported in favor of three new colonies in the American West and a major reduction of the Indian Department. A hostile cabinet quashed his plan for colonies when the Board of Trade opposed it. The Indian Department lost its "commercial" role of regulating the fur trade, but managed to keep its "diplomatic" functions, which enabled it to supervise the acquisition of Indian lands.[108] At last, in June 1768, Gage received orders to withdraw from all but the major posts in North America.[109]

The ironic, perhaps tragic, aspect of the reappraisal of 1767 is that Shelburne in the end planned to retain almost the same Western posts as Barrington had in the beginning, and the Board of Trade concurred. There was disagreement on other matters, but almost everyone thought it would be unwise to evacuate Niagara, Detroit, Michilimackinac, and probably Fort Chartres in Illinois, and agreed that it was unnecessary to garrison much else. Even Richard Jackson, the severest critic of Barrington's plan, agreed with the Secretary at War on the matter of troop disposition.[110] Only Amherst had been clearly opposed: he had advised being "very Cautious about abandoning the least post."[111] Unfortunately, Amherst was the military expert of the Chathamites, and apparently Shelburne paid close attention to his advice.[112] Among all the

---

much upon Lord Shelburne or his friends; besides that, from his youth and want of knowledge, he was hardly of weight, by himself, to maintain any character in the cabinet. The best of him is, perhaps, that he has not acted with greater insincerity to your lordship than to former connections." 2 January 1768, *Chatham Corr.*, III, 303.

[108] Sosin, *Whitehall*, 152-169.

[109] Hillsborough to Gage, 15 April 1768, *Gage Corr.*, II, 61-66.

[110] Jackson's opinion of Western plans, November 1766, *IHC*, XI, 428-430.

[111] "Remarks on Ld Barrington's Plan," Shelburne MSS., L, 65-76.

[112] Amherst was, in effect, Chatham's general, and was treated as such by the Crown in October 1768, when Shelburne resigned from the government and Amherst lost his honorary but lucrative governorship of Virginia.

others, the area of disagreement was negligible, but the question of troop location had imbedded itself in questions of colonial policy and domestic politics, and meanwhile military matters in America had hung fire pending a decision.

From the time that Barrington first had written to Gage about reappraising the missions and deployment of the army in America, it had required three years to reach a decision. Even then, it was not clear cut, for Fort Chartres in Illinois remained a question and protests from those living or investing in West Florida soon forced the return of more troops to Pensacola.[113] In the event, the decision, such as it was, came too late to have much effect at all. Taken in the winter 1766-1767, it would have had a major political impact in both England and America, aside from its economic consequences. It would have had a lesser, yet important, effect if taken soon after the passage of the Townshend Acts. Coming when it did—in the summer of 1768—the decision only made it easier to send troops to Boston that autumn.

[113] See below, p. 322.

VII · Boston: The Turning Point

THE prolonged argument over the West confused both the participants and the issues. In the end, Shelburne, who advocated the creation of Western colonies, and Barrington, who thought the West should be left to the Indians, agreed on the withdrawal of most of the army. Only Amherst, who still believed Indians to be contemptibly unimportant, and Johnson, who still hoped to placate the Indians through trade regulation, opposed the removal of forces. The Board of Trade expressed yet another view, and probably John Pownall was its spokesman. He attacked Shelburne's plan for Western colonies by arguing that only such colonies could justify the retention of troops in the West, because these new settlements would surely goad the Indians to war, and that the government ought to choose one or the other. But even Pownall reunited the two issues in order to sink the colonization scheme, and in the end he had his way.[1]

When seen in a broader frame, the most confusing aspect of the argument was the way it masked the only important disagreement. Surprisingly, that disagreement was between Barrington and Gage. Barrington wanted not only to get the troops out of the West, but out of the older colonies as well. He said repeatedly that troops concentrated in Florida, Nova Scotia, and Canada would be available in case of disorder in the older colonies, but would no longer be a grievance to those colonies.[2] Gage was cautious about

[1] The Board of Trade's report, 7 March 1768, is in *IHC*, xvi, 183-204. See also Sosin, *Whitehall*, 166-169, though I find little evidence to support Sosin's contention that Barrington, through his private correspondence with Gage, was able to "subvert" the "compromise" on interior posts. There was no compromise because there was very little disagreement about those posts that were finally retained.

[2] See, for example, Barrington to Bernard, 13 December 1766, *Barrington-Bernard Corr.*, 119, and Barrington to Gage, 7 August 1771, "Private," Gage MSS.

it, but he never concurred. He argued that troops had to
on the spot if magistrates were to uphold law and order.[3]
The two men were close friends, and agreed on almost
every other facet of colonial and military policy, so that
friendship muted their disagreement in this one case.
Barrington never gave in, but he never pushed his point;
instead, he seemed willing to defer to Gage's superior command of the facts. The result was that three or four battalions remained in Pennsylvania, New Jersey, New York,
and, later, Massachusetts.

One can only speculate about the effect a complete withdrawal of forces from the older colonies might have had.
It certainly would not have made Anglo-American relations any worse.

Another interesting, if less important, speculation is why
Gage never took Barrington's proposal seriously. Gage
already had had some experience with the difficulties involved when magistrates might want military aid, and he
ought not to have been so sanguine about the value of
troops being on the spot when trouble arose. Though it
seems petty when measured against the consequences, Gage
may have been impelled to keep troops in the Middle
Colonies by a desire to keep his headquarters in New
York City. His wife was from New Jersey, and Barrington's plan logically would have entailed banishment for
the Gages to sweltering and primitive St. Augustine, to
cold and equally primitive Halifax, or to snowy Quebec,
where they had not enjoyed their earlier tour of duty.[4]
More tangibly, to divide the army north and south would
have diminished the importance of its Commander in Chief.
It might even have led to a divided command, with

[3] Gage to Barrington, 7 May 1766 and 3 September 1771, "Private," *Gage Corr.*, II, 351 and 589-590, are examples of Gage's
cautious, tactful mode of disagreeing. Lt. Col. Robertson to Haldimand, 29 June 1768, BM Add. MSS. 21666, illustrates the kind of
influence exerted on Gage at New York; Robertson wanted eight
or nine regiments encamped at New York during the summer,
to be quartered at Philadelphia, New York, and Boston during the
winter.

[4] Alden, *Gage*, 59-61.

northern and southern commanders reporting directly to Whitehall.

Instead of withdrawing, part of the army remained in those colonies that were later to form the United States. By mid-1768, more troops were rubbing shoulders with Americans than at any time since the war.

Prelude to the Boston Massacre: The Army in 1768

Five years after the decision of 1763, the mission of an army in America was more obscure than ever. The plan for the regulation of the fur trade had failed, partly because of geographic and legal difficulties, partly because of human weakness in both the military and Indian departments. Even Gage and John Pownall, who had supported the plan, admitted this. The attempt to keep frontiersmen off Indian land by military force likewise had not been a success. The question of the use of troops to support customs officials— an afterthought when proposed in 1763—had not yet arisen in concrete form.

The location of the forces in 1768, at the time of the decision to give up the grand scheme of Indian management and to concentrate the troops, was more a matter of local circumstance than of any over-all plan.[5] Fifteen battalions, each composed of 9 companies, with a nominal strength of 500 men—about 350 soldiers present for duty in practice—were strewn unevenly over half a continent.[6] Since 1766, Gage, acting on his own initiative, had been closing down a few of the smaller posts which had seemed to have little peacetime function. The desire to have greater force available on the seaboard was certainly at the back of his mind in doing this, but the routine problems of administering and supplying tiny, scattered forts and garrisons were the immediate stimulus to the concentration of troops. But he had not dared do much in this way until a

[5] Gage surveyed the stations of the army for Hillsborough, 16 June 1768, *Gage Corr.*, I, 175-179. The fullest statement on the forts is in *ibid.*, II, 318-324.

[6] The best collection of strength reports for regiments in America, from 1768 on, is in BM Add. MSS. 29256-29259.

decision came from Whitehall; meanwhile, expenses of apparently useless garrisons accumulated, the need for major repairs increased, and discipline deteriorated.

Three battalions were in the Nova Scotia-Newfoundland area. Of these, three companies at St. John's and Placentia in Newfoundland policed and defended the fisheries, always in danger from French encroachment.[7] There were also four companies on Cape Breton Island, though, as Gage reported, "the fortifications of Louisbourg having been destroyed, the whole is now a heap of rubbish, and the place entirely defenceless."[8] Likewise, Fort Amherst on Isle St. John (the modern Prince Edward Island), where there were two companies, was in ruins and of no use.[9] In Nova Scotia itself, company-size detachments held Fort Cumberland on the Chignecto Peninsula, Fort Frederick at the mouth of the St. John's River on the Bay of Fundy, and Annapolis Royal on the western shore. Smaller detachments were at Fort Edward on Minas Basin and Fort Sackville at the head of Bedford Basin. The army had occupied these posts in the course of the war with the French, and there was no good argument for their retention, especially after the expulsion of the French population. Now, all of them, outside of Newfoundland, were ordered vacated and the forces, except the three-company detachment for the fisheries, concentrated at Halifax.

There was general agreement that Canada required no less than four battalions because the British government and army command never ceased to fear a rising by the French inhabitants, especially if war should break out.[10] Quebec was the somewhat ramshackle citadel of the province, and always held two battalions. The other two had their headquarters at Montreal, and furnished detachments to Three Rivers, St. John's, and Chambly. Montreal supported the posts on the Great Lakes, but it was necessary to transship supplies from river boats to

[7] *CHOP*, III, 449-451.

[8] Gage to Shelburne, 23 December 1766, *Gage Corr.*, I, 117.

[9] Gage to Shelburne, 3 April 1767, *ibid.*, 125.

[10] Carleton to Gage, 22 November 1768, "Secret," Gage MSS.

lake vessels. At first, both Fort William Augustus on Isle Royale, and Oswegatchie (modern Ogdensburg, New York) were the transshipping points, but Gage had ordered Fort William Augustus given up in 1766 because it was falling down and would have been expensive to repair.[11] The small force left at Oswegatchie came from the Montreal garrison. In general, the decision of 1768 did not affect the deployment of troops in Canada.

During the war, Albany had been the center of British operations in the northern theater. Fort Edward and Fort George at the ends of the 15-mile Hudson River-Lake George portage led north against Ticonderoga; and Fort Stanwix and Fort Ontario east along the Mohawk River-Lake Oneida-Oswego route against Niagara and Frontenac. After the war and the Indian uprising, these posts were of little value. The Hudson and Mohawk Rivers could not compete with the St. Lawrence and Lake Ontario as a peacetime line of supply to the Great Lakes.[12] In 1765, Gage had abandoned Fort Edward; in 1767, Fort Stanwix.[13] Albany remained important only as a way-station between New York and Montreal; Ticonderoga and Crown Point served the same purpose. In 1768, Gage withdrew from Fort Ontario and Fort George, and kept only a few men from Montreal at Ticonderoga and Crown Point. John Bradstreet remained deputy quartermaster general at Albany, but the post had become a virtual sinecure.

No one believed the Great Lakes posts—Niagara, Detroit, and Michilimackinac—ought to be given up. Too many traders came to Michilimackinac each year, too many Frenchmen lived in Detroit, and Niagara was too important as an advanced base for both, to be left without garrisons.[14] All of the other forts that had existed in this

[11] Gage to Conway, 9 November 1765, *Gage Corr.*, I, 74; and Gage to Barrington, 18 December 1765, "Private," *ibid.*, II, 322.

[12] Capt. John Maxwell to Gage, 23 July 1766, and Gage to Bradstreet, 7 June 1773, Gage MSS.

[13] Gage to Conway, 6 May 1766, and to Shelburne, 27 May 1767, *Gage Corr.*, I, 90, 141.

[14] Gage to Barrington, 4 March 1769, "Private," *ibid.*, II, 502.

region had been lost in the Indian uprising and never reestablished. Since 1765, a single battalion had been distributed among the three Lake posts, and there was no change in 1768.

One thousand miles from its base at Philadelphia, 50 miles down the Mississippi from the site of St. Louis, lay the former French Fort Chartres. After the war, it had taken two years to occupy. Two years after that, no one could decide what to do with it. Its garrison had failed to control the shipment of furs down the River, because traders easily went round the fort or drifted by silently in the dark. Its rampart was in danger of collapse as the River undermined the foundation. No extensive repairs were authorized, but, until the government reached a decision, a full battalion continued to hold Fort Chartres.[15]

Fort Pitt was the major link in the supply line to Fort Chartres. Amherst originally had planned to occupy Illinois from Detroit, and perhaps to supply it through there as well. But the Indian war had ended that plan.[16] Then the initial attempt to get to Illinois up the Mississippi had failed, so that the first troops to reach Illinois had come down the Ohio from Fort Pitt; henceforth, that had been the line of communication. Pitt was also the center for dealings with the strong and bellicose Delaware and Shawnee, and it offered some slight protection to the Pennsylvania frontier. Three companies held the fort, and furnished a detachment to Fort Ligonier on the road to Philadelphia. The other forts on that road—Loudoun and Bedford—were vacated by 1766. The fate of Fort Pitt depended on what was decided about Illinois.

At the end of the war, informed opinion regarded West Florida as more valuable to the empire than East Florida.[17] Mobile and Pensacola each had a battalion, while East Florida got only one. But the British government had carelessly failed to secure its right to navigate

[15] Hillsborough to Gage, 4 December 1771, *ibid.*, 137-138.
[16] *IHC*, x, 8.
[17] See "Thoughts concerning Florida," PRO 30/47 (Egremont MSS.), xiv, 88-89, probably written in 1762.

the lower reaches of the Mississippi during the treaty negotiations, and the prospects of West Florida never materialized.[18] For several years, soldiers and slaves labored to cut a channel to link Lakes Maurepas and Ponchartrain to the Mississippi. Small garrisons were established at Fort Bute (near modern Baton Rouge) and Fort Panmure (Natchez). These efforts, as will be seen later, produced nothing. In 1768 it was decided to keep only three companies at Pensacola and a detachment at Mobile, and to concentrate almost three battalions at St. Augustine.[19]

In the beginning, detachments from St. Augustine had occupied the old Spanish fort at San Marcos de Apalache, the island of Bermuda, and New Providence in the Bahamas. Gage received permission to withdraw all these garrisons in 1768.

Three companies had been assigned to South Carolina and Georgia in 1763. They were there to take over the traditional duties of two companies of mounted Georgia rangers, and the three South Carolina independent companies, all of which had been paid by the British government and disbanded at the end of the war. Headquarters for the three regular companies after 1763 were at Charleston, and small detachments were at Fort Augusta (Augusta, Georgia), Fort Charlotte higher up the Savannah River, Fort Prince George in Cherokee country, and Fort Frederica off the Georgia coast. The first three were too weak to protect even themselves against Indian attack, and the fourth was a vestige of the day when St. Augustine was Spanish and a threat to the Carolina coast. The refusal of the South Carolina Commons House to furnish transportation of supplies to the backcountry garrisons gave the British government an excuse to remove all troops from those colonies in 1768.

[18] T. C. Pease, "The Mississippi Boundary of 1763: A Reappraisal of Responsibility," *AHR*, XL (1935), 278-286.
[19] Douglas S. Brown, "The Iberville Canal Project: Its Relation to the Anglo-French Commercial Rivalry in the Mississippi Valley, 1763-1775," *MVHR*, XXXII (1946), 491-516.

A review, post by post, of the withdrawal of 1768 makes it obvious that the military question in fact had been separable, at least in part, from the Indian and western questions. The forts actually given up in 1768 had little bearing on Indian affairs, while the five forts important to Indian relations were kept for the time being. Though the army orginally was meant to deal with the Indian problem, especially in the Old Northwest, the forts best sited for this purpose had been lost in 1763. Amherst thought these posts were unnecessary, but Gage, who might have known better, was working in an atmosphere in which the spirit of economy pervaded every thought, and he would never have dared suggest their reestablishment.

The fairest conclusion is that the army had tried to do what could not be done. Some of the difficulties it encountered have already been discussed. But there were other ways in which rational intentions were being frustrated by unforeseen obstacles. One such problem deserves brief notice, and another more extended treatment.

In early 1764, Secretary at War Ellis had informed Gage that a "general fixed rotation" of regiments was being planned so that each would get its fair share of foreign service, and none would be outside the British Isles for an unduly long time.[20] The plan called for the replacement of five regiments in North America in 1765, five in 1766, and three in 1768.[21] Although troubles in Ireland delayed the dispatch of any troops from that kingdom in 1766, the plan seemed to work fairly well, for by 1769 thirteen regiments had rotated.[22] Various crises, in Boston and elsewhere, prevented further rotation for several years, but three more regiments were replaced in 1773.[23] It was planned to replace four others in 1774, but their orders to return were cancelled for obvious reasons.[24]

[20] 21 January 1764, WO 4/987.
[21] Ellis to Gage, 8 June 1764, *ibid.*
[22] This can be traced through WO 4/987-988.
[23] Gage to Barrington, 7 April 1773, *Gage Corr.*, II, 639.
[24] Barrington to Haldimand, 2 February 1774, WO 4/988.

Because service in North America was more arduous than in the home islands, the rotation policy seemed wise. It contrasts strikingly with the lack of any such policy for the few units in North America before the Seven Years War. But execution of the policy was expensive and often difficult. One difficulty in remote garrisons was that a unit or detachment could not leave its station until another had arrived. This proved impossible at Nova Scotia in 1765 when men-of-war carrying the relief from Ireland could not get around to the minor posts, and the whole 40th Regiment had to embark at Halifax.[25]

On the first occasion, in 1766, when the Great Lakes garrisons had to be relieved, replacements were drawn from the New York area; the second time, in 1772, they were drawn from Quebec.[26] On both occasions when units were relieved at St. Augustine in 1769 and in 1773, the transports could not get across the bar at the mouth of the harbor.[27] In 1769, St. Augustine was so jammed with both arriving and departing garrisons that one battalion had to go to Charleston and demand shelter under the Quartering Act. This occurred at an inopportune time, just as troops in Boston were arousing general resentment in the colonies.[28] Still more difficult was the replacement of the Illinois garrison. It was done only once, in 1768, and required more than six months.[29]

The most serious consequence of the new rotation sys-

[25] Ellis to Halifax, 19 March, and to Gage, 13 April 1765, WO 4/987. A typical comment concerning service in America was that of Lt. Col. Vaughan of the 46th Regiment at Niagara; he wrote to Gage, thanking him for relieving his unit, and adding that "the Regiment might still be made good but with so small a garrison and so much duty they must be intirely lost, banishment having been for the most part there fate since they came to America." 23 November 1764, Gage MSS. Many stations in America amounted to "banishment."

[26] Gage to Barrington, 15 July 1766 and 13 April 1772, *Gage Corr.*, II, 362-363, 601.

[27] Gage to Hillsborough, 6 January 1770, *Gage Corr.*, I, 244; and Haldimand to Dartmouth, 3 November 1773, CO 5/90.

[28] Gage to Gov. Montagu, 8 October 1768, Gage MSS.

[29] Gage to Hillsborough, 5 January 1769, *Gage Corr.*, I, 210.

tem occurred not in America but in Ireland. Regiments on the Irish establishment had been reduced in 1763 to a strength of only 280, compared to the 500 for regiments elsewhere.[30] It will be remembered that the Crown had given up its plan to increase the size of the army in Ireland at that time, and had settled for a large number of regiments there at little more than cadre strength rather than a smaller number of 500 men each. But the annual shift of regiments across the Atlantic under the rotation system had made this arrangement unsatisfactory. Regiments entering and leaving Ireland had to draft almost half their strength out or in, and nothing caused more trouble within the army, and did more to damage unit pride and efficiency, than the practice of involuntary drafting.[31]

In 1767, the Adjutant General finally convinced the King of the evils of the current arrangement, and obtained his consent to "level" all regiments—to bring them to a uniform strength of 484 men in order to make rotation simpler and less painful.[32] Of course it was out of the question for political reasons to disband a number of regiments in Ireland, so the Irish establishment had to be augmented, as originally planned in 1763. A new Lord Lieutenant went to Dublin with royal instructions to get the augmentation through the Irish House of Commons. He succeeded, but it took two years and great effort to accomplish. In the end, it led to a fundamental change in the politics of Ireland, and in the relation of Ireland to England, a change that would still be ramifying when the American Revolution had passed into history.[33]

[30] Barrington to William Mellish, 7 September 1765, WO 4/988.
[31] The Adjutant General in Britain, Edward Harvey, described the practice of drafting men as "this Murdering System of destroying your Regiments"; to Col. Cunnynghame, 28 July 1768, WO 3/24, 56.
[32] Harvey to Granby, 27 August 1767, WO 3/1, 72-73. WO 3/2 contains further evidence that it was Harvey who was pressing for a uniform establishment.
[33] J. L. McCracken, "The Irish Viceroyalty, 1760-1773," *Essays in British and Irish History in Honour of James Eadie Todd,* eds. H. A. Cronne, *et al.* (London, 1949), 158-168.

Some Irishmen at the time, and some historians later, have associated this augmentation of the army in Ireland with the growing fear of an American or Irish insurrection, and with a "conservative" trend in British government. Certainly these forces, as well as the King's general desire for a larger army, made the change acceptable, but documentary evidence points to the administrative demands of the rotation system as the immediate cause of the change.

To sum up: though the plan for rotation of units looks like a reasonable and innocuous measure in general, its actual operation suggests some of the real costs of innovation, however rational, in the old British Empire.

If distance and geography created difficulties for the army in America, its human components were almost as intractable. First thought goes to the individual soldier, who was treated in the eighteenth century little better than an animal, and who behaved like one whenever he dared. It might be assumed that his very presence in the midst of an American community would prove intolerable, and perhaps it would have if events on other fronts had not outraced the growth of animosity between the common soldier and the common American. There was friction before 1768, to be sure, and specific instances will be discussed later, but the general impression is one of comparative civil-military harmony at the lowest levels, at least after the beginning of victories in the Seven Years War until the shipment of troops to Boston in 1768.

Some reasons have previously been advanced for the slowness of Americans to resent the presence of British regulars, but there were others. One unexpectedly grew out of the rotation policy. As during the war, recruits for units in America posed a chronic difficulty. The official policy was that all regiments were to send recruiting parties home whenever necessary.[34] This was expensive and it was resisted, because the regimental recruiting fund had to bear the cost. Some clandestine recruiting of Americans never

[34] Ellis wrote to Amherst, 12 November 1763, that the King desired that the troops in America be "recruited out of his European Subjects, . ." WO 4/987.

ceased, and Gage winked at it, though he believed that American recruits were usually inferior and more likely to desert.[35] The principal solution for the replacement problem seems to have been hit upon almost by accident; it grew out of the traditional practice of "drafting" from one regiment to another. As it developed in America, members of units departing were permitted to volunteer to join units remaining. In the rotation of units that began in 1767, when five battalions departed, about 450 men asked to remain in America.[36] This was about one-third of the effective enlisted strength of these units, and nearly a tenth of the effective strength of the American army itself. When the 9th and 34th Regiments left in 1769, 266 men, almost half their effective strength, stayed behind.[37]

It is reasonable to assume that the British army was becoming Americanized, as a growing body of soldiers declared its preference for life in the colonies, despite the constant danger here of being called to fight Indians or to rot in the Caribbean. These men, half of whom could not write their names, left no documents for the historian, but their action speaks clearly.[38] For the hundreds who volunteered, many more must have been willing to do so if their regiments were called back to England or Ireland. Their readiness to remain in the colonies indicates that they had managed somehow to get along with their civilian neighbors.

[35] Gage to Farmar, 14 March 1766; Gage to Mackay, 15 May 1769; Gage to Haldimand, 31 January 1770; Gage to Carleton, 30 April 1770; Leslie to Gage, 23 May 1773; Gage MSS. Most of these letters record complaints about recruiting in America, but all contain oblique admissions that such recruiting did go on.

[36] Gage to Carleton, 20 July 1767 and 15 August 1768, *ibid.* According to WO 8/5, 121, four of these regiments arrived in Ireland with a total strength of only about 500 men; thus, almost half their strength must have volunteered to remain in America.

[37] Gage to Barrington, 10 June and 2 December 1769, *Gage Corr.*, ii, 512, 529.

[38] The estimate that half could not write their names is based on a study of signatures and marks on the depositions of soldiers in CO 5/88.

A second reason for the relative lack of friction between soldiers and colonists before 1768 lies in the fears of British local commanders. Given the traditional attitude of Englishmen toward standing armies, the unsettled state of British politics in the 1760's, and the specific controversy over the American garrison in Parliament, no commander was happy to see his men in trouble with the local inhabitants. He suspected, with good reason, that the circumstances of any incident were liable to garbling and misrepresentation in London, and that, whoever was at fault, the military was not likely to get the benefit of the doubt. Prudent commanders ruled their men with a hand of iron in matters of this kind, and did what they could to keep the civilian authorities happy.

In 1766, for example, the people of New York City erected a Liberty pole on the Common to celebrate repeal of the Stamp Act. British soldiers cut it down and there were fights between soldiers and civilians. But regimental officers quickly met with the magistrates and the governor, and promised to court-martial soldiers involved or to turn them over to the magistrates, whichever the latter desired. The principal offenders, a drum major and a corporal, accordingly were bound over to the next quarter-sessions. When a soldier tried to resume the quarrel, and assaulted a civilian in the street, a regimental court-martial gave him 500 lashes.[39]

Even when the army went to Boston in 1768, and commanders knew they had gone there to restore order, they began by acting much the same way. Andrew Eliot, a Boston clergyman not at all sympathetic to the British army, reported in early 1769 that "the Town is surprisingly quiet. The discipline is so shockingly severe, that the commen men [i.e., soldiers] are afraid to offer the least insult."[40] In short, the human problems of the army were not primarily those caused by the rank and file.

The weakest part of the army, at least in the years

[39] *Virginia Gazette,* 5 September (supplement), 13 November, and 4 December 1766; *Pennsylvania Journal,* 28 August 1766.
[40] To Thomas Hollis, 29 January 1769, 4 *MHSC* IV, 437-438.

when the West was the paramount concern of military policy, was not the common soldier but the local commanders themselves. They usually kept their men on a tight rein in populated parts of the older colonies, but when in remote stations an unusual number of them proved so contentious, corrupt, or lax, that they were ineffectual, or worse. Only indirectly was it a question of antagonizing future revolutionaries, for there were few Americans involved; rather, the main effect was to impair seriously the efficiency of the army.

The behavior of Burton in Canada, of Howard and Rogers at Michilimackinac, of Lieutenant Grant at Fort Loudoun, of Bradstreet at Albany and Detroit, of Farmar and Wedderburn in West Florida, have all been discussed briefly. It is possible, of course, that some of them were maligned, as all of them claimed to be. It is also no more than just to make Governor Johnstone take most of the blame for trouble in West Florida, and Governor Murray (who was an army officer himself) some of the blame for trouble at Quebec. But when all is said in their favor, local commanders showed an amazing capacity to get into scrapes.

Before 1768, the principal mission of the army was more diplomatic than military: it was to see that the Indians were not abused, either in trade or land. Even after 1768, the army had an important role in this area. Yet Gage had to admonish the commandants at Michilimackinac and Pitt for striking and otherwise abusing Indians.[41] Another commandant at Michilimackinac apparently engaged in the fur trade himself, while there is a reliable report that a commandant at Detroit cleared about £800 Sterling per annum, whether through trading himself, taking bribes to overlook violations of trade regulations, or both, is not clear.[42] One finds recorded in the Thomas Jefferson papers,

[41] Gage to Capt. Glazier, 28 September 1769, and Capt. Edmondstone to Gage, 20 September 1769, Gage MSS.

[42] Robert Roberts to Sir Charles Hotham Thompson, 14 August 1775, East Riding County Record Office, Beverley, Yorkshire, DDHO 4/16. A "Spicemaker" is listed in the "Fur trade returns,

years after the event, that commandants at Fort Pitt were giving Virginians permission, undoubtedly for a consideration, to settle land in the area claimed by the Indians just at the time when Gage and the Secretary of State were trying to stop such settlement.[43]

The most flagrant, and certainly the best-recorded, cases of corruption occurred in Illinois. Lieutenant Colonel John Reed was the first permanent commandant at Fort Chartres. Soon Gage was troubled by the huge expenses in Illinois, and had heard complaints about Reed.[44] But not until the arrival of Reed's successor, Lieutenant Colonel John Wilkins, did the Commander in Chief have his suspicions confirmed. There proved to be large shortages in Reed's accounts, which he simply could not explain.[45] Other sources tell of fee-gouging and arbitrary treatment of traders and the French inhabitants.[46] Reed's successor, however, was even worse. Before he left Philadelphia in 1768, Wilkins signed a contract with the firm of Baynton, Wharton and Morgan. Wilkins was to promote the firm's trade in Illinois, for which he was to receive a 5 per cent commission on profits, with a £1,000 guaranteed annual minimum. It was a fantastic piece of business, and came to light only with the bankruptcy of the firm.[47]

1767," from Michilimackinac, in *Canadian Historical Review,* III (1922), 351-358. Capt.-Lt. Frederick Spiesmacher was on duty there at that time.

[43] *Jefferson Papers,* ed. Boyd, II, 100-102.

[44] In 1768 Gage wrote secretly to Lt. Col. John Wilkins that "great Regulations are wanted to be made at the Illinois, nothing seems to be on a proper footing, and some sensible and discreet Officer is absolutely necessary for the Post. . . ." 5 May 1768, Gage MSS.

[45] Gage to Wilkins, 24 March 1769, *IHC,* XVI, 508-509.

[46] *Ibid.,* 129-30, 162-63, 224, 243; Gage to Barrington, 15 May 1768, "Private," *Gage Corr.,* II, 473.

[47] See Max Savelle, *George Morgan, Colony Builder* (N.Y., 1932), 31-56; and Colton Storm, "The Notorious Colonel Wilkins," *Journal of the Illinois State Historical Society,* XL (1947), 7-22. In 1771, Gage wrote to Haldimand: "There has been strange work at the Illinois, very bad proceedings carried on, indeed most shamefull ones. A Quarrell amongst them has laid open scandalous

Wilkins does seem to have been fairly diplomatic if rather inept in his treatment of Indians, but, like Reed, his handling of all other matters made the post in Illinois an expensive travesty of imperial policy.[48]

Nothing quite so sensational occurred elsewhere, but few local commanders seem to have performed without friction. West Florida and Canada, in particular, remained troublesome.

As has been mentioned, the decision to permit general officers to exercise complete military control when present in a province, but to give the civil governor some military power when troops were commanded by only regimental officers, was of doubtful constitutionality as well as practicality. Moreover, the decision was vitiated by the conflicting intentions of those who made it, Ellis and Halifax. The weakness of the decision, coupled with some bad luck, actually exacerbated conflict despite steps taken to alleviate it. Ultimately, in both West Florida and Quebec, drastic action was required.

It was hoped that the assignment of competent, tactful Henry Bouquet as the southern Brigadier General would rectify the unsatisfactory situation at Pensacola, but Bouquet died of yellow fever within two weeks after his arrival in May 1765. In the following winter, the 21st and 31st Regiments from England relieved the decimated 22nd and 35th under the new rotation system. Not only had the latter two regiments been shattered by their service in Cuba and West Florida, but their officers (like Wedderburn, Farmar, and Mackinen) had become deeply involved in the disputatious politics of the province.[49] But almost immediately after the arrival of the new regiments, Governor Johnstone, who assumed that military command de-

---

scenes, and all is Faction. I am obliged to Superseede Lieut. Colo. Wilkins in the Command of that Country." 13 Sept. 1771, BM Add. MSS. 21665.

[48] Peckham, *Pontiac,* 315.

[49] Gage to Conway, 28 March 1766, *Gage Corr.,* I, 87-88. Major Farmar and the 34th Regiment had gone up the Mississippi to occupy Illinois.

volved upon himself after the death of Bouquet, was engaged in controversy with Lieutenant Colonel Ralph Walsh of the 31st Regiment, stationed at Pensacola. Matters reached such a pass that Johnstone actually used a detachment of the 21st, at Mobile, to besiege Walsh and the 31st.[50] Johnstone later arrested Walsh for high treason and demanded his court martial. When, on Gage's order, Colonel William Tayler of the 9th Regiment, stationed at St. Augustine, sailed to Pensacola to assert his authority as acting Brigadier General for the Southern District, Johnstone refused to accept the idea of an "acting" Brigadier, and challenged Colonel Tayler to a duel.[51] Wearily, Gage told Tayler not to bother trying to convince Johnstone of his errors.[52]

The source of dispute never changed: who was to command the troops? The forms taken by the dispute, however, were kaleidoscopic. Many were clearly frivolous, but some involved questions pertinent to other colonies. When the Governor asserted his right to command the fort, he was on fairly firm ground, and the military knew it. But to command the fort necessarily meant control of the garrison staff, and officers of this staff had to serve both the province and the regular forces stationed within it. An added complication was that the most important members of the staff—the engineer, the barrackmaster, and the ordnance storekeeper—usually reported to the Board of Ordnance in England, completely divorced from the War Office. Repeatedly, members of the provincial military staff refused to obey the orders of superior line officers, and then took refuge under the Governor's wing.[53] Johnstone also

[50] There is a full description of the controversy in Cecil Johnson, *British West Florida, 1763-1783* (New Haven, 1943), 53-56.

[51] Walsh to Gage, 24 January 1766, inclosed in Walsh to Conway, CO 5/84, 153-162; and Tayler to Gage, 31 May 1766, "Private," Gage MSS.

[52] Gage to Tayler, 10 June 1766, Gage MSS.

[53] Gage to the Board of Ordnance, 17 August 1766, *Gage Corr.,* II, 364-365; Lt. Col. Robertson to Gage, 17 February 1768, BM Add. MSS. 21666; Gov. Browne to Haldimand, February 1766, BM Add. MSS. 21677; and Capt. Innis to Haldimand, 22 July

believed, and with some justice, that his hand had been strengthened by the Quartering Act, and he proceeded to reallocate quarters at Pensacola as he saw fit.[54] One can easily imagine what all these events did to military efficiency and discipline in West Florida.

The garrison in West Florida had the special mission of establishing and maintaining a line of communication with the Mississippi, in order both to secure the southwestern corner of the new British empire in North America and to divert the Mississippi fur trade from New Orleans to Mobile. It was soon evident that this was feasible only if the channel provided by the Iberville river between Lake Maurepas and the Mississippi could be cleared and deepened. If it could, West Florida promised to become a prosperous and militarily important province. Obviously, Johnstone had an interest in optimism on this matter, while Gage had at least an equal interest in an accurate assessment. Johnstone attempted to commit the army, as well as the British government, to vigorous action on the "canal" question when he built Fort Bute (near modern Baton Rouge) at the junction of the Iberville with the Mississippi in 1765, and later when he ordered the occupation of Fort Panmure (Natchez). Neither post was tenable without the canal which would eliminate the need to rely on New Orleans. But years elapsed before Gage could obtain from officers there an informed, unbiased, and, as it turned out, decidedly pessimistic estimate of the practicability of the project. Meanwhile, he had no choice but to expend money and manpower in attempting fruitlessly to open the line to Fort Bute.[55]

1769, BM Add. MSS. 21729; and correspondence between Gov. Durnford and Ordnance officers, November-December 1772, BM Add. MSS. 21675.

[54] Walsh to Gage, 24 January 1766, CO 5/84, 153-62.

[55] Farmar had first tried to open the channel with 50 slaves under the direction of Capt. James Campbell, and Johnstone claimed that they had completely succeeded when he established Fort Bute. But it soon became obvious they had not. See Johnstone to John Pownall, 19 February 1765, *Miss. Prov. Arch.*, 271-273, and

The other missions of the army in the South were also affected by these civil-military disputes. Although the economies of both East and West Florida came to depend heavily on the expenditures required by their regular garrisons, the strife (which had spread to East Florida by 1767) connected with the presence of those garrisons undoubtedly discouraged immigration, especially since political instability could jeopardize land titles. In this connection, it is also likely that political jockeying combined with the military land-grant provisions of the Proclamation of 1763 to stimulate an engrossment of the better land by army officers as well as by local officials and their English political "connections."[56]

It was over the Indian question that Johnstone finally fell from power. He decided in 1766 that war with the powerful Creek nation was inevitable, and that the British should have the advantage of striking the first blow, despite Gage's opposition and the manifest weakness of the West Florida garrison.[57] Another Indian war, however, even a small one, had no place in the plans of any Secretary of State, and the Earl of Shelburne told Chatham that Johnstone was a "Perfect Madman." Shelburne got cabinet approval to sack him soon thereafter.[58]

Brown, *MVHR*, XXXII (1946), 491-516. See Gage to Tayler, 26 June 1766, Gage MSS., for the attitude of the Commander in Chief toward these posts. In the spring of 1768 Gage was just beginning to see through the haze of factional conflict within West Florida with sufficient clarity to guess that the canal was impracticable. Gage to Haldimand, 29 April 1768, Gage MSS.

[56] Charles L. Mowat, *East Florida as a British Province, 1763-1784* (Berkeley, 1943), 34-72; Johnson, *West Florida,* 124-129; Alexander Fraser to Haldimand, 29 June 1768, BM Add. MSS. 21728. This is not the conclusion of C. N. Howard, *The Development of British West Florida, 1763-1769* (Berkeley, 1947), 32-41, but I believe his Appendix on land grants (pp. 50-106) supports my assertion.

[57] Alden, *Stuart,* 224-228; Gage to Taylor, 10 December 1766, Gage MSS.

[58] 6 February 1767, PRO 30/8 (Chatham MSS.), III, 189. See also Shelburne to Gage, 19 February 1767, *Gage Corr.,* II, 51-52.

The removal of Johnstone certainly mitigated but it did not end the conflict between the governor and the military commander in West Florida. Frederick Haldimand had received an appointment as the permanent Brigadier General for the Southern District in 1767, and upon his arrival at Pensacola reported that all branches of the service were in such a snarl that he despaired of ever putting them in order. The barracks were so irreparably bad that they did not deserve the name, and the troops, who had buried 500 of their comrades in the past two years without anything being done to improve living conditions, were on the verge of mutiny.[59] Haldimand set to work to bring some order out of near chaos, but George Johnstone continued to cast a long shadow. A year after Johnstone's recall, Lieutenant Colonel James Robertson, now barrackmaster-general for North America on Gage's staff, explained to Haldimand why one Mr. McLellan, barrackmaster for West Florida, could successfully defy his nominal military superiors: "[The Board of] Ordinance persists in supporting McLellan . . . as Johnstone family has receiv'd imminse accessions of wealth, and he is espoused by Administration and supported for the borough of Carlisle [in the election of 1768] in an extraordinary manner."[60]

Even without Johnstone's presence or influence, Haldimand continued to have trouble with other members of the provincial military staff who could claim the protection of the current governor or the Ordnance Board, or both. In fact, despite apparent good will on both sides, Haldimand could not avoid disagreement with the governors themselves, disagreement which seriously weakened the ability of the army to protect the province from foreign attack. Later, Haldimand would feel impelled to separate physically the garrison's military stores from the military stores of the

---

Sutherland, *East India Company,* 167, 170-172, leads one to suspect that the timing of Johnstone's recall was not unrelated to the struggle over the East India Company.

[59] Haldimand to Lt. Col. Robertson, 29 November 1767, BM Add. MSS. 21666.

[60] 17 February 1768, *ibid.*

province in order to avoid disputes.[61] For a similar reason, Gage would later order Haldimand to concern himself no longer with the state of the fortifications in the province.[62] With the arsenal divided into two parts, and with the control of the troops divorced from responsibility for the fortifications, the line eventually drawn between civil and military in West Florida made it less likely that the latter could effectively protect the former in the event of war.

The result of similar trouble in Quebec was somewhat different; there Gage's authority rather than the security of the province suffered. Like Johnstone, Governor Murray had quickly used the Quartering Act of 1765 to strike a blow at military power. The deputy quartermaster general at Montreal was responsible for supplying the Great Lakes posts. In order to do this, he sent supplies by bateau to the head of the St. Lawrence at Fort William Augustus, where they were transshipped to lake schooners. During the period of military government, it had been customary to draft Canadian bateau-men for this service whenever they were needed, in the same way that Bradstreet or Bouquet had drafted wagoners and packhorse men.[63] But the Quartering Act of 1765 said nothing about the bateau service, and Murray abruptly stopped the drafting of bateaumen.[64] Legally, Murray was quite correct, but the manner and circumstances of his doing it had put a crimp for a time in the supply line, and it had looked to Burton and his staff like an act of spite.

As in West Florida, officers of the provincial military staff of Quebec had not been able to obey two masters, and this had angered Burton and Gage.[65] But the quarrel in

[61] Haldimand to Governor Chester, 14 December 1772, BM Add. MSS. 21675.

[62] Gage to Haldimand, 10 June 1772, BM Add. MSS. 21665.

[63] It should be reiterated here that compensation was paid when men, animals, or vehicles were requisitioned, although the fairness of the rate of compensation is open to question.

[64] Lt. Col. Gabriel Christie (DQMG Montreal) to Gage, 26 October 1765, inclosed in Burton to Gage, 29 October 1765, Gage MSS.

[65] The garrison surgeon at Quebec defied Burton. See Burton to Gage, 18 September 1765, *ibid.*

Canada was cut short by action of the British government. It was impossible to tell from London who was at fault in the wrangling among governor, army, and merchants, but the merchants had by far the loudest voice at the Board of Trade, so both Murray and Burton were ordered to England at the end of 1765.[66] Sir Guy Carleton, who had been Wolfe's quartermaster general, received an appointment as both Governor of Quebec and northern Brigadier General.[67] This solved the immediate problem, because Gage and Carleton worked well together, but no one could seriously pretend (as the Secretary at War had tried to do) that Carleton as civil governor of a vast and important province had thereby acquired no *military* power independent of the Commander in Chief.[68] The British government was, in this instance, reverting to the earlier gubernatorial system of colonial military management.[69]

Old disputes, however, did not die easily. As long as the affair of Walker's ear remained unsolved, it was difficult to achieve civil-military harmony in Quebec. At least two important incidents stemmed indirectly from this lack of harmony. On September 2, 1766, a coroner's inquest at Quebec City into the death of Donald McKenzie, a soldier of the 52nd Regiment, concluded that death was the result of a severe whipping imposed by court-martial, and that the president of the court-martial and the regimental adjutant (who supervised the whipping) were guilty of willful murder. Although the officers were eventually acquitted, the incident was reported in the *Virginia Gazette* and became generally known throughout the colonies.[70] As was evident to officials in both England and America, the action at the inquest paralleled a similar incident which had recently occurred at Winchester, England, and which had

[66] Burt, *Quebec*, 124-126.

[67] He did not officially succeed Murray until two years later, but it was generally understood that Murray would not return.

[68] Barrington to Gage, 17 May 1766, WO 4/988.

[69] Governor James Grant of East Florida unsuccessfully attempted to obtain a similar arrangement in that colony. Barrington to Grant, 11 February 1768, *ibid.*

[70] 8 September 1766.

been reported on August 18 in the *Quebec Gazette*.[71] But, as Carleton pointed out to Gage, the prosecution of the two officers (together with the three drummers who had done the whipping) was also "a good deal owing to the Heats and Animosities which have reigned here too long, . . ."[72]

More consequential was the reopening of the Walker case itself when an army deserter, one George McGavock, claimed to know the identity of the assailants of Walker. According to McGavock, this group included certain officers of the 28th Regiment, then in New Jersey. Not only did the Chief Justice of New Jersey thus have to take legal cognizance of the case, but New York newspapers quickly got onto the scent.[73] Carleton protested that the New York press was greatly exaggerating the trouble which Mc-Gavock's accusations were causing in Quebec, but Gage replied from New York that, during the winter 1766-1767, the new developments in the Walker case had "been the Topick of Conversation here; and I understand some of the most Eminent Lawyers of the Place Consulted, and their Opinions may likely Spread abroad. . . . "[74]

Similarly, the disputes of Johnstone with the military, though less publicized, must have been well-known in the older colonies. It would be idle, of course, to pretend that squabbling in either West Florida or Quebec was simply a matter of personalities, or even a consequence of the difficulty in reconciling the military power of the Commander in Chief with that of the royal governor. Murray, Carleton, Johnstone, and his successors had more than enough purely political problems to keep the pot bubbling. But the fact is that conflict tended, in the first instance at any rate, to follow this particular line between civil and military, a line at once vulnerable and sensitive. Moreover, seldom do the

[71] Lt. Col. Valentine Jones to Gage, 8 September 1766, and Barrington to Gage, 8 November 1766, "Private," Gage MSS.

[72] 20 December 1766, *ibid.*

[73] Chief Justice Smyth to Gage, 4 December 1766, and reply, 6 December 1766; Gage to Governor William Franklin, 6 December 1766; *ibid.*

[74] Carleton to Gage, 23 March 1767, and reply, 3 May 1767, Gage MSS.

local commanders seem to have behaved with political finesse.

In following the history of the army in the decade before 1768, one cannot but be impressed by the efforts made to organize the new empire and improve the old. Unlike the past, considerable attention and intelligent thought were given in Whitehall to formulating a sound military policy for the colonies, while all the Commanders in Chief, whatever their personal limitations, strove mightily and honestly to execute policy. But when one looks further down the chain of command, the picture changes. However gallant these field officers may have been in battle, so many seem temperamentally and intellectually unfitted for their peacetime assignment that one seeks some general explanation. Only two Swiss officers, Haldimand and Bouquet, displayed notable vigor, honesty, and good judgment.[75] But Haldimand and Bouquet were pure mercenaries, dependent completely on their performance for success in the British army. The others, with perhaps the exception of Carleton, lacked that ascetic professional attitude, prized in the twentieth century, but scorned as mean and narrow in the eighteenth. Put in charge of a post in the wilderness, British majors and lieutenant colonels thought first how to live nobly, plan grandly, and, if possible, find the fortune that would provide for their heirs. Honor and affluence, not obedience or honesty, were their paramount concerns. They were gentlemen first, officers second. The general explanation, obviously, lies deep within the structure of society in eighteenth-century Europe. The specific effect, however, is plain enough: the army, as an instrument of imperial control in time of peace, had a dull edge.

The Boston Crisis in Whitehall

On the seaboard, in contrast with the remote stations of the army, matters seemed to be going more smoothly in 1768 than ever before. A brief dispute between Gage and

[75] See Jean N. McIlwraith, *Sir Frederick Haldimand* (London and Toronto, 1926); and *DAB*, II, 480-481, for Bouquet.

Governor Moore of New York had flared during the past winter, producing "a true dry politeness" between the two men, but otherwise Gage had little reason to complain.[76] He was reconciled to what the army could not accomplish, and he had learned how to manage the rest. Problems of quartering, supply, finance, and even recruitment had at least shaken down into a workable system. After the long wait, permission had come to rationalize the deployment of his forces, though he was disappointed that Chartres and Pitt were retained pending further study. Most pleasing, he now had friends in power at home.

The creation of a new office, that of Colonial Secretary, had accompanied Shelburne's departure from the scene. Though a reasonable measure on its merits, it was also part of the arrangements to bring the Bedfordite faction into the ministry. Because a Bedfordite was not appointed to the office, and because his commission was poorly drafted, the Colonial Secretary had a weaker position, both politically and constitutionally, in the cabinet than had the Secretary of State for the Southern Department.[77] But, under Shelburne's successor, the Earl of Hillsborough, weakness in the cabinet was initially compensated by strength in the royal closet. Hillsborough was a courtier, a "King's Friend" in politics. Despite later royal disparagement of Hillsborough's ability, it is evident that he possessed the King's confidence at this time. Hillsborough and Barrington had long been close friends, and they both were able to work closely on military matters with a third confidant of the King, Adjutant General Edward Harvey. Moreover, Gage and Hillsborough were old acquaintances.[78]

[76] Capt. Marsh to Haldimand, 22 January 1768, BM Add. MSS. 21728.

[77] Margaret M. Spector, *The American Department of the British Government, 1768-1782* (N.Y., 1940), Chap. V.

[78] In a letter to Governor Bernard of Massachusetts, his brother-in-law, Barrington called Hillsborough "the most intimate friend I have in the world." 23 February 1764, *Barrington-Bernard Corr.*, 73. In contrast, Barrington recalled: "I never lived in any sort of intimacy with Lord Shelburne. . . ." 4 June 1769, *ibid.*, 202. As for Harvey, Charles Jenkinson wrote: "Colonel Harvey says

Hillsborough was also closely tied to the person and policies of the Earl of Halifax, under whom he had served as President of the Board of Trade in 1763-1765, and to John Pownall, long-time Halifax protégé as secretary to the Board, who became Undersecretary of State when Hillsborough acceded to the higher office. Although Halifax had ceased to play a very active role in politics by 1768, Hillsborough and Pownall evidently had been deeply influenced by his plans for a tighter and more rational colonial connection. However one may judge the substance of their ideas, it is clear that these men had an uncommon knowledge of and interest in American affairs.[79]

With Harvey on the military flank, and Pownall on the colonial, Hillsborough, Barrington, and Gage were largely in agreement on the American question, and worked to effect their views. It is not exaggeration to call this little group a camarilla, at least on American colonial and military policy. But its influence would be diminished by the press of circumstances, by its lack of strength in the House of Commons, and by its inability to sway the cabinet.

No historian has had a good word to say for Hillsborough, perhaps because Benjamin Franklin hated him and filled several letters with testimony to the fact.[80] Franklin

---

that nothing satisfactory can be got [by the King] from Mr. Pitt. . . . The Colonel is, you know, the very best authority. . . ." To James Lowther, 3 October 1765, *Jenkinson Papers,* 388-389. When Harvey was appointed royal aide-de-camp in 1760, he was described by a contemporary as "a most worthy, valuable man." *Sarah Lennox Life and Letters,* 20. On the relationship of Gage and Hillsborough, see Barrington to Gage, 8 January 1768, "Private," Gage MSS. Gage himself referred to Hillsborough, Barrington, and Harvey as "so judicious a triumvirate." To Barrington, 17 June 1768, "Private," *Gage Corr.,* II, 478. Barrington's strong position at this time is demonstrated by the rumor that he would become a Secretary of State; see Rockingham to Newcastle, 11 August 1768, BM Add. MSS. 32990, 408.

[79] On Pownall and Halifax, see Richard Cumberland, *Memoirs* (London, 1806), 71-74, 86, 96, 110-111, 130. For Pownall's attitude toward Hillsborough, see Pownall to Gov. Bernard, 9 July 1768, Bernard Papers, XI, Houghton Library, Harvard University.

[80] Typical is the description of Hillsborough in Ritcheson, *British*

had his own reasons for enmity, because Hillsborough never ceased opposing the land promotion schemes with which Franklin was connected. Hillsborough was convinced, in contrast with Shelburne, that western colonies meant Indian war. The opinion of William Samuel Johnson, like Franklin a colonial agent, furnishes a contrast with that of Franklin: "Lord Hillsborough is esteemed a nobleman of good nature, abilities, and integrity; is a man of business, alert, lively, ready, but too fond of his own opinions and systems, and too apt to be inflexibly attached to them; by no means so gentle and easy to be entreated as his predecessor [Shelburne] in that branch of business, but much more to be depended upon if he once adopts your ideas of any measure."[81] As Johnson was to learn, if Hillsborough was willing to listen to the colonial side of the argument, to

---

Politics, 115, as one "whose pomposity and determination to play the strong man could not conceal his want of talent, . . ." There is no doubt that Hillsborough intended to act decisively in American affairs, but in manner he was more suave than pompous, and in talent was clearly superior to his successor, the Earl of Dartmouth, who has been treated gently by historians because of his apparent sympathy for the American position. Franklin described Hillsborough to Dr. Samuel Cooper of Boston: "His character is Conceit, Wrongheadedness, Obstinacy, and Passion." 5 February 1771, *Franklin Writings,* ed. Smyth, v, 298. Franklin added that Hillsborough would soon fall from power, and that the feud with him would then be a political advantage.

[81] To Governor Pitkin, 26 December 1767, 5 *MHSC,* IX, 252. Johnson thought the change from Shelburne to Hillsborough might be "rather beneficial" to the colonies, and also suggested that Hillsborough, because of his Irish origin and property, might have a fairly liberal theory of empire. There is an interesting confirmation of this in Hillsborough to Fox [October 1761?], *Fox Letters,* 152-153. For the way in which Shelburne could be swayed by personal pressure, see R. A. Humphreys, "Lord Shelburne and British Colonial Policy 1766-1768," *EHR,* L (1935), 241-264, and Wainwright, *Croghan,* 242. For other, more balanced, opinions of Hillsborough, see Croghan to Johnson, 24 February 1764, *Johnson Papers,* IV, 341; Francis Maseres to Fowler Walker, 19 November 1767, *The Maseres Letters,* ed. W. Stewart Wallace (Toronto, 1919), 61; *Virginia Gazette,* 15 September 1768; Denys De Berdt to Thomas Cushing, 26 August 1768, *CSMP,* XIII (1910-11), 337-338.

urge the need for better understanding by both parties, and even to deny the propriety of the Townshend duties, he was also determined to brook no denial of Parliamentary sovereignty.[82] This harsher aspect of his character is hinted in the judgment of him by a personal friend, Lady Holland: "He is in the main a good kind of man, and I shall always feel a friendly disposition towards him, but I don't admire his character. He has parts; but there is I think a *petitesse* in his character, nothing open or great in his way of thinking, or acting. His ideas are all little and confined; . ."[83] The King would later write, "I am sorry to say, I do not know a man of less judgment than Lord Hillsborough." But there is reason to suspect that Hillsborough was a different man after he was forced out of office in 1772, and became—what he was not from 1768 to 1772—bitter, cynical, and indolent.[84] While Colonial Secretary, his words and actions reveal him attempting to personify the policy which almost all British politicians agreed was the proper one for America—a firm hand in a silken glove.[85]

[82] Johnson to Pitkin, 13 February, 23 July, and 20 October 1768, 5 *MHSC* IX, 262-263, 290-296.

[83] To Duchess of Leinster, 14 June [1768], *Correspondence of the Duchess of Leinster*, ed. Brian Fitzgerald (Dublin, 1949), I, 539.

[84] To John Robinson, 15 October 1776, 10 *HMC* VI (*Abergavenny MSS.*), 15. This was the last of a series of reasons why the King opposed Hillsborough's appointment as Lord Lieutenant of Ireland. But three years later, George III agreed to the appointment of Hillsborough as Secretary of State. John Robinson to Lord North, 11 May 1779, *ibid.*, 25. See the low estimate of Hillsborough in Ian R. Christie, *The End of North's Ministry 1780-82* (London, 1958), 6. Hillsborough wrote to his friend and former Under secretary William Knox: "Whether I shall ever be a public man again I do not know, nor do I think it of any consequence." 29 December, 1776, *HMC, Various Collections*, VI (*Knox MSS.*), 128.

[85] A few individuals, like Thomas Pownall, did not subscribe to this, but by 1768 every political faction favored a firm American policy. For example, see the illuminating analysis of the American problem in William Dowdeswell to the Marquess of Rockingham, quoted in Brooke, *Chatham Administration,* 369-371. Contemporary criticism of Hillsborough questioned the effectiveness of specific measures, but not the principle behind them. See *Junius* (Philadelphia, 1836 edn.), 2 vols., I, 189-190.

Hillsborough took office just as resistance in America to the Townshend duties began. His first major act was to denounce the famous circular letter of the Massachusetts Assembly in a letter of his own to the American governors; he did this after cabinet consultation and with the full support of the King.[86] Soon thereafter, he received reports from Governor Bernard and the Boston customs officials concerning past and prospective trouble over the collection of duties. Because Bernard made it clear in private letters to his brother-in-law Barrington that he dared not ask for troops without the advice of his Council, which in turn dared not give its consent, Hillsborough issued Gage a secret order to move a battalion to Boston.[87] But before this order could reach America, Hillsborough learned that the customs officials had fled Boston after the riots caused by their attempt to seize John Hancock's sloop *Liberty*. Both Bernard and the customs officials sent loud calls for help to Gage and Hillsborough.

The arrival of news of the *Liberty* affair appeared at first as the match which would ignite a combustible situation. After the vacillation of the Rockingham and early Chatham ministries, Hillsborough, Barrington, Gage, and others of their temper were eager for vigorous action. Had not Chatham himself, in speaking of the possibility of colonial resistance to British commercial regulation, spoken in the House of Commons of "filling their towns with troops and their ports with ships of war?"[88] Writing privately about the event, Gage forgot his usual cautiousness: "If . . . a determined Resolution is taken, to inforce at all Events, a due Submission to that Dependence on the Parent State, to which all Colonies have ever been Subjected, you can not Act with too much Vigour. . . . Quash this Spirit at a

[86] Hillsborough to the King and reply, 27 March 1768, *Geo. III Corr.*, II, #597-598.

[87] Bernard to Barrington, 4 and 28 March 1768, *Barrington-Bernard Corr.*, 147-150, 152; Hillsborough to Gage, 8 June 1768, "Secret and Confidential," *Gage Corr.*, II, 68-69.

[88] George Grenville to William Knox, 27 June 1768, *HMC, Various Collections (Knox MSS.)*, 95.

Blow, without too much regard to the Expence and it will prove oeconomy in the End."[89] King and ministers were in a receptive mood for this sort of talk, because the election of John Wilkes and economic distress had led to serious riots in the spring and summer in London and elsewhere, and to many, of whatever faction, Boston seemed of a piece with events at home. An unusual session of the newly elected Parliament had met in May, primarily to consider domestic disorder.[90] In July, Hillsborough pushed for prompt action to curb disorder in Boston, and quickly secured royal approval for the dispatch of two regiments to Boston from Ireland on the assumption that Gage might have difficulty, similar to that of 1765, in moving a sizeable force in time.[91] Even William Dowdeswell, one of the prin-

[89] Gage to Barrington, 28 June 1768, "Private," *Gage Corr.,* II, 479-480.

[90] The short session of Parliament called in May after the election had spent its time discussing domestic disorder. Even the Chathamite and City Radical William Beckford had said: "Let us, for God's sake, unite: the kingdom is in danger. These men [the rioters] want more money for less labour done. In so doing they take example from their betters. They who raise mobs raise the devil; . . ." Sir Henry Cavendish, *Debates of the House of Commons During the Thirteenth Parliament Commonly Called the Unreported Parliament,* ed. J. Wright (London, 1841), I, 10. Later Horace Walpole wrote in a more humorous vein: "Well! but we have a worse riot, though a little farther off. Boston—not in Lincolnshire, though we have had a riot even there, but in New England, is almost in rebellion, . . ." To Horace Mann, 4 August 1768, *Walpole Letters,* ed. Toynbee, VII, #1223. An exchange of letters between the Duke of Newcastle and Sir Matthew Fetherstonhaugh in May and June 1768 demonstrates how even those in opposition to the government were torn between their fear of anarchy and their fear of military force. BM Add. MSS. 32990.

[91] Hillsborough to the King, 19 and 22 July 1768, *Geo. III Corr.,* II, #637-38; Hillsborough to Gage, 30 July 1768, *Gage Corr.,* II, 72-74. Ritcheson, *British Politics,* 118, believes that the ministry acted very slowly on this matter. In fact, Hillsborough received the news on 19 July and wrote to the King immediately; the Treasury Board considered it on 21 July; decision was made and the letter written to Gage by 30 July. This was prompt action.

cipal members of the opposition Rockinghamites, admitted that "sending . . . two regiments is not I think a reprehensible measure."[92]

No one thought that the mere presence of a strong military force in Boston would settle the problem; the forthcoming session of Parliament would pass the laws which would do that, and then, if necessary, the army would enforce them. Rockingham refused to plan opposition to such government measures, because he knew that some of the most important members of his own party were in sympathy with them.[93] With the anti-Boston tide of opinion running strongly, there was good reason for optimism that the cabinet would formulate a "firm" American policy and that Parliament would enact it.[94] News that the Boston radicals had vainly tried to get colonywide support, by means of an extralegal "Convention," for violent resistance to the landing of the troops only strengthened the prevailing attitude. After the first meeting of Parliament in early November, Barrington saw unanimity in the House of Commons on what had passed in Massachusetts. But within two months, Barrington was dejected. He told Gage that, unless there was a great change in the plan then proposed by the government, one would have to depend entirely on the army to maintain order in Boston.[95] How had this change come about?

[92] Quoted in Brooke, *Chatham Administration,* 371.

[93] The correspondence of Rockingham in Wentworth Woodhouse MSS., Sheffield City Libraries, R 1, and of Newcastle in BM Add. MSS. 32991, shows clearly how the Old Whigs were split on what to do about American affairs during the summer and autumn of 1768. Rockingham was discouraged, ready to acquiesce in coercion, and more interested in hunting than politics.

[94] Barrington wrote to Gage: "I do not find among our Ministers the same erroneous Ideas which operated so fatally at the time when the Stamp Act was repealed." 1 August 1768, "Private," Gage MSS. A month later, George Grenville was informed that "Lord Hillsborough is now the active Minister, and is said to have acquired great favour in the Closet." From William Knox, 8 September 1768, *Grenville Papers,* IV, 360.

[95] Barrington to Gage, 9 November and 31 December 1768, "Private," Gage MSS.

The answer is complex, and the available evidence is not as full as could be desired, but the main lines are discernible. Lord George Sackville saw the basic problem: "They talk of vigour, and two regiments are embarked for Boston ... but ... applying this military force ... is a point of such delicacy in our constitution that I doubt much of its being properly executed."[96] Outside the ministry, the opposition, especially the Rockinghamites, had badly needed a focus and a justification for their activity. Within the ministry, the Chathamite rump (which remained after the resignation of Shelburne and Chatham in the autumn of 1768) was uneasy at signs of its former leader's returning interest in politics; there were rumors of a reconciliation among "the brothers"—Chatham, Grenville, and Temple—preparatory to storming the royal closet.[97] The ministerial Chathamites, although a minority in the cabinet, occupied key positions, especially for a legal attack on the Massachusetts government: Grafton, head of the Treasury and nominal prime minister; Conway, former leader in the House of Commons; and Camden, Lord Chancellor. Moreover, they knew that their party enjoyed the reputation of being friendly toward America. But neither Rockinghamites nor Chathamites finally decided to make a stand on the Massachusetts question until the later reports from Boston began to arrive.[98]

Rockingham learned from Governor Wentworth of New Hampshire, who visited Boston, that the troops had been received quietly and without hostility, that the trouble there appeared to be more the fault of "servants of Government" than of anyone else, and that General Gage, who had him-

[96] Sackville to Irwin, 22 September 1768, *HMC, Stopford-Sackville MSS.,* I, 128.

[97] Horace Walpole to George Montagu, 1 December 1768, *Walpole Letters,* ed. Toynbee, VII, #1242.

[98] William Knox, in a letter to George Grenville, 15 September 1768, *Grenville Papers,* IV, 363-364, states that the ministry was unanimously for coercion, with the exception of Shelburne, who therefore would have to resign. Knox also mentions, without comment, the first hints that the initial accounts of the trouble in Boston were distorted and exaggerated. See also *ibid.,* 367.

self come to Boston, agreed.[99] Gage's official report to Hillsborough, although worded equivocally, gave support to
Wentworth's analysis: "According to the best Information
I have been able to procure, the Disturbance in March was
trifling. That considering what had happened respecting
Seizures, the Commissioners of the Customs had Reason,
to act as they did, respecting the Seizure which occasioned
the Riot on the 10th of June; which was considerable and
tho' I do not find, they were at that time personaly attacked, yet the Assault upon some of their Officers, and
the Threats daily thrown out against Themselves, was certainly a Sufficient Reason to make them apprehensive of
Danger to their own Persons. Whether any harm would
have actualy happened to them had they remained in the
Town, it is not possible to Judge."[100] This report arrived
in London during the Christmas recess of Parliament, just
as the cabinet was considering its policy for Massachusetts. From these letters one acquires a strong impression
that Bernard and the customs officials had acted first in-
temperately, then in panic.[101]

At an earlier cabinet meeting, on December 8, Grafton
had sponsored a plan for Massachusetts which Conway
had found "very hazardous."[102] Perhaps from this meeting

[99] Gov. Wentworth to Rockingham, 13 November 1768, *Memoirs
of the Marquis of Rockingham,* ed. Earl of Albemarle (London,
1852), II, 88. Moses Franks, the army contractor and an important
London merchant, had told Rockingham the same thing on October
3; Wentworth Woodhouse MSS., Sheffield City Libraries, R
I-1101.

[100] Gage to Hillsborough, Boston, 31 October 1768, *Gage Corr.,*
I, 204-205.

[101] As early as November 8, in the debate on the Address from
the Throne, Col. Barré (a Chathamite out of office) stated: "May
we not reasonably suspect, that some of these reports were not
quite fair? May not a little mob have been called a tumult, and a
little insurrection a rebellion?" Cavendish, *Debates,* I, 44. For an
unsympathetic but not inaccurate view of Gov. Bernard, see James
Bowdoin to Thomas Pownall, 10 May 1769, who wrote that
Bernard "has a peculiar knack at making mountains of mole hills,
and idle chitchat, treason"; 6 *MHSC* IX, 143.

[102] Walpole, *Memoirs of Geo. III,* ed. Barker, III, 189-190. As

came the eight resolutions, roundly condemning all that
had been done by the Massachusetts Assembly and the Boston town meeting and magistracy, which Hillsborough had
put through the House of Lords in mid-December. Probably this was contemplated as only a first step, but by the
New Year any further action had encountered strong opposition within the cabinet, apparently from Grafton, Conway, and Camden.[103] One reason why the majority of the
cabinet was unwilling to push the Massachusetts matter as
far as had been originally planned was the growing dimen-
sions of the case of John Wilkes; it necessarily claimed
first priority, and the Opposition was making an uncom-
fortably good showing on the strength of it.[104] But Hillsborough would not—perhaps dared not—relax his demand
for a "firm" American policy. There is one other factor in
this developing situation, and that was the crucial one—
the King.

George III undoubtedly was aware of the growing political dangers, both within and without the ministry. He
saw the government's case against Boston, apparently so
strong at first, weaken as more information arrived. He
probably agreed to the Chathamite argument for delay on
Massachusetts. Finally, in February, Hillsborough attempted to force a decision from the cabinet before the
House of Commons again took up the American question.

Walpole was close to Conway, these factual statements are acceptable. But the other alleged circumstances of the meeting—that
Grafton did not realize that he was offering a plan which had been
substituted for his own by Jeremiah Dyson at the Board of Trade—
sound too much like a Walpolian jibe at Grafton to be accepted
without confirmation.

[103] Wrote Barrington to Bernard: "By some fatal catastrophe,
two or three men there [in the cabinet], with less ability, less
credit, less authority & less responsibility than the rest, have
carry'd their point and produced that flimsey unavailing Address
[the eight resolutions]. . . . I think there is a bare possibility
it may be amended [by the House of Commons]." 2 January 1769,
Barrington–Bernard Corr., 182.

[104] Horace Walpole, in both his memoirs and his letters, gave
far more attention to Wilkes than to Massachusetts, and the same
was true of Parliament; see Cavendish, *Debates*, I.

The cabinet deferred action, and the Colonial Secretary then tried to get royal backing before its next meeting.

In his plan, Hillsborough sought to couple the carrot and the stick. Essentially, he wanted to make the Massachusetts Council appointive and to make opposition to Parliamentary sovereignty by the Massachusetts Assembly an ipso facto forfeiture of the charter, but also to recall Bernard (after knighting him) and to give Gage discretion to withdraw the troops as soon as possible; for the colonies in general, he wanted to quarter troops in private houses when necessary and to put quartering under the control of the governor rather than of the local magistrates, but also to repeal the Townshend tariffs for Virginia, the West Indies, and any other colonies that would cease resistance to them.[105]

The King agreed only to the recall of Bernard and to the instructions for Gage. He remarked that Crown appointment of the Massachusetts Council "may from a continuance of their conduct become necessary," disapproved the remainder of the plan, and did not even mention the recommended revision of the quartering provisions of the Mutiny Act. Whether King George realized it or not, this effectively ended any serious thought of using the American army to enforce British law or royal command prior to 1774-1775.[106]

Certainly implicit in Hillsborough's plan was the possibility of military enforcement; from putting it to the touch, the King recoiled. Almost five years later Hillsborough's successor would be advised by his Undersecretary, in connection with a plea by a colonial governor for military assistance against the populace: "Exclusive of the violence and inhumanity of employing the soldiery upon such occasion I always understood from Lord Hillsborough

[105] 15 February 1769, *Geo. III Corr.*, II, #701. Hillsborough also wanted to remove four New York Councillors and to move a Parliamentary address censuring the conduct of the New York Assembly.

[106] Memorandum by the King, [February 1769], *Geo. III Corr.*, II, #701A. See also Walpole, *Memoirs of Geo. III*, ed. Barker, III, 223.

that the King was particularly averse to the detaching his troops for such purposes, as it serves to make the army odious to the public."[107] It can be argued that it hardly matters, because Hillsborough's plan could no more have succeeded in 1769 without continental rebellion than did the Coercive Acts in 1774-1775. This may be, and yet there are a few facts which argue otherwise: resistance to the troop landing had failed, and Boston radical leaders were clearly discouraged by the Parliamentary prospects; Massachusetts had less support from the other colonies in 1769; and revolutionary organization was more primitive at that time.

In any event, chances for that firm American policy which everyone claimed to desire steadily diminished after February 1769. In England, the Wilkes case continued to grow, and promised trouble from a united opposition in the next session of Parliament. In Ireland, the attempt to increase the size of the Irish army was bringing more trouble, in both traditional and unprecedented forms: riots broke out, and the government managers of the Irish parliament went into opposition. Barrington was so discouraged by the prospects for a strong policy toward the colonies that, without ministerial support, he moved an amendment to stiffen the quartering provisions of the Mutiny Act. His motion was rejected by both government and opposition, but another, making it easier for colonies to comply with the substance of the law while avoiding the question of Parliamentary sovereignty, was accepted.[108] In America, because of the bombastic resolutions passed by Parliament, the British government had paid the cost of moderation without collecting any of its benefits.[109] Bos-

---

[107] William Knox to Dartmouth, 6 October 1773, II *HMC* v (*Dartmouth MSS.,* I), 339.

[108] Some observers thought Barrington's independent action simply a governmental trial balloon. For example, see William Samuel Johnson to Pitkin, 23 March 1769, 5 *MHSC,* IX, 326. But Barrington explained to Gage that his duty to Crown, state, Parliament, and the army made him do it, despite opposition from all quarters. 21 March 1769, "Private," Gage MSS.

[109] Barrington had asserted that not five men in either House

ton leaders at first considered the resolutions a major set-back, but they soon learned from friends in England that no bite was to accompany the bark.

The Massacre and Its Consequences

More than a year before it actually happened, Thomas Cushing of Boston had heard that troops would occupy his town in order to secure obedience to Acts of Parliament. "Nothing," wrote Cushing, "would so soon throw the people into a flame. No one measure I could think of, would so effectually drive them into resolutions, which in the end would prove detrimental to Great Britain."[110] Troops did not come to Boston in 1767, but they came in 1768. By mid-summer people throughout New England had heard that a regiment was under orders to move south from Halifax, and most of them were furious.[111] Lieutenant Governor Thomas Hutchinson heard talk of open resistance, and when Boston leaders called a provincial "Convention," the talk seemed about to lead to action.[112] But the one regiment of July had increased by September. Almost the whole garrison of Halifax, more than two battalions, was coming, escorted by Captain Samuel Hood and the North American squadron. Two more battalions were known to be embarking in Ireland. When the Convention met, ardor if not temper had cooled somewhat.

Boats appeared in Boston harbor at the end of September to take soundings and plan anchorages. The next day, men-of-war sailed in and, one by one, took up position with springs on their anchor cables, so that broadsides faced the town. Then came transports with the 14th and 29th Regiments, and some troops of the 59th. Any man

---

had approved of them. To Gage, 12 February 1769, "Private," Gage MSS. In the following year, Edmund Burke pithily and accurately described them: "You showed your ill-will towards America, at the same time that you dared not execute it." Cavendish, *Debates,* I, 549.

[110] To ———, 9 May 1767, 4 *MHSC* IV, 348.

[111] *Stiles Corr.,* 244-245.

[112] Hutchinson to ———, 27 July 1768, Massachusetts Archives, XXVI (Hutchinson MSS.).

who had been at Louisbourg in 1758 must have remembered as he watched: the ships looked the same, they took station to support an assault landing in the same deliberate way, and the soldiers sitting like rows of red pegs in the barges looked the same as they moved slowly toward the town at noon, Friday, October 1. This display combined order, uncertainty, and menace. It was unsettling, for no imagination was required to see what might happen to this small seaport of less than twenty thousand people. Little wonder then that Boston anger lost its edge, and that talk of fighting in the streets gave way to counsels of fear and prudence.[113]

First resistance to the troops in Boston occurred not on the waterfront but in the Court House. When Lieutenant Colonel William Dalrymple, senior officer present, asked for quarters under Act of Parliament, the Massachusetts Council refused.[114] Its refusal was less a matter of defiance than one of interpretation. According to the law, a province had to provide quarters only after any existing barracks were full. There were barracks on Castle Island designed for a thousand men, though they were of poor wartime construction and now out of repair. The island was several miles from Boston proper, but legally was part of the town. If the troops did not first fill those barracks, said the Council, then any troops quartered in the town itself would be there illegally, and it would be impossible to furnish them anything under the Act. Dalrymple fumed, but, as the Council saw it, law was law and no one could violate it with impunity.

The Council was quibbling, of course, but even Thomas Hutchinson thought the Act left such a loophole.[115] The troops from Ireland, not due for another month, would eventually fill the Castle Island barracks, but the Council was not disposed to be reasonable. Dalrymple could not

[113] There is a detailed account of the landing of the troops in the *Virginia Gazette,* 27 October 1768.

[114] 6 *MHSC* IX, 105-111.

[115] Hutchinson to Thomas Whatley, 5 and 17 October 1768, and to Richard Jackson, 19 October 1768, Massachusetts Archives, XXV (Hutchinson MSS.).

withdraw his troops to the Island without negating the purpose for which they had come to Boston. With the 29th encamped on the Common, and the 14th temporarily in the Court House and Faneuil Hall only as a matter of Yankee courtesy because the regiment had no field equipment, the Colonel had little choice. He and Engineer John Montresor, sent by Gage from New York, began to hire buildings in town to house the soldiers.[116]

James Murray, a Scot recently arrived from South Carolina, let both his own home and his large sugar house, near Dock Square. A Mr. Forrest let his warehouse, and a Mr. Gordon his stores. Officers found lodgings for themselves wherever they could.[117] When Gage arrived for a brief visit in mid-October, the Council retreated somewhat and voted to turn over the provincial "Manufactory House" on condition that Castle Island barracks would be filled. But the manufactory house had occupants, and both the army and the magistracy lost face in trying to dislodge them.[118] Instead, Montresor rented buildings scattered throughout the town: on Water Street; on the wharf of that good Whig, Nathaniel Wheelwright; along Atkinson Street, where the ropemakers worked; and elsewhere.[119]

Within a few days, everyone—officers, soldiers, and civilians—knew the consequence. In the eighteenth century, troops outside of regular barracks or bivouac were hard to hold. While Hutchinson was pleased to report that "these Redcoats make a formidable appearance and there is a profound silence among our Sons of Liberty," he noted also that 70 men had deserted in the first two weeks.[120]

In response, the military command tried to seal the town. Dalrymple placed guards on all the improvised bar-

---

[116] *Virginia Gazette,* 10 November 1768.

[117] Oliver M. Dickerson (comp.) *Boston Under Military Rule [1768-1769] as Revealed in a Journal of the Times* (Boston, 1936), 3.

[118] *Ibid.,* 7-9.

[119] *Ibid.,* 11; Frederic Kidder, *History of the Boston Massacre* (Albany, 1870), 36n.

[120] Hutchinson to Whatley, 17 October 1768, Massachusetts Archives, xxv (Hutchinson MSS.).

racks and around the town itself. Especially important was Boston neck, and he placed a strong guard there. The purpose of the guard was neither ceremonial nor strictly military; rather, it was simply to stop desertion. During darkness, every person near a guard post was suspect, even civilians, because deserters changed clothes if they could. Though Dalrymple liked to believe that Yankees were "seducing" his men, he knew that the scattered situation of his command was the real trouble. But guards at night found it impossible to distinguish spurious from bona fide civilians, and soon zealous sentries were embroiled with sensitive townsmen. Thus it happened that, initially, friction in Boston was a direct product, not of civilian hostility, but of an internal military problem.[121]

There is abundant evidence to reconstruct events in Boston for the eighteen months prior to the Massacre on March 5, 1770. The printers, Edes and Gill, perhaps with Sam Adams behind them, published a "Journal of the Times" intended to expose the evil activities of both the troops and the customs officials.[122] Almost a hundred depositions printed after the Massacre are in the same vein, while Gage had some 70 depositions taken from officers and soldiers in order to counter the Boston version of the truth.[123] Other depositions favorable to the army were printed in London.[124] By looking for mutual agreement and for self-incriminating admissions in this mass of contradictory material, one can winnow a considerable amount of dependable information from the partisan distortion and falsehood. In particular, one fact stands out: most of the incidents between soldiers and civilians, at least

[121] Lt. Col. Dalrymple to Gage, 13 October 1768, and Col. Pomeroy to Gage; 12 December 1768, Gage MSS.

[122] Dickerson, *Boston Under Military Rule,* is a compilation of the "Journal."

[123] The pro-American depositions are printed in Kidder, *Boston Massacre.* The depositions of the British soldiers are in CO 5/88. Alden, *Gage,* 171-172, errs in saying that the latter depositions were never taken.

[124] *A Fair Account of the Late Unhappy Disturbance at Boston* (London, 1770).

in the first year, had their origin in the army's attempt to prevent desertion.

Boston had successfully advertised its peaceful reception of the troops as proof that the town was loyal and tranquil, and that the Governor and Customs Commissioners were liars. We have seen how the British government swung around on this question during December and January. But success in England had meant bruised pride in Boston, for even the inhabitants themselves were unsure of the respective proportions played by policy and by timidity in their behavior. Now that the soldiers were among them, it would be unwise to risk the benefits of prudent conduct, but to answer a sentry's challenge with the traditional cry of "Friend!" was more than most Bostonians could bear.

Incident after incident turned on this apparently trivial point, and it is easy to see why. The officer, sergeant, and corporal of the guard, each in turn, would instruct the sentinel to keep sharp watch, challenge all persons near his post, and let no deserter slip by, on pain of a few hundred lashes for neglect of duty. The sentinel would try to carry out orders, but few townsmen would play the game. When he attempted to stop these unidentified persons who did not answer, as he was obliged to do, they might do one of several things. If they were numerous, rowdy, or drunken, they might seize his musket and beat him with it. If they were few, timid, or respectable, they would get his name and have him before the justice of the peace next day for assault. Another variation, favored by small boys who had observed their elders, was to throw a rock, brick, or snowball, then run.

Morale, never high among troops who may have to fight against civilians, dropped still further, and desertion continued unabated. At first Gage tried to deter it by rigor. Two weeks after his arrival in October, he had a deserter named Ames executed. The inhabitants were horrified to see, on the Lord's Day, this young man, dressed all in white, led to the Common, and, after a lengthy ceremony, shot to death. The regiments then filed by the corpse in case anyone had missed the point.[125] But in May 1769, the commander in Boston persuaded Gage to issue a general pardon for all deserters who would surrender.[126] By September, Gage was back to a policy of no mercy.[127]

Nothing seemed to be effective in stopping desertion. The guards around the town kept it within bounds until February, when a hard freeze set in and the deserters began to go over the ice.[128] When Gage ordered parties of soldiers in civilian clothes out into the countryside to look for deserters, the local magistrates and inhabitants refused to cooperate, and occasionally rescued any deserters caught.[129] The execution of Ames had been widely reported, and had had an effect, but not the one intended. Whatever their opinion of the British government and army, or of Boston radicals, no civilian was willing to turn a soldier over to the firing squad or the hangman. It was this "false Humanity" on the part of New Englanders that eventually led Gage to issue the general pardon in May.[130]

Bostonians were shocked not only by the execution of Ames, but by the frequency and severity of corporal punishment in the army. Boston courts, when sentencing a convict to the lash, reckoned by tens; the army by hundreds. Only a few days after the troops landed, nine or ten men were whipped on the Common, and thereafter this was a regular spectacle.[131] Any offense that was worth a regimental court-martial got at least 100 lashes, and sentences of 1,000 lashes were not uncommon. In the latter cases, Negro drummers took turns whipping a culprit until the surgeon intervened, the trick being to stop before the man was dead but not much before.[132]

[125] Dickerson, *Boston Under Military Rule,* 16.

[126] Gage to Maj. Gen. Mackay, 15 May 1769, Gage MSS.

[127] Gage to Dalrymple, 10 September 1769, *ibid.* Gage MSS. during 1768-1770 are filled with mention of this problem.

[128] Dickerson, *Boston Under Military Rule,* 64.

[129] Pomeroy to Gage, 12 January 1769, Gage MSS.

[130] Gov. Wentworth of New Hampshire to Pomeroy, 20 February 1769, *ibid.*

[131] Dickerson, *Boston Under Military Rule,* 3.

[132] Records of general courts-martial for the American army

As everywhere, whippings and the offenses that earned them were almost completely due to drunkenness, but the situation was unusually bad in Boston because of the cheapness of rum.[133] The nonimportation agreement had depressed the economy, and with it commodity prices.[134] Bostonians may have hated the army in their midst, but they needed the soldier's business, and they were pleased to sell rum to anyone with hard cash. In fact, so many troops in such a small community had a significant economic impact. James Bowdoin, moderator of the town meeting and future governor of the state, wrote in May that complaints of a currency shortage had subsided, "as the new guardians of our liberty and rights scatter with the pox some of their loose money."[135] Unkind reports from New York had it that Boston cleared £250 each week from its soldiers.[136] But the cost of this prosperity was crime, disease, desertion, even death, and a slow deterioration of discipline within the British garrison.

One result of drunkenness was violence. Soldiers began to get into fights, especially with sailors, some of them unemployed, others from His Majesty's Navy. In either case, the sympathies of a maritime town lay with the seafaring men. More serious was the rising incidence of petty crime, especially theft, all of which was blamed on soldiers who were after drinking money. Most offensive to the Puritan conscience was the increase in prostitution, which, combined with drunkenness, must surely have been behind some of the more lurid incidents reported in the

---

are in WO 71/72-80. Regimental courts-martial were not forwarded to the Judge Advocate General, but never in the occasional one that I have found does a convicted man get less than 100 lashes.

[133] Andrew Eliot wrote that "the soldiers are in raptures at the *cheapness* of spirituous liquors among us"; to Thomas Hollis, 29 January 1769, 4 *MHSC* IV, 437-438.

[134] Ruth Crandall, "Wholesale Commodity Prices in Boston During the Eighteenth Century," *The Review of Economic Statistics,* XVI (1934) 117-128.

[135] To Thomas Pownall, 10 May 1769, 6 *MHSC* IX, 140.

[136] *Virginia Gazette,* 10 August 1769, dateline New York.

press. In April, the "Journal of the Times" expressed dismay at what people in Boston would do for money, and shame at the acts of prostitution committed day and night in the streets and on the commons.[137] Here too the depression had its effect, for the number of poor in Boston was rising in these months; high unemployment, low prices and wages, and prostitution were all part of the same economic pattern.

It would be misleading, however, to describe the areas of friction and let it stand as an explanation of the Boston Massacre. A year and a half went by after the troops arrived before there was a Massacre, and that amount of time is itself suggestive. There were forces operating to prevent open conflict. Two of them—Boston fear and the economic value of the garrison—have already been mentioned. Another has been hinted at: a certain humanitarian feeling for these poor creatures who seemed worse off than most slaves. Bostonians saw them beaten, saw their religious life neglected, and came to know them well enough to see fellow human beings under the red coats. When the "Journal of the Times," with its virulently antimilitary views, could refer to the troops in Boston as "the best soldiers of Britain," there is a faint echo of the sentiment prevalent during the Seven Years War.[138]

Finally, there are the commanders in Boston to be considered. After Gage's departure in November 1768, his successors managed to keep reasonably good order for the next six months. Brigadier General John Pomeroy arrived with the major elements of the 64th and 65th Regiments in November, and was in command until the following May. The sister of one of the Customs Commissioners, who did not live in any great harmony with the military officers, decribed him as "an amiable worthy Man," who "takes great care that his men shall give no real Offense."[139] When the county jail caught fire and endangered

---

[137] Dickerson, *Boston Under Military Rule*, 86-87.
[138] *Ibid.*, 28.
[139] Ann Hulton, *Letters of a Loyalist Lady* (Cambridge, Mass., 1927), 18.

neighboring buildings, British soldiers reacted quickly to
put it out and Pomeroy received the thanks of the town.[140]
An enemy of the military called him "prudent, discreet."[141]
When he departed, even the "Journal of the Times" admitted that his conduct had "done honour to the army, and
that as a gentleman he was well respected."[142]

Major General Alexander Mackay had been shipwrecked
in the West Indies with part of the troops from Ireland,
and did not arrive until early May 1769. He stayed in
Boston only a few months, but while there did what he
could to mollify the inhabitants. He stopped some of the
grosser offenses against the Sabbath, like horse racing
on the Common and strolling during divine service, that
had rankled among pious Bostonians.[143] He tried to keep
challenging by sentries within reasonable bounds. As a
result of such actions, Mackay, like Pomeroy, was fairly
popular among the townspeople.[144]

They had courted civilian favor for reasons that do them
little credit, however. Pomeroy had not expected to be in
command at all, and only the accident to Mackay had made
it necessary. He was soon begging Gage for leave because
of pressing personal business at home, to take effect upon
Mackay's arrival.[145] But no sooner had Mackay arrived
than he too wanted leave. He said that the Boston command was really too small for a major general, and there
might be difficulties with the other general officers in
America, who were junior to him but controlled more
troops.[146] These were feeble if traditional arguments, but
for some reason Gage gave in. He let Pomeroy go in June
1769, and Mackay in August. Both officers were bent on
getting out of a potentially nasty situation as quickly as
they could, and the conciliatory policy of each primarily

[140] Dickerson, *Boston Under Military Rule*, 57; Pomeroy to
Gage, 6 February 1769, Gage MSS.

[141] Andrew Eliot to Thomas Hollis, 29 January 1769, 4 *MHSC*
IV, 437-438.

[142] Dickerson, *Boston Under Military Rule*, 112.

[143] *Ibid.*, 108.   [144] 6 *MHSC* IX, 170n.

[145] Alden, *Gage*, 169-170.

[146] Mackay to Gage, 12 June 1769, Gage MSS.

reflects a desire to keep the lid on until he was safely on a ship outward bound.[147] And with Mackay's departure real trouble began.

A violent culmination may have been simply inevitable, but there is a complex, yet discernible, structure to events in Boston between the summer of 1769 and March 5, 1770, that deserves examination. Despite the problems of desertion, challenging, and drunkenness, both sides conceded that it had been a surprisingly quiet winter and spring. In June, a rumor began to circulate: the government was considering withdrawal of the troops from Boston.[148] It was indeed. Growing disorder in Ireland over the proposal to increase its army made the transfer of at least two regiments from North America urgent. When the King, cabinet, and Parliament had rejected his plan to crack down on Boston, Hillsborough did the logical thing by giving Gage discretionary authority to withdraw the troops if the Governor concurred.[149]

Once again the fissure between civil and military power, which had opened with the creation of a single general headquarters, became visible. Gage sent James Robertson to get Governor Bernard's opinion in writing, but Bernard played coy. His own departure was imminent, and he did not relish the prospect of, in effect, deciding on the removal of troops, only to see a mob drive the customs officers out of town again.[150] For the time, it was agreed to send two regiments away with Pomeroy, and keep two in Boston.

When the 64th and 65th Regiments embarked, Bostonians were elated. Their policy of prudence had paid off,

[147] [Henry Hulton], "Some Account of the Proceedings of the People in New England; from the Establishment of a Board of Customs in America, to the breaking out of the Rebellion in 1775," MS. in Princeton University Library, P 850, 147-149, discusses how eager various commanders were to find an excuse to leave Boston.

[148] Dickerson, *Boston Under Military Rule,* 111.

[149] Hillsborough to Gage, 24 March 1769, *Gage Corr.,* II, 87.

[150] Mackay and Lt. Col. Robertson to Gage, 12 June 1769, Gage MSS.; Gage to Hillsborough, 22 July 1769, *Gage Corr.,* I, 229-230.

and it seemed that Benjamin Franklin had been well informed when he wrote that, if only Boston would keep
quiet and avoid tumults, "this Military Cloud that now
blusters over you, will pass away, and do you no more
harm than a Summer Thunder Shower."[151] The Reverend
Samuel Cooper reported to Franklin, "The greater part of
the Military has lately been withdrawn from this Town,
and it is said the remainder will not tarry long among
us."[152] Even the "Journal of the Times" ceased publication
as if the battle had been won.

Elation did not last the summer. Hutchinson, now acting Governor, saw more clearly than Bernard that troops
could not be of any use because no magistrate would ever
call on them for assistance, but no more than his predecessor did he dare take responsibility for their removal.[153]
The Customs Commissioners were the principal target of
Boston's wrath, and Hutchinson was afraid to leave them
without the force they claimed was needed to perform their
duty. Two regiments remained in the town.

The inhabitants, once they thought withdrawal imminent,
had begun to exert more pressure on the garrison, perhaps
to speed its departure. As it dawned on them that there
would be no withdrawal, this pressure increased and turned
uglier. Colonel Dalrymple, again in command after Mackay's departure, wrote Gage that the spirit of the towns-
people had become "so overbearing that I live in hourly
dread of a Disturbance."[154] From the other camp came a
confirming echo: "Our people," wrote the Reverend Andrew Eliot, "begin to despise a military force."[155] The time
for prudence and illusions had passed, and only direct
action now seemed likely to get the army out of Boston.

From the beginning, Bostonians had been probing for
weak spots in the army. They had learned to bring ob-

[151] To Rev. Samuel Cooper, 27 April 1769, *Franklin Writings,*
ed. Smyth, v, 205.
[152] 3 August 1769, CL, Franklin-Pownall-Cooper Letterbook.
[153] Hutchinson to Thomas Whatley, 24 August 1769, Massachusetts Archives, xxv (Hutchinson MSS.).
[154] 19 August 1769, Gage MSS.
[155] To Thomas Hollis, 7 September 1769, 4 *MHSC,* iv, 445.

streperous sentries before a fire-eating magistrate like old
Richard Dana, who would first harangue them: *"What
brought you here, who sent for you,* and by *what authority
do you mount Guard,* it is contrary to the laws of the *Province,* and you should be all taken up for so offending"; and
then fine them as much as they earned in a month or
more.[156] But when soldiers charged with more serious
offenses were turned over to the Superior Court, the Attorney General seems to have been lax in prosecuting
them.[157] Angered by such a frustration of the law, Dana
and Justice Ruddock and others like them levied ever
higher fines. The resources of regimental funds soon gave
out against this kind of attack, and magistrates began to
bind out as servants soldiers who could not pay their
fines.[158]

At this new turn, Gage exploded. "I can hardly write
with Patience on this infamous Affair," was his response
to the first case of a soldier being indented as a servant.
Gage was afraid that the troops, who knew they had some
rights as British subjects, would mutiny.[159] Mackay began
to pay the fines whenever he could, and even to give money
to soldiers who had suffered abuse from the townsmen in
silence.[160] But by mid-summer it was becoming difficult to
keep the soldiers from seeking redress in the streets, and
dangerous for an officer to go too far in ordering them to
turn the other cheek.

A grenadier of the 14th Regiment, John Riley, knocked
a butcher down in the public market after a quarrel on the
afternoon of July 13. Riley seems to have been a popular
man in his unit, and also to have had good reason for his
action. He was brought immediately before Justice Edmund Quincy, who was not one of the "hanging" judges.
Quincy found him guilty of assault, fined him 13*s.* 4*d.*,
and gave him a day of grace to find the money. Both officers

[156] Deposition of Ensign John Ness, 25 August 1770, CO 5/88.
[157] Dickerson, *Boston Under Military Rule,* 91, 105.
[158] Mackay to Gage, 12 June 1769, Gage MSS.
[159] Gage to Mackay, 18 June 1769, *ibid.*
[160] Mackay to Gage, 19 June and 18 August 1769, *ibid.*

and men of the 14th were unusually aroused by this affair. As the butcher drove through town next day in a cart, soldiers jeered him; when he appealed to Dalrymple, who happened to be passing by, the Colonel damned the butcher and said that he, Dalrymple, would have knocked him down if Riley had not done it. In the words of eye witnesses, this so "elevated" the soldiers that they "Swore by God that no Justice nor Constable nor Town people neither Should Commit their fellow Soldier to Goal."[161] About twenty of them went to Quincy's, where Riley had been taken by a constable, to rescue their comrade. In the ensuing melee, the constable called on bystanders for help, and the soldiers drew swords. No one was seriously hurt, and Riley was spirited away and out of Boston, undoubtedly with the connivance of some officers. But the Boston Massacre could have happened on July 14, 1769.[162]

A conviction grew on both sides that there was no way to get justice without violence. Bostonians saw prisoners of the court rescued, others who were accused disappear, and those who came to trial let off by the Attorney General. Soldiers suffered outrageous penalties for obeying orders, and heard magistrates tell juries not to believe the unsupported testimony of military men. Equally ominous was the changing attitude of the military commanders. Gage had lost his temper, and so had Dalrymple.[163] Both felt

[161] Investigation by the House of the rescue of John Ryley, grenadier of the 14th Regiment. Arthur Lee MSS., Houghton Library, Harvard University.

[162] The British version, which has Riley striking the butcher in a quarrel over a little boy being beaten in the market place, is contained in the depositions of Cpl. Samuel Heale, Sgt. John Phillips, Lt. Alex. Ross, Capt. Charles Fordyce, and Pvt. Jonathan Stevenson, 25 August 1770, CO 5/88.

[163] Miss Hulton, the sister of the Customs Commissioner, described Dalrymple as "proud, haughty, and voluptuous, devoted to self, and Self gratification [,] hated in general by those under his Command, and universally despised." Hulton, *Letters, 63.* In fact, he seems to have been an intelligent and popular if hard-bitten officer, nick-named "Steel Breeches" because he reputedly wore one pair of buckskin breeches for thirty years. S. G. P. Ward, *Faithful: The Story of the Durham Light Infantry* (London and Liverpool, 1962), 50.

315

that they had to support their men in order to prevent morale and discipline from declining still further.

Trouble increased during the autumn, until another serious incident occurred at the guard post on Boston Neck. Ensign John Ness, officer of the guard on the night of October 23, apparently had had a quarrel with Robert Pierpoint over the firewood that Pierpoint supplied to the Neck guard house. When a constable tried to serve a warrant on Ness for assaulting Pierpoint and stealing his wood, Ness refused to accept it until he was off duty. Words were exchanged, a crowd gathered, and Ness had to turn out the guard to protect his post. Next morning, during the march back to Boston, angry civilians harassed the column of soldiers. They yelled, pushed, and threw rocks. At last, a blacksmith named Whiston ran into the column and struck Private William Fowler in the face. Fowler, cut badly, staggered on with the help of other soldiers, while the sergeant used the butt of his halberd to keep Whiston from repeating his act. Ness held the soldiers in ranks, and managed to get the column back to barracks. Again, a "massacre" did not happen.[164]

Both Ness and the sergeant were brought before Dana, who lectured them in his usual manner, and did all he could to keep them from being bailed. When Pierpoint and some spectators became abusive toward the two men, suggesting for example that they ought to be "bailed" with a rope, Dana feigned deafness. Eventually both were freed in the Superior Court, perhaps with the help of the Attorney General. When Private Fowler sought to prosecute his assailant, he was told to find some civilian witnesses.[165]

The rule of law was near an end in Boston. Something like gang warfare went on in the streets, and neither side could have stopped if it had tried. Incidents no longer flared and then were forgotten, as they had the previous

[164] Deposition of Ensign John Ness, 25 August 1770, CO 5/88. Pierpoint claimed the land on which the Neck guardhouse had been built. Dalrymple to Gage, 27 September 1769, Gage MSS.

[165] Deposition of Sgt. James Hickman, 25 August 1770, CO 5/88. There are many depositions in CO 5/88 relating to this affair.

winter, but retaliation led to counterretaliation. Bostonians had learned that a sentry dared not fire, no matter what the provocation, and they used this knowledge without mercy to harass the men who had corrupted the law and the morals of the town.

Most of the 14th Regiment was housed in a single building, Murray's sugar house near Dock Square, but the 29th was scattered in barracks along Water Lane and Atkinson Street, down toward the waterfront along the ropewalks.[166] After the New Year, the 29th became the special target of Boston's attack. On Friday, March 2, there was a fight when some ropemakers asked a soldier of the 29th if he wanted work and, when he said he did, suggested that he clean their privy. Soon after, Thomas Walker—drummer of the 29th, Negro, and a big man— met the soldier, who had blood streaming from his head. Walker and some of his comrades then decided they ought, in Walker's words, to "inquire" down at the ropewalk. Next morning as Walker was being carried to the hospital, he remembered hearing some ropemakers ask the litter bearer where the 29th planned to bury its dead.[167]

Fighting continued on Saturday, there was a lull on Sunday, but on Monday, March 5, everyone knew that a crisis was imminent. The ropemakers were using hatchets on their neighbors the soldiers, and other Bostonians travelled the streets in packs with lead-weighted clubs. A sergeant was missing, and Dalrymple thought he had been murdered. If a soldier lived outside barracks, as an undetermined number of them did, with the family of his girl for example, he might be warned to keep off the streets by those who did not want him hurt, or he might pass a similar warning to the household. In the gloom of the late winter afternoon, the first blows were struck at isolated soldiers and officers. Next, the sentries began to suffer. Finally, about eight o'clock, after an affray near Murray's barracks, the gangs converged along the dark

[166] Kidder, *Boston Massacre,* 36n.
[167] Deposition of Drummer Thomas Walker, 24 July 1770, CO 5/88.

and icy streets on the sentry post at that hated building, the Customs House. Earlier, officers had driven their men, hungry for revenge, back into barracks. Soon someone brought word to Captain Thomas Preston, officer of the main guard, that the sentry's life was in danger. Preston at first did nothing, because he could not use force without legal authorization any more than the sentry himself could. Only after a second call for help did he take a file of men up King Street to the Customs House. Meanwhile the bells had begun to ring as if for fire, and Boston knew the time had come.[168]

Whether Preston ordered the shots that killed five men is not a very interesting question. A jury of Massachusetts citizens acquitted him and all but two of his men, who received nominal sentences for manslaughter, and that judgment ought to satisfy historians.[169] Boston had accomplished its purpose, and could only profit by showing magnanimity. Both civil and military authorities had been in a panic during the day and night after the Massacre, and town leaders had successfully exploited their fear. Boston demanded the complete withdrawal of troops, and threatened a rising of the whole countryside if these terms were not met. Hutchinson seems to have frozen into silence, and the Council could not reach a decision. Colonel Dalrymple insisted for the record that he had no authority himself to move the troops. But while the Council recessed, Dalrymple went round to each member and begged him to advise withdrawal. The Council members agreed, made an official recommendation, and Dalrymple complied, grumbling of course to Gage that he had had no choice.[170]

More interesting than the minutiae of the Massacre itself is the question of to what extent it was the work of

[168] Kidder, *Boston Massacre,* and Depositions in CO 5/88.

[169] The record of Preston's trial has been lost, and both the trial of the soldiers and the record of it were perfunctorily executed. See *Diary and Autobiography of John Adams,* ed. Butterfield, 291ff.

[170] This story is told in Thomas Hutchinson, *History of Massachusetts-Bay,* III, 197-198, and is confirmed by Henry Hulton, "Some Account . . . ," Princeton University Library, MS. P 850, 158-159.

Boston leaders. Conspiracies are seldom well documented. Aside from untrustworthy accounts of the rumors running before the Massacre, there is a dearth of extant evidence.[171] But circumstances suggest that there was as much purpose as spontaneity in the events leading up to the Massacre. After the dashed hopes of the past summer for removal of troops, resentment and desperation among the inhabitants had grown apace. One would have expected an explosion no later than November or December, soon after the Pierpoint incident, which in some ways was more incendiary than the attack on the sentry on March 5. It may be, however, that Boston leaders had learned a lesson in 1768—that it was better to have trouble at the end rather than the beginning of a Parliamentary session. At it happened, the Boston Massacre and the vote in the House of Commons to repeal all Townshend duties save that on tea occurred on the same day. When news reached London of the Massacre, at the fag end of the session, there was little response. The House called for all papers on civil-military relations in America, but debate was listless and dull. All the American questions—revenue, army, and the West—seemed stuck on dead center. The truth was that no one knew what to do about them. In any case, at that season no one had the energy or temerity to suggest a strong response to the expulsion of troops from Boston.[172]

After the 1768-69 Parliamentary session, a few diehards had continued to express the need for strong action, but they knew that the moment for it had passed.[173] News

[171] A good deal was made at the time of the coroner's report on Crispus Attucks, a Negro and one of the victims of the Massacre, which said that two musket balls had entered his body at an oblique angle and so must have been fired from an upper window in the Customs House (Kidder, *Boston Massacre,* 102). But buried in the trial record is testimony that seems to explain the angle of entry: "The mulatto was leaning over a long stick he had resting his breast upon it [just before he was shot]." (*Ibid.,* 142).

[172] Thomas Pownall to James Bowdoin, *et al.,* 11 May 1770, *CSMP,* vii (1900-1902), 213-215.

[173] "I entirely agree with you that every act of relaxation in this

of the Boston Massacre caused no demand by the ministry for coercion, but led only to another denunciation by Thomas Pownall of the powers of the staff of American general officers, and to a desultory debate on the ineffectuality of the government's colonial policy.[174] As the agent for Connecticut reported, it was obvious that this debate was not conducted for the sake of the colonies, but only to distress the ministry. After the customs officials had fled Boston a second time in the summer of 1770, Gage advised that it was better to do nothing than to do it by halves; Barrington and, presumably, Hillsborough agreed.[175]

Country towards it's [*sic*] refractory Colonies is destructive: I make no secret of this opinion any where, and I lament that Persons in Stations of more importance do not think as I do." Barrington to Gage, 20 September 1769, "Private," Gage MSS. But in his next private letter (1 November), Barrington admitted that no matter what American measures were planned for the coming session of Parliament, nothing could repair the damage done by inactivity in the previous session.

[174] Barrington to Gage, 2 April and 1 July 1770, "Private," Gage MSS.; William Samuel Johnson to Gov. Trumbull, 28 March and 21 May 1770, 5 *MHSC,* IX, 428, 435-437.

[175] Johnson to Trumbull, 21 May 1770, 5 *MHSC,* IX, 437. Gage to Barrington, 6 July 1770, "Private," *Gage Corr.,* II, 547; Barrington to Gage, 2 September 1770, "Private," Gage MSS.

VIII · A Pause, 1770-1773:

The Army in Retrospect

IF the use of troops to coerce colonists had not become a dead issue for political reasons after the Boston Massacre, other events would have made it a difficult course to follow. Disorder in Ireland became so serious in 1769 that Gage had to send back the two-regiment reinforcement he had received the year before.[1] More threatening was the turn taken by foreign affairs. Since the Seven Years War, Great Britain had remained in a state of apathetic isolation, despite the common assumption that France and Spain would seek revenge at the first opportunity. Nothing had come of Chatham's plan to establish a northern counterweight by allying Britain with Prussia and Russia.[2] Instead, French intervention in Corsica had seemed to bring Britain measurably closer to war in 1768.[3]

From America there were frequent reports of French and Spanish intrigue among the Indians, although both Amherst and Gage generally discounted these reports as the gambits of Indian diplomacy or the complaints of unsuccessful British fur traders.[4] By 1769, however, Hillsborough was showing unusual concern over Spanish activity in America.[5] That activity was apparently innocent of any aggressive intentions, but it looked suspicious at the time, for Gage had reported the arrival of a considerable body of Spanish troops in New Orleans and there was word of Spanish negotiations with the Indians along the Gulf Coast.[6] Though the Spanish soldiers obviously were sent

[1] Barrington to Gage, 21 March 1769, "Private," Gage MSS.

[2] Sir Richard Lodge, *Great Britain and Prussia in the Eighteenth Century* (Oxford, 1923), 139-149.

[3] John F. Ramsey, *Anglo-French Relations, 1763-1770; A Study of Choiseul's Foreign Policy* (Berkeley, 1939), 189.

[4] Gage to Hillsborough, 4 February 1769, *Gage Corr.*, I, 217.

[5] Hillsborough to Gage, 24 March and 9 December 1769, *ibid.*, II, 87, 93-94.

[6] Gage to Hillsborough, 5 March and 7 October 1769, 7 July 1770, *ibid.*, I, 222, 238-239, 262.

to put down a rebellion in Louisiana, their presence made both Hillsborough and the inhabitants of West Florida uneasy. The latter, who were also unhappy at what the withdrawal of troops would do to their primitive economy, succeeded in keeping a full battalion at Pensacola instead of the three companies planned for West Florida in the redeployment of 1768.[7]

Anglo-Spanish relations had been steadily deteriorating since 1766, and it seemed ominous that the new commander at New Orleans was General Alexander O'Reilly, known as one of the most influential members of the "war party" at the Spanish court.[8] O'Reilly had left New Orleans before a major Anglo-Spanish dispute developed over possession of the Falkland Islands in 1770, but by then Gage was reporting friction further up the Mississippi, at Fort Chartres.[9] A month later the British Board of Ordnance decided to fortify St. John's, Newfoundland. All signs pointed to an early war: Parliament voted an augmentation of forces, Gage issued orders to concentrate six battalions and an artillery train at New York, and Hillsborough secretly informed him that New Orleans would be the first British objective if war began.[10]

The war scare had passed by mid-1771, but it made the government readier than ever to liquidate its military commitment in the American West. Hillsborough had gained cabinet approval in early 1768 for the abandonment of all except a few key posts, but local interests in at least four

[7] Hillsborough to Gage, 9 December 1769, *ibid.*, II, 94. For the disgust with this change expressed at headquarters, see Gage to Haldimand, 23 March 1770, Gage MSS.; Lt. Col. Robertson to Haldimand, 26 March 1770, BM Add. MSS. 21666; Haldimand to Gage, 11 June 1771, BM Add. MSS. 21665; and Adjutant General Harvey to Maj. Gen. Mackay, 17 June 1771, WO 3/3, 41.

[8] Vera Lee Brown, "Anglo-Spanish Relations in the Closing Years of the Colonial Era," *Hispanic-American Review*, v (1922), 409-412.

[9] Gage to Hillsborough, 14 May and 2 June 1770, *Gage Corr.*, I, 256-257, 259.

[10] Hillsborough to Gage, 31 July, 28 September ("Most Secret and Confidential"), and 11 November 1770; 2 January ("Most Secret") and 22 January 1771, *ibid.*, II, 110-111, 117-118, 121-126.

colonies fought against it. The citizens of West Florida used the war scare (as already noted), and the Governor of New Providence in the Bahamas used the danger of internal disorder, to prevent the withdrawal of forces in those colonies. Bermuda and Nova Scotia tried to exert similar pressure but without success.[11]

Another obstacle to withdrawal from the interior was that troop deployment remained tied in theory and belief, if not in fact, to the still unsettled problem of Western colonization. The dilemma of Hillsborough was like that faced by Shelburne, for both proponents and opponents of colonization asserted that their own plans would prevent Indian war, and that those of their antagonists would foment it. Hillsborough feared, if an Indian war should follow the abandonment of Fort Pitt and Fort Chartres, that he could and would be attacked for rejecting Shelburne's plan to establish two or three colonies in the West.[12]

Since the winter of 1768-1769, Hillsborough's influence had declined, not only in the cabinet where it had never been large, but also with the King. The plan of early 1768 for the withdrawal of troops and the end of imperial Indian trade regulation had included a new negotiated boundary line with the various tribes. Both Shelburne and Hillsborough had sent exact instructions to Sir William Johnson about how the line should be drawn with the Six Nations so as to meet the southern part of the line and so as not to antagonize the interested Cherokee, Delaware, and Shawnee. Johnson, secretly connected with one speculative group and under pressure from others, violated his instructions and permitted the Six Nations to extend the boundary down the Ohio River to the mouth of the Tennessee River. He

[11] On West Florida and Nova Scotia, see Gage to Hillsborough, 4 March 1769, *ibid.*, I, 218-219, and Hillsborough to Gage, 13 May 1769, *ibid.*, II, 88. On the Bahamas, see Hillsborough to Gage, 4 August 1769, *ibid.*, 91-92. On Bermuda, see Gov. Bruere to Gage, 9 January 1771, Gage MSS.

[12] Samuel Wharton privately reported in 1769 that the ministers were "afraid of each other and dread nothing so much as bringing on an Indian war." Quoted in Wainwright, *Croghan*, 265.

thereby opened most of present day Kentucky to settlement, but he also started a flood of Shawnee-Delaware resentment which, after much bloodshed, was still flowing in the War of 1812. Hillsborough foresaw the consequences of Johnson's action and intended to repair the damage done, but apparently neither the King nor the remainder of the cabinet could understand why the Colonial Secretary should be upset when the Indian agent had done no more than secure an unexpectedly advantageous territorial cession. Hillsborough, who understood the Indian situation as the King and the rest of the cabinet did not, was overruled on this point at about the same time he was overruled on his plan for getting tough with Massachusetts. Whether there was a connection between the two rebuffs, and whether they were cause or result of his loss of influence, is impossible to say. Whatever the answer, in June 1769, the Massachusetts agent reported that Hillsborough no longer seemed to have "the chief ministerial direction of American affairs."[13]

Hillsborough was convinced from the reports of Gage, John Stuart, and Johnson himself that colonies in the Indian country meant war. And yet, Samuel Wharton, London agent for the Grand Ohio Company, reported that an unnamed *"powerful Body"* was watching the Colonial Secretary and would hold him responsible if an Indian war resulted from any of his actions, such as failing to keep Johnson's "promises" to the Six Nations to buy Kentucky.[14] The difficulty was that an Indian war could occur for any of a number of reasons, many of them unconnected with British policy. Although Barrington continually pressed him to withdraw the garrison from Illinois, it is not surprising that Hillsborough moved cautiously.[15] While seeking detailed advice from Gage on this point, he fought those, like Franklin and Wharton, who would establish a colony in the upper Ohio valley.[16] By the end of 1771,

[13] William Bollan to Samuel Danforth, *et al.*, 21 June 1769, 6 *MHSC*, ix, 145.

[14] Sosin, *Whitehall*, 183-184.

[15] Barrington to Gage, 1 July 1770, "Private," Gage MSS.

[16] Sosin, *Whitehall*, 185-195. In general, this account follows Sosin's treatment of Western policy.

Hillsborough had finally decided to withdraw all but a small detachment from Illinois and to abandon Fort Pitt.[17] Perhaps, if he had remained in office, he would have adopted Barrington's plan of getting all troops out of the older colonies, for the Secretary at War had continued to advocate this idea.[18]

Hillsborough did not remain in office, however. He had opposed the plan of the Grand Ohio Company to form a colony in present day West Virginia for over three years; in doing this, he had used fair means and foul. Finally, Samuel Wharton simply bribed several members of the government with shares in the company to override the Colonial Secretary's report on the matter. They had their own political interest in eliminating Hillsborough, and advised Wharton to promote a petition from "experts" in America in order to give the lords an excuse for action. The result was predictable: North gave half-hearted support to Hillsborough, the King was confused by the whole situation but irritated by Hillsborough's intransigence, and Hillsborough, overruled by the cabinet in his own department, resigned in August 1772.[19]

When Hillsborough resigned, Barrington and Gage took up the fight. They had both believed for some time that

[17] Hillsborough to Gage, 4 December 1771, *Gage Corr.*, II, 136-139.

[18] In fact, Barrington suggested to Gage that five battalions be withdrawn from the American garrison to Ireland where (1) they were always needed, (2) they would be immediately available for any emergency, and (3) they would cost much less. 2 July 1771, "Private," Gage MSS. Gage tactfully presented the "facts" which made such a plan impracticable in his opinion. 3 September 1771, "Private," *Gage Corr.*, II, 589-590.

[19] Sosin, *Whitehall*, 195-205; the King to Lord Suffolk, 22 July 1772, *Geo. III Corr.*, II, #1100; "Lord Hillsborough's Resignation, 15 August 1772," *HMC, Various Collections*, VI (*Knox MSS.*), 253-255. In 1774, Thomas Hutchinson heard, "that soon after Lord Hillsborough resigned, one of the Ministry, who he named, and I have forgot, who had greatly promoted it [Vandalia], altered his sentiments; and that if he had done it sooner, Lord H. need not have resigned, . . ." *Hutchinson Diary and Letters*, I, 185. John Pownall called the whole affair "an Infamous Jobb," to Dartmouth, 22 September 1773, Dartmouth MSS., D 1778, I, 882.

Western settlements meant Indian war, and they had used their friendship with the former Colonial Secretary to effect their views. Now that he was gone, they had to act more directly. Together, they could mobilize a modest amount of power: Gage enjoyed a favorable reputation with the King, and Barrington had access to the royal closet and frequently showed the King parts of his private correspondence with the American Commander in Chief.[20] After the Privy Council approved the Grand Ohio Company project, Barrington used Gage's prestige as a weapon by giving North, Hillsborough's well-intentioned but weak successor Lord Dartmouth, and the Lord President of the Council extracts of Gage's condemnation of Western colonization.[21] This was sufficient to delay further action until Gage could return home on leave, and then his personal testimony would kill the scheme.[22] It is interesting to note that the most effective argument in England against colonization was the mercantilistic one—that Western settlement would promote manufacturing—although the immediate, specific objection to interior colonies among those who knew the situation was that they would probably cause an Indian war.[23]

[20] "In the course of this summer the King (who sees most of your private Letters to me) ordered me to tell you how much he was pleased with your whole conduct." Barrington to Gage, 20 September 1769, "Private," Gage MSS.

[21] *Ibid.*, 28 September 1772.

[22] Alden, *Gage*, 149 and note 30; Dartmouth to Gage, 3 March 1773, *Gage Corr.*, II, 156; John Armstrong to George Washington, 24 December 1773, *Letters to Washington and Accompanying Papers*, ed. Stanislaus M. Hamilton (Boston and N.Y., 1898-1902), IV, 290-291.

[23] Gage blamed Johnson's boundary line of 1768 (Treaty of Fort Stanwix) for Indian unrest in the North. Gage to Dartmouth, 8 February 1773, *Gage Corr.*, I, 345. At about the same time, the danger of war with the Creek appeared so serious that General Haldimand (Commander in Chief during Gage's absence) was planning to visit Georgia. Haldimand to Dartmouth, 2 March 1774, CO 5/91, 225-231. See also Randolph C. Downes, "Dunmore's War: An Interpretation," *MVHR*, XXI (1934), 311-330. Perhaps, however, Downes accepts too uncritically the assertions of Sir William Johnson and his deputy Alexander McKee that the Indians desired an English colony on the upper Ohio.

One of Hillsborough's last acts as Colonial Secretary was to order two regiments detached from the American command for service in the so-called "Carib war"—a native insurrection on St. Vincent in the Ceded Islands. Gage sent the 14th Regiment from Castle William in Boston harbor, and the 31st from St. Augustine, with Colonel Dalrymple in command. One would imagine that the four or five battalions always stationed in the West Indies could have handled any such uprising, and that these battalions might even have been able to assist Gage's army in time of emergency. This, however, would be a misconception. By the end of the Seven Years War, the West Indian garrisons had each become immobilized by the danger of slave revolt, which was the principal reason for their presence in any case. Thus, for a few years after 1770, new dangers—Irish disorder, the threat of war with Spain and France, the perils of disengagement in the West, and Caribbean insurrection—drew attention and resources from the task of policing mainland colonies.[24]

The Economic Impact of the Army

Gage faced a number of problems in the spring of 1773, but all of them together were not nearly as pressing or dangerous as the Boston situation had been three years before; under the circumstances, the Commander in Chief felt able to return to England on leave, after almost twenty years of continuous service in America. When he returned to Boston, a year later, soldiers and colonists would be standing on the brink of war. The time of his departure, then, is one of the last tranquil moments to consider in retrospect the British army in peacetime colonial America.

On June 3, 1773, Gage wrote a long memorandum for his deputy, Frederick Haldimand, who would command

[24] An account of the Carib war is in *The Annual Register* for 1773, 82*-92*. For the troops sent from America, see *Gage Corr.*, II, 607-627. The almost exclusive concern of West Indian garrisons with slave revolt can be seen in *CHOP*, I, #111 and #1279; *APCC*, IV, #548; *Stiles Corr.*, 236; and Wilmot (agent for the Leeward Islands) to Ellis, 22 January 1763, WO 1/981. When the 14th went to St. Vincent, the 64th moved from Halifax to Castle William.

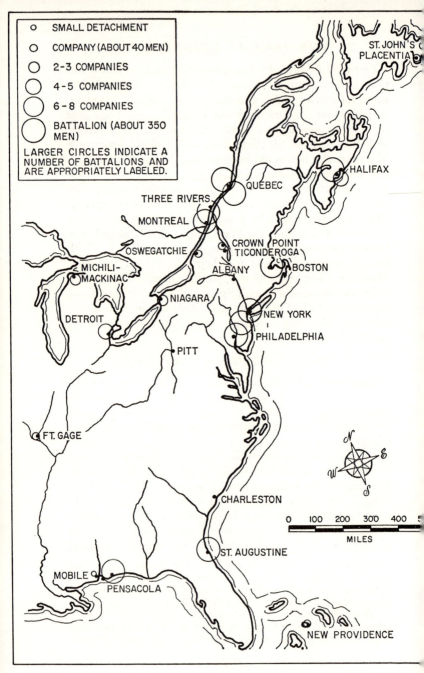

ST. JOHN'S PLACENTIA

HALIFAX

QUEBEC

THREE RIVERS

MONTREAL

OSWEGATCHIE

CROWN POINT
TICONDEROGA

MICHILI-MACKINAC

ALBANY

BOSTON

DETROIT

NIAGARA

NEW YORK

PHILADELPHIA

PITT

FT. GAGE

CHARLESTON

ST. AUGUSTINE

0   100   200   300   400   5

MILES

MOBILE

PENSACOLA

NEW PROVIDENCE

The Army in 1772 after the withdrawal from the West and from Boston (except Castle Island), with several battalions detached to the West Indies.

at New York in his absence.[25] In it Gage discussed the difficulties as well as the routine procedures involved in commanding an army of 6,000 men scattered from New-foundland to Mobile Bay. The memorandum must have been a valuable guide to Haldimand; it is equally valuable —by its omissions as well as its content—to anyone who would know what the army had done for the past decade, and how that army had changed and fitted itself into American life.

As in 1763, no subject was more important than money. "I have found it absolutely necessary," he wrote to Haldi-mand, "to curtail Demands, and as far as possible fix all ordinary Contingencies in such manner as no Alterations may be made, otherwise there is no end to Pretensions and Demands. . . ." Here was a problem that could not be solved. Since 1765, Gage and the Secretary at War had been pressed by the Treasury to bring contingent expenses under strict control. Gage could undertake no new "works" without submitting plans and estimates, and be-fore obtaining the approval of the Treasury. "Accidental repairs" were permissible, but he refused to delegate this power to his subordinates; a local commander was not to incur any expenses without authorization from Gage. But such expenses, especially in an army so dispersed, were almost by definition beyond perfect control. The collapse of a bastion, a fire in a kitchen, shipwreck, spoilage or loss of a ration shipment, an unexpected visit by Indians, even a leaky roof were minor disasters that could hardly wait for orders from headquarters.

The amount of money involved in these contingencies was comparatively small—never as much as 5 per cent of the total cost of the army. Yet it was the one item that could increase sharply if the Commander in Chief permitted dishonesty or extravagance to flourish, as Gage had learned from the conduct of affairs in Illinois by Colonels Reed and Wilkins. On the other hand, the Commander in Chief could prove his zeal for economy if he kept contingent expenses to the barest of minimums, and this is what

[25] Gage to Haldimand, 3 June 1773, BM Add. MSS. 21665.

Gage, like Amherst before him, had done. As long as a few thousand pounds leaked away every year in unexpected ways, Gage strove to tighten the system. The effect in Whitehall may have been all that he could wish, but the results of this policy in America were unfortunate.

From almost every post came a similar story—decay of installations and misery for the men. Living conditions remained so bad in West Florida that Haldimand thought that no council of war would punish the troops if they mutinied; the Lieutenant Governor said the barracks were Negro huts, "I might say worse," he wrote.[26] In Canada, the guard house at Quebec often had a foot of water in it, while the ration storehouse at Three Rivers flooded every spring, causing great losses.[27] Despite occasional repairs, Michilimackinac and Fort Niagara crumbled and rotted away.[28] The commander at Placentia, Newfoundland, violated Gage's standing orders by repairing the broken and fallen gates of the fort simply to keep "the Soldiers to their quarters."[29] Fort Chartres was abandoned just before it collapsed, and an engineer officer reported of Fort Pitt shortly before it was given up that "the name, and Vestiges of it, are all that remains."[30]

The state of the once proud fortresses in the Champlain Valley may be taken as typical of conditions in the early 1770's. Crown Point exploded and burned in April 1773, when fire broke out in an unswept chimney. The subsequent inquiry revealed that the fort and most of the equipment in it had already decayed beyond salvage.[31] When

[26] Haldimand to Robertson, 29 November 1767, BM Add. MSS. 21666; Lt. Gov. Durnford to Gage, 6 March 1770, Gage MSS.

[27] Lt. Col. Jones to Gage, Quebec, 31 October 1772, Gage MSS.

[28] Capt. Glazier to Gage, 4 October 1769, Gage MSS.; Gage to Lt. Col. Caldwell, 5 October 1774, BM Add. MSS. 21678.

[29] Maj. Gorham to Gage, 1 November 1771, Gage MSS.

[30] Capt. Williams to Gage, 23 November 1771, *ibid.*

[31] The proceedings of the court of inquiry are in CO 5/91. Seven years before, the commander reported that Crown Point was falling down; Capt. Hamilton to Gage, 23 June 1766. Gage, in his memorandum to Haldimand, wrote that Crown Point—rebuilt by Amherst in 1759—"began to decay before it was near compleated."

the garrison moved to Ticonderoga, and Haldimand considered making that post the single station for troops on the route to Canada, an inspection report was discouraging: "The fortifications . . . are fast going to ruin, and are involving the barracks in their destruction. The bomb proofs are falling in and lead water into most of the barrack rooms. . . ."[32] The capture of Ticonderoga by Ethan Allen two years later was important psychologically and for the windfall of heavy ordnance it yielded, but, under the circumstances, it was hardly a major military accomplishment.

Perhaps there was little that Gage could have done, or little reason for him to try to do more. Almost every post had been built under wartime conditions—inexpert design, green timber, and hasty construction. More than once, a local commander had said that repairs were simply a waste of money. Since 1766, the existence of every garrison had been under government review, and to at least some officers in America the choice seemed to lie between building more posts or maintaining very few.[33] But when, as often happens to military policy made in time of peace, the criteria for rational choice became cloudy and controversial, economy remained the one clear guideline for decision. The British government had risked the empire to keep a military force in the colonies at great expense, only to sacrifice most of the anticipated gains by trying to reduce that expense by a small fraction. Gage cannot be blamed for failing to solve the problem, but neither do his recorded views show an understanding of it that would deserve praise.

Most of the money spent for the army went to pay and to feed it, though Gage in his memorandum did not emphasize the fact because he was not fiscally accountable for these activities. But, while the maintenance and repair of

[32] Robertson to Haldimand, 21 July 1773, BM Add. MSS. 21666.
[33] Capt. Gordon to Gage, 15 December 1767, Gage MSS. Gordon was an Engineer, and reconnoitered the Ohio and Mississippi valleys. He advised: "One of Two Things should be done—either retire the back Garrisons, or increase their Number."

forts and barracks occasionally employed a few Pennsylvania carpenters or provided a market for New York bricks, rations and pay were major links between the army and the American economy.

The British Treasury made the ration contracts, based on information furnished by the Secretary at War.[34] The American Commander in Chief was authorized to make minor contracts himself, usually in order to meet some special situation or to clarify the terms of an existing Treasury contract. But Gage seldom if ever did this, and all proposals for supplying the army were referred to the Treasury Board. The Board, in order to insure that the terms of the contracts were being fulfilled, appointed commissaries and deputy commissaries to inspect all deliveries of provisions to the various storehouses. Although some contracts had been drawn on a cost-plus-commission basis during the war, after 1760 provision contracts for North America were drawn in terms of a fixed cost per daily ration.[35] That ration, as far as the contractors were concerned, was composed of beef or pork, flour, rice, butter, and peas. For North America, five provision contracts were let after the war: one for each of the Floridas, one for Newfoundland and part of Nova Scotia, another for the other part of Nova Scotia, and the fifth and largest for the remainder of the continent.

Early in the Seven Years War, when fighting was confined primarily to New York and Pennsylvania, and was carried on by a fairly small number of regulars, the contractors were American merchants. After the disastrous campaigns of 1755 and 1756, however, the government decided that a British contractor was essential in view of the number of troops to be employed, and because of

[34] T 29/37, entry for 5 July 1765, exemplifies this.

[35] The men appointed might or might not actually serve. Robert Leake, Commissary General for North America, appears to have always been present at his post in New York. On the other hand, Adam Cunningham did the work for George Allsopp, who in turn held the office of Commissary of provisions at Quebec under one Roberts, the original patentee. Allsopp to Gage, 26 October 1772, Gage MSS. See also Pargellis, *Loudoun*, 135ff.

the unsatisfactory performance of the American victual-lers.[36] Yet these British contractors depended on colonial connections, and the way in which they tied American commerce to Whitehall is of some interest.

Sir William Baker, alderman of London and M.P. for Plympton Erle, and Christopher Kilby, merchant of New London, Connecticut, were the first to be given the job, at 6 pence per ration, to be delivered to general storehouses in North America. Baker and Kilby already were providing food to the Nova Scotia garrison under a similar contract, and may have been selected primarily for their experience in the business.[37]

Baker and Kilby gave up their contract in 1760, apparently without acrimony, and a new one was negotiated with Sir James Colebrooke, his brother George, Arnold Nesbitt, and Moses Franks for 4¾ pence per ration, with all interior transport to be paid by the Crown.[38] The first three of these men were M.P.'s and all were prominent London merchants; Moses Franks was their link to America. His father Jacob was a merchant of New York City while his brother David was one of the largest Philadelphia merchants. Moses' sister had eloped with Oliver DeLancey, member of the New York Council and brother of James DeLancey, Lieutenant Governor until his death in 1759 and one of the most important figures in New York political history before the Revolution.[39] A sister of Oliver and James DeLancey was married to John Watts, merchant and councillor. The firm of Oliver DeLancey and John Watts had acted as New York agents for Baker and

[36] Theodore Thayer, "The Army Contractors for the Niagara Campaign, 1755-1756," 3 *WMQ* XIV (1957), 31-46, attempts to show that the American contractors were falsely maligned. I am not convinced.

[37] Pargellis. *Loudoun,* 72-74, 295; and Gerrit P. Judd, *Members of Parliament 1734-1832* (New Haven, 1955), 110.

[38] Pargellis, *Loudoun,* 296; and Namier, *England,* 280.

[39] Jacob R. Marcus, *Early American Jewry 1649-1794* (Philadelphia, 1951-53), I, 66-67, II, 6-7, 10, 22-23, 26, 93; Edwin Wolf and Maxwell Whiteman, *The History of the Jews of Philadelphia from Colonial Times to the Age of Jackson* (Philadelphia, 1957), 27, 51-52, 66.

Kilby, and they continued to act as such for Colebrooke, Nesbitt, and Franks, while David Franks and various partners served as the Philadelphia agents.[40]

Sir James Colebrooke died in 1761, and George Colebrooke and Arnold Nesbitt lost their contract for adhering to Newcastle in 1762. But Moses Franks appears again as the third partner of the new contractors—Sir Samuel Fludyer, one of the greatest of London merchants, and Adam Drummond, ex-army officer who had served in North America and brother-in-law of the Duke of Bolton.[41] Both Fludyer and Drummond were M.P.'s. Soon thereafter, John Drummond appears in the documents as resident agent for the contractors at Quebec.[42] Because Moses Franks continued as the third partner, DeLancey and Watts in New York, and David Franks and his partners in Philadelphia, continued to act as the principal American agents. The new contract reduced the price per ration to 4 pence.[43] When the Rockingham ministry came into office in 1765, Fludyer had "no pretensions to be well considered by the present Administration," and at the beginning of 1767 the contractors appear as Nesbitt, Drummond, and Franks.[44] There were no further changes until the Revolution.

Of the minor contractors, Chauncy Townshend, M.P., had been involved in supplying Newfoundland and Nova Scotia since 1744. In 1754, he claimed to have spent £6,000 at elections on behalf of the government, and added that "Mony support I allways declined when hinted—half [the] Gibraltar [contract] was my object."[45] His agents in

[40] Virginia D. Harrington, *The New York Merchant on the Eve of the Revolution* (N.Y., 1935), 42-44, 292-293.

[41] Namier, *England*, 281, 282n., 283n. Fludyer, unlike George Colebrooke and Nesbitt, had not abandoned Newcastle for Bute.

[42] John Drummond to Gage, 13 July 1766, Gage MSS.

[43] The old price for Quebec province was 5 1/2 *d.*, the new 4 3/4 *d.* Lower insurance rates as a result of British victories may explain these falling prices. *Jenkinson Papers*, 239-240.

[44] George Colebrooke to Newcastle, 15 July 1765, quoted in Namier, *Structure of Politics*, 52-53. *Commons Journals*, XXXI, 515ff. The Duke of Bolton's interest apparently saved Drummond.

[45] Namier, *England*, 284-285, and *Structure of Politics*, 50.

America before 1764 were the Apthorps and Hancocks of Boston.[46] Townshend kept his contract until he died in 1770, and was succeeded by Robert Jones, M.P., a director of the East India Company, and "man of business" to the Earl of Sandwich, First Lord of the Admiralty during the Revolutionary War.[47] The other half of the Nova Scotia contract was in the hands of Matthew Woodford of Southampton, never an M.P., who began victualling Annapolis, Canso, and Placentia in 1720.[48] When Woodford died in 1768, he was succeeded by Richard Vernon Sadleir.[49]

The West-Florida contract was held by Sir John Major and his son-in-law, John Henniker. Both came into Commons in the election of 1761, and were Treasury "undertakers"—wealthy men who were willing to carry on a campaign in an expensive borough in return for government contracts. Their agent at Pensacola was Jacob Blackwell, member of the Council, collector of the customs, and merchant of West Florida.[50] In 1766 Major and Henniker gave up the contract after wrangling with the Treasury over criticism of their performance, and the contract was given to Edward Codrington, brother of Sir William Codrington—M.P. and Barbadian sugar planter.[51]

[46] W. T. Baxter, *The House of Hancock: Business in Boston 1724-1775* (Cambridge, Mass., 1945), 151-156, 162, 203, 253-255, 299. I have not been able to ascertain who served as his agents after 1764.

[47] *Commons Journals*, XXXIII, 167ff.; and Namier, *Structure of Politics*, 286.

[48] Charles M. Andrews, *Guide to the Materials for American History, to 1783, in the Public Record Office of Great Britain* (Washington, 1912-14), 2 vols., II, 84.

[49] *Commons Journals*, XXII, 276ff. Andrews, *Guide*, II, 85, in his listing of declared accounts at the Audit Office indicates Stephenson and Blackburn as purveyors for Nova Scotia, Newfoundland, and Penobscot 1768-1782.

[50] Judd, *Members of Parliament*, 227, 269; *Jenkinson Papers*, 110, 114, 115-116; and Johnson, *West Florida*, 26.

[51] For the dispute, see T 29/37, entries for 8, 13, and 16 July 1765; 21 and 22 January, and 12 February 1766. For Codrington, see *The Annual Register* for 1775, 205.

For a time, Joseph Garrow was his agent at Pensacola, but, after some trouble with Haldimand, Codrington gave the business back to Blackwell.[52]

The contractors for East Florida were Kinder Mason and Witter Cuming. Little is known of Mason, but Cuming personally transacted the partnership's business in St. Augustine, where he also served as comptroller of the port and a member of the provincial Council.[53] From these brief biographical sketches, it is evident that the commercial activity required by a colonial army took place within a highly political setting.

The same was true of army finance. Most of the ration payments could be made by disbursements in England or through bills of exchange, but there was also a heavy demand for hard currency, especially to pay the troops. Except for the brief period, 1765-1766, when the Treasury hoped to find the needed specie from the Sugar and Stamp Acts revenue, contracts were drawn with City bankers and merchants to provide money to the deputy paymasters in America. The usual commission for this service was 2 per cent.[54] Frequently the provision contractors were connected with the money contract. While Colebrooke, Nesbitt, and Franks held the main provision contract in 1762, Colebrooke, Nesbitt, and John Thomlinson held the money contract. Thomlinson had served New Hampshire as agent since the 1730's, and his son had been elected to Parliament in 1761.[55] When, after the hiatus of 1765-1766, a new money contract was let, it went to Sir Samuel Fludyer, who

[52] Haldimand to Garrow, 28 January 1768, BM Add. MSS. 21674; Haldimand to Edward Codrington, 11 June 1770, Blackwell to Haldimand, 20 March 1771, and Blackwell to Mayor Hutcheson, 3 April 1771, BM Add. MSS. 21729.

[53] For Mason, see the *Gentleman's Magazine* for 1790, 959. For Cuming, see Mowat, *East Florida*, 44; and Wilbur H. Siebert, *Loyalists in East Florida, 1774 to 1785* (Deland, 1929), II, 42. The role of political connection is shown in Henry Kennan to George Grenville, 7 May 1764, *Jenkinson Papers,* 293-294, in which Kennan pleads in vain to be allowed to share the contract with Cuming.

[54] *Jenkinson Papers,* 293n.

[55] Namier, *England,* 246-50; *Commons Journals,* XXIX, 371ff.

had held the provision contract earlier, and to John Drummond, apparently related to Adam Drummond who shared in the provision contract after 1762. Fludyer died in 1768, and was replaced by Thomas Harley, M.P. for London, while Henry Drummond replaced John Drummond around 1770.[56]

The American end of the money contract shows a similar pattern. During the mid-century wars, when Boston had been a major military base, Charles Apthorp of that town was the chief military banker in the colonies. His son-in-law, Barlow Trecothick, was taken into the British side of the business sometime after 1758, and became an M.P. for London in 1768. When the financial center of military affairs shifted to New York in the 1760's, Apthorp was not left out, for two of his children were married to children of James McEvers. McEvers is best known as the quondam Stamp distributor for New York, but far more important was his partnership with John Watts as principal agent in America for Fludyer and Drummond, later Harley and Drummond, money contractors.[57] The clan Drummond took care of the business in Canada, and Edward Lewis, an M.P., had the money contract for West Florida.[58]

There were some lesser contracts putting money into American pockets. The ambitious and talented Colonel James Robertson had found a peacetime job for himself as barrackmaster general, a position created in 1765 when the Quartering Act had passed and all King's barracks in the colonies were brought under central direction. Robertson gave most of the business for barrack furniture and supplies to Hugh and Alexander Wallace, New York mer-

[56] *Commons Journals*, xxxi, 515ff.; *DNB*, xix, 350, and xxiv, 406-407; *Gentleman's Magazine* for 1774, p. 390, for 1794, p. 676, and for 1795, p. 535.

[57] Namier, *England*, 230-233, 249-250; Harrington, *New York Merchant*, 218-219.

[58] Andrews, *Guide*, ii, 85; Gage to John Robinson, 7 October 1772, *Gage Corr.*, ii, 621. Lewis's other activities as government contractor are touched on in Betty Kemp (ed.), "Some Letters of Sir Francis Dashwood, Baron Le Despencer, as Joint Postmaster General, 1766-1781," *Bulletin of the John Rylands Library*, xxxvii (1954), 236-237.

chants. The four supply vessels on the Great Lakes and
Lake Champlain were also maintained by contract with
John Blackburn of Bush Lane, London, who employed the
Wallaces of New York as his agent. Finally, there were
the local provision contractors or subcontractors, like Fen-
wick Bull at Charleston, Robert Callendar in western
Pennsylvania, Joseph Allicocke at New York, James Phyn
at Schenectady, and John Erving, Henry Lloyd, and the
Hutchinsons at Boston.[59]

The impact of this economic activity was considerable,
if difficult to describe precisely. Between 1768 and 1774,
the principal money contractors carried about £94,000
Sterling into North America annually for the payment of
various "extraordinary" expenses. In an economy with a
chronic imbalance of payments and shortage of hard money,
and with total annual imports of roughly £2,000,000, this
injection of specie was of some importance.[60] The effects

[59] On the Wallaces: William M. MacBean, *Biographical Register
of the Saint Andrew's Society of the State of New York* (N.Y.,
1922), I, 127; Lorenzo Sabine, *Biographical Sketches of Loyalists
of the American Revolution* (Boston, 1864), II, 392-393; Gage to
Grey Cooper, 25 December 1766, Gage MSS. On Blackburn: *Commons Journals*, XXXIII, 167ff.; *Gentleman's Magazine* for 1787,
204. On Bull: Gage to Capt. Cochrane, 17 November 1764, Gage
MSS.; Sabine, *Loyalists*, II, 488. On Callendar: "Proposals for
Victualling His Majesty's Troops," 12 February 1766, Gage MSS.
On Allicocke: William Smith, *Historical Memoirs* [1763-1776],
103; *Watts Letter Book*, 301, 372. On Phyn: MacBean, *St. An-
drew's Society*, I, 116-117. On Erving: *Watts Letter Book*, 301,
332; Sabine, *Loyalists*, I, 405-407; J. L. Sibley and C. K. Shipton,
Harvard Graduates (Cambridge, Mass., 1873—), XII, 152-156.
On Lloyd and the Hutchinsons: Gage to Loyd [*sic*] and Hutchin-
son, 22 November 1768, Gage MSS.; Sabine, *Loyalists, II*, 24, and
I, 560.

[60] The Sterling amounts recorded in *Commons Journals* as paid
to the American money contractors after the new money contract
was let in 1766 are as follows: 1767—£50,000; 1768—£85,000;
1769—£76,246; 1770—£100,000; 1771—£111,000; 1772—£92,805; 1773
—£97,600; 1774—£90,500. These are entered against the name of the
contractor for the "Extraordinaries" of each year. On colonial imports, see *Historical Statistics of the United States, Colonial Times
to 1957* (Washington, 1960), 757.

of provision contracting were equally important. Though the nominal cost of rations for 15 battalions was only about £22,000, spoilage, transportation, and other contingencies brought an average of more than £68,000 to the provision contractors in addition to the nominal price. Almost all of this annual total of £90,000, less profits taken in England, found its way into American hands, because after the war the contractors used the colonies as their source of supply.[61]

It is impossible to calculate exactly the amount of pay spent by officers and men stationed in the colonies, but by making a few reasonable assumptions, and by allowing for the intricacies of regimental finance, one may conservatively estimate that 15 infantry battalions annually spent £90,000.[62] The artillery battalion and ordnance services, carried on an account separate from the rest of the army, increased military expenditures in the colonies by another

[61] In the estimate for 1766, rations for 15 battalions, less the 2 1/2d. ration deduction per man, were supposed to cost £22,242. This amount varied only slightly in succeeding years. *Commons Journals*, XXX, 470-471. But I have calculated that an additional £72,729 were actually paid out that year to the American ration contractors. The additional amounts paid out in succeeding years were: 1767— £49,289; 1768—£73,034; 1769—£70,587; 1770—£90,408; 1771—£65,147; 1772—£65,306; 1773—£52,450; 1774—£61,698. These figures are extracted and totaled from the "Extraordinaries" in *Commons Journals*. That contractors used America as their source of supply is clear from the steadily decreasing proportion of British and Irish provisions in the occasional inventories found in Gage MSS.

[62] The daily pay of an infantry battalion was about £26, about £14 of which went to the 423 privates authorized by the establishment in 1763. Ellis to Amherst, 12 February 1763, WO 4/987. The pay of the men was subject to heavy deductions in England, and I estimate that as little as 30 per cent of it (£23,000) may have been spent in America. Officer's pay (£66,000 plus various allowances) was probably all spent in America, plus an unknown additional sum by officers who had an income, minus the pay of officers on leave in England. The pay for men a regiment was short ("wanting to complete") was paid to the regiment (the "non-effective fund") and was to be used primarily for recruiting, but any "excess" was usually divided among the captains annually. See War Office Circular, 27 July 1768, Gage MSS., and Mackenzie Letter Book B, 43-45, in CL.

£40,000. Various miscellaneous expenses, including the lake vessels, certain regimental contingencies, and additional medical services, added at least £6,000. Thus, even when deductions are made for profits taken in England, and for expenses paid by the Commander in Chief though not strictly military (such as for the Indian Department), the army brought about £300,000 Sterling into America every year.[63]

As interesting as the raw economic impact of military expenditures is their political effect within the American business community. Generalizations cannot be made on this question with confidence, but there are some suggestive coincidences that deserve attention. Obviously, political influence and business advantage marched together at the

[63] Ordnance estimate for 1766 was £44,026 (*Commons Journal*, xxx, 482-483) and it changed little from year to year. The £6,000 estimate for contingencies is rough, and is based on a scrutiny of "Extraordinaries." This latter sum does not include any of the money brought to the deputy paymasters in America by the money contractors.

Throughout these calculations, care has been taken to prevent any duplication, though the accounts themselves are not easy to disentangle. Shelburne's "man of business," Lauchlin MacLeane, found he could not determine the cost of the army for one year; Shelburne MSS., LVII, 227. The "Expences of America for One Year" in *ibid.*, 231, jumbles civil and military costs together and omits the bulk of "extraordinary" expenses. Modern historians have had as much difficulty. The figure given in Morgan, *Stamp Act*, 22n. of "only a little over £200,000" obviously fails to take into account the "Extraordinaries." Just as obviously, the estimate in Sosin, *Whitehall*, 132, of "over £700,000" combines the "Extraordinaries" for one year and the total estimates for the next, thus doubling the true total. Though Dora Mae Clark, *Rise of the British Treasury* (New Haven, 1960), discusses the problem of financing the army at some length, she does not discuss fully its annual cost. Beer, *British Colony Policy*, 267-268n., was close with £320,000, but his calculations are incorrect. My own research has impressed me (1) with the difficulty of learning the cost of the army, and (2) with the probable accuracy of George Grenville's estimate of £350,-000 (*Jenkinson Papers*, 306), though even he may have been including civil and Indian expenses, in which case his estimate is perhaps £50,000 too low; £350,000 is about right for the annual cost of the forces under Gage's command. This compares with Clark, *Treasury*, 124n.

Treasury Board, and inevitably the projection of one across the Atlantic brought some of the other with it. A number of American merchants who already had enough of each to become military contractors found themselves drawn into a heady world of power, prestige, and profit. When the Revolution forced them to declare their loyalty, few could decide to leave that world.

A daughter of John Watts would become the mother of General Stephen Kearney, U.S. Army, but Watts himself, though opposed to many aspects of British policy, remained loyal to George III. His friend and business associate, John Erving of Boston, held about the same views, yet made the same decision in 1775. Watts' partner, Oliver DeLancey, became a general in the British army. David Franks of Philadelphia played a more equivocal part in the Revolution: until 1778 he served the Americans as commissary for British prisoners, but then was forced to depart for British lines as a suspected Tory. Alexander Wallace had arrived in New York from Ireland in 1752, set up as a ship chandler, and in partnership with his brother had risen through military contracting to become a member of the Council and one of the wealthiest merchants of the city. There was no question that the Wallaces would remain loyal, nor was there any doubt about the Apthorps of Boston and New York. Other merchants connected with the army who were known Tories are Fenwick Bull of South Carolina and James Phyn of Schenectady. A lone exception may have been Joseph Allicocke of New York, who was subcontractor to Watts and De Lancey, but who was said to have led the mob in 1765-1766.[64]

There were other merchants who supported the Revolution, and whose personal history strengthens an impression that there was a relation between politics and military contracts. Almost without exception, these were men who had left the business or lost out. The American contractors

[64] See note 59. On DeLancey and Watts, see Sabine, *Loyalists*, I, 363-366, and II, 404-405; and *Watts Letter Book*, ix-xvi. On Franks: Sabine, *Loyalists*, I, 444-445.

who had failed to perform satisfactorily early in the Seven Years War included Peter VanBrugh Livingston, Lewis Morris, Jr., and William Alexander. Livingston was a prominent radical on the New York nonimportation committees, Morris signed the Declaration of Independence, and Alexander, under the dubious title of Lord Stirling, was one of Washington's chief lieutenants.[65]

The Philadelphia firm of Baynton, Wharton, and Morgan had lost the provision contract for Illinois to David Franks and his associates, and had gone bankrupt; John Baynton died in 1773, but Samuel Wharton and George Morgan were active in the American cause.[66] Robert Morris, future financier of the Revolution, and Thomas Willing, Philadelphia merchant and later a stanch Whig, had made an unsuccessful attempt to get part of a provision contract in 1772.[67]

Even John Hancock, much of whose fortune was acquired by his Uncle Thomas in military contracting, dropped out at the end of the Seven Years War. There is no evidence that Hancock was forced out, but his associates and successors in the business—the Apthorps and the Ervings—had better business and political connections outside Boston.[68]

Though Philip Schuyler, the future Revolutionary leader, was not strictly speaking a contractor, he had shared largely in the profits of transporting military supplies. But, with the postwar shift in the Great Lakes line of supply from Albany to Montreal, Schuyler and his patron, the quartermaster John Bradstreet, ceased to handle the

[65] Thayer, 3 *WMQ* XIV (1957), 31-46. John Erving, Jr., of Boston was also involved, but was able to stay in the business through his connection with John Watts.

[66] Carter, *Illinois*; Savelle, *Morgan*; and Wainwright, *Croghan*, tell about Baynton, Wharton, and Morgan.

[67] James Willing to Haldimand, 11 November 1772, BM Add. MSS. 21729.

[68] See Baxter, *Hancock*. Capt. G. A. Bruce to Thomas Hancock, 8 March 1762, Private and Business Papers, III, Boston Public Library, suggests that the Hancocks did not simply lose interest in military contracting at the end of the war.

heavy military traffic that had once moved in the Hudson, Mohawk, and Champlain valleys.[69]

When the issue is treason, motives and decisions are not to be understood in terms of monetary profit and loss. Yet the evidence bears out the view that Americans drawn into the world of royal business remained loyal to the Crown.

The Officer Corps and American Society

Not only was the army, from the American point of view, an economic organization that provided opportunities for the influential and enterprising businessman, it was also a social institution that had to be accommodated. Gage, in his memorandum, did not dwell on the personnel of the army or on their relations with the colonists. Part of the explanation is that Haldimand understood the need for civil-military harmony without being reminded of it. More important is the fact that Gage, by comparison with modern practice, had remarkably little to do with the men under his command and their personal conduct.

During the eighteenth century, the British army had been brought under central direction and discipline to an extent that made it an effective instrument of policy in time of war. Like other European monarchies, the Crown, with the help of Parliament, had expunged whatever remained from the age of bastard feudalism and the influence of the *condottiere* spirit among its generals and colonels. But whenever it did not seriously interfere with tactical operations, the proprietorial basis of military organization remained intact.[70] Officers, for the most part, had purchased their commissions, and even those who had not were living in an environment where they could act as if they had. Officers were selected and promoted in ways that had little

[69] On the closeness of the relations between Bradstreet and Schuyler, see Benson J. Lossing, *Schuyler*, I, 179, 216-217, 289-290.

[70] Pargellis, *Loudoun*, and Whitworth, *Ligonier*, are the best published accounts of the internal history of the army. Of special interest is James Hayes, "The Social and Professional Background of the Officers of the British Army, 1715-1763" (unpublished M.A. thesis, U. of London, 1956).

to do with the military or administrative needs of the army itself; if a man had the combination of affluence, influence, and luck needed to enter or rise in the officer corps, only gross lack of discipline or obvious incompetence could stop him—and occasionally not even that could. Gage had lost the wartime power held by Amherst of appointing and promoting officers to fill vacancies, and he had to fight for even the right of selecting his personal staff.[71] When he could issue direct orders, few of his subordinates dared to disobey openly. But in cases where their judgment or discretion was involved, and Gage reduced to giving advice or admonition, nothing except an acute sense of honor controlled their response. And "honor"—a slippery word— had two edges, one of which tended to sever, rather than cut along, the lines of hierarchical obedience and responsibility.

The varieties of eighteenth-century military "honor" can be found in the documents created by courts-martial involving officers, and by protracted *causes célèbres* like that of Colonel Wilkins mentioned above. An officer's "honor" required that he carry out the orders of his superiors and not cheat his brother officers or the army as a whole, but it could also dictate that he refuse to obey "dishonorable" orders or orders from "dishonorable" officers, and that he not "dishonor" his rank or office by living meanly, even if living and entertaining "honorably" required some diversion of military funds or manpower to private uses. More than one junior officer got off lightly by excusing his disobedience or disrespect on grounds of "honor." The hierarchy of military authority was complicated by ideas of social behavior and a belief in the brotherhood of arms to an extent that takes some effort for a twentieth-century mind to imagine.[72]

Similarly, the rank and file were beyond Gage's immediate control. For the most part, recruitment, pay, dis-

[71] Barrington to Gage, 4 February and 6 July 1768, "Private," Gage MSS.
[72] See the courts-martial involving officers in WO 71. The case of Col. John Wilkins, scattered through the Gage MSS., is also typical.

cipline, and conditions of life were regimental matters—
the responsibility of colonels across the Atlantic, the business of their agents in the Strand, and the work of
lieutenant colonels and majors who represented them in
camp and garrison. Regimental courts-martial could do
anything except kill a man, and they were not subject
to higher review short of some unconcealable miscarriage
of justice.[73] Only when problems of recruitment or desertion substantially reduced the army's effectiveness would
Gage interfere. In short, the army, both officers and men,
had a surprising amount of local autonomy. Within limits,
they lived among Americans, not as general headquarters
said they would, but as they pleased.

Basic questions about these men readily come to mind:
who were the people that comprised the army in America,
and did they differ as a group from the character of the
British army as a whole? The stereotype of the eighteenth-
century army is well known: an officer corps recruited
from the aristocracy, a rank and file from the dregs of society, with a gulf between them that was truly inhuman.[74]
As a crude simplification, this stereotype is better than
any other, but it is misleading if treated as more than that.

There were, it is true, a surprising number of army
officers who sat in the unreformed House of Commons.[75]
Few of them had got there because of outstanding military
accomplishment; on the contrary, their relative youth—
the average age was 33, compared to 39 for lawyers and

[73] Early in the century, Judge Advocate Hughes complained to
Henry Pelham, who was Secretary at War, that regimental courts-
martial were out of control because they were trying cases and
awarding punishments that ought to have fallen to general courts-
martial (31 October 1729, WO 72/1). The complaint was repeated
by Judge Advocate Gould to Secretary at War Charles Townshend, 15 June 1762 (WO 81/10). Part of the problem in small
garrisons and remote stations was the requirement for thirteen
officers on a general court-martial.

[74] For one of the most recent surveys of eighteenth-century mili-
tary organization, see Eric Robson's essay in *The New Cambridge
Modern History*, Vol. vii: *The Old Regime, 1713-63*, ed. J. O.
Lindsay (Cambridge, England, 1957), 175-190.

[75] Namier, *Structure*, 24-28.

naval officers—suggests that the army was simply the profession most attractive to the aristocracy.[76] That a commission in the army carried great prestige in a society
traditionally hostile to the army may be a paradox, but
it is also a fact. Nothing in the literature of the century,
from George Farquhar to Jane Austen, contradicts this
conclusion; and, as will be seen, there was an American
version of the same paradox. Many of these military
M.P.'s were colonels, who used their political power to
bring younger sons, friends, and relations into their regiments, thus tending to keep the officer corps an aristocratic
preserve.

There were countervailing forces at work, however. For
all of the early Hanoverian kings, including George III,
the army was the chief source of diversion: it was their
hobby. Louis XV of France had mistresses; Louis XVI
liked to hunt stag and repair clocks; the first three Georges
of England sometimes hunted and the first two kept mistresses—they liked best of all, however, to tinker with the
army. Changing the design of uniforms and watching mock
battles frequently amused them, but there was a more
serious side to their avocation. They worked strenuously,
and usually against the grain of politics, to introduce
efficiency, or at least equity and rationality, as the basis
for officer selection and promotion.[77]

The British army, in the decade before the American
Revolution, was a century old. Like all middle-aged institutions, it had begun to acquire a vitality and direction of
its own, beyond the overt purposes of those who controlled
and financed it. The demands of war had brought in numbers of officers who would never have been admitted otherwise—many from the fringes of the aristocracy, some from
well outside. The army gave these men social reinforce-

[76] Judd, *Members of Parliament*, 25, 49. The cases of Ligonier
and Barré are those of men who moved up to Parliament *through*
the army.

[77] Hayes, *Rylands Library Bulletin*, XL (1958), 328-357; Namier,
Structure, 28, 252-254; Richard Pares, *King George III and the
Politicians* (Oxford, 1953), 17-19, 144.

ment, a precarious financial base, perhaps inward satisfaction, and sometimes a chance for fame and great wealth; in short, they had found a way of life, and they wanted to pass that life on to their sons if they could.

George III and Lord Barrington tried to uphold certain standards for the officer corps: the price of commissions and promotions were fixed to prevent abuses; officers who refused to serve with their regiments were to be cashiered; and when a regimental vacancy occurred, the highest ranking officer in the regiment who could and would purchase the promotion was to be given the opportunity to do so.[78] Officers with little influence or money, and who sought to promote themselves and their kin, usually found their interest in supporting these rules. Commissions in the infantry were least fashionable and most easily obtained, yet an ensigncy (a second lieutenantcy) in a "marching regiment of foot" cost £400 even by the official tariff. To purchase all the steps to lieutenant colonel cost £3,500.[79] The full pay of an ensign was less than £70 a year, part of which would be deducted before he ever received it.[80] Prospects for advancement were discouraging under any circumstances, but without regulations to prevent exorbitant prices and without a system that gave some credit for seniority and attendance to duty, the position of the officer with no outside resources would have been virtually hope-

[78] These points pervade the administrative correspondence of the army, but three documents can be cited to indicate both what the rules were and how they were broken. On fixed prices: Barrington to Gage, 21 February 1766, "Private," Gage MSS. On failure to join regiment: "Warrant for Regulating the Attendance of Officers Belonging to Regiments on Foreign Station," 11 February 1767, LO 6370. On promotion by seniority: Weymouth to the Lord Lieutenant of Ireland, 8 April 1769, *CHOP*, II, #1162.

[79] Royal Order, 10 February 1766, Mackenzie Letter Book B, 47-49, in CL.

[80] Ellis to Amherst, 12 February 1763. An ensign received 3s. 8d. per day, a lieutenant 4s. 8d. and a captain 10s. But captains were expected to bear certain expenses of their companies. By comparison, a common laborer could make 2s. and a "mechanic" 2s. 6d. or 3s. at Boston in 1765. Benjamin Hallowell to Charles Jenkinson, 3 May 1765, BM Add. MSS. 38339.

less. As the army changed, and such officers grew in numbers and visibility, the King and his Secretary at War came to spend much of their energy in trying to protect these vulnerable men.

Career officers—if they may be so called—generally considered North America a congenial station after the war. Distance from Whitehall, St. James, and Westminster Palace would somewhat weaken the pressure their more influential messmates could bring to bear on the War Office. Active service would be more important, especially in isolated posts, and so would count for more with the colonel at home and the Commander in Chief at New York; thus, the one thing the career officer could give in abundance—conscientious application—should be more useful to him if he were in America. There were even chances for promotion without purchase, because most of the commissions in the two battalions of the 60th had been granted free, and were not to be sold.[81] Sometimes also an ensigncy could be had for much less than tariff price when a regiment was stationed in an undesirable place, such as Florida.[82] Finally, there seemed unusual opportunities for financial gain: land grants, many positions with extra pay on the staff or in command of little forts, and daughters of affluent Americans to be married.

The officer corps of the British army before 1775 was a social mélange; indeed, a few of its members had been promoted from the ranks. Only in tone was it truly aristocratic, for it had not yet been fragmented by the intramural class antagonisms that would characterize it in the nineteenth century, and that already afflicted the French army. The useful fiction was still accepted in the regimental messes that only gentility mattered, and that officers

[81] On the King's policy, see Ellis to Gage, 9 October 1764, "Private," Gage MSS. For an exception to the rule, see Ellis to Gage, 8 December 1764, WO 4/987.

[82] Amherst to Robert Napier, 6 April 1761, WO 34/74 (Amherst MSS.); Barrington to Gage, 12 December 1765, WO 4/988; Gage to Wilkins, 5 May 1769, Gage MSS.; Samuel Holland to Haldimand, 16 March 1773, BM Add. MSS. 21730.

were, prima facie if not ipso facto, gentlemen.[83] The officers who served in the colonies after the Seven Years War thus retained their character as gentlemen, but were in fact more socially heterogeneous than the officers corps as a whole. Both their character and their heterogeneity affected their relations with American society.

Perhaps a thousand officers actually served in America between the end of the Seven Years War and the outbreak of the Revolution.[84] Lack of full data prevents systematic study of them all, or of even a selected random sample. But one can learn enough about a number of them to have some confidence in the general picture that emerges.

There were the genuine aristocrats, like Gage himself; or Lieutenant Colonel Thomas Bruce, whom Lord Bruce asked to have sent home from his command of the 65th at Boston; or Major Arthur Brown of the 28th, who was second son of the Earl of Sligo.[85] Major General Alexander Mackay and Colonel John Pomeroy, who both commanded at Boston 1768-1769, were members of the British and Irish Houses of Commons, respectively. The Honorable Lucius Ferdinand Cary was the eldest son of Viscount Falkland. Cary was an ensign in the Guards at 16, a captain in the 14th Foot at 19, a major in the 74th at 25.

---

[83] This judgment is based primarily on reading records of general courts-martial in which officers were involved. More often than not, such courts-martials were really "courts of honor" called to clear an officer's reputation. Though the records are highly circumstantial, there is little in them (at least for the American army) suggesting that social origins had any major effect on the way British officers regarded one another at this time. For the French army, see E. G. Léonard, *L'armée et ses problèmes au XVIIIe siècle* (Paris, 1958). Compare Hayes, "Social and Professional Background of Officers," especially 103-109.

[84] This is a rough estimate, and perhaps a trifle high. Each battalion had 26 officers (not counting the colonel, the chaplain, and the surgeon). Thirty-four different battalions served under Gage, 1764-1774. The product of the two numbers is 884. The figure of 1,000 allows for some turnover within regiments, and assumes that all officers actually served in America with their regiments.

[85] Gage to Barrington, 1 July 1772, "Private," *Gage Corr.*, II, 611. On Browne, see *NYCD*, VIII, 846n.

Put on half-pay when the 74th was disbanded at the peace, he bought a majority in the Royal Americans (60th) in 1765, but sold out in 1768 when there seemed no chance for promotion. After 1774, Cary was a member for Bridport in the House of Commons.[86]

Another group of officers was not quite aristocratic, but had somehow managed to connect themselves with the aristocracy. Amherst was such a man. There were others, like Major William Fleming of the 64th, described by Barrington as a protégé of the Duke of Grafton, First Lord of the Treasury; or Captain John Marsh, whose political interest in the borough of Coventry kept him away from his regiment but did not seem to hurt his military career.[87] Lieutenant Colonel Eyre Massey was the fifth son of an army officer, and was a competent officer himself; but it took more than merit to beg the Secretary at War for an extension of leave in words like these: "Have compassion on a Brother Sportsman, and save him from Transportation, tho' was there good hunting in North America I would return there without regrets."[88]

There were many more who were sons of army officers like Massey, but who did not have connections (which included in Massey's case marriage to the daughter of a baron and the patronage of the Duke of Cumberland). Wolfe and Braddock might easily have remained in this group, but they had escaped through ability or good fortune.[89] More typical was Major Henry Bassett, commanding the 10th Regiment at Detroit. His wife dead, two sons also army officers in America, with only major's pay to support several other children, he pleaded for help from

[86] *Gentleman's Magazine* for 1789, 576; and for 1790, 576.

[87] G. F. R. Barker and Alan H. Stenning (comps.), *The Record of Old Westminsters* (London, 1928), I, 169.

[88] Barrington to Gage, 9 September 1768, "Private," Gage MSS.; Marsh to Haldimand, 22 January and 12 March 1768, BM Add. MSS. 21728. Massey to Ellis, 26 May 1763, WO 1/981. See also *DNB*, XXXVII, 5.

[89] The fathers of both Wolfe and Braddock became general officers through seniority, but neither were well connected politically nor distinguished socially.

Whitehall in return for his long services. He wanted to be made Surveyor of the Woods or even Governor of Detroit, or at least to get a grant of land on Lake Erie or an ensigncy for a third son. Young Bassett got the ensigncy, though Barrington "was not pleased" to stumble on the fact several years later that "he was then a child."[90] But the wrath provoked at the War Office by the connivance of a Bassett was tempered by other feelings in cases like that of Ensign Barbut: "You have done a charitable Deed in getting him a Commission," wrote Gage. "His Father dyed miserably of a wound in the Hospital of Quebec, and left as little for his family as Officers generally do."[91] There were others like young Barbut, serving as "gentlemen volunteers" and hoping that their own zeal and the mercy of Barrington would get them the next vacant ensigncy.[92]

Some few had actually come up through the ranks. James Robertson was one; the master recruiter, George Etherington, was another; the jailer of Robert Rogers, Captain Frederick Spiesmacher, was a third.[93] These promotions had been made under wartime conditions, but in 1771 a Corporal Rimington in the Royal Artillery at New York was promoted to second lieutenant.[94]

The officer corps may be analyzed, not only by class, but by national origin and connection as well. The creation of the four battalions of the 60th Regiment in the Seven Years War had largely been the work of a disastrously

[90] Barrington to Gage, 22 June 1775, Gage MSS.; Scarsdale to Dartmouth, 27 May 1773, and Maj. Bassett to Dartmouth, 2 October 1773, *CHOP*, IV, #179, #301.

[91] 14 December 1774, "Private," *Gage Corr.*, II, 663.

[92] See Gage to Barrington, 10 September 1770, "Private," *ibid.*, 560.

[93] On Robertson, see Hayes, "Social and Professional Background of Officers," 101. On Etherington, see Graydon, *Memoirs* (1846 edn.), 71. On Spiesmacher, see Lt. Grandidier to Bouquet, 26 March 1763, *Bouquet Papers*, BM Add. MSS. 21649.

[94] Adjutant Jacob Schalch to Capt. Gosling, 28 May 1771, BM Add. MSS. 21729. For the relative frequency of such promotions in wartime, see Ward, *Faithful*, 25.

bad officer—Colonel Jacques Prevost of Geneva.[95] But Prevost had brought with him German and especially Swiss soldiers of fortune, some of whom were outstanding. Bouquet and Haldimand were the best of these; another was Augustine Prevost, the younger brother of Jacques.[96] Because they lagged behind continental armies in the development of technical education, the Royal Artillery and Engineers also drew talent from abroad.[97] James and John Montresor, father and son, served as engineers in America for two decades. The father of James came from Caen, and James himself had come up through the ranks of the Royal Artillery.[98] Captain Schalch, who commanded an artillery battery at Halifax, was the grandson of Andrew Schalch, master-founder from Schaffhausen, Switzerland, and known as the father of Woolwich arsenal.[99]

By far the largest contingent of "foreign" officers, however, were Scots.[100] Estimates of the proportion of Scottish officers in the British army at this time range from a fifth to a third. Study of the army in America supports the

[95] On Jacques (or James) Prevost, see Pargellis (ed.), *Military Affairs, passim,* and Wolfe to Sackville, 7 August 1785), in Willson, *Wolfe,* 391.

[96] On Bouquet and Haldimand, see Chapter VII, note 75, above. For information on the career of Augustine Prevost, I am indebted to a seminar paper by Mrs. Helen Hornbeck Tanner (Ann Arbor, 1950) which she has permitted me to read.

[97] Lt. Frederick Mackenzie of the 23rd, an intelligent, competent officer, wrote in 1775 that engineering "is a branch of Military education too little attended to, or sought after by our Officers, . . ." Allen French (ed.), *A British Fusilier in Revolutionary Boston* (Cambridge, Mass., 1926), 27. A similar opinion concerning the British artillery is expressed by Matti Lauerma, *L'artillerie de campagne française pendant les guerres de la révolution* (Helsinki, 1956), 59-60. In neither branch were commissions purchased, and perhaps the onus of that fact outweighed in the minds of men considering a military career the opportunity it created.

[98] *DAB,* xii, 100-102.

[99] Lt. Col. M. E. S. Laws, *Battery Records of the Royal Regiment of Artillery, 1716-1859* (Woolwich, 1952), 37ff.; and *DNB,* xvii, 896-897.

[100] James Hayes, "Scottish Officers in the British Army," *Scottish Historical Review,* xxxvii (1958), 23-33; Namier, *England,* 265-267.

higher estimate. Moreover, an astonishing number of the key positions were held by Scots. Robertson has already been discussed at some length, but Gage's adjutant general was Lieutenant Colonel Richard Maitland, a younger son of the Earl of Lauderdale.[101] Two of the three brigade majors at New York in later years were Scots: Philip Skene, who spent most of his time cultivating his great estate south of Lake Champlain, and John Small, who would raise a corps of Highland emigrants in Nova Scotia during the Revolution.[102] Harry Gordon, the most talented and trusted of the engineer officers, was a Scot, as was Sir John St. Clair, quartermaster general under Braddock and later one of the two Colonels of the 60th.[103] When St. Clair died on his estate near Trenton in 1767, he was succeeded in his colonelcy by another Scot, Gabriel Christie, who had served in the important position of quartermaster general at Montreal.[104] Throughout the army in America, Scots held many of the command positions: John Campbell of Strachur and the 17th Regiment, who commanded at Detroit; William Dalrymple of the 14th, nephew of the Earl of Stair, at Boston, as well as General Mackay and Alexander Leslie of the 65th, Dalrymple's predecessor and successor, respectively; Paulus Aemiluis Irving of the 15th and Valentine Jones of the 52nd, both of whom had been supported by Governor Murray, in Canada; David Wedderburn of the 22nd, who had supported Governor Johnstone in West Florida.[105] Some English officers were in-

[101] *Gentleman's Magazine* for 1772, 439.

[102] On Skene: William F. Skene (ed.), *Memorial of the Family of Skene of Skene* (Aberdeen, 1887), 58-59; and *Bulletin of Fort Ticonderoga Museum*, VI (1943), 161-166. On Small: *NYCD*, VIII, 588.

[103] On Gordon: Constance O. Skelton and John M. Bulloch, *Gordons Under Arms* (Aberdeen, 1912), 136-138. On St. Clair: Charles R. Hildeburn, "Sir John St. Clair, Baronet," *PMHB*, IX (1885), 1-14.

[104] On St. Clair's death: *Virginia Gazette*, 7 January 1768. On Christie: *Burke's Landed Gentry* (London, 1952), 441.

[105] On Campbell: *NYCD*, x, 728. On Dalrymple: Sir James Balfour Paul, *The Scots Peerage* (Edinburgh, 1904-1914), VIII,

clined to see a Scottish conspiracy at work, supported by Lord Bute, the minister supposedly "behind the curtain." A historian is inclined to see Scots, if pushing harder, also working harder and readier to serve in out-of-the-way places like America.

There were, indeed, some officers who were Americans themselves, and many more who acquired close ties to America. Thomas Hutchins, engineer lieutenant and future geographer of the United States, was born in Monmouth County, New Jersey.[106] Captain David Hay of the Royal Artillery appears to have been a native Pennsylvanian.[107] The Captain John Clarke who put down the land rioters in 1766 was the son of a merchant of Salem, Massachusetts, while Gage brought two of his wife's family into the army, and made one his aide-de-camp and another deputy quartermaster general.[108] Applications for commissions— many of them successful—came steadily from the most prominent families in America: Byrd of Virginia, Bayard, Schuyler, and DePeyster of New York, Lyman of Connecticut, Erving and Flucker of Massachusetts.[109]

150-151; *Gentleman's Magazine* for 1807, 280; Ward, *Faithful*, 50. On Mackay: *Gentleman's Magazine* for 1789, 576. On Leslie: *ibid.* for 1794, 1207. On Irving: W. Stewart Wallace, *The Encyclopedia of Canada* (Toronto, 1936), III, 285. On Jones: *Gentleman's Magazine* for 1779, 566. On Wedderburn: G. E. Cokayne, *The Complete Peerage* (London, 1910-59), XI, 172.

[106] *DAB*, IX, 435-436.

[107] *Records of Royal Artillery*, 35-36. Hay transferred in order to remain in America when his battery returned to Woolwich in 1765. On his earlier service, see S. K. Stevens, D. H. Kent, and A. L. Leonard (eds.), *The Papers of Henry Bouquet* (Harrisburg, 1951), II, 20n., 23.

[108] Alden, *Gage,* 69-75. In addition, a brother and a cousin of Mrs. Gage came into the army as ensigns. On Clarke: *Watts Letter Book,* 17, 109, 259.

[109] For these officers, in the order mentioned in the text, see Robertson to Haldimand, 27 May 1770, BM Add. MSS. 21666; *NYHSC for 1898*, 423, and *for 1899*, 140; Gage to Capt. Schuyler, 6 August 1769, Gage MSS.; Gage to Carleton, 15 August 1768, *ibid.*; Leslie to Gage, 10 March 1773, *ibid.*; George Erving to Haldi-

Even more impressive than the proportion of Scots in the officer corps was the number of officers who were bound to America by the strongest of ties—land and marriage. At one extreme was Walter Rutherford, whose brother John had left Scotland for New York early and had become a captain of one of the independent companies there and a member of the provincial Council in 1745. John was promoted to major in the 60th and Walter made a captain in the same battalion. John had married the sister of Andrew Elliot, Collector of New York port, while Walter married the sister of William Alexander of New York, the Lord Stirling of the Revolution. John was killed at Ticonderoga in 1758, but Walter came into an estate of more than £15,000 when his mother-in-law died in 1760. He retired from the 60th after the war—"there is no necessity of being separated from my dear Katie," he wrote to his wife soon after her mother's death, "confined to some disagreeable garrison or dragging you after me through a desert country"—and lived comfortably at his house on Broadway.[110] When the Revolution forced him toward an unwelcome choice, Rutherford avoided it by withdrawing to his farm in New Jersey.

At the other pole was Charles Lee, the eccentric associate and rival of Washington in the early years of the Revolution. Lee, who had come to the colonies as a captain in the 44th with Gage and Braddock, "married" only an Iroquois squaw, and acquired no more than some acres of wilderness. But he came sailing back in 1774 to

---

mand, 7 February 1774, BM Add. MSS. 21731; Haldimand to Amherst, 31 August 1773, BM Add. MSS. 21661. There was another type of American born officer, a man of humbler origins who had wormed his way in during the war and who managed to stay. For an example, see Bernard to Barrington, 11 January 1766, *Barrington-Bernard Corr.*, 103-104.

[110] *NYCD,* VII, 205; Lewis B. Walker (ed.), *Selections from Letters written by Edward Burd, 1763-1828* (Pottsville, Pa., 1899), 19-20; Livingston Rutherford, *Family Record and Events* (N.Y., 1894), 90-117.

stand with America; his true ties were not marital or material, but almost purely ideological.[111]

Three other military leaders of the Revolution fall somewhere between Lee and Rutherford. Horatio Gates, Richard Montgomery, and Arthur St. Clair had each found the prospect for promotion in the 1760's disappointing, and had retired to an American estate—Gates in Virginia, Montgomery in New York, and St. Clair in Pennsylvania. St. Clair had been fortunate enough to marry into the Bowdoin family of Boston, Montgomery into the Livingston of New York.[112] A variation was the case of Major Pierce Butler of the 29th, younger son of a member of the Irish House of Commons. Major Butler married the daughter of Thomas Middleton, a prominent South Carolinian, and retired from the army to Charleston in 1773. He later served eleven years in the United States Senate.[113] In 1764, Governor Murray lamented the "Matrimonial Distemper" which was threatening Montreal; five years before, Colonel John Reid of the Black Watch had diagnosed a similar malady at Philadelphia—Miss Betty Plumsted to marry an ensign in the 17th, her sister engaged to a lieutenant in the 35th; the lovely Miss Willing almost married to Sir John St. Clair, and now with Colonel Bouquet on the string; Dr. Huck pursuing her sister. But all were most surprised to hear of the recent marriage of Margaret Kemble to Gage, "as he had always professed himself an Enemy to that State."[114]

Colonel Reid himself is worth brief attention. Married to Susana, daughter of James Alexander of New York, and owner of 35,000 acres in the unsettled area east of Lake Champlain, he retired rather than return to Britain with the Black Watch in 1768. Not only was Reid an accomplished flutist and composer (he would endow a chair of

---

[111] John R. Alden, *Charles Lee, Traitor or Patriot* (Baton Rouge, 1951).

[112] *DAB*, VII, 184-185; XVI, 293-295; and XIII, 98-99.

[113] *Ibid.*, III, 364-365.

[114] Murray to Burton, 22 March 1764, BM Add. MSS. 21666; Reid to Loudoun, 27 March 1759, LO 6052.

music at the University of Edinburgh), but he became a politician as well. Members of the New York Assembly found that access to Lord Dunmore, Governor 1770-1771, lay through Colonel Reid. He went back to Scotland in 1777, after the death of his wife.[115]

The list of officers known to have socially prominent American wives is too long to set down, and there must have been many more obscure marriages, but a few are of special interest. Major James of the Royal Artillery married a DePeyster and sent three sons into the British army.[116] Brigade Major Thomas Moncrieffe married the daughter of Andrew Barclay; Engineer John Montresor the daughter of Richard Nicholls; Adjutant General Richard Maitland a daughter of William McAdam; and Captain Gabriel Maturin, Gage's secretary, a daughter of Robert J. Livingston and niece of William Smith, Jr.[117] Barclay, Nicholls, McAdam, Livingston, and Smith were wealthy and powerful New Yorkers. Even tension at Boston did not stop the "Matrimonial Distemper"—witness merchant John Rowe's diary entry for April 21, 1769: "Captain Molesworth of the 29th carried off Miss Suky Sheaffe to Hampton."[118]

The list of those who came to own land is far longer than the list of marriages, and one begins to suspect that only unusual sloth or ineptness kept an officer from getting a sizeable grant somewhere in America during his service here. Few could match Captain Philip Skene, laird of Skenesboro (modern Whitehall, New York); or Major Robert Farmar, who retired after his quarrels with Governor Johnstone to the life of a planter at the head of Mobile Bay; or Colonel Gabriel Christie on his estate in the St.

[115] *DNB*, XLVII, 430-431; Rutherford, *Family Record,* 81-83; Smith, *Historical Memoirs* [*1763-1776*], 88-89.

[116] John Watts DePeyster, *Local Memorials Relating to the Depeyster and Watts and Affiliated Families* (N.Y., 1881), 45-46.

[117] On Moncrieffe: *NYHSC for 1899,* 347. On Montresor: *ibid.,* 295. On Maitland: *ibid.,* 61. On Maturin: *ibid.,* 396.

[118] 21 April 1769, A. R. Cunningham (ed.), *Letters and Diary of John Rowe* (Boston, 1903), 186.

Lawrence valley.[119] But many, many dreamed of such possibilities, and worked and schemed to achieve them.

It would be quite wrong to draw simple conclusions from these personal ties that developed between American society and so many army officers. In only a small minority of cases do such ties seem to explain behavior in the Revolution, and even then argument is possible. Whether the officer corps as a whole failed to put its heart into stamping out the insurrection, at least in the early years, because it had been partially Americanized, is an interesting speculation, but not one likely to yield much to further research. A similar speculation concerns the extent to which army officers Anglicized a part of the colonial elite, for one can see in the polemics of the Revolution the fear of some Americans that their society was threatened by the moral decay of creeping cosmopolitanism.[120] Something more will be said about this later. It is sufficient at this point merely to recognize the extent of these ties in the years before Lexington. In general, they appear to have moderated conflict before 1774, and to have weakened the army as an instrument of imperial control and defense.

The Army as a Military Organization

Much less can be learned about the rank and file than about officers. Records of enlisted men were primitive at the regimental level, and none at all were maintained at the War Office. It is known that soldiers as well as officers

[119] On Skene and Christie, see notes 102 and 104, above. On Farmar: *NYCD*, VII, 816; and *Miss. Prov. Arch.*, I, 7-8. The entry under "Samuel Farmar" in *Burke's Landed Gentry* (1952), 808, suggests to me that the obscure Major Farmar may have been American born.

[120] Just one more example indicates how British officers tied themselves to America. Francis Hutcheson was a trusted member of Haldimand's staff; he was "Hutchy" to the inner circle. When Hutcheson died in 1780, he left the bulk of his estate to his sister, the wife of Capt. Magill Wallace, related to the New York mercantile Wallaces, but left 2,000 acres in Albany County to his godson, Hugh Wallace, Jr., son of Alexander Wallace the army subcontractor. Hutcheson's will also indicates that he was close to the Bayard family of New York. *NYHSC for 1900*, 137.

were being Americanized: men were permitted to volunteer to remain in the colonies when their regiments returned to the British Isles, and hundreds of them did so; and considerable if unauthorized recruiting for the army went on within the colonies.[121] But only occasionally is there a glimpse of the soldier himself in an officer's chance remark, a record of a court-martial, or a list of discharged men.[122]

Recruiting, desertion, discipline, and regimental finance were four sides of a single major problem. Unlike the problem of "extraordinary" and contingent expenses, Gage had little to tell Haldimand about this problem of manpower, except to say that when the 21st and 29th departed for home, volunteers could enlist for other regiments.[123] The gaining regiment was to pay a guinea and a half to the volunteer, and £5 to the losing regiment. Every regiment paid such expenses from its "non-effective fund"—the accumulated pay for the number of men it was short of full strength.[124] It cost £12 10s. just to send a recruiting officer to England, not to mention his expenses while there and the bounty paid to every new recruit, so on the face of it the volunteer system seemed the ideal solution to the problem of manpower.[125]

Reality fell short of the ideal, however. As in other areas, traditional British practices and the American environment

[121] "The sending a regular recruiting Party into New Hampshire might occasion Noise as it is not publickly allowed to recruit in this Country, But if you can contrive to recruit there privately, I should be glad that you could procure some good recruits there or elsewhere." Gage to Lt. Col. Leslie at Boston, 14 February 1773, Gage MSS. On volunteering, see p. 278, above.

[122] In 1770, Lt. Col. Leslie discharged six men from the 64th Regiment at Halifax: a sergeant with 36 years service who had "sore eyes" and was "wore out"; a man with 16 years service who had a dislocated shoulder and rheumatism; three others with 2-8 years service who respectively had tuberculosis, rheumatism, and a "Putrified leg and rheumatic pains"; and a sixth whose father was an ensign who had just sold out of the army. 13 January 1770, Gage MSS.

[123] BM Add. MSS. 21665, 152-154.

[124] See the "Royal Warrant for regulating the Non-Effective Fund," 19 February 1766, Shelburne MSS., cxxxvi, 25-26.

[125] WO 3/23, 24.

interacted to frustrate the designs of officialdom. Two sorts of men seem to have "volunteered." One was the man who was either an American himself or who strongly wanted to remain here. The other was the man the losing regiment wanted to be rid of. In 1769, Gage had advised General Mackay, who recently had arrived at Boston, to adapt his ideas about recruiting to conditions in the colonies. It was commendable, Gage wrote, that officers should want to fill up their regiments with good men. But, he continued, "none will effect it in this Country, by Recruits from Europe. Scarse any Recruits at all have come for any Regiment within these Two Years, and most that have been sent over were taken from Prisons." Unfortunately, he concluded, many of the volunteers from homeward bound regiments came from this latter group.[126] Four years later, the 26th refused to accept a number of "volunteers" from the 31st. "The above men declares," wrote Lieutenant Colonel Dudley Templer of the 26th to Gage, "that they were not sent Voluntarily of their own Accord, but were Drafted."[127] Thus the traditional practice of "drafting," so much disliked within the army, had partially thwarted the attempt to adjust recruitment to American conditions.[128]

Tradition had also operated to send convicts from Britain to the American regiments. Normally, such men were brought into the service only under wartime conditions; regimental commanders and recruiting officers tried to avoid jailbirds whenever possible in favor of healthier, less troublesome yeomen.[129] But Barrington or Harvey, as a way of solving the problem of recruitment for the forces in America, in 1766 appointed a recruiting officer for the whole American army, to supplement the efforts of regimental recruiters. Major Barry St. Leger, who would win a clouded fame by leading the unsuccessful invasion of the

[126] 28 June 1769, Gage MSS.

[127] 23 June 1773, BM Add. MSS. 21730.

[128] See Lt. Col. Coningham of the 29th to Gage. 12 October 1765, Gage MSS., on the subject of drafts.

[129] See *CHOP*, II, #1193 and #1200. This incident concerned convicts for African service in 1769, and even so the Secretary at War protested.

Mohawk Valley in 1777, was given the job.[130] The idea of centralizing recruitment at home seemed sound; but it appears that St. Leger, unable to make the paternal promises of regimental care and protection which were the stock in trade of good recruiters, competed unsuccessfully with regiments in Britain, and ended by shipping out the convicts and dregs who would subsequently "volunteer" to remain in America when their regiments returned.

Presumably, the other part of the volunteer system worked better—the genuine volunteers who wanted to remain in the colonies. In 1773, Colonel Valentine Jones at Quebec wrote glowingly of the 30 volunteers expected from the 21st: "some of them the most sightly men in the Regiment, being natives of America, and desirous to stay in the Country."[131] But Gage had learned that native American soldiers could be as troublesome as convicts. The first major effort to recruit Americans after the war (aside from the 60th, which constantly recruited Americans) was made by the 34th in Pennsylvania in 1766. Lieutenant Richard Steele enlisted 50 or 60 men; apparently there were more Americans desperate enough to join the regular army for life than might be imagined.[132] But two years later, Colonel John Reed of the 34th reported that desertion in the regiment was out of hand: "The first beginning of our Desertion . . . was the Recruits raised in this Country; which I never desire or hope to have any more of them."[133] In the following years, Gage echoed Reed's view. "Men of this Country do well enough for the West Indies," he wrote to Mackay, "but they generally Enlist with the Regiments in America with no other Intent than to Desert."[134] Yet the weakness of his regiments, and the lack of alternatives, re-

[130] Barrington to Gage, 8 February 1766, WO 4/988. For St. Leger's expenses, see *Commons Journals*, XXXI, 129, XXXIII, 172, 175, XXXV, 268-269.

[131] To the Commander in Chief, 3 June 1773, BM Add. MSS. 21730.

[132] Gage to Farmar, 14 March 1766; Gage to Governors Penn and Franklin, 29 August 1766; Gage to Capt. Murray, 23 August 1766, Gage MSS.

[133] To Gage, 16 August 1768, *ibid.*

[134] 15 May 1769, *ibid.*

peatedly forced Gage to permit the enlistment of Americans; and, despite his admonitions to accept only the "Clever Lad" and "Boys likely to grow, who will be less liable to Desert," it is a safe assumption that he usually got the drifters and drunkards he told his recruiters to avoid.[135]

The problem of manpower was circular, and it closed in the court-martial. Soldiers were expensive to recruit, so the death penalty for desertion was seldom executed.[136] But neither was there the fine modern distinction between desertion and absence without leave; any man absent was presumed to be a deserter.[137] Punishment for desertion, while seldom capital, was draconian; but, because most men needed to be drunk before they dared desert, punishment, no matter how harsh, could do little to deter them.[138] In fact, because it was uncertain, harsh punishment may well have increased rather than reduced desertion.

Gage never found a solution. He blamed the colonists for concealing deserters but the basic trouble lay within the army itself. He tried making an occasional "example": executing a repeated offender in order to frighten his comrades, as was done with poor Ames on Boston Common in 1768. But "examples" drove some men to desert, and reduced the likelihood that men who had already deserted would turn themselves in or be turned in. As a last resort, he occasionally tried mercy. In the early years, he would issue a general pardon to all who returned to their regiments before a certain date. Later, he merely let regiments

[135] To Carleton, 30 April 1770; Leslie to Gage, 23 May 1773, *ibid.*

[136] My own research in court-martial records confirms this judgment in Pargellis, *Loudoun*, 333.

[137] See the regimental court-martial of 10 October 1766 in BM Add. MSS. 21682, 118, for the one case I have found where absence without leave is distinguished from desertion.

[138] An anonymous observer wrote in 1761 of regiments that had gone to North America: "Before they were Six Months in the country they have had more flogging among them for drunkenness alone, than they would have had in Europe for three years, all occasioned by the immence quantity of cheap Rum." Shelburne MSS., xlviii, 179.

spread the word unofficially that deserters would be welcomed back; in advising a regiment on the question in 1774, he rejected an official general pardon because it would bring in "a Parcell of Trash that wou'd not answer the Expence."[139]

None of these measures was effectual, and it remained to courts-martial to inflict ever greater doses of corporal punishment.[140] Postulate an army organized to expect the worst rather than elicit the best in its soldiers; locate that army in a rich, vast, and wild country; populate the army with its own cast-offs, criminals, and natives of the country itself—given these elements, there was little that could be done. Many soldiers seem to have been happier to be on the American continent than at Chatham, Dublin, or in the West Indies, but they were happier for reasons that did the army no good.[141]

Desertion, discipline, and morale were major problems within the officer corps as well, though they were less obvious. Some officers in effect deserted by never being present for duty. A few posts were understood to be sinecures, but the tendency was to convert every staff position and even regimental offices into mere sources of income; only constant vigilance at the War Office and at general headquarters curbed this tendency. In 1764, Colonel Reed himself, who would complain so bitterly of desertion four years later, was told by the Secretary at War to join the 34th in Florida immediately or to get out of the regiment.[142]

---

[139] To Lt. Prevost, 6 August 1774, Gage MSS. A year later, Adjutant General Harvey summarized his view of the problem in a letter to Col. Francis Smith: "I know of no Cure for Desertion but an Oz. of Lead." 30 September 1775, WO 3/5, 82.

[140] A comparison of general courts-martial in England during the 1760's with those held in North America indicates that a convicted soldier received a heavier punishment for the same offense if committed in America. For example, compare WO 71/26 and WO 71/75.

[141] "The soldiers are in raptures at the *cheapness* of spirituous liquors among us," wrote Andrew Eliot from Boston to Thomas Hollis, 29 January 1769, 4 *MHSC* iv, 437-438.

[142] Ellis to Reed, 16 December 1764, WO 4/982, 103.

This was typical, though seldom was language so blunt; but, in many cases, an officer who had first obtained leave would use every available excuse for an extension or delay. It was well known that extensions of leave, especially for regiments overseas, were "very disagreeable" to the King.[143] But the only effective threat was to cashier the recalcitrant officer, and this was a difficult threat to execute in a society acutely sensitive to the rights of property against a man who owned his commission. For example, Ensign James Segrave failed in 1768 to join the 65th Regiment, bound for Boston, despite repeated orders. Segrave was clearly a candidate for summary dismissal. But, reported the Lord Lieutenant of Ireland, where the 65th had been stationed, Segrave's father "is a gentleman of family and character," who had purchased his son's commission. Accordingly, Segrave was given time and permission to sell out.[144]

In the early nineteenth century, when regiments were ordered to or from India, wholesale exchanges of officers took place; this did not occur for American service in the years before the Revolution.[145] The practice was foreshadowed in some individual cases, however, and it ought to be noted that Gage's command was historically the first large overseas commitment of the British army in which regiments were replaced periodically. Perhaps only more time was needed to let the practice develop and thus split the officer corps into aristocrats and mercenaries, one group serving at home, the other overseas.

As it was, Gage had all he could do to hold many of his officers at their posts. It was general policy that either the lieutenant colonel or the major, and half the company officers, were to be on duty with each regiment, but enforce-

[143] Ellis to Capt. William Hervey, 4 October 1764, *ibid.*, 83-84.
[144] To Shelburne, 30 June 1768, *CHOP*, II, #935.
[145] Cecil Woodham-Smith, *The Reason Why* (N.Y., 1954), 21-25, describes how the purchase and exchange system was working in the first half of the nineteenth century. There *are* indications that wholesale exchanges were occurring in regiments ordered to the West Indies. See WO 1/863, 77-85, 89-93, 97, in which 16 officers exchanged out of four regiments destined for the West Indies in 1764.

ment was often difficult.[146] A genuine emergency or the intervention of some powerful person would sometimes force Gage to grant leave to an officer in a regiment that already had no more than a bare minimum of officers.[147] The War Office tried to keep the unit rotation list confidential, because it feared that regiments scheduled to depart within a year or two would never get officers to join or return from England.[148] Those who willingly stayed with their regiments may be categorized briefly: a few who did so from a sense of duty; some with strong ties to America; many without the money or the motive to go home.

The chief motive to go home was to seek promotion. Though Barrington repeatedly said that he would *"take care of the officer absent and doing his duty,"* and that an officer was better off with his regiment at Michilimackinac than soliciting preferment in Whitehall, he was frequently unable to make good on his promise for reasons which were not his fault.[149] From 1766 until 1770, John Manners, Marquis of Granby, was Commander in Chief of the Army. A brave, skillful cavalry leader, Granby was an amiable, popular man—the number of pubs named for him attest to that.[150] His office was as much political as military, and it was filled only when there was a royal prince or a military hero who could strengthen the King and his ministers by being made Commander in Chief. Otherwise, the King and the Secretary at War ran the army themselves.[151]

When Granby succeeded Ligonier, Lord Chesterfield wrote to his son that it was cruel to replace the old Field

---

[146] Mackenzie Letter Book B, 62-64, in CL.

[147] Gage to Barrington, 3 March 1773, *Gage Corr.*, II, 637.

[148] Ellis to Gage, 9 October 1764, "Private," Gage MSS.

[149] To Gage, 8 April 1768, "Private," *ibid.*

[150] On Granby, see *DNB*, XXXVI, 52-54. For a sketch of Granby which admirably succeeds in conveying his popularity, so inexplicable to all but contemporaries, see Reginald Hargreaves, *This Happy Breed* (London, 1951), 249-265. Whitworth, *Ligonier*, contains some remarks on Granby's reputation at the end of the Seven Years War; also, Namier, *Structure*, 146, 236.

[151] See Charles M. Clode, *The Military Forces of the Crown* (London, 1869), especially vol. II, 689-714, where Palmerston's historical memorandum of 1811 is reprinted.

Marshal with "such a boy."[152] Granby himself was un-
comfortable at the abrupt dismissal of his former patron,
commander, and friend. "I am very conscious how improperly I am plac'd at the head of the Army," he wrote
to Gage. "I never wished for it. As long as I remain my
end will be to be of service to the Army."[153] But Granby
had been put in office to be of service to the ministry and
to his friends, with the army a poor third.

Gage was not under Granby's operational command, but
in 1766 control of commissions and promotions throughout
the army shifted from the War Office to the Horse Guards,
where Granby held court. Before long, Barrington was
complaining to Gage in his private letters that all the salutary rules he had striven to enforce were being broken.[154]
Gage himself shifted with this shift in power: "Get the
Affair transacted with the Marquis of Granby," he advised Colonel Pomeroy in 1769, "for I fear you will meet
with Strong Objections from Lord Barrington."[155] After
Granby's resignation and death in 1770, "Junius" publicly
echoed what Barrington had privately observed some three
years earlier: for all the Marquis's good intentions and
"thousand virtues he has one defect arising from a most
amiable quallity: he finds it very difficult to say *no*."[156]

Barrington was a man who could say "no" whatever else
his faults or limitations, and this partly explains his bitter-
ness at Granby's accession to the supreme command. Some
of his pique was surely because the existence of a Commander in Chief diminished the influence of the Secretary
at War both in the army and in the royal closet. But it was

[152] Quoted in Whitworth, *Ligonier*, 386-387.

[153] 10 July 1767, Gage MSS. I have repunctuated the quotation
for clarity.

[154] See especially Barrington to Gage, 23 May and 14 June 1767,
"Private," *ibid.* Barrington repeated his complaint many times.

[155] 13 March 1769. But Gage also remonstrated with Granby on
occasion; see Gage to Granby, 31 December 1767, *Gage Corr.*,
II, 442.

[156] Barrington to Gage, 9 May 1767, "Private," Gage MSS. The
anonymous "Junius" used almost the same words in describing
Granby; see *DNB*, xxxvi, 52-54.

also a result of Granby's use of the army for political purposes, a practice which the first three Georges disliked thoroughly and fought with limited success. Barrington said in June 1767 that Granby's control accounted for many things that were being done contrary to his own known ideas, and that he had heretofore gone along with Granby to prevent friction in government; but, he continued, his love of peace henceforth would not keep him from trying to prevent what he considered objectionable.[157]

With Granby at the head of the army, many officers found it worthwhile to leave their regiments in America to solicit in person at the Horse Guards.[158] Even when Granby resigned, Barrington had difficulty returning to previous policies, for the King himself, after the bruising political battles of the 1760's, seemed readier to oblige his supporters and their friends.[159] Gage caught the essence of the situation in 1772, writing to an officer who sought exemption from a rule: "Interest will sometimes get the better of all Regulations, but these things must be done in an underhand way, and you know, I am tied down by Rules. . . ."[160] As a result, an extraordinary amount of energy within the officer corps was spent in trying to climb the military ladder by circumventing the rules.

Three rules in particular provided a challenge to the ingenuity of officers, even to those poor career soldiers who as a group benefitted most from the strict enforcement of regulations. One rule, which had been laid down in the

[157] Barrington to Gage, 14 June 1767, "Private," Gage MSS. This side of Barrington's character is well illustrated in a letter to Gage concerning a policy for the West: "If I acted a prudent part, I should leave things to work their own way; but I was born with certain particles of zeal and ardour which will show themselves on some occasions, notwithstanding I am past fifty and have lived more than half of that time among politicians." 4 April 1768, "Private," *ibid.*

[158] For example, Lt. Augustine Prevost to Gage, 10 November 1770, *ibid.*

[159] James Grant to Haldimand, 10 July 1770, BM Add. MSS. 21729.

[160] To Capt. Carden, 13 May 1772, Gage MSS.

debates on the army estimates of 1763, was that vacancies within the army were to be filled from the half-pay list whenever possible. A second was that an officer who had not purchased his rank could not sell it. A third was the requirement that no one under sixteen years of age could receive a commission.

A vacancy, properly speaking, occurred only through death or dismissal, or upon the resignation of an officer who had not purchased his commission.[161] Any other kind of "vacancy" necessarily entailed a purchase, and so was offered by seniority to officers actually serving with the regiment. The latter case, of course, was more frequent than the former in peacetime. Nevertheless, a substantial minority of the officers serving in America had not purchased their rank: some in the 60th, where commissions had gone without purchase; some in other regiments who had been promoted to fill heavy battle losses. Under these circumstances, the first two of the three rules operated to make advancement, always slow in peacetime, unusually slow in the American army.

Almost every officer who had not purchased his rank sought the privilege of selling it; if he were not permitted to sell, he would insist on drawing his full pay until he dropped, thus blocking advancement.[162] When a vacancy eventually occurred, junior officers did not move up but officers were brought in laterally from the half-pay list. In practice, the situation was alleviated somewhat by the War Office permitting money to change hands for an "exchange" between two officers of equal rank, one on active service, the other on half-pay.[163] But even this did almost nothing to speed advancement within a regiment. Accordingly, there was little about active service in America to

---

[161] See for example Gage to Barrington, 25 October 1766 (both letters), *Gage Corr.*, II, 383-384.

[162] Barrington described the situation clearly when he wrote that, where an officer cannot sell out, "the young and healthy, must do the duty of the old and infirm." To Charles Gould, 8 February 1766, Mackenzie Letter Book B, 52, in CL.

[163] Barrington to Gage, 21 February 1766, "Private," Gage MSS.

attract the officers with influence, wealth, or prospects outside the army. The number who left the army after finding
another source of income in the colonies has previously
been noted. The most penurious and the hopeless remained
in the army, however; thus, when a commission was put
up for sale, it became ever less likely that the officer in line
to buy it could actually raise the price.[164]

The net effect was unfortunate, though not unforeseen;
Barrington had analyzed it in a memorandum to the Board
of General Officers: "The senior officers have merit, and
long services, but they have no money; this circumstance
does not prevent the transaction; and the commission is
purchased, perhaps, by the youngest, least steady, and
least experienced of that corps, or of some other, to the
infinite distress of many deserving men, and to the great
scandal and detriment of the service."[165] This described the
situation in the whole army between 1763 and 1775, but
things were worse in the colonies than elsewhere, for the
reasons already mentioned.

As the years passed, and a demoralized, superannuated
core of officers appeared in Gage's regiments, the third rule
came increasingly into play. These men, if they could not
rise themselves, wanted at least to provide for sons and
nephews. By the 1770's, there were few subalterns remaining on the half-pay list who were able and willing to serve
when an ensigncy fell vacant. Few Englishmen wanted a
commission in a regiment in America if there were any

[164] At the end of the war, Capt. William Dunbar had expressed
a view that became endemic within the officer corps of the army
in America: "I have taken my resolution if I can't obtain Leave
to go home, not to remain in the Army; and there is little prospect
of my being preferred [promoted] and I can never think of being
buried for ever in this and such other villianous Quarters. . . ."
Dunbar was writing from Fort William Augustus to Gage, 22 September 1763, *ibid.* (I have repunctuated his statement for clarity.)
On the other hand, it appears to have been easier for an officer
to live within his pay in America than in Britain. See Shelburne
to Chatham, 26 September 1773, PRO 30/8 (Chatham MSS.),
LVI, 126-127.
[165] Barrington to Gould, 8 February 1766, Mackenzie Letter
Book B, 51, in CL.

choice, so pressure mounted to select new ensigns from among the "gentlemen volunteers." These were young men, frequently sons of officers in the regiment, who were carried on the roll as privates, who supposedly performed whatever duty was required of them, and who hoped to earn the approbation of the regiment and eventually a commission.[166]

It might be imagined that Barrington, with his concern for military professionalism, would support the gentlemen volunteers. He did not. "They are all without a farthing, or the means of getting one from their friends," he wrote, "and they are a pernicious set of men in the army." Though he said that he did not "mean this to extend to officers sons of proper age," he was opposed in principle to the commissioning of volunteers.[167] His concern was not with the whiggish doctrine of keeping the aristocracy in control of the army and keeping adventurers out; in part at least, his concern was more humane. Men without money, he argued, however zealous they might be in the beginning, were doomed to a life of disappointment and mortification as younger, less deserving men passed them in the service.[168] But he was also worried about the abuses connected with gentlemen volunteers, for they were the principal way by which children got into the army.[169] An officer, with the connivance of his comrades, could carry his boy on the regimental roll as a gentleman volunteer. The boy would draw private's pay, but never be present for duty. His father, when the opportunity offered, would get the colonel

[166] On the growing pressure created by sons of officers, see Hayes, "Social and Professional Background of Officers," 64-67.

[167] Barrington to Gage, 28 July 1775, "Private," Gage MSS.

[168] Barrington to Gould, 8 February 1766, Mackenzie Letter Book B, 50-53, in CL.

[169] Barrington to Gage, 31 January 1775, "Private," Gage MSS. Almost ten years earlier, Barrington had informed Gage that a volunteer recommended for a commission by Gage was in fact "a boy returned hither with his Mother." 16 December 1765, "Private," *ibid.* For evidence that Barrington had good reason to be suspicious, even of his friend Gage, see Gage to Wilkins, 1 December 1767, *ibid.*

to recommend his son for an ensigncy. If they were lucky, perhaps he got one at ten.[170] In any case, the true strength of the regiment was reduced by one man.

When Gage returned to face trouble at Boston in 1774, he found that this practice had become widespread. He could muster only 1,766 men from six regiments, and "was led to scrutinize every Corps, and discovered that in some Regiments, Young Boys, were returned Volunteers, amongst the Men on Furlough. . . . This Abuse of the Service may have crept into more Corps, than those here. . . ."[171]

There can be little doubt that the army, when considered as a military organization, was slowly rotting. The purchase system increasingly insured that many regimental officers would be too old for their positions, and that many others would be very young men without experience and often without much inclination to learn or to perform their duties. The system of rank-and-file recruitment, especially through volunteers to remain in America, had a similar aging effect on the soldiers. Adjutant General Harvey had begun to worry about the regiments overseas as early as 1767; many of the soldiers were so "Old and Worn out," he believed, that a major recruiting drive would be necessary to bring the regiments up to present authorized strength, much less augment them. The basic problem was "the Difficulty of Recruiting and the unwillingness of Commanders Abroad to part with any Soldiers under their Command while they can Crawl."[172]

Colonel Jones at Quebec confirmed this picture of rot in a letter to Haldimand six years later. He was about to send

[170] For a case in which the son failed to get a commission and was discharged from the regiment when his discouraged father decided to sell out, see Gage to Pomeroy, 20 February 1769, and Leslie to Gage, 13 January 1770, Gage MSS., which describe the affair of Robert Beatson, father and son. The elder Beatson became the well-known chronicler.

[171] Gage to Barrington, 1 November 1774, *Gage Corr.*, II, 658.

[172] Harvey to Barrington, 8 December 1767, WO 3/1, 129-132.

the 8th Regiment out to the Lakes posts. It had 150 "old men," who were inured to the climate but who also had an average of about sixteen years service. Jones went further: officers in Quebec could get credit beyond their means, and then had to sell out to pay their debts. Soldiers made improper connections, and did odd jobs of all kinds to supplement their pay, so that even the most diligent officers could not find them. All extra money went for drink, which was the source of all trouble.[173] Haldimand himself added a touch when he noted that only among the officers of the 60th, recently dispatched to the West Indies, did there remain any substantial amount of combat experience in the American army.[174]

With few exceptions, commanders could not bring themselves to emphasize tactical training; there were more pressing things for the men to do—mounting guard, chopping wood, hauling provisions, repairing roads and fortifications, working for extra money to eke out their pay in whatever time remained. Though Gage and some of his subordinates were competent administrators, there was hardly a flicker of intellectual interest in professional questions within his army. By way of contrast, a great debate over the techniques and philosophy of warfare had begun on the European Continent, a debate of mounting intensity and one that in many ways forecast the revolution in warfare a quarter century in the future. Even the reestablishment of a light infantry company in each regiment during the Falkland Islands crisis, an act sometimes regarded as a landmark in British tactical organization, seems to have had negligible impact. During the Seven Years War, the tenth company of each regiment unofficially had been armed and trained as light infantry. At the peace, when regiments were reduced to nine companies, the tenth, or junior, company had been disbanded. A company was added in the war scare of 1770-1771, and

[173] Jones to Haldimand, 24 December 1773, BM Add. MSS. 21730.
[174] Haldimand to Amherst, 15 December 1774, BM Add. MSS. 21661.

if "light infantry" was more than a convenient label for that company, then documents do not record the fact.[175]

What has been said is not meant to explain British defeat in the American Revolution. As always, the army would expand and change radically under the demands of war. It is true that the army was weaker than it ought to have been at the outbreak of war, and than it was thought to be by the King and others not constantly in touch with the unpleasant truth; this gap between belief and reality would have its effect in 1774-1775. But to speak of military rot in this particular army is to do more than describe the usual neglect of military forces in time of peace, because "rot" in this case has more than military significance. Men in Whitehall had *not* neglected the army; they had sought to rationalize its organization and to use it to solve new imperial problems. Very early they had failed to solve any problems, and in fact had created new ones, confusing themselves in the process. They failed partly because they could not agree on what the problems were, but they failed also because the army failed—it lacked the physical and moral ability to succeed in the face of enormous obstacles. "Rot" meant that the army, despite the unprecedented administrative attention it received, lacked the ability even

[175] Barrington to Gage, 11 December 1770, WO 4/988. On the beginning of controversy over military organization and doctrine in Prussia and France, see Robert R. Palmer's essay in *Makers of Modern Strategy*, ed. Edward Meade Earle (Princeton, 1941), 49-68. On the state of the British army officer corps on the eve of the American Revolution, see [Thomas Erskine] *Observations on the Prevailing Abuses in the British Army, Arising from the Corruption of Civil Government* (London, 1775). Erskine was concerned primarily with low pay in a time of price inflation, and with the pernicious effects of political influence. He wrote of regiments "continually languishing in our baneful colonies." No sooner would there be a vacancy in one of these regiments "than the levee rooms shine with cosmetic complections, and unsullied scarlet; the votes of their kindred are weighed in the ministerial balance, and the parchment is deposited in the sinking scale." (p. 30) Erskine, like Barrington, lamented the fate of the poor officer without political connections.

to *survive* in the American environment; to survive, that is, by the new standards of enlightened thought and practice. The problem was too great, the men too weak, the traditional system too strong, the plans and estimates too optimistic and narrow.

Rot meant more than mere administrative failure. To change the metaphor, it meant that the army, while bringing many individual colonists within its orbit, was itself overpowered by colonial conditions and whirled into the greater orbit of American life. What this signified for the larger question of political upheaval would depend on the response to it by men in London and in the cities of the American seaboard.

IX · The Road to Lexington

THE time between the Boston Massacre and the Boston Tea Party is often treated as a false calm before the storm, marred only by the rumble of thunder when Rhode Islanders burned the schooner *Gaspée*, and Thomas Hutchinson argued with Samuel Adams. The metaphor is surely misleading in many respects, but for understanding the role of the British army in the coming of the Revolution it makes a certain amount of sense. The Massacre removed troops from the place where violence was most likely to occur, and discouraged all those who had hoped that the army would enforce new laws in America. These men now understood that, short of rebellion, troops would not use force against civilians. After the brief flurry of discussion in Parliament in the spring of 1770, no one agitated the issue any longer. Americans, pleased to have most Townshend duties repealed and the troops out of Boston, did not try to drive the army from the other colonies. Both Gage and Barrington, representing military command and administration, seemed chastened. They were more cautious, less optimistic, and sought tranquility rather than trouble. They had lost their zest for analyzing and improving the situation of the army itself. No more sweeping plans issued from the War Office; few pleas for action came from headquarters at New York.

But this was no reversion to the placid days before the Seven Years War. The army remained in America and, however untroubled it might be, its presence was a fact of the first importance. In the military as in other areas of conflict, the events of the past five years had peeled away most hopes and illusions, only to leave a dangerously inflexible residue of aspirations and demands. Both sides sensed this brittleness, and if they were quiet for a while it was because the alternative seemed awful. And yet, within the new hardness of opinion toward the army, there remained traces of older feelings about redcoats. Not until the few months before Lexington did Americans become as clearly and simply hostile to the army as one might imagine they had been all along.

The New American Attitude

In his compendium of American political thought before the Revolution, Clinton Rossiter has noted various denunciations of a standing army.[1] It is interesting, though not surprising, to find that only a few antedate the Boston Massacre. In fact, there were a number of attacks on the very idea of regular troops in America *before* the Massacre, but one has to search for what few are extant. After the Massacre, it is impossible to miss the argument, repeated many times, that a standing army is a cancer in the body politic.

March 5 was the holiday of patriotic celebration in Boston from 1771 to 1783, when July 4 took its place.[2] On that day in March, an orator would remind his audience of the Bloody Massacre and its meaning, while a pictorial display often provided a visual encore. The speeches were published, and newspapers outside Massachusetts noted the anniversary.[3] In the years before the outbreak of war, young James Lovell delivered the first Massacre Oration, a brief and inferior performance; Dr. Joseph Warren, the second, which set a high standard for those that followed; Dr. Benjamin Church, who would betray the Revolution, the third; John Hancock, the fourth; and Warren again, the last, six weeks before Lexington, and less than four months before he would die at Bunker Hill. Taken together, they are the most obvious expression of a new and sterner American attitude toward the British army.

One expects to find in them the hackneyed arguments of English political folklore, and is not disappointed. Standing armies are always dangerous to liberty, and are un-

[1] Clinton Rossiter, *Seedtime of the Republic* (N.Y., 1953), 143, 277-278, 331, 386-388, 400, 437, 443.

[2] Wesley Frank Craven, *The Legend of the Founding Fathers* (N.Y., 1956), 61-62, for a general discussion of patriotic celebration.

[3] The speeches are conveniently reprinted in Hezekiah Niles (ed.), *Principles and Acts of the Revolution in America* (Baltimore, 1822; 1876 edn.), 15-79.

constitutional when kept up in peacetime without the consent of the governed. Standing armies tempt governors to rule by arbitrary force when their true strength lies in the love and cooperation of the people. Standing armies are themselves tyrannical organizations which ought not to exist in free societies. Most of the argument is predictable. But occasionally one finds a fresher point, while nuance and emphasis reveal the way Americans applied hoary precepts to their own situation. These orations expose, fleetingly and incompletely, the roots of both conflict with Great Britain and a national military tradition.

"The true strength and safety of every commonwealth or limited monarchy," pronounced James Lovell in 1771, "is the bravery of its freeholders, its militia."[4] This, too, was a standard argument, rediscovered by Machiavelli and repeated by the *philosophes,* but the American context gave it a new meaning. The qualities of militia may have been a subject of controversy, but its existence was not in doubt; Americans had weapons and a rudimentary military organization. In any other setting, Lovell's argument was a call for military reform, for replacement of an unconstitutional force by a constitutional one. In America, though Lovell may not have fully realized it, the argument could just as well be understood as a call to arms.

Not the Massacre, but the movement of troops to Boston had first provoked the thought that the colonies might have to use force, not sporadically and ambiguously, but openly and as a matter of right. Talk that the "Convention" would advocate armed resistance may have been loose and irresponsible, yet two pamphlets had appeared in 1768 that argue otherwise. Someone thought Jonas Clark's sermon to the Artillery Company of Boston on *The Importance of Military Skill* worth printing, though these annual sermons had not been published since the war. Likewise, for the first time since the war, appeared a new manual of militia drill and tactics, extracted for Massachusetts from William Windham's *Plan of Discipline* for the Nor-

[4] *Principles and Acts,* 18.

folk militia.[5] Dr. Warren made the point clearly in 1772 when he asserted that, exactly two years before, nothing had saved the 14th and 29th Regiments from a true massacre except the uniform of the King.[6]

A second argument also harks back to 1768 rather than to 1770. Benjamin Church, after setting forth the contractual basis of political obligation, implied that the use of force by one party against the other breaks the contract: "Breach of trust in a governor, or attempting to enlarge a limited power, effectually absolves subjects from every bond of covenant and peace; the crimes acted by a king against the people, are the highest treason *against the highest law among men. . . .* When rulers become tyrants, they cease to be kings."[7] More than one American saw the events of 1768 in almost the same terms. Governor Bernard had broken his trust when he asked for troops that he himself would not be able to control, while pretending that he had not made any such request. Far worse, the Crown had convicted itself of sustained bad faith when, after asserting for five years that regulars were in America for defense, it sent them to Boston as police. Charles Thomson, a leader of resistance in Philadelphia, conceded that the taxes laid so far were "not very grievous," but argued that there would be no security if the principle of taxation were ever established, for "the army which was left in America after the late war under pretence of securing and defending it, is now publickly declared to be for the purpose of enforcing obedience to the authority of Parliament."[8] That the army was responsible to no colonial civil authority, neither to royal governor nor to elective assembly, added to this sense of insecurity. Henceforth it would be difficult to accept any act of Crown or Parliament, whether repeal of import duties or a new government for Canada, at face value.

[5] They are number 10856 and 11121, respectively, in Charles Evans, *American Bibliography* (Chicago and Worcester, Mass., 1903-1959).

[6] *Principles and Acts*, 22-23.   [7] *Ibid.*, 34-35.

[8] To Benjamin Franklin, 26 November 1769, *NYHSC for 1878*, 28.

But the note most frequently sounded in the American attack on the British army is that of corruption. After sketching the inherently corrupt nature of any standing army, Warren asked his audience in 1772 to remember the night of March 5, "When our alarmed imagination presented to our view our houses wrapt in flames, our children subjected to the barabarous caprice of the raging soldiery,—our beauteous virgins exposed to all the insolence of unbridled passion,—our virtuous wives, endeared to us by every tender tie, falling a sacrifice to worse than brutal violence, and perhaps like the famed Lucretia, distracted with anguish and despair, ending their wretched lives by their own fair hands."[9] It was crude, but presumably effective.

More sophisticated, and more revealing, were the words of John Hancock in 1774: "All the arts which idleness and luxury could invent, were used to betray our youth of one sex into extravagancy and effeminacy, and of the other to infamy and ruin; *and did they not succeed but too well?* . . . Have there not been some, few indeed, I hope, whose youth and inexperience have rendered them a prey to wretches, whom, upon the least reflection, they would have despised and hated as foes to God and their country? I fear there have been some such unhappy instances; or why have I seen an honest father clothed with shame; or why a virtuous mother drowned in tears?"[10] Soon after troops arrived in Boston, "A Citizen" writing in the *New York Journal* had said about the same thing: many of us, he wrote, would like *more* troops "for the sake of the Paltry Six Pence per day they spend amongst us." But, he warned, it is not worth the "luxury, debauchery, extravagance, &c."[11]

As might be expected, the army was seen as a threat to chastity and sobriety, but more surprising is the American concern with frugality and simplicity. The recurrent use of words like "luxury" and "extravagance" in con-

[9] *Principles and Acts,* 22.
[10] *Ibid.*, 39. Italics mine.
[11] Reprinted in the *Boston Evening Post,* 31 October 1768.

nection with the army raises the question of exactly what Americans were talking about. It is impossible to be sure. The life of a common soldier could hardly have been considered luxurious or extravagant.

Dr. Benjamin Rush of Philadelphia provided a clue in a letter written soon after the arrival of troops in Boston. The "strict discipline kept up in armies," he wrote, ". . . disposes military gentlemen, above all others, to contract an arbitrary temper. . . ." This is always disagreeable, and often dangerous, because these men are essential to the defense of their country and they "naturally claim a superiority over the rest of their countrymen. They feel their own importance . . . [and] their knowledge in arms and their popularity with the soldiers and common people . . . give them great advantages over every other citizen."[12] The operative words are *gentlemen, arbitrary, superiority, popularity,* and *advantages.* Rush, of course, was referring to officers; and here the argument begins to acquire a historical richness that makes it much more than a mere parroting of pamphlets written in the reign of William III.

In truth, Americans were less afraid of regular soldiers in the classic, Praetorian sense than were Englishmen; Charles I, Cromwell, and James II had used soldiers to intimidate an unarmed population, but Americans had at least the means of resistance. The most frightening feature of the army for Americans seemed to be its corps of officers, and not so much in their official as in their private capacities. John Hancock and "A Citizen" knew the social and economic attraction of these men; Ezra Stiles had confessed to the power of their skeptical outlook; Benjamin Rush admitted their "superiority" and "popularity." Worldly, dissolute, charming, violent, occasionally wealthy, and often cynical, British officers presented a prospect for provincials that was at once tempting and disgusting.

In 1762, when Rush had joined American clergymen in confusing the Anglo-American force that had just cap-

[12] To Catharine Macaulay, 18 January 1769, *Letters of Benjamin Rush,* ed. Lyman H. Butterfield (Princeton, 1951), I, 70.

tured Havana with the hand of God, a smaller segment of the British army had made a different sort of impression on another Philadelphian.[13] Alexander Graydon's mother kept a boardinghouse where British officers stayed, and long after the Revolution he remembered two of them, incredibly named Captain Ogle and Lieutenant Friend. Ogle and Friend had frequently "plunged themselves into an excess of intemperance; and in the plentitude of wine and hilarity, paraded the streets at all hours, . . to the no small terror of the sober and the timid." On one occasion, after they had talked themselves out of being arrested for "extremely disquieting and insulting" conduct at a coffeehouse, they drove wildly through the city, smashed all the bottles in an apothecary shop, and roughed up a fellow boarder— a parson from Maryland—when they returned home. Though Graydon told the story as if amused in spite of himself, he concluded by generalizing the anecdote and pointing the moral: "The common observation, that when men become soldiers they lose the character and feelings of citizens, was amply demonstrated by the general conduct of the British officers in America. Their studied contempt of the *mohairs*, by which term all those who were not in uniform were distinguished, was manifest: and it is by no means improbable, that the disgust then excited, might have more easily ripened into that harvest of discontent, which subsequent injuries called forth. . . ."[14]

Some officers who offended influential Americans have been noted earlier in this book: Colonel Dalrymple at Boston, with his quick temper, who was described even by one of the Customs Commissioners as "proud, haughty, and voluptuous, devoted to self and Self gratification . . ."; Captain Clarke of the 46th, who made the Berkshire County posse back down in 1766; Major James of the Royal Artillery, who published his contempt for New York courage during the Stamp Act troubles. One group of officers in particular, who had earlier drawn the wrath of

[13] For Rush's attitude, see his letter to Ebenezer Hazard, 27 September 1762, *ibid.*, 5-6.
[14] Graydon, *Memoirs* (1846 edn.), 51-54, 63ff.

Daniel Dulany for their misconduct, wrote a sequel to their bad reputation.

In 1767, several presumably intoxicated officers of the 28th Regiment conducted a small riot at Elizabeth, New Jersey, on the night before the embarkation of their unit for Ireland. The *New York Mercury* described the affair, which somehow never found space in Gage's official dispatches: "As the inhabitants had used them so very ungenteely as to make them pay their debts . . . the officers seemed determined upon revenge." Windows were broken at the jail, the alarm was rung, blows were struck, and someone fired a load of bird shot into the legs of one of the officers. When the local magistrates went to Perth Amboy for help, the officers fled to their waiting transports. But Colonel Sir John St. Clair, Gage's quartermaster general, ordered them to disembark, appear before the Elizabeth court, apologize, and pay £25 damages. The *Mercury* concluded: "It is a pity, that men, who call themselves men of honour, should leave a place with such an odious name behind them."[15]

It will be recalled that the 28th had been troublesome in Quebec in 1764 and 1765, and perhaps had gotten out of hand during the Hudson valley insurrection of 1766. Then, in August 1766, after it had pacified Dutchess County and arrived in New York City, it had been in another scrape. Soldiers of the 28th Regiment had cut down the Liberty pole on the Common, and two major fights had occurred the following day when townsmen tried to erect it again.[16] For the rest of the year, there had been intermittent violence between soldiers and New Yorkers, and one might compare this situation with that obtaining in Boston two years later.[17] But there were some differences, for Gage had moved quickly in 1766 to prevent trouble before it could grow, and he must have been happy to see the 28th go back to Ireland in 1767. It is little

[15] I *N.J. Archives*, XXV, 432-435.

[16] *Virginia Gazette*, 5 September 1766 (supplement).

[17] *Ibid.*, 13 November and 4 December 1766.

wonder that the lower House of the New York Assembly, in December 1766, had rejected a reward of 10s. per man of the 28th and 20s. per man of the 46th for their campaign of the previous summer up the Hudson; the wonder is that the vote was nine to eight.[18] Although Governor Moore attempted to blame "the Populace" and to defend the soldiers in his official report to the Secretary of State, it is fairly evident from its record that the 28th—officers and men—was an undisciplined regiment.[19]

There are scraps of evidence which indicate that the officers of the 28th were merely worse than most, and not unique, in their misbehavior. After the small garrison had been withdrawn from South Carolina in 1768, Gage learned that its commandant had borrowed new muskets from the provincial armory, but had turned in worn out King's arms upon his departure.[20] A young buck of Philadelphia bragged to his sister in London how "we—with four or five young Officers of the regiment in barracks—drink as hard as we can to keep out the cold, and about midnight sally forth, attended by the Band . . . march through the streets and play under the window of any lady you choose to distinguish. . . ."[21] When Gage and Governor Moore began to debate their legal relationship to one another, some officers of the New York garrison made it a public issue, first by arguing in city taverns that Gage commanded all colonial governors, then by arranging a dance in such a way that the Governor and his lady were snubbed.[22] A year later Major Henry Pulleine ordered a file of regulars to protect a friend and New York merchant, Simeon Cooley, who had been accused of violating the nonimporta-

[18] *N.Y. Assembly Journal, 1766-1767*, 215, 219 (Jenkins microfilms, N.Y., Reel A.1b).

[19] To the Duke of Richmond, 23 August 1766, *NYCD*, VII, 867-868.

[20] Gage to Carleton, 25 September 1769, and Governor Bull to Gage, 3 November 1770, Gage MSS.

[21] Alex. MacKrabie to Mrs. Francis, 9 March 1768, *The Francis Letters*, eds. Beata Francis and Eliza Keary (N.Y., n.d.), I, 91.

[22] Moore to Hillsborough, 19 August 1768, *NYCD*, VIII, 98-99.

tion agreement; though when Gage heard of it, he immediately countermanded the order.[23]

In Boston, soon after the arrival of soldiers, people were alarmed to read that Captain John Wilson of the 59th had been heard, probably in his cups, telling Negro servants they ought to rise against their Puritan masters and win their own freedom.[24] A month later, the insulting letter of another officer was widely quoted in American newspapers to the effect that Massachusetts was a pleasant country, "But the men are all hypocrites, and the women wh---s; there is not an officer in the sea or land service, nor a common man, down to a drummer, that cannot have his bedfellow for the winter." The writer went on to suggest that a "Yankey war" would produce more births than burials.[25] The Reverend Andrew Eliot, commenting on drunkenness in the army, wrote: "The officers are most troublesome, who, many of them, are as intemperate as the men."[26] An unusually large proportion of the military incidents at Boston during 1768-1769, as reported by the "Journal of the Times," involved officers. Thomas Hutchinson may have been right when he said that nine-tenths of the "Journal" was distortion or outright falsehood, but, true or false, it was a fair indicator of how Bostonians regarded army officers.[27]

If resentment were the only or even the principal feeling toward the army and especially its officers, then the question would be simple. But there was another sentiment that tempered animosity, at least for a time: many Americans could not help liking the color and pomp of military organi-

[23] *Virginia Gazette*, 10 August 1769 and 22 February 1770.

[24] Denys DeBerdt to Richard Cary, 3 January 1769, *CSMP*, XIII (1910-1911), 352.

[25] Dated 22 December 1768, *Virginia Gazette*, 1 June 1769 (supplement).

[26] To Thomas Hollis, 29 January 1769, 4 *MHSC*, IV, 437-438.

[27] Thomas Hutchinson to Israel Williams, 26 January 1769, Israel Williams MSS., Letters and Papers, II, 162, Massachusetts Historical Society. For the "Journal of the Times" itself, reprinted in a number of colonial newspapers, see *Boston Under Military Rule*, ed. Oliver M. Dickerson (Boston, [1936]).

zation, nor help envying army officers and wanting to meet and please them. In the spring of 1772 John Adams asked his fellow citizens at Braintree, "What is the Tendency, what has been the Effect of introducing a standing army into our Metropolis? Have we not seen horrid Rancour, furious Violence, infernal Cruelty, shocking Impiety and Profanation, and shameless, abandoned Debauchery, running down the Streets like a Stream?" The following autumn, after an hour's chat with Major William Martin, Adams noted in his diary: "A Sensible Soldier is as entertaining a Companion as any Man. They acquire an Urbanity, by Travel and promiscuous Conversation, that is charming." Even though Major Martin later spoke of his friendship with the hated Thomas Hutchinson, Adams had him to dinner and wrote: "The manners of these Gentlemen are very engaging and agreable."[28]

When John Adams himself had trouble distinguishing between urbanity and debauchery, how many other Americans up and down the seaboard felt the same tension? Officers could make shocking spectacles of themselves, but they also sought whatever comforts provincial society had to offer. Accordingly, they usually held their men on a tight rein, worked to charm the local gentry, and in general tried to keep service in the colonies as pleasant as possible. The American response to their efforts, even after the Massacre, can only be described as ambivalent. To compare the rhetoric and the reality of housing regulars in colonial towns is perhaps the best measure of this ambivalence.

The Quartering Act had ceased to be a source of controversy in South Carolina after its regular garrison withdrew in 1768. But, as mentioned previously, troops returned to Charleston the following year when the difficulty of navigation and the shortage of quarters at St. Augustine forced General Haldimand to send part of his command northward temporarily during the rotation of regiments. There were barracks in Charleston, and the

[28] *The Diary and Autobiography of John Adams*, ed. Lyman H. Butterfield *et al.* (Cambridge, Mass., 1961), II, 58, 68, 71-72.

soldiers moved into them. One officer wrote that the arrival of regulars was "not very pleasing to the people of this place at present," and another that "the people here would proceed to as great lengths in a short time as they have done at Boston—were they not affraid of Military force. . . ." When the Governor asked the Commons House to support these troops according to law, it failed to act and then made its failure well known outside South Carolina.[29]

In fact, however, the army did not fare badly during its brief return to South Carolina. There were other reports from officers: "The people are very civil and polite," and "We receive all kinds of civilities from the hospitable inhabitants of this pretty Town. . . ."[30] Somehow the barracks got supplied, for Gage had no real complaint to make when the regulars again departed Charleston.[31] The main desire of the citizens had been, not to harass the soldiers out of the colony, but to take a stand in sympathy with Boston and against Parliamentary authority. It was South Carolina's gesture of resistance, however, rather than the fact of its acceptance of troops, that had an effect in the North.

The New York Assembly had conformed to the Quartering Act well enough to avoid the penalties set down in the Restraining Act of 1767. It had continued to do so into 1768 under its popular Governor, Sir Henry Moore. Divided almost evenly between two political factions, and with enough purely local problems to hold its attention, New York seemed little inclined to join its sister colonies in a crusade against British policy and authority. The leaders of the colony mistrusted Philadelphia, and believed

[29] The reports are by Major Chisholm to Haldimand, 28 March 1769, and Captain Hodgson to Haldimand, 22 July 1769, BM Add. MSS. 21729. General accounts, which stress South Carolina resistance, are by Edward McCrady, *The History of South Carolina under the Royal Government, 1719-1776* (N.Y., 1899), 617-622, and W. Roy Smith, *South Carolina as a Royal Province, 1719-1776* (N.Y., 1903), 358-359.

[30] Major Chisholm to Haldimand, 25 February 1769, and Major Whitmore to Haldimand, 23 November 1769, BM Add. MSS. 21739.

[31] Gage to Hillsborough, 7 October 1769, *Gage Corr.*, I, 239-240.

that trouble in Massachusetts had more to do with hatred for Governor Bernard than with any larger issue.[32] But the movement of troops to Boston aroused New York. In November 1768, a crowd burnt effigies of Bernard and Sheriff Greenleaf, whose part in trying to evict the tenants of the Boston "Manufactory House" had received wide publicity.[33] The fiery Major James, who had returned from England and commanded the garrison while Gage was in Boston, put his men under arms and had them patrol the streets, though Moore had not asked for military assistance. For a few days, the situation seemed as delicate as in Boston.[34]

Gage smoothed matters over upon his return, but could not restore the old tranquility. When the Assembly again voted supplies for the army in 1769, there were accusations that New York had failed to follow the courageous example of South Carolina and Massachusetts, and so had played the ministry's game by splitting the colonies.[35] Troops in Boston, the nonimportation movement, the intricacies of local politics—all now combined to make the Quartering Act a livelier issue than in 1765. At the end of 1769 when the bill for supplying the troops passed by a single vote, "A Son of Liberty" proclaimed in a broadside that New York had been betrayed.[36] The Assemblymen from New York City received identical letters listing four reasons why money for the army was a mistake: (1) "luxury and voluptuousness will be the certain concomitants of a standing army; commerce, industry, and frugality will be despised, together with mechanism and agriculture, the two grand sources of wealth and independence"; (2) it would give up New York's principal weapon in the colony's fight for a paper currency; (3) it would "annihilate the

[32] William Smith, *Historical Memoirs* [*1763-1776*], 44.

[33] *Virginia Gazette*, 1 December 1768.

[34] Major James to Gage, 15 November 1768, Gage MSS.

[35] William Smith, *Historical Memoirs* [*1763-1776*], 66-70.

[36] The text is reprinted in Thomas Jones, *History of New York during the Revolutionary War* (N.Y., 1879), I, 426-430. The author, of course, was Alexander MacDougall, who would become famous as the "Wilkes of New York."

freedom, honour, dignity" of the Assembly itself; and (4) it would "forfeit all federal confidence of the colonies," now so necessary.[37] Soon the rancour created by the quartering issue spilled into the streets.

As they had in 1766 when feeling ran high, redcoats cut down the Liberty pole in the Fields. The Sons of Liberty responded violently in the "Battle of Golden Hill," where heads were broken but no one was killed. A mass meeting voted that the conduct of the soldiers was "an incontestable proof that they are not only enemies to the peace and good order of this city," but are enemies of liberty and must henceforth be treated "as enemies, to all that is dear and valuable to Englishmen."[38] It seemed to some that New York would have a massacre before Boston. But once again Gage and the officers intervened to avert a disaster. The 16th Regiment (like the 29th in Boston), the center of most of the trouble, was shipped off to Pensacola. Colonel Robertson, whose smooth tongue concealed his harsh opinions, was so effective in calming all parties that he won the public gratitude of New Yorkers.[39] The army got its supplies, and in return the colony got permission to issue paper money. Three years later, when Gage departed for England on leave, he was given the freedom of the city.[40] Somehow the major violence that one would have expected in New York never occurred; it is difficult to believe that a large part of the explanation does not lie in the close personal relations between army officers and New York gentry.[41]

Elsewhere, civil-military conflict never reached the intensity that it did in New York and Boston. In Virginia

[37] *Virginia Gazette*, 22 February 1770.

[38] *Ibid.*

[39] *Ibid.*, 19 April 1770: "The behavior of Colonel Robertson on the occasion has earned him the good will of the inhabitants." Robertson's private views are in his letter to Haldimand, 26 March 1770, BM Add. MSS. 21666.

[40] *Minutes of the Common Council of the City of New York, 1675-1776* (N.Y., 1905), VII, 424-427.

[41] Isaac N. P. Stokes, *The Iconography of Manhattan Island* (N.Y., 1915-1928), IV, 795-831.

and North Carolina, where there were no troops, there was little interest in the question of standing armies. Though the *Virginia Gazette* reported the troubles to the northward, it also saw no harm in praising the Black Watch when that battle-scarred regiment sailed for home in 1767: "It has ensured to us peace and security; and along with our blessings for those benefits it has our thanks for that decorum in behavior which it maintained during its stay . . . giving an example that the most amiable conduct in civil life is in no way inconsistent with the character of the good soldier."[42] One may reasonably believe that such sentiments, even if held, would not have appeared in print after 1768. In Pennsylvania and New Jersey, however, where troops were always on the scene, some of the same benevolent attitude toward regulars is visible as late as 1774.

In 1766, Justice Bowers of Morris County, New Jersey, and a posse had rescued a number of recruits from Captain George Etherington and a party of regulars. Four of the regulars required hospital treatment.[43] But Etherington was a notoriously skillful recruiting officer, and too much can be made of this incident.[44] Far more important was the support furnished annually by the New Jersey Assembly to the regular garrisons of the colony. Nevertheless, New Jersey, like New York and South Carolina, refused to obey the Quartering Act in every point, and tried to trade strict compliance for royal permission to emit bills of credit. Each year the struggle grew a little sharper.

When Governor Franklin summoned the Assembly to meet in the fall of 1769, he expressed fear that its mood boded ill for the King's business. Not only had the Board of Trade refused in the previous winter to approve the issuance of £100,000 in bills of credit, considered essential to the economy of the province by the legislators, but the public assertion of South Carolina that the expenses of quartering the British Army should be paid from the

[42] *Virginia Gazette*, 30 July 1767.
[43] Gage to Governor Franklin, 3 July 1766, Gage MSS.
[44] Graydon, *Memoirs* (1846 edn.), 71-72.

Townshend Acts revenue seemed to have "an ill Effect on the Minds of the Assembly."[45] Although Franklin persuaded the Assembly to vote the required funds in 1769 and, after a struggle, in 1770, the Assembly balked in 1771. Bluntly alluding to the Crown's refusal to permit bills of credit or a loan office, the Assembly resolved: "That the Colony is *not* of *Ability* to make *any further Provision* for the Supply of His Majesty's Troops stationed in this Colony."[46] Hillsborough informed Gage that there were only two alternatives: to deal with New Jersey by act of Parliament, or to remove troops from the province. He suggested the latter if it could be done without loss of face, so Gage found an excuse to withdraw all troops from New Jersey in the fall of 1771.[47]

In that same year, some of the citizens of the province awoke to the political and moral menace posed by a standing army. The freeholders of Hunterdon County asked their representatives in the Assembly whether the presence of British troops was useful, constitutional, safe, and would not "spread Vice and Immorality in a Country where they are maintained in idleness."[48] Yet, when troop movements made it necessary, the colony permitted the return of a regiment in 1772, and another in 1774, without serious complaint or resistance.[49] Moreover, in the year of the Boston Massacre the corporation of New Brunswick sent a warm letter of praise and gratitude to the 26th Regiment upon its departure after thirty-four months' residence in the town. After its involvement in the Massacre, the 29th Regiment moved from Boston to New Jersey; when it departed in the general exodus of 1771, both New Brunswick and Perth Amboy publicly thanked the officers and men for their good behavior.[50] When all redcoats were gone

[45] Franklin to Hillsborough, 27 September 1769, 1 *N.J. Archives*, x, 130-131.

[46] *Ibid.*, 243.

[47] Hillsborough to Gage, 19 July 1771, and Gage to Hillsborough, 6 November 1771, *Gage Corr.*, I, 135, and II, 312.

[48] 1 *N.J. Archives*, x, 269-273.

[49] *Ibid.*, 321-323, 378-379; xxviii, 584-585; xxix, 454.

[50] *Ibid.*, xxvii, 161-162, 640-643.

from the province, Gage heard from Franklin that "one half of New Jersey is now complaining that they have no Troops."[51]

Philadelphia was, if possible, more placid than New Jersey as a home for His Majesty's forces. There appear to have been no ugly incidents, no sharp words, only polite answers to polite requests. When the 18th Regiment arrived from Ireland in the summer of 1767 and Gage came down to Philadelphia to review it, Thomas Willing, future financier of the Revolution, wrote that the men "made a fine appearance, and acquited themselves to admiration." Willing added that they "are very orderly people; so that we are very happy together."[52] John Dickinson, in his *Letters from a Farmer In Pennsylvania,* deplored the Quartering and Restraining Acts; but he thought that New York had "acted imprudently, considering all circumstances, in not complying so far as would have given satisfaction, as several colonies did."[53] Joseph Fox had been provincial barrackmaster since 1758, and he kept the 18th Regiment happy. In July 1774, its commander praised Fox in a message to the Pennsylvania Assembly: in the past seven years, he wrote, "no troops have been better supplied, nor applications from commanding officers more politely attended to than here."[54]

The safest conclusion about the American attitude toward British troops is that, though hardening noticeably after 1768, it contained almost as much sympathy as hostility until late in the prewar struggle. An event soon after the Boston Massacre confirms this conclusion.

At the time of the crisis between England and Spain over possession of the Falkland Islands, Parliament voted to increase the size of the army, and Gage received orders

[51] Gage to Hillsborough, 5 February 1772, *Gage Corr.,* I, 316.
[52] To Haldimand, 26 October 1767, BM Add. MSS. 21728.
[53] *The Writings of John Dickinson,* ed. Paul L. Ford (*Memoir ; of the Historical Society of Pennsylvania,* XIV [Philadelphia, 1895]), 308-309.
[54] Major Hamilton to the Assembly, 21 July 1774, quoted by Anne H. Cresson, "Biographical Sketch of Joseph Fox," *PMHB,* XXXII (1908), 186-187.

in early 1771 to bring his battalions up to wartime strength.[55] The crisis had actually passed by then, but he did not learn of it until late spring. Meanwhile, he had sent recruiting parties into most of the colonies. The results were surprising. Though in some cases the recruiting parties had hardly begun to work when they were recalled, the reports were favorable from every quarter. The governors of New Hampshire, Massachusetts, Connecticut, New York, New Jersey, Pennsylvania, Virginia, and South Carolina promised their best assistance, and none warned him that local reluctance or resistance was likely.[56] The five battalions recruiting in the Middle Colonies did very well by all accounts, though no exact figures are available.[57] The 31st Regiment, at St. Augustine, got 15 men at Charleston the first week, and at Norfolk and Williamsburg local officials cooperated fully; after a few weeks, the 31st had about 50 new American soldiers.[58] Even in New England there were no complaints, except at Boston itself where Governor Hutchinson was pleased that recruiting parties did not go.[59] Results were good enough so that later, after his extraordinary instructions had been cancelled, Gage permitted recruiting in Connecticut and New Hampshire *sub rosa*.[60] The fact that numbers of Americans would enlist under British officers even after the Boston Massacre (and that other Americans would let them do it) is a fact that can be explained in several ways, but it cannot be ignored.

It is tempting at this point to go beyond the bounds of prudence in assessing the part played by the British army

[55] Barrington to Gage, 11 and 29 December 1770, WO 4/988.

[56] Gage to Hillsborough, 7 May 1771, *Gage Corr.*, I, 298; Governor Bull to Gage, 6 May 1771, Gage MSS.

[57] Gage to Dalrymple, 21 April 1771, Gage MSS.; Robertson to Haldimand, 15 May 1771, BM Add. MSS. 21666. The units were the 18th, 26th, 29th, and both battalions of the 60th.

[58] William Nelson to Gage, Virginia, 24 June 1771, and Major Mackenzie, St. Augustine, 1 July 1771, Gage MSS.; Major Mackenzie to Haldimand, 7 September 1771, BM Add. MSS. 21729.

[59] Hutchinson to Gage, 13 May 1771, Gage MSS.

[60] Gage to Lt. Col. Leslie, 14 February 1773, and Leslie to Gage, 10 March 1773, Gage MSS.

in early American history. Relationships suggest themselves that, if valid, are of major importance; but they cannot be proved, at least not by this author, and they must remain suggestions only.

There was, for example, an atavistic, puritanical strain in the American Revolution. It seems to have been largely a response to an American society that was getting richer, more tightly structured, and in many ways more Anglicized. It perhaps best expressed itself in the nonimportation movement, which was not only an instrument of policy but the road back to a simpler, more frugal and self-sufficient way of life. Ambivalent feelings toward the British army, and particularly the emphasis and fear of military "luxury" and "voluptuousness," fit this puritanical strain.[61] The army officer corps was the true danger personified—an aristocracy by definition corrupt, yet far more attractive than the swarm of Crown officials who had begun to lure Americans long before the army appeared. The number of American names in the Army List—Apthorp, Butler, Byrd, DeLancey, DePeyster, Lyman, Schuyler, and others —testified to the great temptations. The name Washington was missing only because he never managed to get a commission.

A related phenomenon is the almost hysterical attack on the Society of Cincinnati in the 1780's. Again there was talk of Roman history and Praetorian dangers, but the emotional spring was social rather than political—a powerful image of what American society ought not, dare not, contain. Everyone knew that military officers as a group, whether British or American, deserved no more than pity or scorn. But some also knew, and many must have suspected, that too often, as individuals, they would win flattery, servility, and imitation. Indeed, the thought might have crossed the mind of John Adams, for one. An armed citizenry had early bred a certain contempt for the function

[61] Listen to Dr. Joseph Warren: ". . . if you, from your souls, despise the most gaudy dress that slavery can wear; if you really prefer the lonely cottage (whilst blest with liberty) to gilded palaces, surrounded with the ensigns of slavery . . ." *Principles and Acts*, 24.

of a professional officer, but the very flatness of American life seems to have nurtured a fascination with his role. Perhaps the vestiges of these attitudes have always haunted American politics.

Whether these reflections on American ambivalence toward the army are sound or not, ambivalence itself is incontestable. Moreover, it has meaning quite apart from the contours of the American psyche. Not all Americans were torn; some simply liked the army, some did not. The army brought money into depressed economies, especially in New York, which had something to do with the reluctance of leading New Yorkers to become revolutionaries. Some army officers were charming and intelligent without being debauchees, while others were scoundrels; it was reasonable to make distinctions between one sort and the other. Soldiers tended to be drunken and disorderly, but then so did many Americans. Many soldiers seemed to like the colonies and their inhabitants; in fact, some soldiers were Americans, though just how many is hard to say. Soldiers often worked as laborers and journeymen in their free time; this brought them into local life, but it could also lead to trouble, as in Boston and New York. And, finally, Gage was tactful and most of his commanders careful in dealing with Americans, while the government had shown a great reluctance to use force against colonists. But Americans were not being hypocritical, or frightened by mere shadows, when they expressed concern about a standing army, for events in England seemed to tell them what *could* happen.

Between the Seven Years War and 1775, civil disorder in England repeatedly required the use of military force.[62] Unlike the situation in the colonies, a minister had few inhibitions about making troops available, and a magistrate even fewer compunctions about using them, when rioters threatened peace or property. Much of the trouble was economic: unemployment, strikes, high food prices,

[62] See *An Alphabetical Guide to Certain War Office and Other Military Records Preserved in the Public Record Office* (London, 1931), 77-79; George Rudé, *Wilkes and Liberty* (Oxford, 1962), *passim*.

and enclosure of common land. Weavers at Spitalfields and Tiverton, coal-heavers at Wapping, tinners in Cornwall, miners in Durham and Northumberland, farmers in Denbighshire—all rose up in anger or despair, and had to be put down by force. But there was also a newer, more clearly political wave of disorder, a wave set off by the protracted affair of John Wilkes. For Wilkes and his cause, civilians faced soldiers at Westminster, Bloomsbury, and Brentford. To the troops, however, these distinctions made little difference; once the magistrate had read the Riot Act and given the signal, they could shoot to kill.

Almost all of the clashes between soldiers and civilians in England were reported in colonial newspapers, and these reports were amplified by a transatlantic correspondence. The obstacles to using force in the colonies as it was used in England are apparent—though not obvious—to historians, but Americans can be excused if they did not see them. On the contrary, it seemed that only a cabinet meeting and a letter to Gage, or even a reckless local commander, could have British soldiers killing unruly Americans in the same way that unruly Englishmen (not to mention Irishmen) were being killed at home.

Probably the ugliest such incident occurred in May 1768, when economic distress and Wilkite agitation fused to produce a period of intense disorder. Soldiers fired on a mob in St. George's Fields, killing seven persons and wounding a number of others. Particularly flagrant was the killing of a young man by a soldier who apparently had run amok.[63] The news reached America in August, just before troops went to Boston, and was reported as follows by the *Virginia Gazette*: "The soldier who shot Mr. Allen's only son on Tuesday quitted his rank, crossed the two high roads, pursued the young man down a lane into a cow house, then levelled his piece, took aim, and shot him through the heart, and another soldier ran his bayonet into his shoulder."[64] The accuracy of the account is not important; its impact was all that mattered.

[63] Rudé, *Wilkes*, 37-56.
[64] *Virginia Gazette*, 18 August 1768. See also 25 August, 8 Sep-

The "Massacre of St. George's Fields" aroused English-men almost as the Boston Massacre would soon arouse Americans. Both Wilkites and Rockingham Whigs attacked the government for its tendency to use military force as a substitute for political action. The published views of both these groups were transmitted across the ocean to an audience already prepared to believe that the government was not merely stupid or inept, but malevolent. William Bollan, former agent for Massachusetts, published a pamphlet in London in 1768 on *Continued Corruption, Standing Armies, and Popular Discontents.* . . . The first pages do not make clear whether he is discussing the problems of England or America. In a passage that might have referred to the tactful, cautious behavior of Gage, Bollan argues that no one should be deluded by "the accident of person, which is ever subject to mutation," but rather should "consider things as they are in their nature and institution." Armies are naturally corrupt, he continues, and easily used for arbitrary purposes. But then follows an unmistakable reference to the affair at St. George's Fields, which Bollan calls plain murder, and it is evident that he has been talking about England all along.[65]

When Americans saw what was happening at home, concern over the army lost some of its speculative and doctrinaire quality, and became more tangible and immediate. By its physical presence in many places at once, and by its uniform and centralized administration, the army forced its neighbors to think in general and comparative terms. Through the army, Americans could literally see similarities between England and America, and between one colony and another, when they might otherwise have gone on seeing differences. In fact, the Massacre of St. George's Fields was fairly typical of events in Britain, while the Boston

---

tember, 13 October, 3 and 10 November 1768; and *Pennsylvania Journal*, 8 August 1765.

[65] Pages 10-11, 18-19. The copy used was that in the Boston Public Library. In the report of the Boston Massacre, the *Virginia Gazette*, 5 April 1770, explicitly compared it with the earlier massacre in St. George's Fields.

Massacre was atypical for the colonies. But under the circumstances, it was not surprising that the extreme cases—London and Boston—seemed similar.

These years of political conflict had leached away much of the sentimental, wartime affection for the army. Even the ambivalent feelings about it that troubled some Americans could be mastered if, with Bollan, one kept straight the difference between persons and institutions. Toward the end, in 1774, young Josiah Quincy, who had helped defend Preston and his soldiers after the Massacre, could speak about the army in the accents of bitter radicalism. Boston should be grateful to the army, he said, for "the permission of an early carnage in our streets," which had made plain to everyone the real intentions of the British government. All America should be grateful that Providence had caused the army "to scatter much wealth and diffuse abroad a martial passion." Without the army's money, nonimportation might have collapsed; without the "martial passion," there might have been no revived militia to make armed resistance possible. But now armed resistance was the only course, because the British resort to force had broken the contract forever.[66]

Whether Quincy could speak for America is another, and more difficult, question; the evidence is fragmentary and contradictory. Though attitudes toward the army had obviously hardened, they never crystallized around the army as a major grievance in itself. Instead, the hardening seems only to have reinforced American attitudes on other issues—legislative autonomy, individual rights, and British corruption. Largely without conscious intent, the British government had communicated with its colonial subjects through the medium of the army; read in the visible results of military policy, the message had betrayed ignorance, weakness, procrastination, and malice. Most of the American response to this message was directed, not back to the army, but toward the sender through other channels—

[66] *Observations on . . . the Boston Port Bill; with Thoughts on Civil Society and Standing Armies* (Boston, 1774), reprinted in his *Memoirs* (Boston, 1875), 325, 342, 349.

against the customs officials, for example. This is easily understandable, once it is recognized, but more needs to be said about it, for Americans acted as if they did not truly *want* to make the army a major issue. The reason is obscure, but surely involves an intricate tangle of fondness and fear. Even today, in "colonial" societies, discontented people feel a need to act as if soldiers are themselves not the target of political attack, and they assert that troops are the guiltless instruments of an oppressive government. Americans did about the same thing, and for about the same reasons.

The one exception was Boston, but that exception is all important. There, where no regular garrison had been since the war, soldiers had come again to disrupt the life of the city; there, the danger of coercion had been faced squarely, rather than obliquely as elsewhere, because it could not be deflected by the habitual presence of regulars or by the question of defense against external attack. The result was to stifle fondness and to transform fear from an inhibition into a new source of energy and determination. There, in 1775, war would begin. It could have begun nowhere else.

The End of the Road

It would be difficult to overstate the importance of Boston in the few years before the clash at Lexington. Opposition to British policy and legislation was widespread, but resistance—the readiness to push opposition to any necessary length—centered in the capital of Massachusetts. Elsewhere even the hardiest Whigs refused until late 1774 to contemplate rebellion as a deliberate act that might soon present itself as the lesser evil among several alternatives, but in Boston there were many who saw the likelihood of something more than accidental violence, and they began to prepare for it, psychologically as well as physically.

Two minor and almost simultaneous incidents point up this contrast between Boston and the rest of America. When the 23rd Regiment embarked at New York in July 1774, on its way to join the army gathering at Boston, the *New York Mercury* dared to wish it *bon voyage* : "The Harmony which, ever since their Arrival, has subsisted betwixt the Citizens and this very respectable Corps of his Majesty's Troops, cannot be exceeded in the Chronicles of any other Garrison."[67] A fortnight earlier, James Warren, Boston radical, had written to John Adams about British political leaders and the chances for a peaceful outcome of the current crisis : ". . . we have nothing to expect from their Justice, and every thing to hope from their fears."[68] More was involved here than differing political opinions ; rather, these words describe different political atmospheres, and only in the latter—at Boston—could armed resistance to British soldiers readily be imagined.[69]

The British government had done all it could to sharpen this difference between Boston and the rest of the colonies. From the time that Shelburne sponsored the attack on the New York Assembly in 1767 over the Quartering Act, the British policy line had been one of isolating and punishing the most obnoxious colony, while conciliating the others. There was, of course, no explicit agreement on this line over the years, but the acts of the government reveal a fairly consistent adherence to the concept. With the accession of Hillsborough, the target had changed from New York to Massachusetts, never to change again. Other colonies and other problems, however, were competing for similar attention from the North ministry : a complete collapse of representative government in South Carolina, backcountry insurrection in both Carolinas, continued defiance from the Virginia Burgesses, land grabbing in both western Pennsylvania and Illinois that could cause a major Indian uprising, a dispute over land between New York and

[67] *New York Mercury*, 1 August 1774, as quoted in Stokes, *Iconography*, IV, 861.

[68] 14 July 1774, *MHSC*, LXXII, 27.

[69] Even Connecticut was not ready for war. "The people here are full of phlehm," Col. Robertson wrote to Haldimand from New Haven, "their passions are not easily roused but by interest, they talk with more warmth about Susquehannah than Boston." 23 May [1774], BM Add. MSS. 21666. Robertson conceded that an attack on provincial charters would "rouse" them. He was right.

New Hampshire that had led to guerrilla war, and the destruction of one of His Majesty's Ships by the inhabitants of Rhode Island. But competition was in vain, because British ministers and officials were no longer willing to attack any but what they considered the principal problem. The experience of the army in the few years before the outbreak of war exemplifies this course of action.

When, in 1770, Governor Penn asked Gage to intervene militarily against a new wave of Connecticut immigrants settling Indian land in the upper Susquehannah valley, the Commander in Chief displayed none of his aggressiveness of 1763 or 1767, and instead turned a deaf ear to Penn's request.[70] Gage had learned what Amherst had suspected in 1763, that this was at bottom not a question of imperial Indian policy but an intercolonial dispute over property, and that he and the army could only get into trouble by mixing in it. Of more importance, Gage had become pessimistic about preventing white encroachment on Indian land, although he continued to believe that continued encroachments meant eventual war. When Stuart and Johnson were negotiating the new and supposedly definitive Indian boundaries in April 1769, Gage wrote gloomily to Governor Grant of East Florida that the line "I fear . . . will not produce the good Effects expected from it, the Frontier People will never be restrained to Boundary's."[71]

Perhaps Governor Tryon of North Carolina apprehended Gage's newfound caution, for when disorder in the backcountry reached a dangerous level in 1770, he did not bother to ask Gage for the assistance of regular troops, but requested only colors, drums, two light field pieces, and some artillery ammunition for his expedition against the Regulators.[72] The handling of rural disorder was the one police function that the British army in America had proved it could perform—at least in narrow military terms—in New York in 1766. But it could succeed in this, whereas it failed elsewhere, only because it could obtain local support. But if

[70] Gage to Hillsborough, 24 April 1770, *Gage Corr.*, I, 254-255.
[71] 24 April 1769, Gage MSS.
[72] Tryon to Gage, 19 March 1771, *ibid.*

government could find sufficient local support, it hardly needed the assistance of regulars, because under those circumstances the provincial militia would act to restore order. This was the situation in North Carolina, where Tryon found enough willing militiamen to defeat the Regulators at the Alamance River in May 1771.

While Gage was on leave in England and General Haldimand temporarily commanded the army, the conflicting claims of New York and New Hampshire in the region of future Vermont reached violent proportions. Once again, Tryon was the governor concerned, having been transferred from North Carolina after the end of the Regulator War. But this time, he was under pressure from both his Council and the House to get help from the British army. Militia from the area around New York City could hardly be raised to march to Vermont, and the New York claimants on the spot were outnumbered and outgunned by New Englanders like Ethan Allen and his Green Mountain Boys. But General Haldimand had learned as well as Gage; he coolly informed Tryon that there was a dangerous tendency in employing regular troops against civilians when militia were available, and said he would refer the matter to England for decision. The decision supported Haldimand.[73]

The change of attitude in Whitehall and at general headquarters in New York was nicely measured by the *Gaspée* incident. In June 1772, Rhode Islanders had attacked and burned this customs schooner, wounding its commander in the process, when it ran aground near the Narragansett shore. No act short of open rebellion could have been more outrageous; even the Boston Tea Party destroyed only private property, care being exercised not to damage the ships themselves nor to injure persons. But the British response to the destruction of the *Gaspée* was curiously weak. The investigatory commission was composed of men who almost certainly would learn nothing and do nothing

[73] Haldimand to Dartmouth, 1 September 1773, with 3 inclosures; and Dartmouth to Haldimand, 14 October 1773, CO 5/90 ff. 375-388, 391-393.

about the incident, and no effective measures were taken to assist them if they did.[74] Rear-Admiral John Montagu on the North American station declined a suggestion from Lord Sandwich to go to Rhode Island with warships in order to support the investigation. "I am clear nothing will ever come of that commission," Montagu wrote, while he considered the Bostonians "almost ripe for independence, and nothing but the ships prevents their going greater lengths. . . ."[75] Though Gage was also ordered to stand by to render military assistance in case the commission should arrest anyone, he was no more eager than Montagu to intervene: "If the Commissioners should be obliged to apply for the Aid of the Troops I must no doubt send a Force to protect them, tho' I am confident, when the Troops arrive, that no magistrate will ask their Assistance."[76] He agreed with Montagu that, no matter what happened, Boston was the heart of the problem: "The Boston Assembly has now thrown off all Dependence upon the Supreme Legislature . . . ," but "The Principle is not yet generally adopted in the other Provinces. . . ."[77] There seemed to be a working consensus that the next crisis had to come in Massachusetts.

On a vaster scale, Gage and the government declined to be concerned any longer about another acute problem—the West. As the British military presence withdrew from the Ohio Valley, disruptive American forces surged into the vacuum of power. Sir William Johnson had been first to

[74] Documents concerning the affair are in *Records of the Colony of Rhode Island . . .* , ed. John R. Bartlett (Providence, 1862), VII, especially pp. 92, 102-104, 182-187. See also *Peter Oliver's Origin & Progress of the American Revolution*, eds. Douglass Adair and John A. Schutz (San Marino, Calif., 1961), 98-99. Oliver was one of the commissioners. For the indecision concerning the affair, see Josiah Quincy's account of his discussion with Lord North in 1774, *MHSP*, L (1917-18), 440-441.

[75] Montagu to Sandwich, 18 March and 1 June 1773, *The Private Papers of John, Earl of Sandwich*, eds. G. R. Barnes and J. H. Owen (London, 1932), 49-50.

[76] Gage to Barrington, 6 January 1773, "Private," *Gage Corr.*, II, 632.

[77] Gage to Barrington, 8 February 1773, *ibid.*, 636.

take his cue from the decision to withdraw, when he extended the northern Indian boundary down the Ohio to the mouth of the Cherokee (Tennessee) in the Treaty of Fort Stanwix in 1768. John Stuart, Indian Superintendent for the South, had accordingly been forced to allow the southern half of the line to bend westward by 1771. Hillsborough had fought to prevent colonization of this area until his resignation in 1772, but hundreds of settlers on the move made a joke of paper barriers erected in England; nevertheless, crumbling forts and weak garrisons of regulars had done more to control the situation than discouraged British officials may have imagined.

When Fort Chartres was razed, and only a token force of regulars remained at Fort Gage (Kaskaskia) downriver, speculators rapidly moved into Illinois and began buying land directly from the Indians.[78] The sheer distance of Illinois from settled areas and the outbreak of war at Boston prevented what must surely have been a violent result. But in the upper Ohio valley, regulars had hardly left Fort Pitt when Governor Penn was pleading for their return, because Virginia settlers in the area had formed an association to resist Pennsylvania authority.[79] The situation was not unlike that in the "New Hampshire Grants," where a dispute over political control and the uncertainty of land titles interacted to produce a confused and violent struggle. Pennsylvania had substantially cooperated with the imperial aim of restricting settlement on land claimed by the Indians, but neither Gage nor Haldimand would use force to support that province in its quarrel with aggressive, land-hungry Virginians. By 1774, the Indian war, so long predicted if expansion were not controlled, was at hand. Lord Dunmore, Governor of Virginia, led several thousand of his militia against the Shawnee while the British army, which had already begun to concentrate at Boston, did nothing.[80]

[78] The fullest discussion of this episode is in Sosin, *Whitehall*, 222-238.

[79] Percy B. Caley, "Lord Dunmore and the Pennsylvania-Virginia Boundary Dispute, *The Western Pennsylvania Historical Magazine*, XXII (1939), 87-100.

[80] Downes, *MVHR*, XXI (1934), 311-330.

In retrospect, the priorities followed by the British government after 1770 seem self-evident: the seaboard was more important than the interior, Boston was more dangerous than any other place on the seaboard. But it should be noted how the priorities had become reversed in the course of a decade. No longer were the threat and expense of an Indian war the principal dangers to be avoided; no longer were "friends of government," the royal prerogative, and the power of Parliament to be supported wherever they might be in jeopardy. Even the Quebec Act of 1774, which Gage warmly supported after his arrival in London, can be seen in part as a negative measure intended to dump the problem of governing the interior into the hands of Carleton, who seemed to want the job.[81] It was one more step in eliminating all military functions that could interfere with action in Massachusetts. Of course, the decision to resist was made in Boston, but the decision to meet resistance head on was made in London.

No candidate for the role of such a decision-maker could have been less likely than William Legge, Earl of Dartmouth, Hillsborough's successor as Secretary of State for the Colonies.[82] For those who would see a growing "conservatism" within the British government brought about primarily by the American question, with men of similar views clustering around Lord North after 1770, Dartmouth is an anomaly.[83] No man appeared more sympathetic to the American cause. He had acquired this reputation by being President of the Board of Trade in the Rockingham government, when the Stamp Act was repealed,

[81] On the Quebec Act, see Sosin, *Whitehall*, 239-255. Sosin does not make the point in this way, but he does demonstrate that Boston and the backcountry were related problems, and that the timing of the Quebec Act was not accidental.

[82] The fullest account of Dartmouth is Bradley D. Bargar, "The Administration of Lord Dartmouth in the American Department: 1772-1775" (unpublished thesis, U. of Toronto, 1952).

[83] This view is argued in Ritcheson, *British Politics*, 136 and *passim*. See also Bernard Donoughue, *British Politics and the American Revolution: the Path to War 1773-75* (London, 1964), which appeared too late to be of use.

and he had sustained the image by keeping up a correspondence with various leading Americans. Above all, he was known for his Methodist piety. Americans, of course, believed that a true Christian and a genuine humanitarian could only support their cause.

Unfortunately, Dartmouth believed in Parliamentary supremacy almost as firmly as he believed in God, though he did not flaunt his belief as did many British politicians.[84] He was also the step-brother of Lord North, and maintained a close personal relationship with him. And, finally, Dartmouth was a weak man who occupied a weak political position as Secretary of State.

When Dartmouth was at the Board of Trade, he was not consulted by the cabinet on colonial business. The old Duke of Newcastle, noting that both Halifax and Hillsborough had insisted on attending cabinet meetings concerning American affairs when they were at the Board of Trade, thought that Dartmouth also should attend. But, Newcastle concluded, "My Lord Dartmouth is a quiet man. He did not complain."[85] After the fall of the government in 1766, Dartmouth was content to slip out of active political association with the Rockinghamites and into a life of semiretirement.

When Britain decided to negotiate rather than fight in the Falkland Islands crisis of 1770, Lord Weymouth, a Secretary of State, had resigned. North asked his step-brother, as a reliable and noncontroversial figure, to succeed Weymouth. Dartmouth refused, preferring his quiet life, but was wounded by general criticism of his "irresponsible" conduct in doing so. When, two years later, North asked him to succeed Hillsborough, Dartmouth seemed to feel he could not refuse again.[86]

North's purpose in appointing Dartmouth was primarily to keep the office out of the hands of his political rivals, and secondarily to make a conciliatory gesture toward America.

[84] Bargar, "Dartmouth," iv.
[85] Newcastle to Rockingham, 10 December 1765, Wentworth-Fitzwilliam MSS., R1-539.
[86] Bargar, "Dartmouth," 100-103.

Neither purpose was successfully accomplished. The very office of Colonial Secretary was vulnerable, and for some time had been under fire from the two "ancient" Secretaries as an innovation of dubious legality. Hillsborough had asserted his right to direct both colonial affairs and the army within the colonies, but Dartmouth, upon his accession, had agreed to something less than full equality of status with his two rivals and colleagues.[87] Moreover, a Hillsborough appointee remained at the Board of Trade and was prepared to combat Dartmouth's known "softness" on the American question.

Gage, upon his return to England, found Dartmouth not only a victim of his own contradictory attitudes toward America, but also so lacking in power that colonial affairs were in danger of slipping from his hands. One of Dartmouth's Undersecretaries informed the other in mid-1773: "Our business has hitherto been as light as you could wish, and I think it is likely to continue so, for what can Lord Dartmouth have to do whilst Bamber Gascoigne is minister for America at the Board of Trade and Lord Suffolk [Secretary of State for the Southern Department] at the Colonial Office, where they will not let us have anything to say, all Councils for American business being in Lord Gower's [Lord President] absence held by Lord Suffolk. . . ."[88] These Undersecretaries themselves, John Pownall and William Knox, upon whom the inexperienced Dartmouth had to lean heavily, were also legacies of the Hillsborough era, thus further confusing the question of where power lay and how policy was made.

When news arrived at London in January 1774, that Bostonians had violently resisted the attempt to import duty-free East India Company tea, this internal confusion in government had major consequences. All knew that something had to be done, but there was disagreement about specific measures. Pownall wanted to shut the port of Boston, while Dartmouth and Knox thought it would be enough

[87] On this dispute, see Spector, *American Department*, 66-78.
[88] John Pownall to William Knox, 23 July 1773, *HMC, Various Collections*, VI (*Knox MSS*), 110.

to make the Massachusetts Council appointive rather than elective, thereby increasing the power of the governor. But a former governor, Francis Bernard, got to Lord North with his old plan to curb town meetings. With no real center of decision, it was easier to accept all proposals in order to win broader support.[89] Dartmouth, in particular, feared to alienate anyone by opposing coercive measures. As William Knox recalled, Dartmouth was trying "to exculpate himself for having formerly moved the repeal of the Stamp Act in the Lords."[90]

Gage himself, more cautious than ever, may have adjusted his conversation to suit his audience. To the King in February he swore he could control Boston with four regiments.[91] But when the idea of making him governor of Massachusetts arose a few days later, he supposedly expressed "indifference" to John Pownall.[92] Probably he cooled as he saw what the government was going to do but apparently there was no escape after having committed himself to the King. This being the case, he made the best of it. With Amherst, Gage appeared before the cabinet on March 30.[93] He surely must have been behind the passage of a new Quartering Act, the last of the "intolerable acts," and perhaps pushed also for an "Act for the Impartial Administration of Justice . . ." which would take soldiers out of the clutches of Suffolk county justices and Boston juries.[94] Years later, he said that he had been averse to being governor of Massachusetts, had wanted more than four "weak" regiments sent out as reinforcements, and, on the advice of one of the greatest lawyers in the kingdom, had sought to have Massachusetts declared in rebellion.[95]

[89] "Proceedings in Relation to the American Colonies," *ibid.*, 257.

[90] "Lord Chancellor Thurlow," *ibid.*, 270.

[91] King to North, 4 February 1774, *Geo. III Corr.*, III, #1379.

[92] *Hutchinson Diary and Letters*, I, 259.

[93] Ritcheson, *British Politics*, 161.

[94] Cabinet minute, 7 April 1774, 14 *HMC* x (*Dartmouth MSS.*, II), 208.

[95] "Queries of George Chalmers with the Answers of General Gage . . . ," 4 *MHSC* IV, 366, 371.

This last was a ticklish point. Gage had asked the cabinet to define exactly his authority to use force in quelling disturbances without the advice and consent of his Council, a fine but crucial question of law.[96] Understandably, Gage wanted all ambiguity, vagueness, and doubts about it removed. The last explicit pronouncement concerning it had in fact represented a distinct shift from traditional practice, which made a military commander and his forces the passive instrument of the civil magistrate who was wholly responsible for the maintenance of law and order. But in 1773, on the occasion of Tryon's request for military assistance in the "New Hampshire Grants," Dartmouth had signed the following instruction to Haldimand: "It is the King's Pleasure that his Troops should not upon any requisition whatever be drawn out, without His Majesty's express Command, in aid of the Civil Magistracy in the Colonies, unless in cases of absolute & unavoidable Necessity, nor until it has been clearly shewn that every Power existing in the Colony where the Danger arises has been exerted without effect."[97] No longer was the military commander to remain passive; he was now expected to judge the propriety of the magistrate's request. The cabinet's reply, made through Dartmouth, to Gage's query seemed to solve the problem: "Your Authority as the first Magistrate, combined with your Command over the King's Troops, will, it is hoped, enable you to meet every opposition, and fully to preserve the public peace, by employing those Troops with Effect, should the madness of the People on the one hand, or the timidity or the want of Strength of the peace officers on the other hand, make it necessary to have recourse to their assistance." But the cabinet quickly hedged: "The King trusts however that such necessity

[96] Cabinet minute, 7 April 1774, 14 *HMC* x (*Dartmouth MSS.*, II), 208.

[97] Dartmouth to Haldimand, 14 October 1773, CO 5/90ff. 391-393. On this affair, see Franklin B. Wickwire, "John Pownall and British Colonial Policy," 3 *WMQ* xx (1963), 551. I doubt that either Dartmouth or Pownall intended to alter traditional practice, but that was the effect of the instruction.

will not occur. . . ." Eight paragraphs later, Dartmouth blurred the answer still further when he referred to the Council: "I do not mean that any Constitutional power or Authority, vested in them, should be set aside by any part of these Instructions. . . ."[98] Constitutionally, a colonial governor could employ military force only with the advice and consent of his council.[99]

In the event, the outbreak of war would not turn on this question of law. The legal question, however, played a part in the deterioration of British control. Both Gage and the cabinet had persisted in the error that marked more than a decade of military policy: they had failed to distinguish between the legality and the capability of using force. Gage, after saying more to the King than he really believed about the capability of controlling colonists with soldiers, had emphasized the legal obstacle in his discussion with the ministers. The latter thought they had met his objections by making him both Commander in Chief for North America *and* Governor of Massachusetts, and by deriving a third office for him from the second—"first Magistrate," though they failed to make clear whether explicit legal restrictions on one office could be circumvented by invoking the powers of another.

It is not known whether this fuzziness created doubts or inhibitions in Gage's mind about his proper course in Massachusetts; once he had returned to Boston, his behavior suggests that it did. But clearly the whole emphasis on legalities created strong expectations in the minds of the cabinet. If Gage *could* control disorder, then surely most Americans were not so blind to realities that they would actually make war; in the end, they would back down. When Gage reported that the arrival of troops had "given Spirits to the Friends of Government," ministers found confirmation for their belief.[100] Henry Ellis, intelligent and more knowledgeable about American affairs than most men, expressed this view in a letter to his former protégé, Knox:

[98] Dartmouth to Gage, 9 April 1774, *Gage Corr.*, II, 158-162.
[99] See p. 44, above, on martial law.
[100] Gage to Dartmouth, 26 June 1774, *Gage Corr.*, I, 358.

"I by no means think the case so desperate or irremediable as many people imagine. We know the real inability of the Americans to make any effectual resistance. . . ."[101]

Beneath this estimate lay the assumption that Boston would remain isolated, cut off from support in the hinterland or in the other colonial cities.[102] Dartmouth, Knox, and Pownall were committed to this view, for they saw little else to be done until the rest of America brought Boston to its senses. Dartmouth went on writing unofficial conciliatory letters to his friends in the colonies, but he expected that the decisive break would come in the Continental Congress.[103]

Gage, if he ever truly held such a view, soon gave it up. Excerpts from his reports to Dartmouth, when read in sequence, are illuminating:

July 5—"The Terror of Mobs is over, the Press is becoming free."

July 20—"The virulent party at New York is routed, and we are told that Philadelphia is moderate. . . . The League and Covenant has not succeeded as the Faction expected."

July 27 [some musing doubts]—"Men who hold Employments and receive Salaries under Government fear that the Administration might relax from the Vigour now adopt'd, and that there might be a Change of Measures, when they should be left as they have been before, to the Mercy of their Opponents and their Mobs. . . . If the Opposers of Government may be called only a Faction in the Province . . . they are at least a very numerous and powerful Faction."[104]

August 27 [privately to Barrington]—If it comes to war with New England "you wou'd be able to overcome them, no doubt, in a year or two."[105]

[101] Ellis to Knox, 23 March 1774, *HMC, Various Collections,* VI (*Knox MSS.*) 111.

[102] See Ellis to Knox, 15 July 1774, *ibid.*, in which Ellis said that America could not be coerced if it were united.

[103] *Hutchinson Diary and Letters,* 261, 273.

[104] *Gage Corr.,* I, 359, 361, 363-364.

[105] 27 August 1774, "Private," Gage MSS. For some reason, this letter is not in *Gage Corr.,* II; but it is quoted in Alden, *Gage,* 212.

September 2—"I mean my Lord . . . to avoid any bloody Crisis as long as possible. . . . His Majesty will in the mean Time Judge what is best to be done. . . . Nothing can be done but by forceable Means. Tho' the People are not held in high Estimation by the Troops, yet they are numerous, worked up to a Fury, and not the Boston Rabble but the Freeholders and the Farmers of the Country."[106]

Here was Gage, so it must have seemed to those in London, changing his estimate of the situation and trying to pass responsibility back to the King's ministers.

The final shock came with his dispatch of September 25. In a private postscript, Gage suggested that Dartmouth look at a letter he had just sent to Thomas Hutchinson, then in England.[107] William Knox described both its contents and its effect: "What turned us all so much against Gage was his telling Governor Hutchinson that, in his opinion, the only thing to be done was to suspend the Acts, and, in the mean time, make preparation for enforcing them . . . it was absolutely necessary to make an entire conquest of the New England Governments, and not less than twenty thousand men could venture to take the field."[108] Not long thereafter, the last hope of Dartmouth and his Undersecretaries was shattered by the news that the Continental Congress had adopted the radical Suffolk county resolutions.[109] Gage discredited and Dartmouth demoralized, all remaining power to control the situation passed from their hands.

Once Gage had decided that Bostonians would fight rather than back down, and that armed men from all over New England would support them, his sole aim seems to have become that of postponing conflict as long as possible. Whether he hoped mainly for a miracle, or for major reinforcements, or simply for someone else to make the final

[106] *Gage Corr.*, I, 371.
[107] *Gage Corr.*, I, 375. See 14 *HMC* x (*Dartmouth MSS.*, II), 226, for a description of the letter to Hutchinson, dated 17 September.
[108] *HMC, Various Collections*, VI (*Knox MSS.*) 257.
[109] *Hutchinson Diary and Letters*, 273.

decision, is not known. During the summer of 1774, he had played his new role with firmness and dignity. But by the end of August his attitude had changed dramatically. The last three of the "Intolerable Acts" arrived on August 6, and he had tried to put them into execution. Under the alteration in the Massachusetts Charter, he appointed a new Council, only to see intimidation successfully used against his appointees. He soon was hearing reports that the courts were being closed in the western counties.[110] His last shred of optimism vanished when he personally tried to break up the town meeting at Salem (where his head-quarters were located) with two companies of the 59th Regiment on August 25. The meeting called his bluff, militia swarmed in from neighboring towns, and Gage decided to release the seven men he had ordered arrested by the sheriff.[111] On the 27th, after being warned that his person was not safe, he moved to Boston and began to fortify the town.[112]

Gage was not preparing to declare war, however; he was preparing to defend himself and his army. While he built fortifications, he also adopted a policy toward the towns-people of conciliation. No repetition of the Massacre of 1770 would occur if he could help it. At the same time, he began to bombard the ministry with letters saying that, as matters now stood, war was inevitable; only some bold stroke or change in policy could prevent it.[113]

Not only did his dispatches after September discredit him in the eyes of the government, but his conciliatory attitude in Boston went far toward discrediting him in the eyes of his own army. After October, there were nine

[110] Gage to Dartmouth, 27 August and 2 September 1773, *Gage Corr.*, I, 365-372.

[111] *MHSP* for 1864-1865, 347-348. These letters of John Andrews to William Barrell are a detailed and reliable source for events in Boston, 1774-1775.

[112] Alden, *Gage*, 212.

[113] His official letters to Dartmouth are in *Gage Corr.*, I, 369ff., and his private letters to Barrington in *ibid.*, II, 654ff. The latter were markedly more candid and pessimistic than the former.

battalions and parts of two others in Boston, over 3,000 men added to a town of about 15,000. Four of these battalions had come directly from the British Isles, four others from the rawness of Canada, Nova Scotia, and Newfoundland.[114] Only the 23rd from New York, the 47th from New Jersey, and the 18th from Philadelphia had been seasoned by service among Americans in the older colonies. Living conditions were miserable, and officers and men, cooped up in the seaport, soon became bored and restless. Even without the imminence of civil war, a commander would have been hard pressed to maintain discipline and morale under such circumstances; for Gage, in the winter 1774-1775, it was nearly impossible.

Many of the scenes of 1768-1770 were repeated. Soldiers deserted at a rapid rate, carousing officers got into affrays with townsmen, and civilians were horrified anew at the drunkenness and harshness of discipline within the army. Merchant John Andrews was pleased to hear that a recaptured deserter was not to be executed; "but when we find that a thousand lashes is the substitute, we are equally shock'd. . . . Early this morning a poor culprit received 250 lashes, which number he is to receive four successive weeks. . . ."[115] But any number of lashes, and even an occasional execution on the Common, could not stop desertion. And this time Bostonians were actively pleading with the soldiers to desert. "Friends and Brothers," read a handbill addressed to the soldiers of the 4th and 43rd Regiments, ". . . you may have Liberty and by a Little Industry may obtain Property. . . . March up either Singly or in Companys. . . . The Country People are Determind to Protect you and Screen you. . . ."[116] Many soldiers took advantage of the offer. Colonel Leslie of the 64th was convinced that social equality

[114] The 4th and 43rd from England; the 5th and 38th from Ireland; the 10th and 52nd from Canada; the 59th from Nova Scotia; two companies of the 65th from Newfoundland. The 64th remained at Castle William in Boston harbor where it had been for several years.

[115] *MHSP* for 1864-1865, 341.

[116] Dated June 1774, Gage MSS.

in Massachusetts was the true cause of desertion, because it removed the feeling of subordination.[117]

Though many of the troubles seemed the same as those that had occurred a few years earlier, they now had aspects —like the handbill and Leslie's remark on desertion—that were more ominous. In particular, when officers got into scrapes, Gage was quick to placate the town. Repeatedly he ordered them to apologize or otherwise make amends for misdemeanors, and, if blame were divided, he was reluctant to let them prosecute civilians. Consequently, almost no Bostonian recorded a harsh sentiment about Gage, but few officers recorded a favorable one. In the diary of Ensign John Barker of the 4th, fresh from Ireland, Gage was *"Tommy"* who "feels no affection for the army." When soldiers could not get into winter quarters because workmen could not be hired to build them, or when officers did not get the extra allowances they thought they deserved, it was Tommy's fault, who was "attach'd to a paltry Oeconomy, both in Publick and Private."[118] Most certainly Barker, and all those among some three hundred officers who agreed with him, sent similar sentiments home to England.

It also rankled to see that the Yankees were no longer merely hiding behind the law; they were openly arming and training. One could laugh at a militia company awkwardly learning the drill, but the several thousand musketeers who had descended on Salem in late August were not funny, nor was it amusing to see the steady stream of weapons moving out through Boston Neck. It hurt most of all to read a pamphlet by a battle-scarred British officer, Charles Lee, in which he told these Americans that, as free men, they could become better soldiers than the regulars, and that anyone who disagreed with him misunderstood the reasons for the poor American showing in the Seven Years War.[119] Haldimand, in private, seemed to confirm

[117] Leslie to Haldimand, 17 April 1774, BM Add. MSS. 21731.
[118] "A British Officer in Boston in 1775," *Atlantic Monthly,* xxxix (1877), 390.
[119] Lee's pamphlet, *Strictures on a Pamphlet, Entitled, A "Friendly Address to All Reasonable Americans . . ."* (Philadelphia, 1774), is reprinted in *NYHSC for 1871* (N.Y., 1872).

Lee's opinion: if the Americans had a regular army, he thought, they would be less dangerous.[120]

Through a long if unusually mild winter, the situation slowly grew worse. In January, the 10th Regiment was on the verge of mutiny. "Throat distemper," smallpox and "putrid fever," ran through the garrison. Officers quarreled, gambled, and caroused more publicly and with less restraint than ever. By March, John Andrews could summarize the situation in two letter-book entries: "The officers in general behave more like a parcell of children, of late, than men"; and "the officers and soldiers are a good deal disaffected towards the Governor, thinking, I suppose, that he is partial to the inhabitants, many of the latter have made no scruples to call him an Old Woman."[121] Gage had won nothing but faint praise for his efforts to scrupulously perform the office of Governor, and in so doing was on the brink of failure as Commander in Chief.[122]

Nothing that happened in the army during this last winter could make much difference, however, except in a negative way. Gage, by preventing any accidental outbreak of violence, ensured that King George would make the decision.

A subtle change had been taking place in the attitude of the King. From George the well-beloved who hated to use soldiery against civilians however unruly, his self-image was shifting to that of George the strong, first soldier of the Empire, whose army faced disgrace at the hands of an armed rabble. This change was encouraged by the warrior-

---

[120] Allen French, "General Haldimand in Boston," *MHSP*, LXVI (1936-41), 91.

[121] *MHSP* for 1864-1865, 400-401. See *ibid.*, 303, for near-mutiny in the 10th Regiment.

[122] For other indications that Gage was losing control of his army, see Charles Stuart to Lord Bute, 24 July 1775, *A Prime Minister and his Son*, ed. the Hon. Mrs. E. Stuart Wortley (London, 1925), 68; and a letter written by Earl Percy (third-ranking officer at Boston), 10 October 1774, quoted in H. M. Walker, *A History of the Northumberland Fusiliers, 1674-1902* (London, 1919), 143-144. Gage appears as a desperate man, aged beyond his years, in *Hutchinson Diary and Letters*, I, 184n., 224.

courtiers, men who had acquired their opinions, at first or second hand, of colonial military ability in the Seven Years War. They remembered the volunteer regiments, recruited by high enlistment bounties or occasionally by draft from the militia, that gave more trouble than assistance in the conduct of the war. They remembered the judgment of British officers like James Wolfe on these untrained, apathetic, usually poorly equipped, and often poorly led soldiers; Wolfe had called them "the dirtiest most contemptible cowardly dogs that you can conceive. There is no depending on them in action. They fall down dead in their own dirt and desert by battalions, officers and all."[123] They unwisely equated these units with the angry militia Gage faced in Massachusetts.

The King had joked in May that *"he had as lief fight the Bostonians as the French,"* but he was no longer joking by autumn.[124] "Blows must decide," he wrote to North in deadly earnest, "whether they are to be subject to this country or independent."[125] When he heard about the heavy desertion from his regiments, the King wept with General Howe (who would succeed Gage).[126] The reports from Gage that Boston was no longer isolated and that the province was arming and training itself served to harden rather than change minds at Court. Only Barrington and Harvey, who had watched military affairs in the colonies more closely than anyone else, did not let emotion cloud their reason; they considered a land war against the united colonies madness, but their views were unheeded.[127] Every-

[123] Wolfe to Lord George Sackville, 7 August 1785, *The Life and Letters of James Wolfe*, ed. Beckles Willson (London, 1909), 392.

[124] Horace Walpole, *Journal of the Reign of George the Third*, ed. John Doran (London, 1859), 1, 366.

[125] The King to North, 18 November 1774, *Geo. III Corr.*, III, #1556.

[126] Walpole, *Journal*, 445.

[127] Alden, *Gage*, 234-35. Also, see Harvey to General Irwin, 30 June 1775, and to Lt. Col. Smith, 3 November 1775, WO 3/5, pp. 36-37, 92-93; and Barrington to Dartmouth, 12 November and 24 December 1774, *Barrington-Bernard Corr.*, x-xiii.

one else, military and civilian, thought Gage's inaction and conciliatory behavior inexcusable, and they howled for his head. The information he was sending back should have called the feasibility of military coercion into question. Instead, it made the affair one in which the honor of the King's army was at stake, and in which retreat was unthinkable.

For the last act, William Pitt, Earl of Chatham, unintentionally joined George III. In 1763, they had unwittingly collaborated to keep an army in America; now, together, they would send it to war. By January 1775, the government, convinced that Gage would do nothing, was ready to order stronger action. But the Earl of Chatham had not yet been heard from, and, though his lustre had tarnished somewhat, the rumor that he would present a plan for America was enough to make the ministry hesitate, for he still carried weight on military and American affairs. He was careful to keep the details of his plan to himself, and when he rose in the House of Lords on January 20 all listened with anticipation. The plan, however, offered no answer to the question of empire; rather, it was a single, bald proposal: remove the troops from Boston. Chatham, lofty and arrogant as ever, made no attempt to gain prior support for it from North, Dartmouth, or the Rockinghamites. He offered no broad solution, toward which this would have been the first step. Horace Walpole described its effect: "The Court could so justly show the unseasonableness of the motion, that all who wished to pay court had better excuse for it than they generally cared whether they had or not; the wavering went after them, and even the Opposition could scarce bring themselves to swallow either Lord Chatham's haughtiness or absurdity."[128] Chatham actually exacerbated the situation because his plan was the only chance to avoid war, yet was proposed in the worst way imaginable.[129]

[128] Walpole, *Journal*, I, 447. See also Burke to Citizens of Bristol, *The Correspondence of Edmund Burke*. ed. Thomas W. Copeland, *et al.* (Chicago, 1958—), II, 101-102.

[129] Versions of this speech are discussed in Robert R. Rea, "Parliamentary Reporting," *Bibliographical Society of America Papers*, XLIX (1955), 219-229.

When, almost two weeks later, he presented a comprehensive bill to conciliate the colonies, his moment had passed, and new instructions, destined to be decisive, had already been written for Gage.

The evidence is far from conclusive, but it appears that, while Dartmouth continued to explore all available paths toward a settlement, the attitude of the King and the colonial Undersecretaries toward the situation of the army and toward Gage's pusillanimity, as well as Dartmouth's own desire to get right with the King and his colleagues, inspired Dartmouth to write or to approve the letter that sent troops to Concord. It told Gage to use his own discretion, but it also criticized him for inactivity, and it clearly demanded some military action.[130] That action began on April 19 at Lexington, and thenceforth problems of British military policy became the comparatively straightforward ones of how to make war.

Some Observations

Looking back from Lexington, one can see the story of the British army in colonial America as, in microcosm, the story of the coming of the Revolution. War had produced a basic change in military policy, and that change raised constitutional problems that could not be solved. But beyond the mere assertion of the ultimately military origins of the Revolution, there are more interesting questions about institutions, intentions, and motives that get specific if tentative answers from a study of the army.

One is impressed anew by the reasonableness of the British decision to keep an army in America after the Seven Years War. It was obvious that the colonies, expanded enormously as they were, required some kind of permanent military establishment; it was also obvious that the militia could not provide that establishment. Moreover, according to all information then available, the Indians promised great (and expensive) trouble if past prac-

[130] Dartmouth to Gage, 27 January 1775, "Secret," *Gage Corr.*, II, 179-183. A convincing discussion of the circumstances surrounding this letter is in Alden, *Gage*, 233-234.

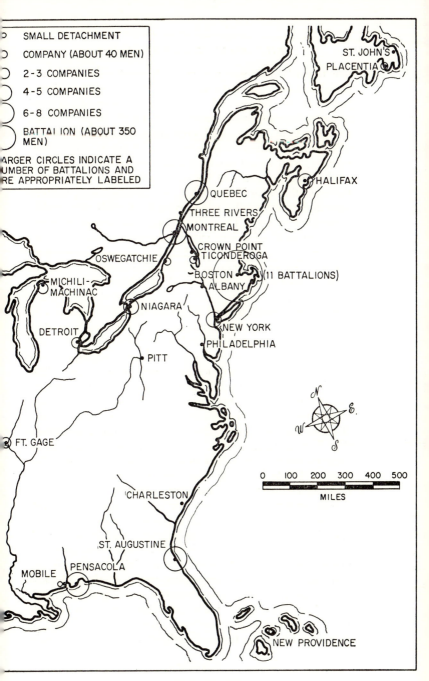

SMALL DETACHMENT

COMPANY (ABOUT 40 MEN)

2-3 COMPANIES

4-5 COMPANIES

6-8 COMPANIES

BATTALION (ABOUT 350 MEN)

LARGER CIRCLES INDICATE A NUMBER OF BATTALIONS AND ARE APPROPRIATELY LABELED

ST. JOHN'S
PLACENTIA

HALIFAX

QUEBEC

THREE RIVERS
MONTREAL

CROWN POINT
TICONDEROGA

OSWEGATCHIE

BOSTON (11 BATTALIONS)
ALBANY

MICHILI-MACHINAC

NIAGARA

NEW YORK

DETROIT

PHILADELPHIA

PITT

N
E
W
S

FT. GAGE

0 100 200 300 400 500
MILES

CHARLESTON

ST. AUGUSTINE

MOBILE PENSACOLA

NEW PROVIDENCE

The Army in early 1775, on the eve of the battle of Lexington and Concord.

tice toward them was not radically improved. Thus imperial economy—a vital concern in 1763—as well as simple justice to the Indians and security for the colonists, seemed to argue for the maintenance of a much larger colonial garrison than had existed previously.

The organization of that garrison under a single commander, who would devote his full energy to its administration and who would be responsible to Whitehall for the execution of military policy, has an appealing, modern look to it, especially when compared with the earlier haphazard system. There had ceased to be any military policy to speak of before 1754; the colonies that had small regular garrisons sometimes had less claim to them than colonies without garrisons, while gubernatorial control of regular troops was characterized by jobbery, neglect, and inefficiency.

But no sooner has one admitted the reasonableness of the new British policy after the Seven Years War than one is forced to concede that it was also fundamentally absurd. It rested on assumptions about men and power that had little basis in fact or historical experience. The readiness to "new-model" political and military organization, the new sense of responsibility and desire for efficiency, which impelled British leaders to adjust in order to meet changed circumstances, also encouraged them to believe that their good intentions would not be misunderstood or their measures resisted on either side of the Atlantic. For men so deeply involved in politics, they had a shockingly unpolitical conception of what was possible.

The sanguine plan to prevent future Indian grievances impinged on the interests and ambitions of fur traders, land speculators, westward-moving farmers, and colonies with claims to expansion; it required delicate political and legal arrangements, not to mention financial support; it demanded a level of communications, transportation, administrative skill, military professionalism, and linguistic knowledge that did not exist. Living at a time when it is possible to fly anywhere in the world and return the next day, or to talk to a man on the spot without moving from a chair, one can only marvel at what these eighteenth-century men aspired to do in an age when the Secretary of State asked a question about Illinois and hoped for an informed answer within a year. Equally fascinating is their expectation that the Indian plan could operate outside politics, which they must have known had the capability of bringing the whole scheme down in ruins.

Perhaps it is unfair to emphasize the Indian plan so heavily, for originally it was only a minor part of the new military policy. Fortuitous events, like Pontiac's rebellion, and unpredictable circumstances, especially the weakness and instability of the government, gave the Indian plan an importance far beyond the intentions of the men who promoted and supported it. But even a broader view of the army's place in America after 1763 raises questions about what was happening in the minds of those who were directing the British empire.

The attempt to rationalize and centralize the defense of North America, if judged by results, was a mistake. Both George Johnstone and Thomas Pownall warned the government that such a change would do more harm than good. Johnstone argued that treating the colonies as a unit was certain to induce them eventually to behave as a unit, with all the potential dangers such behavior implied.[131] He might have added that a single policy would do violence to the fact of colonial diversity. But Johnstone's motives were transparently obvious—he wanted maximum freedom as the new Governor of West Florida—and no one listened to him. Pownall's argument was less dramatic but more pointed. Unfortunately, it smelled of the lamp, and it reeked of his own personal quarrel with Loudoun. It was discounted at the time, and appears to have been ignored

[131] "Thoughts concerning Florida," PRO 30/47 (Egremont MSS.), xiv, 88-89. It is conjecture on my part that Johnstone wrote this document. But its emphasis on sea-power and on the importance of leaving the governor as free as possible leads me to this conclusion. The document seems related to "Somes Thoughts on the Settlement & government of our Colonies in North America," 10 March 1763, in both Shelburne MSS., xlviii, 525-542, and BM Add. MSS. 38335, 69-77.

by historians. Yet it has more to recommend it than
Pownall himself knew.

Pownall argued that a single military establishment
would weaken the power and the position of royal governors, and he was right. Just how much it weakened the
governors, and whether that weakening really mattered in
the coming of the Revolution, are of course the crucial questions, and they cannot be answered with confidence. But
the very presence of regular troops in any colony auto-
matically introduced a center of authority that lay outside the political structure of the colony, and reduced the
prestige of the governor accordingly. His superiors in London now had another way of checking his performance,
and though Gage was the soul of discretion in political
matters his potential power would have been important
even if it had *never* been exercised. No American Commander in Chief ever lost a battle with a royal governor,
and that was what Pownall meant when he attacked military centralization.

Like Johnstone, it is possible that Pownall did not go
far enough. Perhaps the most important political effect of
centralizing control of the colonial army was also the most
subtle: it led governors to see their task in a slightly different way. Now, in time of crisis, Colden, Bernard, even
Hutchinson, saw that they *shared* responsibility for what
happened in their province. Gage and his army fostered an
unhealthy illusion that there was, if worst came to worst, an
available reservoir of emergency power. One suspects, but
cannot prove, that this illusion made governors, and some
other civil officials, both more aggressive and more complacent than they ought to have been—aggressive toward
American resistance and complacent about the possible consequences of aggressiveness. No longer did a governor have
to accept full responsibility when force was used in his
province. Without an army at his back, but with a handful
of regulars under his own control, Colden or Bernard
either would have forced a confrontation much earlier in
the struggle or would have behaved more circumspectly.

Of course the most dangerous illusions about the army flourished in England. There the men with power, including the King, were unable to learn what could (and could not) be done by the army, and to decide what they ought to do about the army; the two questions kept blurring and running together in their minds. Their intentions were benevolent—no one wanted to use force if it could possibly be avoided—but their premises were stern: Parliamentary sovereignty was not negotiable, and it was dangerous to seem to back down on any question. The formulation of policy after 1765 reflected this tension. Divided among themselves for other reasons, they could not find it in themselves or in their system to choose one of two alternatives: use the army, or remove it. Events finally made the decision for them.

The story of the army also illuminates the American side of the pre-Revolutionary struggle. Colonists emerge, not as patriots or as radicals and conservatives, but as reasonable and unexceptionable Englishmen for the most part. They reveal themselves in their words and behavior as less violent and doctrinaire, more willing to compromise and be practical, than they are usually depicted. They are, in fact, as reasonable as the government that is oppressing them. Their attitudes and actions, however, suggest that more than conscious grievances are working on their minds. Hutchinson, Otis, Dulany, Watts, and William Smith of New York were, after all, as upset as anyone about the new British policies, but their loyalty remained unshaken. Benjamin Franklin, by contrast, displayed a certain amount of numbness to early grievances, but eventually committed treason.

More decisive than a growing list of grievances was an increasing sense that the British government did not know what it was doing; that it was ignorant, mean, and hopeless; in short, that it was no government at all. Nothing could have done more to foster such a sense of estrangement than the army. What *was* the army doing in the colonies? No one seemed to know. Defense—as is so often the case when no one is attacking—looked a little ridiculous. The plan for Indian management, not quite defense in the usual meaning of the word, was difficult to grasp, and would not have pleased those Americans who did understand it. And there was always the hint of duplicity—that the British government wanted an army not to defend but to control the colonists. The hint concealed a grain of truth, but what seemed a half-hearted attempt to garrison the backcountry led Americans to suspect more than was there. All lingering doubts were removed when troops went to Boston: the government had played false all along. The government, in fact, hardly knew more than the colonists what it was doing with the army, but its vacillation and weakness could be interpreted as some kind of dark cunning. Even Gage, tactful and cautious, the perfect peacetime commander under normal circumstances, did not improve the situation by concealing his views from both the Americans and the government. In the end, Americans were alienated; they did not come to hate the British government any more than they hated the British army, but they did cease to believe that the government had any necessary, organic part in their own existence.

Abbreviations

Acknowledgments

and

A Note on Sources

Abbreviations

AHR *American Historical Review.*

Amherst-Gage MSS. Papers transmitted to Thomas Gage by Jeffery Amherst, three bound vols., with schedule, William L. Clements Library, Ann Arbor, Michigan.

Annual Register *The Annual Register; or a view of the history, politicks and literature of the year.* . . .

APCC *Acts of the Privy Council of England, Colonial Series.* Edited by W. L. Grant and James Munro. 6 vols. London: 1908-1912.

Barrington-Bernard Corr. *The Barrington-Bernard Correspondence . . . 1760-1770.* Edited by Edward Channing and A. C. Coolidge. Cambridge, Massachusetts: 1912.

Bedford Corr. *Correspondence of John, Fourth Duke of Bedford.* . . . Edited by Lord John Russell. 3 vols. London: 1842-1846.

BM Add. MSS. British Museum, Additional Manuscripts.

Bouquet Papers *The Papers of Colonel Henry Bouquet.* Edited by S. K. Stevens and Donald H. Kent. 19 vols., mimeographed. Harrisburg, Pennsylvania: 1940-1943. Volume numbering follows arrangement of originals in the British Museum.

Chatham Corr. *Correspondence of William Pitt, Earl of Chatham.* Edited by W. S. Taylor and J. H. Pringle. 4 vols. London: 1838-1840.

CHOP *Calendar of Home Office Papers of the Reign of George III, 1760-1775.* Edited by Joseph Redington and Richard A. Roberts. 4 vols. London: 1878-1899.

CL William L. Clements Library, Ann Arbor, Michigan.

CO 5 British Public Record Office, Colonial Office Papers, Class 5.

Colden Letter Books *New York Historical Society Collections for 1876-1877.* 2 vols. New York: 1877-1878.

Colden Papers *The Letters and Papers of Cadwallader Colden. New York Historical Society Collections for 1917-1923, and for 1934-1935.* 9 vols. New York: 1918-1937.

Commons Journals *Journals of the House of Commons.*
Conn. Public Records *The Public Records of the Colony of Connecticut.* Edited by J. H. Trumbull and C. J. Hoadly. 15 vols. Hartford: 1850-1890.
CSMP *Colonial Society of Massachusetts, Publications.*
CSPC *Calendar of State Papers, Colonial Series, America and West Indies, 1660-.* Edited by William Noel Sainsbury *et al.* 35 vols., in progress. London: 1860-.
Dartmouth MSS. Dartmouth papers, William Salt Library, Stafford, County Record Office, England.
DCH Canada *Documents Relating to the Constitutional History of Canada, 1759-1791.* Edited by Adam Shortt and Arthur G. Doughty. 2nd edition. Ottawa: 1918.
EHR *English Historical Review.*
Gage Corr. *The Correspondence of General Thomas Gage . . . 1763-1775.* Edited by Clarence E. Carter. 2 vols. New Haven: 1931-1933.
Gage MSS. The papers of General Thomas Gage, William L. Clements Library, Ann Arbor, Michigan.
Geo. III Corr. *The Correspondence of King George the Third from 1760 to December, 1783.* Edited by Sir John Fortescue. 6 vols. London: 1927-1928.
Grenville Papers *The Grenville Papers.* Edited by W. J. Smith. 4 vols. London: 1852-1853.
HL Henry E. Huntington Library and Art Gallery, San Marino, California.
HM Manuscript prefix, Henry E. Huntington Library and Art Gallery, San Marino, California.
HMC British *Historical Manuscripts Commission.* Prefix is number of *Report.* Suffix is number of *Appendix.*
IHC *Illinois Historical Collections.*
JBT *Journal of the Commissioners for Trade and Plantations.* 14 vols. London: 1920-1938.
JCHA *The Journal of the Commons House of Assembly.* Nov. 10, 1736— Edited by J. H. Easterby. 9 vols., in progress. Columbia, South Carolina: 1951-.
Jenkins microfilms The Microfilm Collection of Early State Records. Compiled by William S. Jenkins. Pre-

pared by the Library of Congress in association with the University of North Carolina.

Johnson Papers The Papers of Sir William Johnson. Edited by Alexander C. Flick, James Sullivan, and Milton W. Hamilton. 13 vols., in progress. New York: 1921-.

LC Library of Congress.

LO The Loudoun papers, Henry E. Huntington Library and Art Gallery, San Marino, California.

Massachusetts Archives State House, Boston, Massachusetts.

MHSC Massachusetts Historical Society, Collections. Prefix is series number.

MHSP Massachusetts Historical Society, Publications.

MVHR Mississippi Valley Historical Review.

N.J. Arch. Archives of the State of New Jersey. Edited by William A. Whitehead *et al.* 33 vols. Newark: 1880-1928. Prefix is series number.

NYCD Documents Relative to the Colonial History of the State of New York. Edited by E. B. O'Callaghan and B. Fernow. 15 vols. Albany: 1856-1887.

NYHSC New York Historical Society, Collections.

Pa.Arch. Pennsylvania Archives. 119 vols. Philadelphia and Harrisburg: 1852-1935. Prefix is series number.

PAC Report Public Archives of Canada Report (title varies). Published annually at Ottawa.

Pa.Col.Rec. Minutes of the Provincial Council of Pennsylvania. 10 vols. Philadelphia and Harrisburg: 1852.

Pa. Statutes at Large The Statutes at Large of Pennsylvania . . . to 1801. Edited by James T. Mitchell and Henry Flanders. 15 vols. Harrisburg: 1896-1911.

PMHB Pennsylvania Magazine of History and Biography.

PRO 30 British Public Record Office, Gifts and Deposits. Second number indicates particular collection.

PRO-SC Records in the British Public Record Office relating to South Carolina, 1663-1782. Prepared by William L. McDowell. Microfilm, 6 reels. Columbia, South Carolina: 1955.

PROSC Records in the British Public Record Office relating to South Carolina. Indexed by A. S. Salley, Jr., 5 vols. Columbia, South Carolina: 1928-1947.

SCCJ Journal of the South Carolina Commons House of Assembly. See Jenkins microfilm.

SC Council Journal Journal of the South Carolina Governor's Council. See Jenkins microfilm.

Shelburne MSS. The Shelburne papers. William L. Clements Library, Ann Arbor, Michigan.

SP British Public Record Office, State Papers.

Stiles Corr. Extracts from the Itineraries and Other Miscellanies of Ezra Stiles . . . 1755-1794. Edited by Franklin B. Dexter. New Haven: 1916.

T British Public Record Office, Treasury papers.

Walpole Corr., ed. Lewis *The Yale Edition of Horace Walpole's Correspondence.* Edited by W. S. Lewis, *et al.* In progress. New Haven: 1937-.

Walpole Corr., ed. Toynbee *The Letters of Horace Walpole. . . .* Edited by Mrs. Paget Toynbee. 16 vols., Oxford: 1903-1905.

Watts Letter Book Letter Book of John Watts [1762-1765]. Edited by Dorothy C. Barck. *New York Historical Society Collections for 1928.* New York: 1928.

WMQ William and Mary Quarterly. Prefix is series number.

WO British Public Record Office, War Office papers.

Acknowledgments and A Note on Sources

A CASUAL remark, made years ago, started this work on its way. To Professor Harold Schultz of the University of Vermont, who thought an army in peacetime might be more interesting than an army at war, I owe a great debt for his friendship and teaching as well as for the idea of this book. His colleague, Professor Paul Evans, encouraged my study of military history in the first years of graduate school, and I am grateful to him for it. Dean Robert Palmer of Washington University, Professor Gordon Craig of Stanford, and Professor Robert Lively read the original manuscript and gave good advice, while Professor William B. Willcox of the University of Michigan improved the final version substantially through his shrewd judgment and staggering knowledge of the subject. Professors Peter Paret, Jack P. Greene, Clyde R. Ferguson, and Frederick S. Allen; Messrs. John R. Cuneo, John C. Long, and Adolph G. Rosengarten; the New Jersey Society of Colonial Wars, and the thesis-writers' seminar of Princeton's History Department each helped me, for which I thank them. And, finally, Professor Wesley Frank Craven gave me what only a master teacher has to give—direction, criticism, and a sense of freedom.

A Note on Sources

Another group of people—those who care for manuscripts—was indispensable to this work. The core of the book is the collection of Thomas Gage papers in the William L. Clements Library at Ann Arbor, Michigan; Professor Howard H. Peckham and Mr. William S. Ewing, Director and Curator of Manuscripts respectively, were kind, helpful, and, what is more, genuinely interested in the book. It must be said that Clarence E. Carter's *Correspondence of Thomas Gage* (2 vols., New Haven, 1931-1933), while providing a reliable text, is only a small part of the Gage papers, includes some trivia, silently and inexplicably omits several letters from an ostensibly complete run of correspondence, and does not include the most interesting series in the Gage papers: Lord Barrington's private letters to his friend Gage. Other manuscript collections at the Clements Library were useful: the incomplete papers of the Earl of Shelburne; the papers of William Knox, Lord George Germain, Frederick Mackenzie, Alexander Wedderburn, and Sir Henry Clinton, in about that order of importance. The Clements Library also has a set of Army Lists for the period, and Mr. John C. Long's typewritten catalogue of the Amherst papers (WO 34, below), which is much more detailed than the useful description in Lester K. Born, *British Manuscripts Project* (Washington, 1955).

The staff of the Henry E. Huntington Library and Art Gallery at San Marino, California, helped me to use the large Loudoun collection and the much smaller Abercromby collection, as well as the enormous and uncatalogued Stowe collection which contains some important papers of George Grenville. The Loudoun and Abercromby papers were valuable primarily in exploring the wartime experience of the army; Loudoun's especially, unlike other collections, contains a considerable number of revealing private letters from various correspondents.

The official papers of Jeffery Amherst, who succeeded Abercromby and preceded Gage as Commander in Chief in America, are in the British Public Record Office as WO 34. They are also available on microfilm, and it was mainly in this form that I used some but far from all of them. The staff of the Public Record Office did, however, provide assistance in the use of other manuscripts, particularly War Office and Colonial Office papers, and the papers of the Earls of Chatham (PRO 30/8) and Egremont (PRO 30/47). I am likewise grateful to the staff of the British Museum where the papers of Henry Bouquet, Frederick Haldimand, Charles Jenkinson (later Earl of Liverpool), and the Earls of Hardwicke and Newcastle proved most valuable. Copies of some of these Public Record Office and British Museum manuscripts are in the Library of Congress, and I thank its staff, especially for sending so many of them to me on interlibrary loan. One can learn most quickly about the location of these manuscripts and manuscript copies by consulting, in conjunction with one another, several invaluable guides: Charles M. Andrews, *Guide to the Materials for American History, to 1783, in the Public Record Office of Great Britain* (2 vols., Washington, 1912-1914) ; Charles M. Andrews and Frances G. Davenport, *Guide to the Manuscript Materials for the History of the United States to 1783, in the British Museum, in Minor London Archives, and in the Libraries of Oxford and Cambridge* (Washington, 1908) ; Grace Gardner Griffin, *A Guide to Manuscripts Relating to American History in British Depositories Reproduced for the Division of Manuscripts of the Library of Congress* (Washington, 1946) ; and B. R. Crick and Miriam Alman, *A Guide to Manuscripts Relating to America in Great Britain and Ireland* (London, 1961).

Finally, I must thank the present Earl of Dartmouth for letting me use some of his ancestor's papers in the William Salt Library, Stafford, England, and its staff for their helpfulness; the staff of the Sheffield City Library, England, and Mr. Thomas W. Copeland, who were kind to me during a brief visit to read some letters of the Earl of Rockingham in the Wentworth Woodhouse Muniments; and the staffs of the Massachusetts Archives, the Boston Public Library, the Massachusetts Historical Society, the New Jersey Historical Society, the Burton Historical Collection in Detroit, the East Riding Record Office in Beverley, Yorkshire, England, the National Register of Archives and the Royal United Services Institution in London, and Princeton's Firestone Library. Last of all, Mr. A. T. Milne and the Institute of Historical Research in London have on several occasions given me tea, a place to work, and the run of their excellent library.

The general bibliography of published material, both sources and secondary work, is vast, but it is listed and described in many places. There are good bibliographies in Lawrence H. Gipson, *The Coming of the Revolution, 1763-1775* (N.Y., 1954); David C. Douglas (ed.), *English Historical Documents* (N.Y., 1953—), vols. VIII and X for the army and vol. IX for the American colonies; and especially Bernhard Knollenberg, *Origin of the American Revolution: 1759-1766* (N.Y., 1960). Moreover, the notes of the present book provide bibliographical guidance, and may be used by consulting the index and the list of abbreviations. It should be said, as it has been many times before, that research in this general field would be far more difficult without the great collections of documents whose publication was begun on a large scale in the mid-nineteenth century. To a legion of editors, compilers, and antiquarians, I give thanks.

In contrast with the wealth of material on the coming of the Revolution, the special bibliography on the army and its problems is quite small, and here my debt is almost personal, though none of my creditors is known to me personally. Stanley M. Pargellis, *Lord Loudoun in North America* (New Haven, 1933), is not a sprightly book; its organization is curious and its range is fairly narrow. But it is a thorough piece of research, and it is rich in understanding how the British army actually worked. The longer I have labored myself, the more I have been impressed by Pargellis' achievement. A few years after the publication of *Lord Loudoun*, John R. Alden began to blaze the first major trail through the Gage papers. His biography, *General Gage in America* (Baton Rouge, 1948), is not sufficiently critical of its subject for my taste, but it is eminently sound and it has let me direct most of my attention toward other aspects of the army's history. Likewise, Alden's *John Stuart and the Southern Colonial Frontier* (Ann Arbor, 1944), together with Jack M. Sosin's *Whitehall and the Wilderness* (Lincoln, Nebraska, 1961), have helped me to find my way through the tangles

of British policy for the West, which was so intimately related to the story of the army. Unlike the books of Pargellis, Alden, and Sosin, the work done on eighteenth-century British political history by Sir Lewis Namier, his
disciples, and his critics, has not yet provided any clear
account of its subject; but at least it has exposed the complexity of British politics in this period, and has kept me
from falling into the trap of oversimplification.

Index

Bibliography, as well as the conventional place, name, and subject headings, will be found in this index. Any work cited more than once, and which is not listed under "Abbreviations" above, has a short-title reference to the page of the text where it is fully described. There are also references to other works which have been of particular importance in this study.